CAREER
OPPORTUNITIES
IN SCIENCE

CAREER
OPPORTUNITIES
IN SCIENCE

Susan Echaore-McDavid

Ferguson
An imprint of ☑® Facts On File

Career Opportunities in Science

Ferguson
An imprint of Facts On File, Inc.
132 West 31st Street
New York NY 10001

Library of Congress Cataloging-in-Publication Data
Echaore-McDavid, Susan.
    Career opportunities in science / Susan Echaore-McDavid.
        p. cm.
Includes bibliographical references and index.
    ISBN 0-8160-4905-X
    1. Science—Vocational guidance.   I. Title.
    Q147.E24   2003
    502′.3—dc21   2003054270

Ferguson books are available at special discounts when purchased in bulk quantities for businesses, associations, institutions, or sales promotions. Please call our Special Sales Department in New York at (212) 967-8800 or (800) 322-8755.

You can find Ferguson on the World Wide Web at http://www.fergpubco.com

Cover design by Nora Wertz

Printed in the United States of America

VB Hermitage 10 9 8 7 6 5 4 3 2 1

This book is printed on acid-free paper.

Dedicated to
Frank Percy Yoon
Chemist, Environmentalist, Humanitarian
1920–1995

CONTENTS

ACKNOWLEDGMENTS

Producing this book was challenging work, and it could not have been done without the help of many people. First off, I would like to thank James Chambers, my editor, for his confidence in me and my work.

My sincere thanks to the many individuals who took the time out of their busy schedules to answer my questions. In particular, I would like to express my gratitude to Alan A. Andolsen, CMC, CRM, President, Naremco Services Inc.; American Geophysical Union; Dr. Russ Altman, President, International Society for Computational Biology; Dr. Daniel Baker, Director, Laboratory for Atmospheric and Space Physics, University of Colorado; Dr. Francis Belloni, Chair of the American Physiological Society Career Opportunities in Physiology Committee.

Jeanine L. Bussiere, Ph.D., DABT, Director, Pharmacology/Toxicology, Immunex Corp., Seattle; John A. Boyle, Professor and Head of the Department of Biochemistry and Molecular Biology, Mississippi State University; Dr. James L. Carew, Department of Geology, College of Charleston, South Carolina; Nick Claudy, Manager, Human Resources, American Geological Institute.

Mike Dion, National Weather Service; Betty J. Eidemiller, Ph.D., Director of Education, Society of Toxicology; Richard A. Engberg, RPH, Technical Specialist, American Water Resources Association; Ken Goddard, Lab Director, National Fish and Wildlife Forensics Laboratory; Kelly A. Gull, Manager, Meetings and Educational Programs, American Society for Biochemistry and Molecular Biology.

Dr. Jill Karsten, Manager, Education and Career Services, American Geophysical Union; Paul R. Koch, Ph.D., P.E.; Penelope Jones, Director of Education and Customer Services, American Board of Clinical Chemistry; Dr. Gene Likens, International Association of Theoretical and Applied Limnologists; Melinda E. Lowy, Higher Education Programs Coordinator, American Physiological Society.

Timothy B. Mihuc, Chair of the North American Benthological Society Publicity and Public Information Committee; Dr. Elizabeth Murray, College of Mt. Saint Joseph, Cincinnati, Ohio; Sharlotte Neely, Ph.D., Professor of Anthropology, Northern Kentucky University; North American Benthological Society; Alan Rowen, Technical Director, Society of Naval Architects and Marine Engineers.

Dr. Wendy Ryan, Department of Biology, Kutztown University, Pennsylvania; Suzanne Scarlata, Department of Physiology & Biophysics, S.U.N.Y. Stony Brook; Joshua M. Scott, P.E.; Frank Shephard, Executive Secretary of the Society of General Physiologists; Professor Marjorie Skubic, Computer Engineering and Computer Science Department, University of Missouri at Columbia, Missouri; Rosalyn Snyder, Homepage Editor, IEEE Robotics and Automation Society.

Society for Integrative and Comparative Biology (SICB) Education Council; Society of Toxicology; Marvin Specter, Executive Director, National Academy of Forensic Engineers; Lisa Spurlock, Entomological Society of America; Dr. Paula Stephan, Andrew Young School of Policy Studies, Georgia State University; Lance Strawn, P.E.

Hilary Troester, Research Assistant, Research and Publications, Association of Science-Technology Centers; Dr. C. Susan Weiler, Whitman College, Walla Walla, Washington; John Winchester, P.E., Water Resources Engineer; and Alan C. York, Professor, Department of Entomology, Purdue University.

Thank you also to all the web developers and webmasters of the numerous websites that I visited in researching this book.

And, finally, I wish to express my gratitude to my husband Richard McDavid for reading over my manuscript and for continually encouraging me with his humor and love.

HOW TO USE THIS BOOK

In *Career Opportunities in Science,* you will learn about more than 80 professions that you can enter in the scientific and technical fields. You'll learn about many types of scientists, engineers, specialists, and technicians. In addition, you'll learn about some career options that are available to individuals with scientific training and a background in such areas as business, education, law enforcement, and communications.

Career Opportunities in Science provides basic information about the different professions described in this book. You'll read about what the occupations are like, what job requirements are needed, and get a general idea of the salaries, job markets, and advancement prospects for each occupation.

Sources of Information

The information presented in *Career Opportunities in Science* comes from a variety of sources—scientists, engineers, educators, professional societies, trade associations, government agencies, and so on. In addition, books and periodicals related to the different occupations were consulted as well as brochures and other written materials from professional associations, federal agencies, businesses, and other organizations. Job descriptions, work guidelines, and other work-related materials for the different professions were also studied.

The World Wide Web was also a valuable source. A wide range of websites were visited to learn about each of the professions that are described in this book. These websites included professional societies, trade associations, law schools, universities, government agencies, social service agencies, law firms, businesses, and on-line professional periodicals.

How This Book Is Organized

Career Opportunities in Science is designed to be easy to use and read. Altogether there are 82 profiles in 13 sections. A section may have as few as four profiles or as many as 12 profiles. The profiles are usually two or three pages long. The profiles all follow the same format so that you may read the job profiles or sections in whatever order you prefer.

Sections one through four describe opportunities in the biological sciences, physical sciences, and earth sciences. Sections five and six cover occupations in the fields of mathematics and computer science. Sections seven through ten discuss professions in applied sciences while sections eleven through thirteen describe nontraditional options that are available for individuals with scientific backgrounds and training.

The Job Profiles

The job profiles give you basic information about more than 80 career opportunities. Each profile starts with the *Career Profile,* a summary of a job's major duties, salary, job outlook, and opportunities for promotion. It also sums up general requirements and special skills needed for a job, as well as personality traits that successful professionals may share. The *Career Ladder* section is a visual presentation of a typical career path.

The rest of the occupational profile is divided into the following parts:

- The "Position Description" details major responsibilities and duties of an occupation. Some profiles discuss several options that are available within a profession.
- "Salaries" presents a general idea of the wages that professionals may earn.
- "Employment Prospects" provides a general idea of the job market for an occupation.
- "Advancement Prospects" discusses possible ways that professionals may advance in their careers.
- "Education and Training" describes the type of education and training that may be required to enter a profession.
- "Experience, Skills, and Personality Traits" generally covers the job requirements needed for entry-level positions. It also describes some basic employability skills that employers expect job candidates to have. In addition, this section describes some personality traits that successful professionals have in common.
- "Special Requirements" lists any professional license, certification, or registration that may be required.
- "Unions and Associations" provides the names of some professional associations and other organizations that professionals are eligible to join.
- "Tips for Entry" offers general advice for gaining work experience, improving employability, and finding jobs. It also provides suggestions for finding more career information on the World Wide Web.

The Appendixes

At the end of the book are six appendixes that provide additional resources for the professions described in *Career Opportunities in Science.* You can learn about resources for educational training for some professions. You can also find contact information for professional associations and other organizations that can provide you with additional career information. Further, you can find a list of books, periodicals, and websites that may give you further information about and insight into the occupations that interest you.

The World Wide Web

Throughout *Career Opportunities in Science,* website addresses for various professional organizations and other resources are provided so that you can learn more on your own. All the websites were accessible as the book was being written. Please keep in mind that the website owners may change website addresses, remove the webpages to which you have been referred, or shut down their websites completely. Should you come across a URL that does not work, you may still be able to find the website by entering the website title or the name of the organization or individual in a search engine.

INTRODUCTION

You are interested in a career in science. That's great!

What is science? A year ago I put that question to my then 15-year-old niece, Amanda. "Science is a question that is never fully answered," she said, "only pieces are discovered."

Science is an awesome and amazing endeavor. It is about research, experimentation, and discovery in a wide range of subjects such as atoms, bacteria, plants, animal behavior, human systems, artificial intelligence, fossils, volcanoes, and outer space.

Science is also about applying scientific knowledge to solve problems, invent new technologies, and develop new products. Look around you, and you can see the results of science: the food we eat; the clothes we wear; the vehicles we ride in; the computers, telephones, and electronic gadgets that we use for work and play; the medicines we take to treat our illnesses; and much more.

You will find that many career opportunities are available in science and technology. The more familiar occupations are those of scientists, engineers, and technicians. They work in academic and government settings as well as in the different industries, including biomedicine, health, biotechnology, agriculture, food processing, energy, aviation, chemical manufacturing, and telecommunications industries.

Additionally, there are careers that you may not have considered to be part of science because they are found in such fields as business, finance, law, education, and communications. However, these professions also require scientific training and skills. For example, you might choose to become a patent agent, science writer, science curator, actuary, regulatory affairs specialist, forensic psychiatrist, technology policy analyst, science educator, or management consultant.

In *Career Opportunities in Science* you can read 82 profiles about different scientific and technical careers. These profiles are designed to introduce you to basic career information and to encourage you to continue investigating the professions that you might choose to pursue.

Explore Your Career Options

As you come across occupations that interest you, take the time to learn more about them. Read books that explore a profession in more depth and read professional newspapers, magazines, and journals. If possible, talk with professionals about their jobs and, perhaps, observe them at work.

Take advantage of the career center at your school or library. Browse through the various resources that are available about colleges, scholarships, careers, job search skills, and so on. If you can't find what you're looking for, ask a career counselor or librarian.

The World Wide Web is also a valuable resource for career exploration. Visit websites for professional societies, trade associations, and other organizations that are related to the occupations in which you are interested. Also go to websites of employers—colleges, universities, hospitals, research institutes, government agencies, businesses, companies, and so forth—to get an idea of what it may be like to work in such a setting. At many websites, you will find articles posted about occupations and the industry along with links that lead to other related websites or webpages. Many employers and organizations also include career information and job listings on their websites.

Get hands-on experience working in the fields and settings in which you're interested. High school students: find out if there is a work experience program for which you qualify. Talk about your interests with the program coordinator and see if you can be placed in an appropriate work setting such as a science lab, hospital, or science center.

College students: Find out about internship or work-study programs that are available in the fields and settings that interest you.

As you explore different career possibilities, you will discover the kind of careers you might like—and don't like. Furthermore, you will also be gaining valuable experience and building a network of contacts for future references.

Good luck with your career exploration!

—Susan Echaore-McDavid

BIOLOGICAL SCIENCES

BIOLOGIST

CAREER PROFILE

Duties: Conduct basic or applied research; design and conduct research projects; may teach college or university students; research assistants and technicians provide research and administrative support; perform duties as required of position

Alternate Title(s): Life Scientist, Biological Scientist, Medical Scientist, Research Scientist; Botanist, Microbiologist, Entomologist, or other title that reflects a specialty

Salary Range: $42,000 to $153,000

Employment Prospects: Good

Advancement Prospects: Good

Prerequisites:

Education or Training—Bachelor's or master's degrees for research assistant and technician positions; Ph.D. required to conduct independent research, teach in universities and colleges, or hold top management positions
Experience—Work and research experience related to position usually required; postdoctoral experience may be required for research scientists
Special Skills and Personality Traits—Math, computer, communication, writing, interpersonal, teamwork, and self-management skills; analytical; creative; clever; flexible; persistent
Licensure/Certification—None required

CAREER LADDER

```
┌─────────────────────────────────────┐
│          Senior Biologist            │
└─────────────────────────────────────┘

┌─────────────────────────────────────┐
│         Research Biologist           │
└─────────────────────────────────────┘

┌─────────────────────────────────────┐
│   Postdoctoral Research Associate    │
└─────────────────────────────────────┘
```

Position Description

Biology is a life science. It is the study of how all living organisms function. They may be one-celled organisms (such as bacteria and algae), plants, animals, or humans.

Biologists are concerned with understanding the structure and life processes of all living organisms. They are also involved with the classification of plant and animal species, as well as with examining the distribution of the different species. In addition, Biologists investigate the relationships that living organisms have with each other and with their environments. Further, Biologists seek to understand plant, animal, and human diseases and search for ways to prevent and cure diseases.

Biology covers many disciplines and subdisciplines, and together these various fields are referred to as the biological sciences. From time to time, new biological fields emerge to

meet challenges of new health and environmental problems, or new subdisciplines develop as a result of scientific discoveries and technological advancements. The following are some of the biological fields in which Biologists specialize:

- taxonomy, the study of how organisms are classified into certain categories
- anatomy, the study of an organism's structure, such as the human skeleton
- microbiology, the study of bacteria, viruses, fungi, and other organisms that can only be seen through microscopes
- botany, the study of the plant world
- zoology, the study of the animal kingdom
- physiology, the study of the life processes (such as the respiratory system or circulatory system) that keep organisms alive

- cell biology, the study of the smallest units of life that make up all organisms
- genetics, the study of how characteristics (or traits) are passed on through generations
- molecular biology, the study of how genetic information is read and controlled
- biochemistry, the study of how chemicals combine and react within the cells
- ecology, the study of how ecosystems are organized and how plants and animals interact with each other in their surroundings

Most Biologists are research scientists who work in academic, government, industry, nonprofit, or nongovernmental settings. Some Biologists conduct basic research, seeking further knowledge about living organisms. They search for answers to such questions as: How does the human brain work? How does a virus cause disease? How are trees affected by air pollution? How do apes communicate with each other? Oftentimes, Biologists work on research projects that involve the collaboration of various biological scientists or with scientists from other disciplines, such as chemists, physicists, or geologists.

Other Biologists are involved in research and development in such applied fields as medical science, agriculture, environmental science, and conservation. Applied researchers use the findings of basic biological research to develop products and processes for practical uses. For example, applied Biologists might work on the development of new medicines, disease-resistant crops, better food processing techniques, or methods for saving endangered species.

Biologists work in offices and laboratories. Depending on their specialty, their research might involve any of the following: manipulating cells, examining tissues and organs, devising experiments that involve greenhouse plants or lab animals, or conducting tests on human subjects.

Many Biologists also conduct research in the field to make observations and to gather samples to study when they return to their laboratories. Sometimes they travel to remote locations, such as wildernesses, islands, rain forests, or oceans, and spend several days or months working and living there.

Biologists' duties vary, depending on their position and experience. In general, research Biologists are responsible for designing and conducting research projects. Senior researchers and principal investigators may perform supervisory and management duties. Some of the general tasks that research scientists perform include: conducting experiments, gathering data, analyzing and interpreting data, writing reports, and performing administrative tasks. Biologists who conduct independent research are usually responsible for seeking research grants from the federal government and other sources to fund their research projects. This involves writing grant proposals that describe goals, methodologies, budgets, and other aspects about their proposed projects.

Most Biologists share the results of their research work with colleagues. They might write scientific papers which they submit to scientific journals or make presentations at scientific conferences that are sponsored by professional associations.

Many Biologists are employed as professors at colleges and universities. They teach basic biology courses as well as advanced courses in their areas of expertise. Their duties include conducting independent research, preparing for and teaching courses, advising students, supervising student research projects, writing scholarly works, performing administrative duties, and participating in community service.

Biologists are also technicians and research assistants. They provide scientists with research and administrative support. Their tasks include setting up experiments, collecting specimens in the field, making observations, analyzing data, writing reports, handling and caring for lab animals or greenhouse plants, maintaining laboratory equipment and facilities, performing routine administrative tasks, and so on.

Salaries

Salaries vary, depending on such factors as education, experience, position, employer, and geographical location. According to a 2001 salary survey by the American Association for the Advancement of Science, the median salary for life scientists in academic settings ranged from $42,000 to $112,000, and for those in nonacademic settings, from $76,000 to $153,000.

Employment Prospects

Biologists are hired by government agencies, businesses, industries, educational institutions, research institutions, nonprofit groups, and nongovernmental organizations.

According to the Bureau of Labor Statistics, job growth for biological scientists is expected to grow faster than average through 2010. Many opportunities will arise as a result of Biologists retiring, transferring to other positions, or leaving their fields.

Job prospects vary, depending on the biological field, job positions, and work settings. For example, research opportunities for marine biologists are limited in comparison to those for molecular biologists. In general, the greatest number of opportunities are found in the biotechnology and pharmaceutical industries for research scientist, research assistant, and technician positions. However, the competition for employment in these industries is strong. Research opportunities in academic and nonprofit settings are also highly competitive.

Biologists can also find employment in other positions that utilize their biological training. Some occupations are: high school biology teacher, environmental educator, biological sales representative, conservationist, park ranger, museum curator, technical writer, safety and health inspector, health care provider, and medical laboratory technologist.

With additional education and training, Biologists can pursue careers in the medical and health professions. For example, they can become medical doctors, dentists, veterinarians, physical therapists, and psychologists.

Advancement Prospects

Biologists with administrative or management ambitions can advance to such positions within their specialty. Research scientists can become project leaders, program managers, laboratory directors, executive officers, and so on. Technicians and research assistants can advance to managerial positions as laboratory managers and nonlaboratory administrative positions. Some Biologists become consultants. Professors receive promotional rankings as assistant professors, associate professors, or full professors.

Many Biologists achieve advancement by earning higher pay, by conducting independent research projects, and through receiving professional recognition.

Education and Training

A bachelor's degree in a biological science is usually the minimum requirement for research assistant and technician positions. Some employers may require or prefer that candidates have earned master's degrees. Research scientists must hold either a master's or a doctoral degree in their specialties. A Ph.D. degree is required in order to teach in universities and four-year colleges, to conduct independent research, or to obtain top management positions. Some Ph.D. scientists also earn medical degrees (M.D.) to obtain additional training for careers in medical research.

Experience, Skills, and Personality Traits

Requirements vary for the various positions as well as among the different employers. For entry-level positions, employers generally choose candidates who have related work and research experience, which may have been gained through research projects, internships, fellowships, part-time employment, and so on. Many employers expect Ph.D. candidates for research scientist positions to have several years of postdoctoral experience.

Biologists need strong math and computer skills for their work. They also need excellent communication and writing skills as they must be able to report their results and conclusions clearly to fellow scientists and to nontechnical personnel. Additionally, Biologists need strong interpersonal, and teamwork skills as well as self-management skills such as being able to meet deadlines, prioritize tasks, work independently, and make sound judgments.

Some personality traits that successful Biologists share are being analytical, creative, clever, flexible, and persistent.

Unions and Associations

Many Biologists join professional societies to take advantage of professional services and resources such as training programs, education programs, and current research information. Membership also provides them with opportunities to network with their colleagues. Biologists are eligible to join societies that serve scientists from all disciplines, such as the American Association for the Advancement of Science, or societies that serve Biologists in general such as the American Institute of Biological Sciences.

In addition, many Biologists join associations that serve their particular fields. For example, animal biologists might join the Society for Integrative and Comparative Biology while microbiologists might join the American Society of Microbiology. See Appendix III for contact information.

Tips for Entry

1. As an undergraduate student, take a wide variety of biological courses to get an idea of the variety of career paths that are available.
2. To gain experience, work as an intern in several settings or become a research assistant with a professor in whose work you are interested.
3. You can learn more about various biology careers on the Internet. Many professional associations provide career information on their websites. (For a list of associations and their URL addresses, see Appendix III.) You can also find relevant websites by entering the key word *biology careers* in a search engine.

MICROBIOLOGIST

CAREER PROFILE

Duties: Conduct basic or applied research; design and conduct research projects; may provide clinical laboratory services; research assistants and technicians provide research and administrative support; perform duties as required of position

Alternate Title(s): Virologist, Medical Microbiologist, or other title that reflects a specialty

Salary Range: $31,000 to $87,000

Employment Prospects: Good

Advancement Prospects: Good

Prerequisites:

Education or Training—Bachelor's or advanced degree in biology, microbiology, or related field

Experience—Postdoctoral experience may be required for research scientists

Special Skills and Personality Traits—Math, computer, writing, communication, interpersonal, and teamwork skills; precise; creative; flexible; self-motivated

Licensure/Certification—Licensure or certification may be required for Clinical Microbiologists; board certification required to run clinical laboratories

CAREER LADDER

```
┌─────────────────────────────────┐
│      Senior Microbiologist       │
└─────────────────────────────────┘

┌─────────────────────────────────┐
│          Microbiologist          │
└─────────────────────────────────┘

┌─────────────────────────────────┐
│  Postdoctoral Research Associate │
└─────────────────────────────────┘
```

Position Description

Microbiology is the study of microbes (or microorganisms) such as bacteria, viruses, molds, yeast, algae, and protozoa. These are very tiny living organisms that can be only seen with the help of microscopes.

Microbiologists seek to understand how microbes exist by studying their characteristics as well as how they function, grow, develop, and reproduce. Additionally, these scientists examine how the different microbes interact with other living organisms. Microbiologists are also concerned in understanding how some microbes act as infectious agents and affect the health of plants, animals, and humans.

Many Microbiologists are research scientists who conduct basic research to gain further knowledge about microorganisms and infectious agents. Microbiologists also develop new methodologies and techniques by which to study the various microbes.

Some Microbiologists devote themselves to a specialty. Some specialize in the type of microbes that they study. For example, bacteriologists examine bacteria, parasitologists study tiny parasites, and virologists investigate viruses that are active inside living cells. Other Microbiologists concentrate in a particular specialty of biology. For example, they might study only the physiology, cytology, biochemistry, immunology, or genetics of microorganisms.

Microbiologists sometimes collaborate on projects with other microbiologists, biologists, and scientists from other disciplines.

Microbiologists' duties vary, depending on their position and experience. In general, they are responsible for designing and conducting research projects. Some of their tasks include conducting experiments, gathering data, analyzing and interpreting data, writing reports, and performing administrative tasks. Most senior researchers and principal investigators also perform supervisory and management duties. Many Microbiologists are responsible for obtaining research grants to fund their projects. This involves learning about available grants from the federal government and other sources, as well as writing grant proposals that describe the methodologies, budgets, and other aspects of their projects.

Microbiologists typically exchange information about their research results with colleagues. They might submit articles, or scientific papers, to scientific journals or give presentations at scientific conferences that are sponsored by professional associations.

Some Microbiologists provide technical and administrative support to scientists. They're usually called research associates or technicians. Some of their duties include conducting experiments, collecting specimens, analyzing data, writing reports, maintaining laboratories, and performing routine administrative tasks.

A large number of Microbiologists are involved in medicine, industry, agriculture, and other areas of applied microbiology. These scientists and technologists use the findings of basic microbiological research to solve problems in their respective fields.

The duties of applied Microbiologists vary, depending on their specialty. Medical and veterinary Microbiologists work closely with physicians, dentists, and medical scientists. These Microbiologists identify and examine microbes that cause diseases in humans and animals. In addition, they investigate ways to prevent, treat, and eliminate those diseases.

Clinical Microbiologists provide laboratory services to physicians. They perform tests to identify pathogenic microbes in specimens from patients; assist physicians with the interpretation and evaluation of tests; and suggest further test procedures.

Public health Microbiologists provide laboratory services to local public health agencies. They perform testing and other services to detect, diagnose, treat, and control infectious diseases and other health hazards in the community.

Industrial Microbiologists are involved in the research and development of new products and production methods in pharmaceutical, biotechnology, food, dairy, cosmetics, and other industries. These products include medicines, antibiotics, foods, beverages, and health care products.

Agricultural Microbiologists are concerned with ways to improve the production of crops and livestock. Some Agricultural Microbiologists may work on projects that use microbes to increase crops or to control insect pests. Environmental Microbiologists are involved in the protection of ecosystems. Their jobs may involve the inspection of manufacturing plants, testing bodies of water for pollutants, or controlling disease that is spread by wildlife, insects, or rodents infected with pathogenic microbes.

Microbiologists mostly work in sterile laboratories and offices. They use computers, electron microscopes, and other sophisticated laboratory equipment. They wear protective clothing and follow strict safety rules and regulations to minimize the risks that are involved in handling microbes, chemicals, and other potentially dangerous elements.

Salaries

Salaries vary and depend on education, experience, type of employer, duties, geographical location, and other factors. The Bureau of Labor Statistics reports that the estimated annual salary in 2001 for most Microbiologists ranged from $30,740 to $87,220.

Employment Prospects

Microbiologists work for universities, colleges, government agencies, agricultural companies, biotechnology firms, pharmaceutical companies, hospitals, research institutes, nonprofit organizations, and so on.

Job prospects for experienced Microbiologists are reported as being favorable by many in the field. However, competition for jobs is keen. Most opportunities will become available as Microbiologists retire, transfer to other positions, or leave their fields.

With additional education and training, Microbiologists can pursue careers as medical doctors, dentists, veterinarians, and lawyers.

Advancement Prospects

Microbiologists can pursue management and administrative positions in any work setting. Experienced Microbiologists can become consultants to businesses, government agencies, and policy makers. An advanced degree is usually required for advancement to higher positions.

Education and Training

Educational requirements vary for different positions and with various employers. A bachelor's degree in biology, microbiology, or related field qualifies individuals for research assistant and technician positions. Some employers may prefer or require a master's degree. Usually, Microbiologists are required to have doctorate degrees in order to conduct independent research, teach in colleges and universities, and obtain top management posts.

Experience, Skills, and Personality Traits

In general, employers choose candidates who have related work and research experience to the positions they are applying for. Recent college graduates may have gained experience through student research projects, internships, fellowships, part-time employment, and so on. Many employers require or prefer that Ph.D. candidates have several years of postdoctoral experience.

Microbiologists need strong math and computer skills as well as excellent writing and communication skills. In addition, they need effective interpersonal and teamwork skills. Being precise, creative, flexible, and self-motivated are a few of the personality traits that successful Microbiologists share.

Special Requirements

Clinical and public health Microbiologists are required to be licensed in some states. A state may allow professional certification from an approved professional board as a substitute for licensure. (Two such professional boards are the American College of Microbiology and the American Society of Clinical Pathologists.)

To become clinical and public health laboratory directors, Microbiologists must be board-certified Ph.D.s or board-certified physicians. The American Board of Medical Microbiology and the American Board of Medical Laboratory Immunology grants certification to Ph.D. Microbiologists.

Unions and Associations

Many Microbiologists join societies to take advantage of professional services such as education programs, professional certification programs, and networking opportunities. Some professional associations are the American Society for Microbiology, the Society for Industrial Microbiology, and the American Society for Virology. See Appendix III for contact information.

Tips for Entry

1. College and university career centers provide services to both students and alumni. Take advantage of your school's career center when searching for internships, cooperative education programs, fellowships, part-time work, and permanent positions.
2. Use the Internet to learn more about microbiology. Two websites you might visit are American Society for Microbiology, http://www.asmusa.org and Microbe World, http://www.microbeworld.org/mlc.

BOTANIST

CAREER PROFILE

Duties: Conduct basic or applied research; design and conduct research projects; may teach college or university students; perform duties as required of position

Alternate Title(s): Plant Biologist; Plant Scientist; Marine Biologist; Plant Physiologist; Plant Pathologist; or other title that reflects a specialty

Salary Range: $32,000 to $117,000

Employment Prospects: Good

Advancement Prospects: Good

Prerequisites:
Education or Training—A bachelor's or advanced degree in botany or related field
Experience—Postdoctoral experience may be required for research scientists
Special Skills and Personality Traits—Math, computer, communication, writing, interpersonal, teamwork, and self-management skills; patient; ambitious; creative; flexible
Licensure/Certification—None required

CAREER LADDER

```
+--------------------------------------+
|           Senior Botanist            |
+--------------------------------------+

+--------------------------------------+
|          Research Botanist           |
+--------------------------------------+

+--------------------------------------+
|    Postdoctoral Research Associate   |
+--------------------------------------+
```

Position Description

Botany is the biological study of plants—lichens, mosses, ferns, flowers, shrubs, grasses, vines, trees, and so on. Basic botanical knowledge is applied in such fields as agriculture, medicine, biotechnology, forestry, horticulture, and conservation.

Botanists, or plant biologists, are concerned with the identification and classification of the thousands of plant species. They seek to understand the structure and life processes of plants, as well as how plants relate to each other and to other living organisms. Botanists also study how plants have developed and changed through time and how plants adapt to their surroundings. Biologists also investigate the practical uses of plants and study the causes and cures of plant diseases.

Many Botanists devote themselves to studying the biology of particular plant species. For example, biologists study the biology of mosses, mycologists study fungi, and marine biologists study different plant species that live in the oceans.

Other Botanists specialize in studying one (or more) biology fields, such as:

- anatomy, the structure of plants
- physiology, the internal processes that take place in order for plants to grow and reproduce
- biophysics, the application of physics principles to study how plants function
- cytology, the biology of plant cells
- biochemistry, the study of how chemicals combine and react in plant cells
- plant genetics, the heredity of plants (how plants pass their traits to the next generation through genes)
- molecular biology, the study of how genes affect the form and function of plants and how genes may be altered to change plants or to create new plants
- taxonomy, the identification and classification of plant life
- plant ecology, the relationships between plants as well as with their surroundings
- paleobotany, the biology and evolution of fossil plants

Many Botanists specialize in the applied plant science fields—biotechnology, horticulture, medical botany, natural resources management, and so on. For example: plant breeders develop better types of plants; plant pathologists study plant diseases and how to manage, prevent, or control them; horticulturists investigate ways to improve the production of ornamental plants, fruits, and vegetable crops; food technologists are concerned with the development of food products; agronomists study how to increase crop production; and conservationists study and manage natural resources such as rangelands and forests.

Most Botanists are research scientists who conduct basic or applied research in academic, government, industry, nonprofit, or nongovernmental work settings. Basic researchers seek further knowledge about the biology of plants, while applied researchers use the findings of basic botanical research to develop products, processes, methodologies, and techniques for practical purposes.

Academic Botanists usually choose their own research topics while those who work in nonacademic settings typically perform research that is determined by their employers. Those who conduct independent research are usually responsible for seeking research grants from the federal government and other sources to fund their projects.

In general, research Botanists are responsible for designing and conducting research projects. They study plants in controlled conditions in greenhouses as well as in their natural habitats. They also examine plant cells and tissues under microscopes. Some of their tasks include conducting experiments; collecting, analyzing, and interpreting data; preparing reports; and performing administrative tasks. Sometimes Botanists conduct field expeditions to remote areas, such as deserts, rain forests, islands, wildernesses, seas, and islands. They may spend several weeks or months working and living there.

Botanists often share information about the results of their research work with their colleagues. They might write scientific papers which they submit to scientific journals or make presentations at scientific meetings that are sponsored by professional associations.

Most academic Botanists are employed as professors in colleges and universities. In addition to conducting research, they are responsible for planning and teaching undergraduate and graduate courses. They also advise students, supervise student research projects, perform administrative duties, and participate in community service.

Salaries

Salaries vary, depending on such factors as education, experience, position, employer, and geographical location. In a 2001 salary survey by Abbot, Langer, and Associates, the median salary for life scientists by type of job positions ranged from $32,000 for postdoctoral researchers to $116,500 for executive-level administrators.

Employment Prospects

Botanists work for universities, colleges, government agencies, research institutes, conservation organizations, biotechnology firms, pharmaceutical companies, seed companies, nurseries, agricultural companies, food processing plants, and so on.

Opportunities are expected to grow during the next few years due to the continuing need for better food supplies and the increased public sensitivity to environmental problems. The best opportunities should be in the areas of agronomy and biotechnology.

Botanists can also seek other occupations in which they may use their training. Some of these occupations are: science teacher, botanical garden director, naturalist, landscape designer, farmer, seed company sales representative, botanical illustrator, and environmental scientist.

Advancement Prospects

Botanists with administrative or management ambitions can advance to such positions within their specialty. They can become project leaders, program managers, laboratory directors, executive officers, and so on. Some Botanists become consultants. Professors receive promotional rankings as assistant professors, associate professors, or full professors.

Education and Training

Educational requirements vary, depending on the position and employer. In general, a bachelor's or master's degree in botany or a related field is required for research assistant, technician, and technologist positions. Doctorate degrees are required in order to conduct independent research, teach in universities and four-years colleges, or to obtain most top management positions.

Experience, Skills, and Personality Traits

Employers typically choose candidates for entry-level positions who have related work and research experience, which may have been gained through student research projects, internships, fellowships, part-time employment, and so on. Ph.D. candidates for research scientist positions are usually expected to have a few years of postdoctoral experience.

Botanists need basic math and computer skills for their work. They also need excellent communication and writing skills to report their results clearly to fellow scientists and others. In addition, they need strong interpersonal and teamwork skills as well as self-management skills, such as being able to work independently, meet deadlines, and prioritize tasks.

Some personality traits that successful Botanists share are being patient, ambitious, creative, and flexible.

Unions and Associations

Many Botanists join professional associations to take advantage of education programs, networking opportunities, and other professional services and resources. Some societies that serve the diverse interests of Botanists are the American Society of Plant Biologists, the Botanical Society of America, the American Society for Horticulture Science, the American Society of Agronomy, and the American Institute of Biological Sciences. See Appendix III for contact information.

Tips for Entry

1. Gain research experience as an undergraduate by doing independent research projects or working as a research assistant for a professor whose work interests you.

2. Summer jobs and internships are available with government agencies, private companies, research laboratories, and other settings. Start searching for positions early as many are often filled by late spring.

3. Use the Internet to learn more about Botanists. One website you might visit is the Botanical Society of America, http://www.botany.org. To get a list of other relevant websites, enter the keyword *botany* or *botanists* in a search engine.

ZOOLOGIST

CAREER PROFILE

Duties: Conduct basic or applied research; design and conduct research projects; may teach college or university students; research assistants and technicians provide research and administrative support; perform duties as required of position

Alternate Title(s): Animal Biologist; Entomologist; Invertebrate Scientist; Wildlife Biologist; or other title that reflects a specialty

Salary Range: $29,000 to $114,000

Employment Prospects: Good

Advancement Prospects: Good

Prerequisites:
　Education or Training—A bachelor's or advanced degree in zoology or related field
　Experience—Postdoctoral experience may be required for research scientists
　Special Skills and Personality Traits—Math, computer, data management, problem-solving, communication, and technical writing skills; curious; creative; analytical; committed; flexible
　Licensure/Certification—None required

CAREER LADDER

```
┌─────────────────────────────────────┐
│          Senior Zoologist           │
└─────────────────────────────────────┘

┌─────────────────────────────────────┐
│         Research Zoologist          │
└─────────────────────────────────────┘

┌─────────────────────────────────────┐
│   Postdoctoral Research Associate   │
└─────────────────────────────────────┘
```

Position Description

Zoology is the biological study of the animal kingdom. It deals with the origin, characteristics, life processes, and behavior of animals. Additionally, it is concerned with the identification, classification, and distribution of the many thousands of different animal species.

The animal biologists who study this science are Zoologists. People often confuse them with zookeepers. Although zookeepers usually have a background in zoology, their primary job is to take care of the animals in aquariums and zoological parks. Zoologists, on the other hand, are research scientists. Some conduct basic research to add further knowledge about the biology of animals, while others apply the findings of basic research to develop useful products or find solutions to problems in such applied fields as agriculture, medical science, biotechnology, conservation, and environmental science.

Many Zoologists focus their studies in one or more biology specialties, such as:

- taxonomy, the naming and classification of animals
- comparative anatomy, examining how body structures are different or the same
- physiology, the study of animal life processes such as the nervous and muscular systems
- endocrinology, the study of the tissues and glands that produce and secrete hormones
- genetics, the study of how characteristics are passed from one generation to the next
- animal behavior, the way animals behave
- animal ecology, the relationship of animals to their environment
- phylogeny, the evolution of animals

Some Zoologists study the overall biology of particular types of animals. For example: protozoologists examine protozoa; invertebrate Zoologists study animals without a backbone; herpetologists examine amphibians and reptiles; ornithologists investigate the world of birds; and primatologists study apes and other primates. Other Zoologists specialize in studying animals within a particular environment. For example, wildlife biologists study animals in the wilderness while limnologists examine animals that live in freshwater bodies.

Many Zoologists work in the applied sciences, such as conservation or animal husbandry (the management of animal welfare and breeding). Conducting basic or applied research may be their primary duty or one of many duties. Some applied Zoologists are employed as animal breeders, fisheries biologists, dairy scientists, food technologists, and wildlife forensic scientists.

Zoologists often conduct more than one research project at a time. They sometimes collaborate on projects with other zoologists, biological scientists, and scientists from other disciplines.

Zoological research involves designing and conducting research projects. Their duties include conducting experiments; collecting, interpreting, and analyzing data; preparing reports; and performing administrative tasks. Those who conduct independent research are usually responsible for seeking research grants from the federal government and other sources to fund their projects. Senior researchers and principal investigators may perform supervisory and management duties.

Zoologists often exchange research information with their colleagues. They might write articles, or scientific papers, which are published in scientific journals. Some might make presentations at scientific meetings that are sponsored by professional associations.

Zoologists observe animals in controlled environments such as zoos or laboratories as well as in their natural habitats (such as seas, jungles, and wilderness areas). Some Zoologists conduct field expeditions to remote locations, such as wildernesses, rain forests, islands, or seas. They often spend several days or months working and living there as they complete their field research.

Many Zoologists are employed as university and college professors to teach zoology courses to undergraduate and graduate students. Zoologists juggle various tasks each day. Their duties include conducting independent research, preparing for and teaching courses, advising students, supervising student research projects, writing scholarly works, performing administrative duties, and participating in community service.

Zoologists also work as technicians and research assistants. In these positions they provide research scientists with research and administrative support. Their tasks include conducting experiments, making observations, analyzing data, writing reports, handling and caring for lab animals, maintaining laboratory equipment and facilities, completing routine administrative tasks, and so on.

Salaries

Salaries vary, depending on education, experience, geographical location, and other factors. According to the Bureau of Labor Statistics, the estimated annual salary in 2001 for most Zoologists ranged from $28,650 to $69,760. The estimated annual salary for most postsecondary instructors of biological sciences (which includes zoology) ranged from $31,240 to $114,080.

Employment Prospects

Zoologists are employed by colleges, universities, government agencies, research institutes, nongovernmental organizations, agricultural research stations, fisheries, agricultural companies, pharmaceutical companies, medical laboratories, conservation organizations, zoological gardens, consulting firms, and so forth.

Opportunities generally become available as individuals retire, transfer to other positions, or leave the profession for any number of reasons. Job candidates can expect keen competition, particularly for research and teaching positions. Zoologists with advanced degrees increase their chances of employment.

Zoologists can also seek other occupations in which they may use their training. Some of these occupations are science teacher, environmental educator, zookeeper, animal trainer, veterinary assistant, environmental scientist, park naturalist, pharmaceutical salesperson, and biological technician. With additional education and training, Zoologists can pursue careers as veterinarians, medical doctors, dentists, or other medical or healthcare professional.

Advancement Prospects

Opportunities vary with the different positions. Research Zoologists can advance to management and administrative positions by becoming project leaders, program managers, and executive officers. Technicians and research assistants can advance to managerial positions as laboratory managers or other nonlaboratory administrative positions. Professors can rise through the ranks to full professorship.

Education and Training

A bachelor's degree in zoology, biology, psychology, anthropology, or related field can qualify Zoologists for research assistant or technician positions. Having a master's degree typically offers candidates a wider range of opportunities. A Ph.D. is required to teach in universities and four-year colleges, to conduct independent research, or to obtain top management positions.

Experience, Skills, and Personality Traits

Requirements vary for the different positions as well as among the various employers. For entry-level positions, employers generally choose candidates who have related work and research experience. This may have been gained through research projects, internships, fellowships, part-time employment, and so on. Ph.D. candidates for research scientist positions may be required to have a few years of postdoctoral experience.

Zoologists need strong math, computer, data management, and problem-solving skills for their work. In addition, excellent communication and technical writing skills are needed in order to write and present comprehensible reports to others.

Being curious, creative, analytical, committed, and flexible are a few of the personality traits that successful zoologists share.

Unions and Associations

Professional societies offer Zoologists many professional resources and services such as current research information and networking opportunities. Zoologists can join general scientific societies such as the American Association for the Advancement of Science or the Society for Integrative and Comparative Biology. They can also join professional societies that serve their particular interests such as the Animal Behavior Society, the Society for Marine Mammalogy, the American Society of Animal Science, or the American Physiological Society. See Appendix III for contact information.

Tips for Entry

1. You can begin acquiring practical experience in high school. Do volunteer work at zoos, nature centers, aquariums, or animal shelters.
2. Contact professional societies for leads to internships, fellowships, postdoctoral positions, and permanent positions.
3. Use the Internet to learn more about zoology. To start, you might visit these websites: Society for Integrative and Comparative Biology, http://www.sicb.org and Biosis, http://www.Biosis.org.

AQUATIC BIOLOGIST

CAREER PROFILE

Duties: Conduct basic or applied research; design and conduct research projects; may teach college or university students; research assistants and technicians provide research and administrative support; perform duties as required of position

Alternate Title(s): Marine Biologist, Limnologist, Fisheries Biologist, or other title that reflects a specialty

Salary Range: $20,000 to $80,000

Employment Prospects: Good

Advancement Prospects: Good

Prerequisites:

Education or Training—A bachelor's or advanced degree in biology, aquatic biology, or related field

Experience—Practical laboratory and field research experience; postdoctoral experience for research scientists may be required

Special Skills and Personality Traits—Laboratory, statistics, computer, data management, communication, technical writing, organizational, interpersonal, and teamwork skills; independent; flexible; persistent; creative; enthusiastic; self-motivated

Licensure/Certification—None required

CAREER LADDER

```
┌─────────────────────────────────┐
│    Senior Aquatic Biologist     │
└─────────────────────────────────┘

┌─────────────────────────────────┐
│   Research Aquatic Biologist    │
└─────────────────────────────────┘

┌─────────────────────────────────┐
│ Postdoctoral Research Associate │
└─────────────────────────────────┘
```

Position Description

Aquatic Biology is the scientific study of plants and animals that live in oceans, estuaries, lakes, rivers, and other bodies of water.

Aquatic Biologists are concerned with understanding the structure and life processes of the various aquatic plants and animals, as well as learning about their origins and evolution. These scientists also are involved in the classification and distribution of the aquatic species. Many examine how aquatic organisms behave and relate to each other as well as with their surroundings. In addition, Aquatic Biologists study problems such as the effects of pollution, the invasion of exotic species into an ecosystem, diseases of aquatic plants and animals, and how to increase production in fish farms.

Aquatic Biologists typically focus their research in areas that most interest them. The following are a few specialties:

- marine biology, the study of bacteria, plankton, worms, fish larvae, and other small creatures that live in oceans and other saltwater bodies (Note: marine biologists rarely work with whales and other large sea animals.)
- biological oceanography, the interaction of organisms with each other and with their saltwater surroundings
- limnology, the study of organisms that live in inland water systems such as lakes, ponds, rivers, and wetlands
- benthology, the study of organisms that live on, in, or near the bottom of seas, lakes, streams, ponds, and other bodies of water
- aquatic invertebrate zoology, the study of aquatic animals without backbones
- aquatic botany, the study of algae and other aquatic plants
- fisheries biology, the scientific management of fish programs

- aquaculture, the study of farming fish, shellfish, and aquatic plants for food, aquarium fish tanks, ornamental purposes, sportfishing, and other purposes

Most Aquatic Biologists work as research scientists in universities, government, industry, research institutes, zoological parks, and other work settings. They may handle one or several research projects at a time, and sometimes collaborate with other scientists on a project. They conduct their research in laboratories as well as in the field on small boats or large research ships. The amount of fieldwork varies with different projects. For example, field expeditions may be conducted on a weekly basis or last for several weeks or months.

Specific duties vary, but in general, Aquatic Biologists are responsible for designing and conducting their research projects. Some of their tasks include conducting experiments, collecting samples, analyzing and interpreting data, writing reports, and performing administrative tasks.

Many independent research projects are funded through grants from the federal government and other sources. Thus scientists must seek out appropriate research grants and write grant proposals.

Many Aquatic Biologists are employed as professors at colleges and universities. Along with conducting their research projects, they prepare for and teach courses to undergraduate and graduate students. Their other duties include advising students, supervising student research projects, writing scholarly works, performing administrative duties, and participating in community service.

Some Aquatic Biologists are research assistants and technicians. They provide research scientists with support in both the laboratory and out in the field. Under the scientists' direction, they perform such duties as conducting experiments, collecting data, analyzing data, writing reports, maintaining laboratory equipment, and performing routine administrative tasks.

Salaries

Salaries vary, depending on such factors as education, experience, employer, and geographical location. According to a membership survey by the North American Benthological Society, the annual salary for 88 percent of the respondents ranged between $20,000 and $80,000.

Employment Prospects

Aquatic Biologists work for colleges, universities, government agencies, research institutions, aquariums and zoological parks, environmental organizations, environmental consulting firms, and various businesses and industries.

Overall, opportunities become available as Aquatic Biologists retire, transfer to other positions, or resign. Some Aquatic Biologists expect opportunities to increase in the next decade due to the large number of colleagues reaching retirement age.

Competition for jobs is strong, especially in the field of marine biology. According to a survey of its members by the North American Benthological Society, the demand for wetlands scientists is stronger than for stream biologists, and that scientists with experience in herpetology (frogs) and ichthyology (fish) are more in demand than those with experience in other fields.

With a background in aquatic biology, individuals can pursue careers in other occupations. For example, they can become fish farmers, fish and game wardens, animal trainers, animal health technicians, animal care specialists, museum curators, science writers, aquarium educators, or biology teachers.

Advancement Prospects

Aquatic Biologists are generally required to pursue management positions in order to earn higher salaries. A typical career path would be 10 to 15 years of field experience followed by 10 years of management experience.

Education and Training

Educational requirements vary with the different positions. For research assistant and technician positions, candidates need a bachelor's degree in biology, chemistry, or other discipline with relevant course work in aquatic biology. Having a master's degree in the appropriate field is usually more desirable with most employers.

Aquatic Biologists who wish to conduct independent research or advance to management positions must obtain a master's or doctoral degree in aquatic biology, limnology, oceanography, or other related field. A Ph.D. is required to teach in universities and four-year colleges.

Experience, Skills, and Personality Traits

Entry-level candidates need practical research experience in the laboratory and the field. This could be in the form of internships, summer jobs, student research projects, and postdoctoral training.

Aquatic Biologists need strong laboratory, statistics, and computer skills and must possess basic data management skills. In addition, they should have proficient communication and technical writing skills. Good organizational, interpersonal, and teamwork skills are also important.

Successful Aquatic Biologists share personality traits such as being flexible, creative, persistent, enthusiastic, and self-motivated.

Unions and Associations

Most Aquatic Biologists join professional associations to take advantage of professional services and resources such as continuing education programs, professional publications, and networking opportunities. Some national societies that serve Aquatic Biologists are the American Society of Limnology and Oceanography, the North American Benthological Society, the Society for Integrative and Comparative Biology, the Society of Wetland Scientists, and the American Fisheries Society. See Appendix III for contact information.

Tips for Entry

1. The more experience you can get in the field, the greater chances you have of being hired. Remember, volunteer work in research programs and for individual Aquatic Biologists also counts as experience.

2. Having skills in any of the following may strengthen your employability: computer programming, Global Information Systems (GIS), photography, boat handling, engine maintenance, and scuba diving.

3. Learn more about aquatic biology on the Internet. Here are some websites that you might visit: Aquatic Network, http://www.aquanet.com, National Marine Educators Association, http://www.marine-ed.org, and LakeNet, http://www.worldlakes.org.

ENTOMOLOGIST

CAREER PROFILE

Duties: Conduct basic or applied research; design and conduct research projects; may teach college or university students; perform duties as required of position

Alternate Title(s): Forensic Entomologist or other title that reflects a specialty

Salary Range: $42,000 to $153,000

Employment Prospects: Good

Advancement Prospects: Good

Prerequisites:

Education or Training—A master's or doctoral degree in entomology, biology, or related field

Experience—Work and research experience related to position one is applying for

Special Skills and Personality Traits—Communication, writing, teamwork, interpersonal, math, statistics, and computer skills; creative; dependable; flexible; self-motivated; persistent

Licensure/Certification—None required

CAREER LADDER

```
┌─────────────────────────────────┐
│      Senior Entomologist        │
└─────────────────────────────────┘

┌─────────────────────────────────┐
│     Research Entomologist       │
└─────────────────────────────────┘

┌─────────────────────────────────┐
│  Postdoctoral Research Associate │
└─────────────────────────────────┘
```

Position Description

Entomology is the biological study of insects, the largest group of animals in the animal kingdom. Insects are tiny, six legged-animals such as ants, flies, beetles, crickets, grasshoppers, bees, locusts, butterflies, and moths. Entomology also includes the study of related arthropods such as spiders, ticks, and centipedes.

Entomologists are concerned with the taxonomy (or classification), distribution, and evolution of the many thousands of species of insects. They examine the morphology (structure) and physiology (life processes) of insects, as well as study their life cycle, behavior, and ecology. Entomologists also study the genetics of insects along with their cellular and molecular composition. In addition, Entomologists investigate the relationships that insects have with each other and with their physical surroundings. Furthermore, many study how insects are beneficial or harmful to humans and the environment.

Many Entomologists are research scientists who work in academic, government, industry, nonprofit, and nongovernmental settings. Some are basic researchers, seeking further knowledge about the various species of insects. Many devote themselves to studying the biology of specific insects; for example, lepidopterists study moths and butterflies while coleopterists study beetles.

Many research scientists conduct applied research. They apply findings of basic research to find solutions to problems and issues in various fields. For example, entomological studies have helped prevent the spread of diseases among humans, solve crime, increase crop production, protect the environment, and so forth.

Applied entomologists usually specialize in a subfield, such as:

- conservation entomology, the restoration of habitats or ecosystems
- agricultural entomology, the study of insects that benefit agriculture, insect pests that affect crops, and pest management
- forest entomology, the study of insects that benefit timber, insect infestations, and pest management
- medical entomology, the study of disease-carrying insects that affect the health of humans as well as pest management strategies

- veterinary entomology, the study of insects that spread disease among domestic animals such as dogs, birds, horses, cattle, and sheep; this field also includes the study of pest management strategies
- forensic entomology, the use of entomology to help solve criminal investigations

Entomologists work in offices and labs where they design and conduct research projects. Their tasks include conducting experiments, examining specimens, analyzing and interpreting data, writing reports, reading scientific journals and other works, performing administrative tasks, and so on. Those who conduct independent research are usually responsible for writing grant proposals and seeking research grants from the federal government and other sources to fund their projects.

Their research involves the use of computers, electron microscopes, and other sophisticated scientific equipment. Many Entomologists go out in the field to collect samples and observe insects in their natural habitats. Field trips may involve living and working in forests, wilderness areas, and other remote locations for several days, weeks, or months at a time.

Entomologists often collaborate on research projects with colleagues and other biological scientists. In addition, Entomologists share their research findings with colleagues by writing papers for publication in scientific journals or by making presentations at scientific meetings that are sponsored by professional associations.

Many Entomologists are employed as professors at colleges and universities. They teach entomology courses to undergraduates and graduates. Professorial duties include conducting their research projects, preparing for and teaching courses, advising students, supervising student research projects, writing scholarly works, performing administrative duties, and participating in community service.

Salaries

Salaries vary, depending on education, experience, geographical location, and other factors. According to a 2001 salary survey by the American Association for the Advancement of Science, the median salary for life scientists in academic institutions and settings ranged from $42,000 to $112,000, and for those in nonacademic settings, from $76,000 to $153,000.

Employment Prospects

Research Entomologists are employed by universities, colleges, government agencies, military services, research institutes, environmental organizations, agricultural companies, biotechnology firms, pest control companies, pest management consulting firms, and so on.

The job outlook is favorable for Entomologists, particularly in areas of applied entomology. Many opportunities will be created to replace individuals who retire, advance to other positions, or resign from the field.

Furthermore, Entomologists can pursue other careers; for example, by becoming science teachers, cooperative extension agents, technical writers, insect zoo directors, beekeepers, pest control specialists, sales representatives (pesticides company), technical directors (pest control firm), vector control specialists, or public health inspectors.

Advancement Prospects

As in any field, Entomologists can advance to become project leaders, program managers, department administrators, and top officers. The highest ambition for some Entomologists is to become consultants.

Education and Training

A master's or doctoral degree in entomology, biology, zoology, or related field is required for most research and teaching positions. Most graduate programs require that applicants have earned a bachelor's degree in entomology, biology, or zoology.

Experience, Skills, and Personality Traits

Employers typically look for candidates who have previous experience in the area in which they would be working. This may be in the form of internships, summer jobs, undergraduate or graduate research projects, postdoctoral research positions, and so on.

Entomologists need strong communication and writing skills for their work. They also need good teamwork and interpersonal skills to be able to work well with others. Entomologists should also have a good grasp of math and statistics as well as have adequate computer skills.

Being creative, dependable, flexible, self-motivated, and persistent are some personality traits that successful Entomologists share.

Unions and Associations

Entomologists can join professional associations to take advantage of networking opportunities, education programs, professional certification, and other professional services and resources. Some societies are the Entomological Society of America, the American Institute of Biological Sciences, and the Society for Integrative and Comparative Biology.

Many Entomologists join societies that serve their particular interests—such as the Association of Applied Insect Ecologists, the Coleopterists Society, the American Arachnological Society, and the American Mosquito Control Association. See Appendix III for contact information.

Tips for Entry

1. You can begin training for a career in entomology while still in high school. Learn about the insect

world through books, videos, software, museums, and so forth. Start your own insect collections. Join youth groups that have entomological activities such as 4-H or the Young Entomologists' Society.

2. Professional societies are good sources of information on internships, postdoctoral positions, and permanent positions. Some societies have websites which include job listings.

3. Use the Internet to learn more about entomology. One website you might visit is the Iowa State Entomology Index of Internet Resources, http://ent. iastate.edu/list. To get a list of other pertinent websites, enter the keyword *entomology* or *entomologists* in a search engine.

PHYSIOLOGIST

CAREER PROFILE

Duties: Conduct basic or applied research; design and conduct research projects; may teach college, university, or medical school students; perform duties as required of position

Alternate Title(s): Endocrinologist, Cardiovascular Scientist, Exercise Physiologist, or other title that reflects a specialty

Salary Range: $43,000 to $163,000

Employment Prospects: Good

Advancement Prospects: Good

Prerequisites:
   Education or Training—A doctoral or master's degree in physiology
   Experience—Postdoctoral experience may be required
   Special Skills and Personality Traits—Communication, writing, interpersonal, teamwork, and self-management skills; innovative; creative; flexible; analytical; persistent
   Licensure/Certification—Medical (M.D.) licensure required for those planning to work with patients

CAREER LADDER

```
┌──────────────────────────────────┐
│        Senior Physiologist        │
└──────────────────────────────────┘

┌──────────────────────────────────┐
│      Research Physiologist        │
└──────────────────────────────────┘

┌──────────────────────────────────┐
│  Postdoctoral Research Associate  │
└──────────────────────────────────┘
```

Position Description

Physiology is the study of how living organisms (microbes, plants, animals, and humans) function. All organisms are made up of cells, tissues, and organs that form different life systems (or processes) such as the respiratory, circulatory, digestive, excretory, and reproductive systems. These life systems all work together to keep organisms healthy, fit, and alive.

Physiologists are research scientists who mostly work in academic, government, medical, and industry laboratories. They are concerned with understanding how the different life systems work individually and with each other. They also seek to understand how tissues or organs can become dysfunctional and cause abnormal conditions or disease in living organisms. In addition, many are involved in the practical applications of physiology in such fields as medicine, agriculture, or environmental science.

Physiology is an interdisciplinary science in which Physiologists apply the knowledge and methodologies of biology, chemistry, and physics to their studies. They focus their research in any number of ways. Many Physiologists concentrate on studying only plants, animals, or humans. Some

focus further by specializing in particular plant or animal species. Some Physiologists concentrate on studying how life functions at the molecular, cell, tissue, or organ level. Others investigate a particular life process; for example, plant photosynthesis, the animal or human endocrine system, or the human cardiovascular system.

Some Physiologists confine their investigations to certain applications. For example, medical Physiologists are concerned with the physiology of diseases such as diabetes, hypertension, and atherosclerosis; exercise Physiologists examine how the body responds to various forms of physical activities; and space Physiologists study how the different life processes handle the stresses of space travel.

Physiologists use a wide variety of tools in their research, including computers, polygraphs, electron microscopes, and nuclear magnetic resonance machines. Depending on the nature of their research, Physiologists may manipulate cells by extracting molecules from the cell nucleus, for example, or devise experiments that involve greenhouse plants or laboratory animals. Some Physiologists examine the life processes in a different species to gain a better understanding of how the processes work in the particular species that they are studying. For example, a Physiologist might study the cardiovascular system of a mouse to understand how that system would function in the human body.

Physiologists are responsible for designing and conducting research projects. Some of their general duties include designing and conducting experiments, analyzing and interpreting data, and performing routine administrative tasks. In addition, Physiologists write scientific papers or give presentations at scientific meetings about their research results. Senior research scientists and principal investigators usually have additional supervisory and project management duties.

Physiologists sometimes handle more than one research project at a time, and often collaborate with other Physiologists and bioscientists on projects. Academic Physiologists are able to choose the topics in which they wish to research, while most nonacademic Physiologists conduct research that is determined by their employers. Physiologists who conduct independent research are usually responsible for obtaining grants to fund their research projects. This involves preparing grant proposals and seeking out scientific grants from the federal government and other sources.

Many Physiologists are full-time professors or adjunct instructors in colleges, universities, and medical schools. Depending on their expertise, professors teach courses in animal, human, or plant physiology, as well as related courses, such as biology, molecular biology, botany, biochemistry, anatomy, and zoology.

As full-time professors, Physiologists must juggle research and teaching duties with other responsibilities. Professors are also involved in advising students and supervising student research projects. Further, they are obligated to write scholarly works, as well as fulfill administrative and community services duties that are required by their positions.

Salaries

Salaries vary, depending on such factors as experience and geographical location. According to a 2000 survey by the Association of Chairs of Departments of Physiology, the mean salaries for academicians (in medical and nonmedical schools) ranged from $43,442 for instructors to $163,416 for department chairpersons.

Employment Prospects

Physiologists are employed by universities, colleges, medical schools, medical centers, hospitals, pharmaceutical firms, biotechnology companies, agricultural companies, and government laboratories. Many also work for the U.S. Air Force and with the U.S. Food and Drug Administration, the U.S. Environmental Protection Agency, and other government agencies that are concerned with health, medicine, epidemiology, pollution, or toxicity.

Most academic positions become available as individuals retire, resign, or transfer to other positions.

With a background in physiology, individuals can pursue career paths in other areas such as medicine, veterinary medicine, pharmacy, law, or journalism.

Advancement Prospects

Positions as laboratory directors, research managers, and executive-level administrators are available to Physiologists who wish to pursue management and management careers. Academic professors can advance in rank (assistant, associate, and full professor) as well as by obtaining job tenure.

Education and Training

Physiologists must have doctoral degrees in physiology or a related field in order to conduct independent research, teach in four-year colleges, universities, and medical schools, or to pursue top management posts.

Physiologists who wish to work with patients, must complete an M.D. program. Some universities offer programs that grant a joint M.D. degree and Ph.D. in physiology.

Experience, Skills, and Personality Traits

Requirements vary with the various employers. In general, Physiologists should have appropriate work and research experience related to the positions for which they are applying. Many employers generally require or prefer to hire Ph.D.s who have worked in one or more postdoctoral positions.

Physiologists need excellent communication and writing skills as they must be able to report their results and conclusions clearly to fellow scientists as well as to nontechnical personnel. Additionally, they need strong interpersonal and teamwork skills and such self-management skills as being able to meet deadlines, prioritize tasks, work independently, and make sound judgments.

Some personality traits that successful Physiologists share are being innovative, creative, flexible, analytical, and persistent.

Special Requirements

Physiologists who wish to work with patients must obtain the proper medical licensure in their states.

Unions and Associations

Many Physiologists join local, state, or national professional organizations to take advantage of professional services and resources, such as networking opportunities. Some of the various national societies that serve Physiologists are:

• American Physiological Society
• Society of General Physiologists
• American Society of Plant Biologists
• Society for Comparative and Integrative Biology

- American Institute of Biological Sciences
- American Association for the Advancement of Science
- American Association for Higher Education.

See Appendix III for contact information.

Tips for Entry

1. When you complete graduate school, your résumé should show that you have completed independent research in addition to the laboratory or research work you have done for others.

2. Get experience writing grant proposals while you are an undergraduate or postdoctoral fellow.

3. Use the Internet to learn more about physiology. One website to visit is the American Physiological Society, http://www.the-aps.org. To get a list of relevant websites to read, enter the keyword *physiology* in any search engine.

GENETICIST

CAREER PROFILE

Duties: Conduct basic or applied research; design and conduct research projects; may work with patients, providing diagnosis, treatment, education, or counseling services; may perform laboratory services; may teach college or university students; perform duties as required of position

Alternate Title(s): Plant Geneticist, Medical Geneticist, or other title that reflects a specialty

Salary Range: $32,000 to $117,000

Employment Prospects: Good

Advancement Prospects: Good

Prerequisites:
> **Education or Training**—A master's degree, Ph.D., or M.D., depending on occupation
> **Experience**—Postdoctoral experience for research scientists may be required
> **Special Skills and Personality Traits**—Communication, writing, computer, statistics, analytical, interpersonal, and teamwork skills; creative; persistent; precise; detail-oriented; dedicated
> **Licensure/Certification**—A medical (M.D.) license may be required for clinical Geneticists

CAREER LADDER

```
┌─────────────────────────────────┐
│        Senior Geneticist        │
└─────────────────────────────────┘

┌─────────────────────────────────┐
│       Research Geneticist       │
└─────────────────────────────────┘

┌─────────────────────────────────┐
│  Postdoctoral Research Associate │
└─────────────────────────────────┘
```

Position Description

Genetics is the study of heredity. That is how an organism's characteristics, or traits, are passed from one generation to the next through its genes. Genes are found in the nucleus of every cell of an organism, and contain the DNA (deoxyribonucleic acid) code which defines the organism's traits. For example, the genes of an orange tree determine its size, the shape of its leaves, the type of fruit it bears, the color of its fruit, and so forth.

Geneticists are interested in learning about the structure and function of genes. They also investigate how genes duplicate within the cell and form organisms, as well as study how genes evolve through generations. In addition, Geneticists are involved in mapping the genetic code of humans, animals, and plants.

Geneticists are also concerned with understanding gene mutations, the changes that occur within the genetic code. They investigate how gene mutations cause diseases in organisms, and examine how organisms inherit genetic disorders. Their studies may involve examining the genes of plants or animals over several generations, which requires the successful mating of organisms.

Most Geneticists are research scientists who work in academic, government, and private research labs. Many Geneticists conduct basic research to gain further knowledge about genes and the genetic process. Some are devoted to studying the genetics of only plants, animals, or humans. Some basic researchers further specialize by examining genetics at the molecular level. For example, many Geneticists are concerned with studying only human DNA.

Many other Geneticists are involved in applying genetic research to the development of useful products and practical methodologies in such industries as biotechnology, biomedicine, pharmaceuticals, and agriculture. For example, some plant Geneticists might seek ways to alter certain genes in tomatoes to create a species that is resistant to pests.

Another example would be Geneticists in a biomedical company who develop diagnostic tests that identify various genetic disorders that people can inherit.

Geneticists sometimes handle several research projects at a time. They often collaborate on research projects with colleagues, other biological scientists, and scientists (such as chemists and physicists) from other disciplines.

Research scientists are in charge of designing and conducting research projects. Their duties vary, depending on their position and experience. Some of their tasks include conducting experiments or tests, gathering data, analyzing and interpreting data, writing reports, and performing administrative tasks. Geneticists who conduct independent research are usually responsible for seeking research grants from the federal government and other sources to fund their projects. Most senior researchers and principal investigators also perform supervisory and management duties.

Research scientists typically exchange information about their research with each other. Many write scientific papers about their research, which they submit to scientific journals. Some give presentations at scientific meetings that are sponsored by professional associations.

Geneticists also perform other roles besides research scientists. Geneticists known as research assistants and technicians provide research and administrative support roles in research projects. Their duties include performing experiments, analyzing data, writing reports, caring for greenhouse plants or laboratory animals, and performing routine tasks.

Other Geneticists are health professionals. They are medical (M.D.) and Ph.D. doctors specializing in the application of human and medical genetics to clinical practice. Clinical Geneticists diagnose, test, manage, and treat patients who have inherited genetic conditions. Some patients are pregnant women whose unborn babies are at risk of birth defects. Some clinical Geneticists work directly with patients, providing medical care along with genetic counseling services. Other clinical Geneticists work in the laboratory performing and interpreting biochemical, molecular, or cytogenetic analyses. In addition, they act as consultants regarding genetic disorders.

Medical Geneticists provide assessment and education services to patients. They generally have doctoral degrees. These specialists work closely with patients, conducting risk assessments and informing them about their disorders and their medical options. Medical Geneticists also provide patients with supportive counseling, as well as refer patients to appropriate health-care resources.

Many research scientists, clinical Geneticists, and medical Geneticists are employed as adjunct instructors or full-time professors at colleges, universities, and medical schools. Full-time professors have a number of responsibilities, which include conducting independent research; preparing for and teaching courses; advising students; supervising student research projects; writing scholarly works; performing administrative duties; and participating in community service.

Salaries

Salaries vary, depending on experience, position, geographical location, and other factors. In a 2001 salary survey by Abbot, Langer, and Associates, the median salary for life scientists ranged from $32,000 for postdoctoral researchers to $116,500 for executive-level administrators.

Employment Prospects

Geneticists work in universities and colleges, medical schools, hospitals, clinical laboratories, private research institutions, government agencies, biotechnology firms, pharmaceutical companies, and so on.

Typically, job openings become available as scientists transfer to other positions, retire, or resign. Employers may create additional positions to meet their growing needs, if funds are available. Opportunities in the private sector are particularly good in the agricultural, biotechnology, pharmaceutical, and biomedical industries.

New opportunities, as well as new fields, in genetics are expected to increase in the coming years because of the recent discoveries in the Human Genome Project (the identification of the human genetic code).

With a background in genetics, individuals might obtain nonresearch positions as quality assurance, regulatory, sales, or marketing professionals in the pharmaceutical, biotechnology, or other industry. With additional training, Geneticists can seek other career paths by becoming physicians, nurses, technical journalists, or museum curators.

Advancement Prospects

Geneticists with administrative or management ambitions can advance to such positions within their specialty. Professors receive promotional rankings as assistant professors, associate professors, or full professors.

Many Geneticists achieve advancement by earning higher pay, by conducting independent research projects, and through receiving professional recognition.

Education and Training

Research scientists must hold either a master's degree or a Ph.D. A Ph.D. is required to teach in universities and four-year colleges, to conduct independent research, and to pursue top management positions.

Clinical Geneticists complete either M.D. or Ph.D. programs. (Geneticists must earn a medical degree if they wish to work with patients.) Upon finishing their M.D. or Ph.D. programs, they complete genetics fellowships (or residencies).

Experience, Skills, and Personality Traits

Requirements vary with the different positions as well as among various employers. In general, Geneticists should have appropriate work and research experience related to the positions for which they are applying. Most employers prefer or require that candidates have several years of post-doctoral experience.

Geneticists need excellent communication, writing, and computer skills. They should be knowledgeable about statistics and have the ability to analyze data. They also need excellent interpersonal and teamwork skills as they must be able to work well with scientists and others.

Successful Geneticists share personality traits such as being creative, persistent, precise, detail-oriented, and dedicated.

Special Requirements

Clinical Geneticists who work with patients must hold valid medical (M.D.) licensure.

Unions and Associations

Many professional societies are available to Geneticists. By joining local, state, or national associations, they can take advantage of various professional services and resources, such as networking opportunities and professional certification. Some national societies are the American Society of Human Genetics, the Genetics Society of America, and the Association of Professors of Human or Medical Genetics. See Appendix III for contact information.

Tips for Entry

1. Talk with Geneticists to learn more about the work they do, the types of courses they took in college, and what their career path has been like so far.
2. Learn more about Geneticists on the Internet. Two websites you might visit are the Genetics Societies, http://www.faseb.org/genetics and Genetic Education Center (Kansas Medical Center), http://www.kumc.edu/gec/geneinfo.html.

MOLECULAR BIOLOGIST

CAREER PROFILE

Duties: Conduct basic or applied research; design and conduct research projects; may teach college or university students; research assistants and technicians provide research and administrative support; perform duties as required of position

Alternate Title(s): Professor of Molecular Biology

Salary Range: $42,000 to $153,000

Employment Prospects: Good

Advancement Prospects: Good

Prerequisites:

    Education or Training—A bachelor's or advanced degree in biochemistry, biology, or related field

    Experience—Postdoctoral experience for research scientists may be required

    Special Skills and Personality Traits—Writing, communication, interpersonal, teamwork, and self-management skills; creative; analytical; persistent; flexible

    Licensure/Certification—None required

CAREER LADDER

```
┌─────────────────────────────────┐
│   Senior Molecular Biologist     │
└─────────────────────────────────┘

┌─────────────────────────────────┐
│  Research Molecular Biologist    │
└─────────────────────────────────┘

┌─────────────────────────────────┐
│ Postdoctoral Research Associate  │
└─────────────────────────────────┘
```

Position Description

Molecular Biology is the study of life at the chemical, or molecular, level. It deals with the study of these basic molecules that reside in the nucleus of all living cells:

- DNA (deoxyribonucleic acid), the genetic code of a living organism; it expresses what genes (characteristics) an organism has inherited from its parents
- RNA (ribonucleic acid), which transmits the DNA code to other parts of the cell where it is translated and forms appropriate protein molecules
- proteins, the different types of molecules that form the various parts (tissues, enzymes, hormones, and so on) of a living organism

Molecular Biologists are concerned with understanding how the basic molecules combine and interact so that living organisms grow, develop, reproduce, and stay alive. They seek answers to such as questions as: How do protein molecules determine what functions they do in a cell? How do cells know when to divide and when to stop dividing? How do cells recognize one another? What causes DNA to become damaged? How can mutant genes be suppressed so that disease does not occur? How can DNA or proteins be altered to produce better or stronger organisms (such as crops)?

Molecular Biologists typically conduct in vitro experiments in which they extract molecules from cells to study. In addition, they are involved in mapping the genetic code of microbes, plants, animals, and humans.

Most Molecular Biologists conduct basic research to further knowledge in this field. Some biologists specialize in developing new methodologies and techniques for conducting cellular investigations. Because molecular biology is such a fundamental biological discipline, Molecular Biologists are also involved in basic research in diverse fields such as ecology, botany, zoology, microbiology, medical science, genetics, immunology, and forensic science.

Many other Molecular Biologists are part of research and development teams in biotechnology, biomedicine, pharmaceutical, agriculture, and other industries. They apply findings of basic research to the development of new foods, medicines, vaccines, and other practical products; the development of medical diagnostic tests, treatments, and cures for inherited diseases; the creation of environmental plans to clean up pollution; and so forth.

Duties for Molecular Biologists vary, depending on their positions and experience. In general, research scientists are responsible for designing and conducting research projects. Some of their tasks include conducting experiments or tests, gathering data, analyzing and interpreting data, writing reports, and performing administrative tasks. Many Molecular Biologists present their research results to their colleagues. They might write scientific papers which they submit to scientific journals or give presentations at scientific meetings that are sponsored by professional associations.

Usually, Molecular Biologists who conduct independent research are responsible for obtaining research grants to fund their research projects. This involves seeking research grants from the federal government and other sources to fund their projects. In addition, Molecular Biologists prepare grant proposals that describe the missions, methodologies, budgets, and other aspects of their projects.

Many research scientists are employed as professors at colleges and universities. Along with their research duties, they are responsible for teaching molecular biology and other biology courses to undergraduate and graduate students. Their other duties include advising students, supervising student research projects, performing administrative duties, and participating in community service.

Research assistants and technicians who work in this field are also considered Molecular Biologists. They provide research scientists with research and administrative support. Their tasks include conducting experiments, analyzing data, writing reports, maintaining laboratories, completing routine administrative tasks, and so on.

All Molecular Biologists are responsible for keeping up with developments in their fields as well as updating their skills. They might read professional journals and books, network with colleagues, enroll in training programs, attend professional conferences, and so on.

Salaries

Salaries vary, depending on such factors as education, experience, type of employer, and geographical location. According to a 2001 salary survey by the American Association for the Advancement of Science, the median salary for life scientists in academic settings ranged from $42,000 to $112,000 and for those in nonacademic settings, from $76,000 to $153,000.

Employment Prospects

Opportunities for experienced Molecular Biologists are good, particularly in the biotechnology and pharmaceutical industries. The demand is also strong for Molecular Biologists who have experience in bioinformatics (the scientific management of biological data that is stored in computers).

Most academic positions become available as individuals retire, resign, or transfer to other positions. Some experts report that the completion of the Human Genome Project (the identification of human genes) should open up more research opportunities in all settings.

With a background in molecular biology, individuals can pursue career paths in other areas such as chemical engineering, medicine, veterinary medicine, pharmacy, law, technical sales, or journalism.

Advancement Prospects

Positions such as project leader, program manager, laboratory director, and executive officer are available for those who wish to pursue supervisory or administrative careers. Professors can advance in rank (assistant, associate, and full professor) as well as obtaining job tenure.

Education and Training

Research assistants and technicians must have a bachelor's degree in biochemistry, molecular biology, biology, or related field. Research scientists must hold either a master's degree or a Ph.D. in molecular biology, biochemistry, or related field. A Ph.D. is required in order to teach in universities and four-year colleges, to conduct independent research, or to pursue top management posts.

Experience, Skills, and Personality Traits

Employers generally choose candidates who have related work and research experience, which may have been gained through research projects, internships, fellowships, part-time employment, and so on. Ph.D. candidates for research scientist positions may be required to have a few years of postdoctoral experience.

Molecular Biologists need excellent writing and communication skills to report their results clearly to fellow scientists and others. In addition, they need strong interpersonal and teamwork skills as well as self-management skills, such as being able to work independently, meet deadlines, and prioritize tasks.

Being creative, analytical, persistent, and flexible are some personality traits that successful Molecular Biologists share.

Unions and Associations

Molecular Biologists join professional societies to take advantage of professional services and resources such as education programs and networking opportunities. Some associations that they might join are the American Society for Biochemistry and Molecular Biology, the American Institute of Biological Sciences, or the American Association for the Advancement of Science. See Appendix III for contact information.

Tips for Entry

1. Many universities offer doctoral programs in molecular biology. Carefully choose the school that fits your needs; for example ask yourself: Are there faculty with whom I would like to work? Does the program offer specialties that interest me? What kind of support does the school's career center offer? If you can, visit schools and talk with professors in the molecular biology departments.

2. Many universities and colleges offer certificate programs in laboratory techniques. These programs may enhance employability for those who want to enter the job market after completing their bachelor's degrees.

3. Use the Internet to learn more about molecular biology. Two websites you might visit are American Society for Biochemistry and Molecular Biologists, http://www.asbmb.org and Cell and Molecular Biology Online, http://www.cellbio.com.

BIOINFORMATICS SCIENTIST

CAREER PROFILE

Duties: Conduct basic or applied research; manage biological information systems; perform analysis of biological information in computer databases; develop new technologies and methodologies; may teach college or university students; perform duties as required

Alternate Title(s): Bioinformatician, Bioinformatics Research Analyst, Bioinformatics Associate

Salary Range: $30,000 to $100,000 or more

Employment Prospects: Excellent

Advancement Prospects: Good

Prerequisites:

Education or Training—A bachelor's or advanced degree in molecular biology or related field

Experience—Previous work experience in bioinformatics is required or preferred

Special Skills and Personality Traits—Biology background; programming, database management, math, statistics, interpersonal, teamwork, problem-solving, and communication skills; creative; flexible; curious; self-motivated

Licensure/Certification—None required

CAREER LADDER

```
┌─────────────────────────────────┐
│  Senior Bioinformatics Scientist │
│       or Project Leader          │
└─────────────────────────────────┘

┌─────────────────────────────────┐
│    Bioinformatics Scientist      │
└─────────────────────────────────┘

┌─────────────────────────────────┐
│          Trainee or              │
│ Postdoctoral Research Associate  │
└─────────────────────────────────┘
```

Project Description

Bioinformatics is the scientific management of biological information that is stored in computer databases. The field is a new one, having emerged in the 1990s from the need for biologists with computer programming skills to store and catalog vast data of human DNA code in the Human Genome Project. The parameters of this young field are still evolving. Some scientists define bioinformatics as the computational management of genetic data only. Other scientists define this field as including the management of all kinds of biological information—such as data about whole organisms or ecological systems, or data from clinical trials or diagnostic tests

Regardless of how Bioinformatics Scientists may define the parameters of their field, their primary responsibilities are the same. They are concerned with the management and analysis of the biological data in public and proprietary databases. They are also involved in the development and application of effective information technology and compu-

tational tools to store, catalog, retrieve, and analyze biological data more efficiently.

Because they have expertise in both the biology and computer science disciplines, Bioinformatics Scientists are considered a new breed of researchers. Usually working as part of multidisciplinary research teams, their role is to apply computational approaches to biological experiments. They work on various types of basic and applied research projects, such as identifying the genetic code in various plant species, seeking the cause of Alzheimer's disease, or working on the development of new drug treatments.

Bioinformatics Scientists work in academic, industry, government, nongovernmental, and nonprofit settings. Their duties vary, depending on their positions and experience. Academic scientists work on the development of new forms of technologies and processes for the bioinformatics fields. Many also teach bioinformatics, as well as biology or computer science courses, to students in undergraduate and graduate programs. As professors, Bioinformatics Scientists also advise students, supervise student research projects, write scholarly works, perform administrative duties, and fulfill community service obligations.

Most Bioinformatics Scientists work in industry settings as part of research and development teams. They collaborate with other scientists to generate and analyze biological information. Depending on the size of the employing company or department as well as their education and experience, Bioinformatics Scientists may be responsible for some or all of the following duties:

- set up and maintain databases
- assess the needs of other scientists in regards to data submissions and retrievals
- set up and run experiments—searching (or mining) databases for the appropriate data (for example, searching for specific gene sequences)
- analyze and interpret data
- identify new areas for bioinformatics investigations
- develop new bioinformatics approaches for analyzing data in proprietary and public databases
- develop and apply computer programs and software to store, organize, manage, retrieve, and analyze data

Bioinformatics Scientists are usually involved with several projects at a time. Senior scientists may have the additional duties of leading and managing projects, as well as training and supervising new and junior scientists.

All Bioinformatics Scientists are responsible for keeping up with new technologies and developments in their fields. They participate in training programs, enroll in continuing education programs, attend professional conferences and meetings, network with colleagues, and so forth.

Salaries
Salaries vary depending on education, experience, employer, geographical location, and other factors. Annual salaries have been reported as ranging anywhere from $30,000 to $100,000 or more.

Entry-level salaries are generally higher for Bioinformatics Scientists than for scientists in other disciplines because the demand is greater than the number of available experienced Bioinformatics Scientists. As more trained Bioinformatics Scientists enter the field, the starting annual salaries will most likely decrease.

Employment Prospects
Bioinformatics Scientists are employed by colleges, universities, pharmaceutical companies, biotechnology firms, government agencies, research institutions, nongovernmental agencies, and so on.

Although bioinformatics is a small field, it is growing rapidly each year. Opportunities are particularly strong in the pharmaceutical and biotechnology industries for qualified applicants.

Advancement Prospects
Bioinformatics Scientists can advance in any number of ways, depending on their ambitions and interests. Those interested in management and administrative work can pursue such positions as project leader, program manager, and executive officer. Professors can advance in rank (assistant, associate, and full professor) as well as by obtaining job tenure.

Education and Training
Educational requirements vary, depending on the position and the employer. For most data analysis and programming positions, Bioinformatics Scientists need a bachelor's degree in molecular biology, other biological science, or computer science. Biology majors should have training in programming while computer science majors should have completed course work in biology. For research and senior-level scientist positions, a master's degree or a Ph.D. is required. Employers often hire candidates with degrees in other disciplines as long as they have qualifying experience.

Because bioinformatics is such a new field, many have learned it on the job, but the number of formal training programs are increasing. Certificate programs in bioinformatics are available for those wishing a concentration in the field rather than a full degree. In the last few years, many universities and colleges have established bachelor's, master's, and Ph.D. programs in bioinformatics.

Experience, Skills, and Personality Traits
Employers look for candidates who have previous experience in bioinformatics. Candidates for entry-level positions may have obtained experience through research projects, internships, part-time employment, postdoctoral training, and so on.

Bioinformatics Scientists must have basic knowledge and skills in biology, particularly in molecular biology. In addition, they need basic math (especially algebra and logic), statistics, programming, and database management skills. Because they must be able to work well with other scientists, engineers, project managers, and others, Bioinformatics Scientists need excellent interpersonal and team work skills. Furthermore, they need effective problem-solving and communication skills for their work.

Being creative, flexible, curious, and self-motivated are a few personality traits that Bioinformatics Scientists share.

Unions and Associations
Many Bioinformatics Scientists join professional associations to take advantage of professional resources and services such as education programs and networking opportunities. Some societies that they might join are: the International Society for

Computational Biology, the American Society for Biochemistry and Molecular Biologists, the American Institute of Biological Sciences, the Association for Computing Machinery, or the American. Association for the Advancement of Science. See Appendix III for contact information.

Tips for Entry

1. Remember: The bioinformatics field is a new discipline. Thus, types of opportunities and requirements for positions will change to reflect the evolving needs of employers.

2. Talk with your college adviser to develop an education program that reflects your interests and ambitions in bioinformatics.

3. Smaller companies are more willing to hire bioinformatics applicants with little work experience.

4. Use the Internet to learn more about bioinformatics. Some websites you might visit are International Society for Computational Biology, http://www.iscb.org, BioPlanet—The Bioinformatics Homepage, http://www.bioplanet.com; and Bioinformatics.org, http://bioinformatics.org.

ECOLOGIST

CAREER PROFILE

Duties: Conduct basic or applied research; design and conduct research projects; may teach college or university students; research assistants and technicians provide research and administrative support; perform duties as required of position

Alternate Title(s): Environmental Scientist; Animal Ecologist, Plant Ecologist, or other title that reflects a specialty

Salary Range: $32,000 to $117,000

Employment Prospects: Good

Advancement Prospects: Good

Prerequisites:

Education or Training—A bachelor's or advanced degree in ecology, biology, or related field

Experience—Postdoctoral experience usually required for research scientists

Special Skills and Personality Traits—Math, statistics, computer, writing, communication, organizational, teamwork, and interpersonal skills; being in good health and physically fit, for those planning to do fieldwork; flexible; determined; creative; analytical; resourceful

Licensure/Certification—None required

CAREER LADDER

```
┌─────────────────────────────────────┐
│         Senior Ecologist             │
└─────────────────────────────────────┘

┌─────────────────────────────────────┐
│        Research Ecologist            │
└─────────────────────────────────────┘

┌─────────────────────────────────────┐
│   Postdoctoral Research Associate    │
└─────────────────────────────────────┘
```

Position Description

Ecology is the study of ecosystems. An ecosystem is a geographical area and all the living organisms and nonliving things (water, air, and soil) that reside within that location. Ecosystems can be small or large; for example, backyards, ponds, suburban hillsides, urban parks, cities, beaches, estuaries, wetlands, oceans, lakes, forests, mountains, canyons, and valleys are all ecosystems.

Ecologists are concerned with the diversity of life within ecosystems. They study the different plant and animal species that live within an ecosystem, how many there are of each species, and how they are distributed within the ecosystem. Ecologists also seek to understand how different organisms interact with each other and with their physical surroundings. In addition, Ecologists examine how ecosystems provide humans, animals, and plants with food, shelter, and other natural resources. Further, they investigate how environmental problems and issues affect ecosystems and what can be done to restore, protect, and preserve them.

Many Ecologists are research scientists. Basic researchers conduct investigations to expand our knowledge about various ecosystems. They ask questions such as: How is a particular wetland affected by elevated levels of carbon dioxide? or What are nonnative species within an ecosystem and how do they affect native species?

Some Ecologists work in the applied field of environmental science. They seek practical solutions to environmental problems and issues such as energy, air quality, water pollution, land use, and hazardous waste management. In addition to conducting research, they might perform other duties. For example, they monitor natural resources within an ecosystem, design plans to restore ecosystems, write environmental impact statements, or advise lawmakers on the best practices for healthy ecosystems within their local communities.

Research Ecologists work in academic, government, nongovernmental, nonprofit, and industry settings. They often collaborate on research projects with other Ecologists, biological scientists, and scientists from other disciplines such as geologists, chemists, and physicists.

In general, research scientists are responsible for designing and conducting research projects. They may handle one or more research projects at a time. Some of their tasks include conducting experiments or tests, gathering data, analyzing and interpreting data, and performing administrative tasks. In addition, they share the results of their research with colleagues by writing scientific papers for science journals or giving presentations at professional conferences.

Ecologists who conduct independent research are usually responsible for obtaining grants from the federal government and other sources to fund new or current projects. This involves writing grant proposals that describe the various aspects of their projects, such as objectives, methodologies, and budgets.

Ecologists work in offices and laboratories, as well as conduct research in the field. Field expeditions may sometimes require working and living for several weeks or months in remote locations such as islands, deserts, rain forests, and wildernesses.

Many Ecologists are employed as professors at colleges and universities. They teach ecology courses, and sometimes teach biology or other courses, to undergraduate or graduate students. As professors, their duties include conducting independent research, preparing for and teaching courses, advising students, supervising student research projects, writing scholarly works, performing administrative duties, and participating in community service.

Many Ecologists perform research and administrative support roles to research scientists. They are known as technicians and research assistants. Some of their tasks include conducting experiments, collecting samples in the field, making observations, analyzing data, writing reports, maintaining laboratory equipment, and completing routine administrative tasks.

Salaries

Salaries vary, depending on such factors as experience, education, employer, and geographical location. According to a 2001 salary survey by Abbot, Langer, and Associates, the median salary for life scientists ranged from $32,000 for postdoctoral researchers to $116,500 for executive-level administrators.

Employment Prospects

Some employers that hire Ecologists are colleges, universities, government agencies, nongovernmental organizations, research institutes, natural history museums, zoos, environmental organizations, agricultural companies, and environmental consulting firms.

With the growing awareness of the environment and the need to manage it more carefully, opportunities are expected to be good for Ecologists. However, keep in mind that job opportunities go up and down, depending on the changes in the economy, political administrations, and other factors. The best opportunities are predicted to be in the private sector and with nongovernmental organizations.

With their background, Ecologists can also pursue other career paths such as becoming high school biology teachers, environmental educators, naturalists, museum curators, land planners, environmental analysts, conservationists, lobbyists, environmental lawyers, or science journalists.

Advancement Prospects

Advancement opportunities vary. Research Ecologists can advance to management and administrative positions, such as project leaders, program managers, and executive directors. Professors can advance in rank (assistant, associate, and full professor) as well as obtain job tenure. Technicians and research assistants can advance to managerial positions as laboratory managers and to other nonlaboratory administrative positions.

Education and Training

The minimum requirement is a bachelor's degree in ecology, biology, or a related discipline. With a bachelor's degree, Ecologists can qualify for research assistant and technician positions. Some employers require or prefer that candidates have earned a master's degree.

Research scientists must hold either a master's degree or a Ph.D. in ecology or a related discipline. To become professors, conduct independent research, or obtain top management positions, Ecologists must hold a Ph.D.

Experience, Skills, and Personality Traits

For entry-level positions, employers generally choose candidates who have related work and research experience, which may have been gained through research projects, internships, fellowships, part-time employment, and so on. Many employers expect Ph.D. applicants to have worked in one or more postdoctoral positions.

Ecologists need strong math, statistics, and computer skills as well as excellent writing, communication, and organizational skills to effectively do their work. They must also have good teamwork and interpersonal skills as they often work with other scientists and staff.

Being flexible, determined, creative, analytical, and resourceful are some personality traits that successful Ecologists share.

Unions and Associations

Many Ecologists belong to professional societies to take advantage of resources and services such as education programs, professional certification and networking opportunities. Some associations that serve the various interests of Ecologists are the American Association for the Advancement of Science, the American Institute of Biological Sciences, the Ecological Society of America, the Society of Wetland Scientists, and the Society for Conservation Biology. See Appendix III for contact information.

Tips for Entry

1. You can start getting involved in ecology while in high school. You might join ecological or environ-

mental organizations, as well as participate in activities that support the environment.

2. You can learn about internships and jobs from various sources, such as professors, college career centers, professional ecological societies, and conservation organizations.

3. Use the Internet to learn more about Ecologists. Two websites you might visit are the Ecological Society of America, http://www.esa.org, and the Environmental Careers Organization, http://www.eco.org.

CHEMISTRY

CHEMIST

CAREER PROFILE

Duties: Conduct basic or applied research; design and conduct research projects; may teach college or university students; research assistants and technicians provide research and administrative support; perform duties as required of position

Alternate Title(s): Organic Chemist; Polymer Chemist; Analytical Chemist; Biochemist; Forensic Chemist; Quality Control Chemist; or other title that reflects a specialty

Salary Range: $30,000 to $93,000

Employment Prospects: Good

Advancement Prospects: Good

Prerequisites:
   Education or Training—A bachelor's or advanced degree in chemistry
   Experience—Postdoctoral experience for research scientists may be required
   Special Skills and Personality Traits—Self-management, mathematical, computer, analytical, problem-solving, communication, writing, interpersonal and teamwork skills; curious; creative; self-motivated; persistent; flexible
   Licensure/Certification—State licensure or professional certification may be required

CAREER LADDER

```
┌─────────────────────────────────────┐
│           Senior Chemist            │
└─────────────────────────────────────┘

┌─────────────────────────────────────┐
│          Research Chemist           │
└─────────────────────────────────────┘

┌─────────────────────────────────────┐
│   Postdoctoral Research Associate   │
└─────────────────────────────────────┘
```

Position Description

Chemistry is a physical science that deals with the substances (or chemicals) which make up matter. All matter, whether it forms living organisms or nonliving things, is composed of chemical compounds. A compound is made up of elements, which are chemicals that cannot be broken down any further. For example, when the elements hydrogen and oxygen combine in a certain way, the compound known as water is formed. So far, 110 natural and man-made elements have been discovered.

The scientists who study elements and compounds are called Chemists. They seek to understand the chemical composition, structure, and properties (or characteristics) of living organisms or nonliving things. Chemists are also concerned with understanding how substances behave under certain conditions and how different chemicals interact with each other. In addition, Chemists investigate what occurs during chemical changes. For example, food goes through several chemical changes in the body in order for the body to absorb nutrients from the food.

Most Chemists work in research labs in academic, government, industry, nonprofit, and nongovernmental settings. Some of them conduct basic research to further scientific knowledge about chemical elements, compounds, interactions, chemical processes, and so forth. Other Chemists are involved in applied research. They use findings of basic research to solve problems in fields such as medicine, the environment, and agriculture.

Chemistry is divided into several major fields of study, and Chemists may work in more than one field throughout their careers. Some of these major fields are:

• organic chemistry, the study of carbon compounds (carbon is an element that is found in all living organisms)

- inorganic chemistry, the study of substances (such as minerals and metals) that are made up of elements other than carbons
- physical chemistry, the application of physical laws and mathematical formulas to study the physical and chemical characteristics of matter
- analytical chemistry, the precise investigation into the composition, structure, and properties of matter
- biochemistry, the study of the chemistry of living organisms

Many Chemists concentrate on devoting their studies to a particular type of matter or a chemical process. Geochemists, for example, examine substances in rocks and minerals; surface Chemists study the surface properties of chemical compounds; and synthetic Chemists investigate the possibility of creating new chemical compounds. Some Chemists specialize in the method they use to approach their studies. For example, computational Chemists use computer technologies to solve problems in chemistry.

Chemists also specialize in one of the various applied fields of chemistry. The following are just a few examples: forensic Chemists analyze physical evidence (such as blood stains, human hair, glass fragments, paint chips, or soil) found at crime scenes. Clinical Chemists apply their expertise to the health field by evaluating blood and tissue samples. Medicinal Chemists work in the area of pharmaceuticals, studying the structural properties of compounds to develop new drugs and medicines. Agricultural Chemists, on the other hand, focus their training in developing new products (feed, fertilizers, and pesticides) that improve the production, protection, and use of crops and livestock. Environmental Chemists are involved in the protection of the environment, where they conduct or develop pollution monitoring or remediation programs.

Chemists work in laboratories and offices. Their duties vary, depending on Chemists' positions. Technicians and research assistants typically work under the supervision of research scientists. They provide research and administrative support in chemical labs. Their duties include conducting experiments or tests, analyzing data, writing reports, maintaining laboratory equipment, performing routine administrative tasks, and so on.

Research Chemists (or research scientists) are responsible for designing and conducting research projects. Some of their tasks include conducting experiments or tests, gathering data, analyzing and interpreting data, writing reports, and performing administrative tasks. Senior researchers or principal investigators typically perform supervisory and management tasks. In addition, Chemists who conduct independent research are usually responsible for obtaining grants to fund their research projects. Their tasks involve seeking out available grants from the federal government and other sources and writing grant proposals that describe the goals, objectives, methodologies, and other aspects of their projects.

Chemists often collaborate on research projects with other chemists as well as with scientists from other disciplines—such as biologists, physicists, and geologists. Many Chemists share the results of their research with colleagues by writing articles (or scientific papers) for scientific journals or giving presentations at scientific meetings that are sponsored by professional associations.

Many Chemists are adjunct instructors and full-time professors at colleges and universities. They teach basic chemistry courses as well as advanced courses in their areas of expertise. Full-time professors must juggle various tasks each day. Their responsibilities include conducting independent research, preparing courses, teaching classes, advising students, supervising student research projects, and performing administrative duties. In addition, professors are required to publish scholarly work and to participate in community service.

All Chemists use a variety of specialized computers and instruments to help them identify, measure, and evaluate chemicals. Further, they must follow specific safety measures while handling chemicals to keep health and safety hazards down to a minimum.

Salaries

Salaries vary, depending on education, experience, geographical location, and other factors. According to the Bureau of Labor Statistics, the estimated annual salary in 2001 for most Chemists ranged from $30,450 to $89,830. The estimated annual salary for most postsecondary chemistry instructors ranged from $31,700 to $93,450.

Employment Prospects

The major employer of Chemists is the chemical manufacturing industry which produces a wide range of chemical products, such as plastics, synthetics, soaps, cosmetics, paints, industrial gases, adhesives, printing inks, and pesticides. Chemists are also employed in pharmaceutical, biomedicine, biotechnology, agriculture, and other industries, and by private firms that provide research and testing services. Additionally, they are employed by colleges and universities. Further, many Chemists work for local, state, and federal government agencies in such areas as consumer protection, public health, safety and inspection, environmental protection, and forensics.

Typically, job opportunities become available as Chemists retire, transfer to other positions, or resign. Experts report that opportunities for experienced Chemists (with bachelor's or advanced degrees) in pharmaceutical and biotechnology companies are especially good and should continue to be favorable for a number of years.

With a chemistry background, individuals can follow other career paths by becoming high school chemistry teachers, environmental lawyers, patent agents, quality control personnel, technical sales representatives, technical writers, software developers, museum curators, safety and health inspectors, physicians, and pharmacists.

Advancement Prospects

Chemists with management or administrative ambitions can advance to such positions in any work setting. Professors receive promotional rankings as assistant professors, associate professors, or full professors.

Many Chemists measure their success by being able to conduct independent research, by making discoveries or inventions, by making higher earnings, and through gaining professional recognition.

Education and Training

Bachelor's and advanced degrees may be earned in chemistry or another discipline—such as biochemistry, toxicology, or materials science—that is related to the area in which Chemists wish to work.

For technician and research assistant jobs, candidates need a bachelor's degree. Many employers prefer or require that candidates have a master's degree. For research scientist positions, a master's degree or a Ph.D. is typically required. To teach at the university level, conduct independent research, or advance to top management posts, a Ph.D. is a mandatory requirement.

Experience, Skills, and Personality Traits

Employers generally choose candidates who have work and research experience related to the position for which they are applying. For example, a job applicant for a position in a pharmaceutical company should have previous work experience in the industry. Experience may have been gained through student research projects, internships, fellowships, part-time employment, and so on. Ph.D. candidates for research scientist positions may be required to have several years of postdoctoral experience.

Chemists need good self-management skills, including the ability to work independently, organize and prioritize tasks, and make appropriate decisions. In addition, they must possess strong mathematical and computer skills, excellent analytical and problem-solving skills, and effective communication and writing skills. Furthermore, Chemists must have good interpersonal and teamwork skills in order to work well with others.

Some personality traits that successful Chemists share are being curious, creative, self-motivated, persistent, and flexible.

Special Requirements

Chemists who work in specific occupations, such as marine chemists and directors of clinical laboratories, are required to obtain appropriate state licensure or professional certification. (For information about a specific occupation, contact professionals in the field, professional societies, or chemistry professors.)

Unions and Associations

Many Chemists belong to professional associations so that they can take advantage of education programs, professional certification, networking opportunities, and other professional resources and services. The American Chemical Society, the American Institute of Chemists, and the American Association for the Advancement of Science are three of the general scientific societies that many Chemists join. Many professional associations serve specific interests in chemistry, including the American Association for Clinical Chemistry, the Society of Cosmetic Chemists, the Geochemical Society, the Association of Formulation Chemists, and the American Association of Cereal Chemists.

Chemistry professors are eligible to join professional societies such as the American Association of University Professors or the National Association of Scholars. See Appendix III for contact information.

Tips for Entry

1. You can find out about scholarships, internships, fellowships, postdoctoral positions, and permanent jobs from college career centers and professional associations.
2. Contact employers for whom you would like to work, and ask about current openings.
3. Learn more about Chemists on the Internet. One website you might visit is the American Chemical Society, http://www.chemcenter.org. To get a list of other relevant websites, enter the keyword *chemistry* or *chemists* in a search engine.

CHEMICAL ENGINEER

CAREER PROFILE

Duties: Research, design, operate, and maintain equipment and plants for industrial chemical processes; may conduct basic research; may teach college or university students; perform duties as required

Alternate Title(s): Process Design Engineer, Polymer Engineer, Operations Engineer, or other title that reflects a specialty

Salary Range: $47,000 to $107,000

Employment Prospects: Good

Advancement Prospects: Good

Prerequisites:
 Education or Training—A bachelor's degree in chemical engineering or related field
 Experience—Relevant work experience required
 Special Skills and Personality Traits—Critical thinking, problem-solving, writing, communication, interpersonal, and teamwork skills; enthusiastic; flexible; innovative; detail-oriented; creative; self-motivated
 Licensure/Certification—Professional Engineer (P.E.) license may be required

CAREER LADDER

```
┌─────────────────────────────────────┐
│   Supervising or Project Engineer    │
└─────────────────────────────────────┘

┌─────────────────────────────────────┐
│          Chemical Engineer           │
└─────────────────────────────────────┘

┌─────────────────────────────────────┐
│ Junior or Assistant Chemical Engineer│
└─────────────────────────────────────┘
```

Position Description

Chemical engineering deals with the design, production, and operation of equipment and plants for industrial chemical processes which change raw materials into final products.

The creation of any product is made in the scientist's lab in small batches. Thus, Chemical Engineers have the responsibility of scaling up the chemical processes in the scientist's operations to industrial size. Chemical Engineers must solve questions such as: What quantity of chemicals are needed? Will the company buy them or make them? How should the chemical processes be done on a large scale? What types of equipment and facilities will be needed? What kind of safety measures must be put in place? How should waste materials be treated and disposed of? How much will it cost to build and run the operations?

Most Chemical Engineers work in various private industries. Many work in chemical processing industries, where they are involved in the manufacturing of such products as plastics, polymers, rubber products, paper, gasoline, petroleum products, paints, inks, soaps, cosmetics, synthetic fibers, industrial gases, and specialty chemicals. Many other Chemical Engineers work in the pharmaceuticals industry to develop processes for the mass production of drugs and medicines. Still others are employed in other industries such as biotechnology, health care, food processing, electronics, design and construction, and environmental protection.

Chemical Engineers typically work in teams comprised of scientists, engineers, project managers, and others, in different areas of production. They may be involved in researching the production of new or modified products. Some are concerned with the development of new or improved chemical processes. Others work on the design of equipment, pilot plants (testing facilities), or manufacturing plants. Some Chemical Engineers design computer applications and technology systems to control and monitor processes. In addition, Chemical Engineers develop budgets, make capital projections, buy equipment, create marketing strategies, and perform other business-oriented tasks.

Chemical Engineers are also involved with the management of day-to-day plant operations. They troubleshoot problems with chemical processes as they occur and provide technical support to staff. Other duties may include monitoring production to ensure products are manufactured according to specification; testing sample products to ensure quality control; conducting safety analyses of equipment; analyzing operations procedures and making recommendations for improving existing methods, processes, or equipment; and so on.

Chemical Engineers also make sure that chemical processes as well as facilities are safe for employees, the environment, and surrounding communities. Some are involved in the development of pollution control strategies or in the design of waste storage and treatment facilities. Others are responsible for monitoring operations to ensure that companies are complying with environmental laws and regulations.

Some Chemical Engineers are involved in basic and applied research, and work in academic, government, or private research laboratories. They study a wide range of topics. For example, they might look for new ways to use or produce chemicals; create products that can be used in health care, biotechnology, space research, environmental protection, and other areas; develop better methodologies or techniques for chemical processes; search for solutions to control environmental problems, and so on.

Research Chemical Engineers in nonindustry settings are usually responsible for obtaining grants from the federal government and other sources to fund their projects.

Many Chemical Engineers are employed as full-time faculty at colleges and universities where they teach undergraduate and graduate courses as well as conduct independent research. Professors also have additional responsibilities. These include supervising student research projects, advising students, and performing administrative tasks. They also are required to write scholarly works and participate in community service.

All Chemical Engineers are responsible for keeping up with developments in their field. Their activities might include reading professional journals and books, networking with peers, enrolling in continuing education courses, and attending professional conferences.

Salaries

Salaries vary, depending on such factors as education, experience, industry, employer, and geographical location. According to the Bureau of Labor Statistics, the estimated salary in 2001 for most Chemical Engineers ranged between $47,490 and $106,680.

Employment Prospects

In general, most opportunities become available as Chemical Engineers retire or transfer to other positions. The best opportunities are predicted to emerge in the areas of phar-

maceuticals, biotechnology, electronics, plastic materials, and specialty chemicals. In addition, opportunities should increase with engineering firms that provide research and testing services. Some experts report that the continuing need to protect the environment should create additional opportunities for Chemical Engineers.

With their background, Chemical Engineers can also seek positions as technical sales engineers, environmental engineers, compliance inspectors, patent agents, technical writers, and finance consultants.

Advancement Prospects

Chemical Engineers can advance to managerial positions such as project leader, project manager, chief engineer, plant manager, director of research, and executive officer.

Education and Training

A bachelor's degree in chemical engineering, chemistry, math, or other major with course work in engineering is required for entry-level positions. A master's degree or Ph.D. is required for independent research, consulting, and management positions. To teach in universities and four-year colleges, a doctoral degree is needed.

Entry-level engineers are given on-the-job training. Many employers also provide some type of classroom training.

Experience, Skills, and Personality Traits

Entry-level candidates should have related work and research experience gained through completion of undergraduate research projects and internships. They should have a full grasp of the fundamentals of chemistry and have skills in laboratory testing and chemistry techniques.

Chemical Engineers need excellent critical thinking and problem-solving skills. In addition, they must have the ability to write effective reports and to communicate clearly to various people such as scientists, technicians, managers, production workers, and customers. Further, they should have excellent interpersonal and teamwork skills.

Some personality traits that successful Chemical Engineers share are being enthusiastic, flexible, innovative, detail-oriented, creative, and self-motivated.

Special Requirements

All 50 states and Washington D.C. require that Chemical Engineers who offer their services directly to the public be licensed as professional engineers (P.E.). Some employers may require or strongly prefer that candidates also hold P.E. licensure. Many Chemical Engineers obtain P.E. licenses voluntarily so as to enhance their employability,

Requirement for P.E. licensure varies with the different states. For specific information, contact the board of examiners for professional engineers in the state where you wish to practice.

Unions and Associations

Many Chemical Engineers join professional associations to take advantage of professional resources and services. Some societies that serve the particular interests of this profession are the American Institute of Chemical Engineers, the American Chemical Society, and the Society of Women Engineers. See Appendix III for contact information.

Tips for Entry

1. Try to get a variety of internships and part-time work experience in various workplaces to get an idea of which settings interest you the most.

2. Many employers attend campus job fairs, career days, or other special events on college campuses to recruit for entry-level Chemical Engineer positions. Contact college career centers for information.

3. You can learn more about chemical engineering on the Internet. Two websites that you might visit are the American Institute of Chemical Engineers, http://www.aiche.org and Chemical Engineers' Resource Page, http://www.cheresources.com.

BIOCHEMIST

CAREER PROFILE

Duties: Conduct basic or applied research; design and conduct research projects; may teach college, university, or medical school students; research assistants and technicians provide research and administrative support; perform duties as required

Alternate Title(s): Research Scientist, Professor

Salary Range: $34,000 to $98,000

Employment Prospects: Good

Advancement Prospects: Good

Prerequisites:

Education or Training—Ph.D. required to conduct independent research work, teach in universities or colleges, or hold top management positions

Experience—Postdoctoral experience for research scientists may be required

Special Skills and Personality Traits—Writing, communication, interpersonal, and teamwork skills; cooperative; creative; imaginative; hardworking; persistent; flexible

Licensure/Certification—None required

CAREER LADDER

```
┌─────────────────────────────────────┐
│         Senior Biochemist            │
└─────────────────────────────────────┘

┌─────────────────────────────────────┐
│        Research Biochemist           │
└─────────────────────────────────────┘

┌─────────────────────────────────────┐
│   Postdoctoral Research Associate    │
└─────────────────────────────────────┘
```

Position Description

Biochemistry is the chemical study of microbes, plants, animals, and humans. Biochemists seek to understand the chemical composition and structure of living organisms. In addition they are interested in learning about the chemical reactions that are involved in reproduction, heredity, metabolism, and growth.

Many Biochemists are involved in basic research, seeking to further scientific knowledge. They study questions such as: How does plant photosynthesis work? How do chemical changes take place during digestion, muscle contraction, and other body functions? What is DNA's role in heredity? How do drugs affect an animal's life systems? How do harmful toxins break down in the human body?

Many other Biochemists are involved in applied research in fields such as pharmacology, physiology, toxicology, veterinary science, microbiology, genetics, agriculture, food science, biotechnology, clinical chemistry, and environmental science. Applied Biochemists use the findings of basic research to solve problems within their specialty. For example, Biochemists have helped medical scientists develop treatments and cures for diseases. Additionally, Biochemists

have contributed to the development of drugs, medicines, foods, and many consumer products. They are also involved in finding solutions to air and water pollution problems.

Responsibilities for Biochemists vary, according to their position, employer, work setting, and other factors. Some Biochemists are research assistants and technicians. They provide research and administrative support in science labs, normally working under the supervision of research scientists (or Research Biochemists).

Research Biochemists are responsible for designing and conducting research projects. Some of their tasks include conducting experiments, gathering data, analyzing and interpreting data, writing reports, and performing administrative tasks. Senior researchers and principal investigators usually perform supervisory and management duties. Biochemists who conduct independent research are usually responsible for seeking research grants from the federal government and other sources to fund their projects. This involves preparing grant proposals that include the goals, methodologies, budgets, and other aspects for their projects.

Biochemists sometimes collaborate on research projects with scientists from other disciplines and with specialists, such as engineers and physicians. Many Biochemists are also faculty members at universities, colleges, and medical schools. They teach biochemistry courses in chemistry and biochemistry departments as well as in such departments as medicine, veterinary science, pharmacy, and agriculture. They are responsible for planning and teaching courses in addition to conducting independent research projects. Their duties also include advising students, supervising student research projects, writing scholarly work, performing administrative duties, and participating in community service.

Most Biochemists share and exchange information with each other as well with other scientists. Many Biochemists write scientific papers which they submit to scientific journals for publication. Some might also give presentations at scientific conferences that are sponsored by professional associations.

In addition, Biochemists are responsible for keeping up with new technologies and developments in their fields. They participate in training programs, enroll in continuing education programs, attend professional conferences and meetings, network with colleagues, and so forth.

Salaries
Salaries vary, depending on experience, education, geographical location, and other factors. The Bureau of Labor Statistics reports that the estimated annual salary in 2001 for most biochemists ranged from $33,930 to $97,710.

Employment Prospects
Typically, most positions become available as individuals retire, resign, or transfer to other positions. Some experts report that the completion of the Human Genome Project (the identification of human genes) should open up more research opportunities in all settings.

With a background in biochemistry, individuals can pursue career paths in other areas such as medicine, dentistry, veterinary medicine, pharmacy, public health, chemical engineering, law, technical sales, or journalism.

Advancement Prospects
Many research Biochemists seek management or administrative positions, such as project leader, program manager, research director, and executive officer. Technicians and research assistants can advance to a managerial position as a laboratory manager or to other non-laboratory administrative positions.

Most Biochemists measure their success by being able to conduct independent research, through earning professional recognition, and by earning higher wages.

Education and Training
Most research associates and technicians hold a bachelor's degree in biochemistry or in biology or chemistry with course work in the other disciplines. Research scientists usually hold a master's or doctoral degree in biochemistry, molecular biology, or a related field.

Doctoral degrees are usually required to teach in universities and four-year colleges, to conduct independent research, and to pursue top management positions.

Experience, Skills, and Personality Traits
Employers generally choose candidates who have related work and research experience, which may have been gained through research projects, internships, fellowships, part-time employment, and so on. Many employers prefer or require that Ph.D. applicants have relevant postdoctoral experience.

Biochemists need effective writing and communication skills, as they must be able to present their findings clearly to others. Strong interpersonal and teamwork skills are also important for their work.

Some personality traits that successful Biochemists share are being cooperative, creative, imaginative, hardworking, persistent, and flexible.

Unions and Associations
Many Biochemists join professional associations to take advantage of professional services and resources, such as education programs and networking opportunities. One national association that serves Biochemists is the American Society for Biochemistry and Molecular Biology. Biochemists are also eligible to join general biology or chemistry societies such as the American Institute of Biological Sciences, the American Institute of Chemists, or the American Chemical Society. Academic Biochemists may join professional societies, such as the American Association for Higher Education, that serve their academic concerns. See Appendix III for contact information.

Tips for Entry
1. Many universities and colleges offer cooperative education programs in which undergraduate students integrate their academic study with supervised work experience in government, industry, or business settings. The work experience may be full-time or part-time. Often, employers hire students for full-time positions after they have completed their bachelor's degree. Speak with your chemistry adviser or a career placement counselor for more information.
2. You can find job listings for biochemistry positions on the Internet. Some sources are professional societies, college and university departments, and general job banks such as Monster.com, http://www.monster.com; or America's Job Bank, http://www.ajb.org. In addition, many employers post job openings on their websites.
3. Learn more about Biochemists on the Internet. To get a list of relevant websites to read, enter the keyword *biochemistry* or *biochemists* in any search engine.

TOXICOLOGIST

CAREER PROFILE

Duties: Conduct basic or applied research; design and conduct research projects; may perform other major responsibilities, such as teach college and university students, provide laboratory analysis services, or provide consulting services; perform duties as required of position.

Alternate Title(s): Toxicologist Assistant; Forensic Toxicologist, Environmental Toxicologist, Clinical Toxicologist, or other title that reflects a specialty

Salary Range: $42,000 to $153,000

Employment Prospects: Good

Advancement Prospects: Good

Prerequisites:
   Education or Training—Ph.D. required to conduct independent research work, teach in universities or colleges, or hold top management positions
   Experience—Postdoctoral experience may be required
   Special Skills and Personality Traits—Interpersonal, teamwork, communication, writing, math, and computer skills; flexible; creative; organized; analytical
   Licensure/Certification—Clinical toxicological chemists may be required to be licensed or obtain professional certification; clinical directors and consultants must be certified by an acceptable professional board

CAREER LADDER

```
┌─────────────────────────────┐
│   Senior Toxicologist or    │
│  Supervising Toxicologist   │
└─────────────────────────────┘

┌─────────────────────────────┐
│        Toxicologist         │
└─────────────────────────────┘

┌─────────────────────────────┐
│ Research Assistant or Associate │
└─────────────────────────────┘
```

Position Description

Toxicology is the study of poisons, which may be solid, liquid, or gaseous substances. All chemicals are potentially toxic and any substance absorbed in excess can be extremely harmful.

Toxicologists identify the toxicity of substances and determine their levels of safe and dangerous use. They also investigate how poisons or pollutants can affect living organisms and ecosystems. In addition, they are concerned with the safety of drugs, cleaning supplies, pesticides, paints, fuel, cosmetics, and dyes, and other products as well as natural and industrial chemicals to which living organisms and the environment are constantly exposed.

Many Toxicologists are involved in basic research. They continually add to the body of knowledge about different poisons, the risks of using various chemicals, how substances cause injury or disease, what are safe conditions for using various chemicals, and so forth. Typically, basic toxicology research is used to solve various problems in medicine, agriculture, environmental science, and other fields.

Many basic researchers work in academic laboratories, and usually have the additional duty of teaching toxicology courses to graduate and medical students. On smaller campuses, Toxicologists might also teach basic chemistry or biology courses to undergraduate students. As faculty members, their duties include advising students, supervising student research projects, writing scholarly work, performing administrative duties, and participating in community service. Further, they are responsible for obtaining grants for their research projects.

Toxicologists also conduct applied research and work on product development teams in chemical, pharmaceutical, biotechnology, and other industries. These Toxicologists are responsible for researching harmful effects of potential products. They identify any risks (such as birth defects, cancer, or illnesses) that may occur if a product is used under certain conditions. For example, a Toxicologist might determine that a new drug for allergies may cause such side effects as nausea or headaches. With approved products, Toxicologists design and conduct various tests to ensure that they are safe for consumers to use and that they meet industrial standards.

Toxicologists also work in other applied areas. Their duties may include conducting research, performing analysis services, and so on. The following are a few other types of toxicologists:

- Forensic Toxicologists are involved in criminal and post-mortem investigations. They perform chemical analyses on human and animal corpses to determine the type and amount of poisons that caused their deaths.
- Medical and clinical Toxicologists are concerned with how poisons and pollutants affect human health. Many are directly involved with the diagnosis and treatment of human diseases. Some are medical doctors who work with patients; other Toxicologists work in hospital labs where they analyze the levels of medication or other substances in blood and tissue samples.
- Veterinary Toxicologists study the effects of poisons and pollutants on animals, both domestic and wild; many are involved with the diagnosis and treatment of diseases.
- Environmental Toxicologists study the effects that chemical pollutants have on humans, animals, plants, and the environment.
- Food safety Toxicologists are concerned with understanding how poisons or pathogens (such as bacteria or viruses) in food affect human health.
- Regulatory Toxicologists work for local, state, and federal government agencies. They assist in the enforcement as well as development of laws and regulations that protect human health and the environment.

Some Toxicologists are consultants, as independent contractors or employees of consulting firms. They offer research, analytical, and other services to private industries and public agencies on a contractual basis.

Toxicologists work in laboratories and offices. Some Toxicologists take field trips to conduct research and testing services. Their field work may involve traveling to isolated areas, such as forests and wilderness areas.

Salaries

Salaries vary, depending on such factors as education, experience, position, type of employer, and geographical location. According to a 2001 salary survey by the American Association for the Advancement of Science, the median salary for life scientists in academic settings ranged from $42,000 to $112,000 and for those in nonacademic settings, from $76,000 to $153,000.

Employment Prospects

Toxicologists are employed by colleges, universities, and medical schools. They also work for a wide range of local, state, and federal government agencies (for example: public health, regulatory, law enforcement, and defense agencies). Many Toxicologists work in pharmaceutical, chemical, biotechnology, manufacturing, and other industries. In addition, many are independent consultants or employed in consulting firms, providing services to local public agencies, industries, and attorneys. Some Toxicologists work for nonprofit research foundations.

Job opportunities are generally stronger in nonacademic settings than in academic settings. Most job openings are created to replace individuals who retire, transfer to other positions, or resign.

Advancement Prospects

In any setting, Toxicologists can advance to supervisory and administrative positions, such as project leader, program manager, lab director, and executive officer. As professors, Toxicologists can move up through the ranks as assistant professor, associate professor, or full professor.

Education and Training

Toxicologists have a bachelor's, master's, or doctoral degree in toxicology or other disciplines such as biology, chemistry, biochemistry, medicinal chemistry, experimental pathology, pharmacology, epidemiology, or cell biology.

Research scientists must possess either a master's degree or a Ph.D. Doctoral degrees are required to teach in universities and four-year colleges, to conduct independent research, and to pursue top management positions.

Experience, Skills, and Personality Traits

Employers generally choose candidates who have related work and research experience, which may have been gained through research projects, internships, fellowships, part-time employment, and so on. Many employers prefer or require that Ph.D. applicants have a few years of postdoctoral experience.

Along with being able to work independently, Toxicologists can work collaboratively with others in team projects. Thus, having effective interpersonal and teamwork skills is important. Toxicologists also need strong communication and writing skills and should have good math and computer skills.

Being flexible, creative, organized, and analytical are a few of the personality traits that successful Toxicologists share.

Special Requirements

Clinical Toxicologists may be required to obtain state licensure or appropriate professional certification from the National Registry in Clinical Chemistry or other organization.

Toxicologists who plan to become clinical laboratory directors or consultants must obtain proper board certification from the American Board of Toxicology or the American Board of Clinical Chemistry.

Toxicologists can obtain professional certification on a voluntary basis from organizations that offer credentials for their field. For example, forensic Toxicologists may seek board certification from the American Board of Forensic Toxicology while veterinary Toxicologists may apply for board certification from the American Board of Veterinary Toxicology.

Unions and Associations

Many Toxicologists join professional associations to take advantage of education programs, professional publications, networking opportunities, and other professional resources and services. Some of the various societies that serve the diverse interests of Toxicologists are: the Society of Toxicology, the American College of Toxicology, the Society of Forensic Toxicologists, the Association for Government Toxicologists, and the Society of Environmental Toxicology and Chemistry. See Appendix III for contact information.

Tips for Entry

1. Contact government and private sector employers directly for information about available internships, postdoctoral opportunities, and permanent positions.
2. Admission requirements for graduate programs in toxicology vary from school to school. Get an early start learning about the programs that interest you so that you can be sure to take appropriate courses during your undergraduate years.
3. Use the Internet to learn more about toxicology. Two websites you might visit are Society of Toxicology, http://www.toxicology.org; and Toxicology Online, http://www.toxicologyonline.com.

PHYSICS AND ASTRONOMY

PHYSICIST

CAREER PROFILE

Duties: Conduct basic or applied research; design and conduct research projects; may teach college or university students; research assistants and technicians provide research and administrative support; perform duties as required of position

Alternate Title(s): Experimental Physicist, Theoretical Physicist; Optics Physicist, Nuclear Physicist, Biophysicist, or other title that reflects a specialty

Salary Range: $35,000 to $123,000

Employment Prospects: Good

Advancement Prospects: Good

Prerequisites:

Education or Training—A bachelor's or advanced degree in physics or subfield of physics

Experience—Postdoctoral experience may be required for research scientists

Special Skills and Personality Traits—Math, computer, problem-solving, analytical, self-management, interpersonal, teamwork, writing, and communication skills; imaginative; persistent; inquisitive; self-motivated

Licensure/Certification—None required

CAREER LADDER

```
┌─────────────────────────────────────┐
│          Senior Physicist           │
└─────────────────────────────────────┘

┌─────────────────────────────────────┐
│         Research Physicist          │
└─────────────────────────────────────┘

┌─────────────────────────────────────┐
│    Postdoctoral Research Associate   │
└─────────────────────────────────────┘
```

Position Description

Physics is the study of matter and energy. It deals with the structure and properties of matter and the various forms of energy, as well as the relationships between matter and energy. It is a fundamental science that has helped solve diverse problems in such fields as medicine, engineering, chemistry, technology, communications, biotechnology, energy, and environmental science. The scientists who work in this physical science are called Physicists. They seek to understand how everything works on all possible levels, from atoms and molecules to living cells and tissues to electrical circuits and supercomputers to liquid, solid, and gaseous matter to the Earth and outer space, and so on.

Most Physicists are involved in research, working in academic, government, industry, nongovernmental, and nonprofit research laboratories. Some Physicists conduct basic research to increase scientific knowledge in their areas of interest. Through observation and analysis, Physicists continue to discover physical laws and theories that explain gravity, electromagnetism, chemical reactions, the transfer of energy, nuclear reactions, and various other processes and interactions that occur in the world.

Other Physicists are involved in applied research. They are typically employed in government and industry research departments, and they work on the design and development of new or improved devices, products, and processes. For example, Physicists have contributed to the development of many technologies such as lasers, radar, X-ray machines, navigation equipment, and atomic power.

Physicists usually specialize in performing experimental or theoretical research. Experimental Physicists design and run experiments and make careful observations and measurements to explain what happened in the experiments. Theoretical Physicists, on the other hand, analyze the results of experiments (usually done by other Physicists) and determine whether the experiments obey particular theories. Theoretical Physicists create computer models (sets of mathematical equations) to help them with their investigations.

Many Physicists also specialize in one of the many subfields of physics. Some Physicists switch from one subfield to another throughout their careers. The following are some of the major specialties.

- Mechanics is the study of the interaction of force and matter, whether matter is at rest or in motion.
- Acoustics is concerned with sound and sound waves.
- Optics is the study of light (including ultraviolet and infrared radiation) and the phenomena related to its generation, transmission, and detection.
- Thermodynamics is the study of heat, its movement from one body to another, and the relationships between heat and other forms of energy.
- Electrodynamics is the study of electricity and magnetic fields.
- Atomic physics is the study of atoms and their properties, as well as their interactions with atomic particles and fields.
- Particle physics (or high-energy physics) deals with the study of electrons, neutrons, protons, and hundreds of other elementary particles that are the building blocks of all matter in the universe.
- Solid-state physics (or condensed-matter physics) is the study of solid matter and its properties, such as optical and acoustic properties.
- Plasma physics is the study of highly ionized (electrically charged) gases, which are found in space as well as in thermonuclear reactors. Plasma is sometimes called the fourth state of matter. (Solids, liquids, and gases are the three known states of matter.)
- Cryogenics is the study of very low temperatures (near absolute zero) and the techniques for producing them.
- Vacuum physics deals with space (vacuum) that contains very few atoms or molecules.
- Nuclear physics is the study of atomic nuclei and their interactions, as well as of nuclear energy.

Some Physicists work in a field that combines physics with another scientific discipline. For example, biophysicists apply physics to biological problems, geophysicists study the physics of the earth, and astrophysicists incorporate the principles and theories of physics to the study of astronomy.

Most Physicists collaborate on research projects with other Physicists as well as with other scientists, engineers, and specialists. Physicists usually share the results of their research work with colleagues. Many write scientific papers which they submit to scientific journals. Some also make presentations at scientific meetings that are sponsored by professional associations.

Physicists' duties vary, depending on their position. Technicians and research assistants typically work under the supervision of research Physicists. Their duties may include: performing experiments, analyzing data, writing reports, maintaining laboratory equipment, performing routine administrative tasks, and so on.

Research Physicists are responsible for designing and conducting research projects. They work in laboratories to conduct their research, but also work in offices to analyze data, write reports, and perform other research and administrative tasks. Physicists sometimes are involved in designing complex equipment (such as lasers, telescopes, radiation detectors, and particle accelerators) for their particular type of research. They might also create computer software programs necessary for data analysis, modeling, and other purposes.

Many Physicists are responsible for obtaining research grants to fund their projects. This involves learning about available grants from the federal government and other sources, as well as writing grant proposals that describe the objectives, methodologies, budgets, and other aspects of their projects.

Many research Physicists are also faculty members at colleges and universities. In addition to conducting independent research, they are responsible for teaching physics courses to undergraduate and graduate students. They also perform other duties that include advising students, supervising student research projects, writing scholarly works, fulfilling administrative duties, and participating in community services.

Physicists sometimes travel to laboratory facilities in other cities or countries to use special equipment for their research projects. They may be exposed to radiation, toxic materials, and high-voltage electrical equipment in the laboratory. Thus, they follow specific safety measures to keep health and safety hazards to a minimum.

Salaries

Salaries vary, depending on education, experience, employer, geographical location, and other factors. According to the Bureau of Labor Statistics, the estimated annual salary for most Physicists in 2001 ranged between $49,320 and $123,220, and for most postsecondary Physicist instructors, between $34,650 and $105,850.

Employment Prospects

Most job opportunities become available as Physicists retire or transfer to other positions. Some experts report that openings should increase in the coming years due to the large number of scientists who will be retiring.

In general, most basic research opportunities are dependent on the availability of research grants from the federal government. Thus, if the federal government increases the budget for physics-related research, more opportunities usually become available.

With a background in physics, individuals can pursue career paths in various areas, such as engineering, computer science, energy, education, medicine, law, finance, and journalism.

Advancement Prospects

Physicists with management and administrative interests can pursue such positions in any work setting. For example, research scientists in industry or government settings may advance by becoming a project leader, program director, or executive officer. Professors receive promotional rankings as assistant professors, associate professors, or full professors.

Education and Training

Research Physicists must possess either a master's degree or a Ph.D. in physics, a subfield of physics (such as biophysics), or other related field (such as engineering). A Ph.D. is necessary for those wishing to teach in universities and four-year colleges, to conduct independent research, or to pursue top management positions.

A bachelor's degree in physics is usually the minimum requirement for research assistant and lab technician positions.

Experience, Skills, and Personality Traits

Employers generally choose candidates who have previous work experience as well as research experience related to the positions being sought. Entry-level applicants may have gained experience through research projects, internships, fellowships, part-time employment, and so on. Many employers generally prefer or require that Ph.D. applicants for research scientist positions have a few years of postdoctoral experience. Candidates for industry positions should have some related industry experience or some background in business or economics.

Physicists should have strong math and computer skills. They need strong problem-solving and analytical skills and good self-management skills, such as being able to work independently, meet deadlines, concentrate on details, and prioritize tasks. They also need good interpersonal and teamwork skills, as they must be able to work well with others. In addition, they must have excellent writing and communication skills.

Some personality traits that successful Physicists have in common are being imaginative, persistent, inquisitive, and self-motivated.

Unions and Associations

Most Physicists join professional organizations to take advantage of professional services and resources such as education programs and networking opportunities. Some general societies are the American Institute of Physics, the American Physical Society, and the American Association for the Advancement of Science. Physicists might also join professional societies that serve their specialties, such as the American Geophysical Union, the Biophysical Society, the Acoustical Society of America, or the American Association of Physicists in Medicine. (See Appendix III for contact information.)

Academic faculty might join professional societies such as the National Association of Scholars or the American Association for Higher Education.

Tips for Entry

1. Talk with physicists of various specializations and in various settings to learn about the types of opportunities that are available.
2. Many sources can provide you with information about job openings. For example, you might talk with physics professors, visit college and university placement centers, contact professional societies, or check out the Internet for job listings. You might also contact human resource departments of those employers for whom you would like to work.
3. To learn about job openings with the federal government, contact the nearest U.S. Office of Personnel Management. Check out the white pages in your telephone directory. Or visit its website at http://www.usajobs.opm.gov.
4. The Internet can provide you with more information about physics. Two websites you might visit are American Institute of Physicists, http://www.aip.org; and PhysLink.com, http://www.physlink.com.

BIOPHYSICIST

CAREER PROFILE

Duties: Conduct basic or applied research; design and conduct research projects; may teach college and university students; research assistants and technicians provide research and administrative support; perform duties as required

Alternate Title(s): Physicist, Staff Scientist

Salary Range: $34,000 to $98,000

Employment Prospects: Good

Advancement Prospects: Good

Prerequisites:

    Education or Training—Ph.D. required to conduct independent research work, teach in universities or colleges, or hold top management positions

    Experience—Postdoctoral experience for research scientists may be required

    Special Skills and Personality Traits—Math, computer, critical thinking, problem-solving, communication, writing, interpersonal, and teamwork skills; inquisitive; determined; creative; self-motivated

    Licensure/Certification—None required

CAREER LADDER

```
┌─────────────────────────────────┐
│      Senior Biophysicist        │
└─────────────────────────────────┘

┌─────────────────────────────────┐
│     Research Biophysicist       │
└─────────────────────────────────┘

┌─────────────────────────────────┐
│  Postdoctoral Research Associate │
└─────────────────────────────────┘
```

Position Description

Biophysics is an interdisciplinary science that applies the knowledge and techniques of physics to the study of life processes, such as the muscular, nervous, and cardiovascular systems.

Biophysicists are concerned about understanding how life processes function in humans, plants, and animals. They study the physical properties and structures of life processes, as well as examine the interrelationships among the life systems. Biophysicists seek answers to such questions as: What is the structure of the cell membrane? How do nucleic acids get their shapes? How do animals respond to light? How do plants make food? How does the brain send messages to the body? How does a wound heal? Will damaged cells in an organism make cells in future generations be unstable? What causes disease at the molecular level?

Most Biophysicists conduct basic or applied research in various areas, including medical science, pharmaceuticals, nutrition, biotechnology, agriculture, clinical chemistry, food science, toxicology, and environmental science. Their research projects often involve collaboration with biologists, chemists, geneticists, and other scientists and engineers.

Biophysicists can focus their studies in several ways. Some choose to conduct only molecular or cellular investigations. Others specialize in the type of organ (such as brain or heart) or type of organism (such as a plant or microbe) that they study. Some Biophysicists are involved in the development of instruments and methodologies that other Biophysicists can use in their research work.

Many Biophysicists choose to specialize in one of two approaches that is used to explore the mechanisms of life. Experimental Biophysicists design and run experiments and make careful observations and measurements to explain what happened in the experiments. Theoretical Biophysicists, on the other hand, analyze the results of experiments to see whether or not they obey particular theories, and to explain what happened in the experiments in mathematical equations.

Biophysicists use a variety of techniques and technologies in their research. For example, they use electron microscopes, magnetic resonance spectroscopy, X-ray crystallography (the use of X rays to determine the structure of molecules), and particle accelerators. It is common for Biophysicists to design and build new or improved instruments and equipment for their research, as well as to design computer software that specifically meets their needs for data analysis, data transference, modeling, or other purposes.

Duties for Biophysicists vary, depending on their position. As research scientists, they are responsible for designing and conducting research projects. Some of their tasks include conducting experiments, gathering data, analyzing and interpreting data, writing reports, and performing administrative tasks. Those who conduct independent research are usually responsible for writing grant proposals and seeking research grants from the federal government and other sources. Most senior researchers and principal investigators also perform supervisory and management duties.

Some Biophysicists are research assistants and technicians. Their role is to provide research and administrative support. Some of their duties include conducting experiments, analyzing data, writing reports, maintaining equipment and facilities, performing routine administrative tasks, and so on.

Many research Biophysicists are faculty members at colleges, universities, medical schools, and dental schools. In addition to their research duties, they are responsible for planning and teaching undergraduate and graduate courses. They may teach biophysics, physics, chemistry, biology, engineering, and other subjects. Their duties also include advising students, supervising student research projects, writing scholarly works, performing administrative duties, and participating in community service.

Research Biophysicists typically share information about their research work with their colleagues. Most Biophysicists write scientific papers which they submit to scientific journals for publication. Some also make presentations at scientific conferences that are sponsored by professional associations.

Salaries

Salaries vary, depending on experience, job duties, geographical location, and other factors. According to the Bureau of Labor Statistics, the estimated annual salary for most Biophysicists in 2001 ranged between $33,930 and $97,710.

Employment Prospects

Some major employers of Biophysicists are universities, medical schools, hospitals, drug companies, biotechnology firms, agricultural companies, government research labs, environmental health laboratories, and private research foundations.

Biophysics is not a new field, but it has been developing rapidly in recent years due to technological advancements and the discoveries in genome research. Some experts report that biophysics is one of the most marketable science degrees

in the biotechnology industry, and that job opportunities are available for technicians as well as for research scientists.

With a background in biophysics, individuals can pursue careers in various other fields, including pharmacology, medicine, veterinary science, agricultural science, oceanography, fisheries and wildlife, toxicology, nutrition, and so on.

Advancement Prospects

Management and administrative positions are available to research scientists who have managerial ambitions. For example, they can advance to positions like project leader, program director, laboratory director, and executive officer. Technicians and research assistants can advance to a managerial position as laboratory manager or to other nonlaboratory administrative positions. Academic faculty members receive promotional rankings as assistant professors, associate professors, or full professors.

Education and Training

The minimum requirement for research assistant or technician positions is a bachelor's degree. Because few undergraduate programs in biophysics are available, many Biophysicists earn majors in such disciplines as physics, chemistry, biology, mathematics, computer science, and engineering.

Research scientists possess either a master's degree or Ph.D. in physics, biophysics, or related field. A Ph.D. is necessary for those wishing to teach in universities and four-year colleges, to conduct independent research, or to pursue administrative positions.

Joint medical and doctoral degree programs are available for individuals interested in pursuing careers in biomedical sciences. In these programs, Biophysicists earn a medical degree as well as a doctorate degree in biophysics, physics, physiology, or related field. The programs are usually seven years long. Students complete medical courses during their first two years, followed by two to three years fulfilling their doctoral program requirements. The last two years are comprised of clinical training.

Experience, Skills, and Personality Traits

Entry-level candidates should have relevant work and research experience. This may have been gained through research projects, internships, summer employment, and so on. Ph.D. candidates for research scientist positions should have postdoctoral experience.

Biophysicists need strong math and computer skills. Also essential are critical thinking, problem-solving, communication, and writing skills. Biophysicists also need to have strong interpersonal and teamwork skills, as they must be able to work well with others from diverse backgrounds.

Being inquisitive, determined, creative, and self-motivated are a few personality traits that successful Biophysicists have in common.

Unions and Associations

Biophysicists can join professional associations to take advantage of networking opportunities, education programs, and other professional services and resources. Some societies that specifically serve the interests of Biophysicists are the Biophysical Society, the Division of Biological Physics (American Physical Society), and the International Union for Pure and Applied BioPhysics. See Appendix III for contact information.

Tips for Entry

1. If you think you would like to pursue a Ph.D., talk with your college adviser to learn what courses would best prepare you for a graduate program.

2. Graduate programs in biophysics are interdisciplinary and usually sponsored by various departments. Some universities and medical schools have departments of biophysics; biophysics and biochemistry; or biophysics and physiology. In some institutions, biophysics programs may be part of the biochemistry, chemistry, pharmacology, physics, physiology, or other department.

3. Use the Internet to learn more about biophysics. To get a list of relevant websites to read, enter the keyword *biophysics* or *biological physics* in any search engine.

NUCLEAR PHYSICIST

CAREER PROFILE

Duties: Conduct basic or applied research; design and conduct research projects; may teach college or university students; perform duties as required of position

Alternate Title(s): Physicist, Research Scientist, Professor of Nuclear Physics

Salary Range: $35,000 to $123,000

Employment Prospects: Fair

Advancement Prospects: Good

Prerequisites:

Education or Training—A master's or doctoral degree in nuclear physics or related field

Experience—Postdoctoral experience may be required

Special Skills and Personality Traits—Communication, interpersonal, teamwork, problem-solving, analytical, writing, and laboratory skills; creative; determined; self-motivated; curious

Licensure/Certification—None required

CAREER LADDER

```
┌─────────────────────────────┐
│   Senior Nuclear Physicist   │
└─────────────────────────────┘

┌─────────────────────────────┐
│  Research Nuclear Physicist  │
└─────────────────────────────┘

┌─────────────────────────────┐
│ Postdoctoral Research Associate │
└─────────────────────────────┘
```

Position Description

Nuclear Physics is the study of the atomic nucleus, the most basic level of matter. All matter (living organisms and non-living things) are made up of billions of tiny atoms. At the core of each atom is the nucleus which contains most of an atom's mass. The nucleus consists of neutrons, protons, and other elementary particles which are the building blocks of all matter. Nuclear Physicists seek to understand the structure and properties of atomic nuclei as well as to learn about their reactions and interactions.

Most Nuclear Physicists conduct research in academic, government, military, industry, nongovernmental, and non-profit labs. Those involved in basic research are concerned with extending knowledge about nuclear science. Their studies range from examining the interactions of elementary particles at the subatomic level to studying astrophysical questions about the formation of stars.

Nuclear Physicists also conduct applied research, contributing to such fields as medicine, electronics, communication, energy, national security, the environment, and archeology. Many Nuclear Physicists are part of research and development projects, and they usually work with teams of scientists, engineers, and other specialists. They are involved in the design and development of new processes, devices, analytical tools, or products, such as:

- nuclear medicine procedures that help physicians diagnose and treat patients by taking internal images of patients' bodies without performing surgeries
- research tools that help environmental scientists to monitor air quality, learn more about global warning or ozone depletion in the stratosphere, search for alternative water supplies, and so on
- processes used to enhance the safety of nuclear power plants and to treat radioactive waste from power plants
- processes that are used for quality control and quality assurance testing of materials and products in the automobile, aircraft, construction, and other industries
- nuclear techniques, such as radioactive dating, to help archeologists and other scientists determine when artifacts and artwork were made

Nuclear Physicists, like other physicists, generally specialize in one of two types of research methods. Some are experimental Nuclear Physicists. They design and run experiments and make careful observations and measurements to explain what happens in the experiments. Others are theoretical physicists. They use computer models to analyze the results of completed experiments to determine whether certain physical laws are being followed.

The most common tools that Nuclear Physicists use in their research are computers, radiation detectors, nuclear reactors, and particle accelerators (which induce nuclear reactions). Nuclear Physicists sometimes build instrumentation and write computer software programs that are needed for their research.

All researchers have virtually the same duties. These include designing research projects, gathering data, conducting experiments, analyzing and interpreting research data, and preparing reports. Senior researchers and principal investigators might also perform supervisory and administrative tasks. Many Nuclear Physicists are involved in writing research proposals and seeking research grants from the federal government and other sources to fund their projects. In addition, Nuclear Physicists write scientific papers or make presentations at scientific conferences to share the results of their research work with colleagues. Some Nuclear Physicists develop websites where they post their research data and information.

Many Nuclear Physicists are employed as faculty members at universities and colleges. In addition to conducting research, they are responsible for teaching physics courses to undergraduate and graduate students. Professors also juggle other responsibilities, including writing scholarly works, advising students, supervising student research projects, performing administrative tasks, and fulfilling community service obligations.

Nuclear Physicists often work long hours to complete research or administrative tasks. Many of them sometimes travel to laboratory facilities in other cities or countries to use special equipment for their research projects.

Salaries

Salaries vary, depending on such factors as education, experience, employer, and geographical location. According to the Bureau of Labor Statistics, the estimated annual salary for most physicists in 2001 ranged from $49,320 to $123,220, and for most physics postsecondary instructors, from $34,650 to $105,850.

Employment Prospects

In general, most Nuclear Physicists work in universities and colleges as faculty members or in large government research laboratories and centers. Many Nuclear Physicists are employed by the U.S. Department of Defense and U.S. Department of Energy. Some Nuclear Physicists work in research and development laboratories in private industries.

Most positions become available as individuals retire or transfer to other positions. The competition for permanent positions in all work settings is high. Some experts have reported that increasingly more Nuclear Physicists work in several postdoctoral or temporary positions before obtaining permanent positions.

Many nuclear physics graduates have been able to apply their skills and training to careers in such other fields as engineering, computer science, finance, business, medicine, environmental science, policy-making, and journalism.

Advancement Prospects

Most Nuclear Physicists measure their success by being able to conduct independent research, through making discoveries, and by earning professional recognition among their peers. Positions such as program director, laboratory director, and executive officer are available for those with management and administrative ambitions. Faculty members may advance through the academic ranks as assistant professors, associate professors, or full professors.

Education and Training

Nuclear Physicists must hold either a master's degree or Ph.D. in nuclear physics, physics, or a related field. A Ph.D. is required in order to teach in universities and four-year colleges, conduct independent research, or pursue top management positions.

Experience, Skills, and Personality Traits

Employers generally choose candidates who have previous work and research experience related to the position being sought. Entry-level applicants may have gained experience through research projects, internships, part-time employment, and so on. Many employers prefer to hire Ph.D. applicants who have a few years of postdoctoral experience.

Nuclear Physicists must have good communication, interpersonal, and teamwork skills, as they must be able to work well with others. In addition, they need strong problem-solving, analytical, and writing skills. Further, they should have developed excellent laboratory skills.

Being creative, determined, self-motivated, and curious are a few personality traits that successful Physicists share.

Unions and Associations

Many Nuclear Physicists join societies to take advantage of networking opportunities, education programs, and other professional resources and services. The American Nuclear Society, the Institute for Nuclear Theory, and the Division of Nuclear Physics (part of the American Physical Society) are some of these professional associations. Faculty members are eligible to join professional societies that serve their interests such as the National Association of Scholars and the American Association of University Professors. See Appendix III for contact information.

Tips for Entry

1. To prepare yourself for graduate school, obtain a summer internship with a university or government lab or get a lab assistant position with a physics professor.
2. The U.S. Department of Energy and the National Science Foundation both sponsor research programs that offer opportunities for undergraduates to participate in nuclear science projects. For help learning more about such programs, talk with your physics adviser or contact your college career center. You can also contact the agencies directly.
3. Join a professional association, and participate in its activities. This is one way to begin building a network of contacts for current and future job searches.
4. Use the Internet to learn more about nuclear physics. Here are some websites that you might visit: Division of Nuclear Physics (U.S. Department of Energy), http://www.sc.doe.gov/production/henp/np/index.html, The ABCs of Nuclear Science, http://www.lbl.gov/abc; and Division of Nuclear Physics (The American Physical Society), http://nucth.physics.wisc.edu/dnp.

ASTRONOMER

CAREER PROFILE

Duties: Conduct research; design and conduct research projects; may teach college or university students; may manage programs, observatories, or labs; perform duties as required of position

Alternate Title(s): Astrophysicist, Observational Astronomer, Theoretical Astronomer

Salary Range: $40,000 to $115,000

Employment Prospects: Fair

Advancement Prospects: Good

Prerequisites:

Education or Training—A doctoral degree in astronomy or related field

Experience—Postdoctoral experience in specialty

Special Skills and Personality Traits—Highly skilled in computers, computer programming, math, and statistics; analytical, problem-solving, observation, writing, communication, and interpersonal skills; patient; precise; determined; curious; self-motivated; imaginative

Licensure/Certification—None required

CAREER LADDER

```
┌─────────────────────────────────┐
│       Senior Astronomer         │
└─────────────────────────────────┘

┌─────────────────────────────────┐
│          Astronomer             │
└─────────────────────────────────┘

┌─────────────────────────────────┐
│  Postdoctoral Research Associate │
└─────────────────────────────────┘
```

Position Description

Astronomy is the scientific study of the solar system and the universe. It is an ancient science, but over the years this discipline has evolved from solely an observation science to a discipline that uses the principles and techniques of physics and mathematics to understand the phenomena of the universe. Today, astronomy is considered to be a subdiscipline of physics, and the terms astronomy and astrophysics are used interchangeably.

Astronomers (or astrophysicists) seek to understand the physical nature, origin, and development of stars, planets, and other celestial bodies as well as of galaxies and the universe. Their studies involve such questions as: How are stars born? What happens when stars die? Where do comets come from? What is the surface like on other planets in the solar system? Does life exist elsewhere in our solar system, the Milky Way, or in other galaxies? Are there other planets in the solar system? How does a star system form? How did the universe begin?

Professional Astronomers work in offices, laboratories, and observatories, mostly in academic and government settings. Academic Astronomers normally research topics within their own interests, while most nonacademic Astronomers conduct research in areas that fulfill their employers' specific goals and missions.

Astronomers gather data about their subject matter by making direct observations of the skies or from information gathered by colleagues, amateur astronomers, and other scientists. They also use various instrumentation to gather data about celestial bodies and phenomena, which include high-powered optical telescopes, radio telescopes, X-ray spectrometers, radar, magnetometers, special cameras, and so on. Furthermore, Astronomers obtain data from observations made by satellites and other spacecraft traveling through the solar system.

Astronomers are often characterized by their method of study, either theoretical or observational. Theoretical Astronomers conduct much of their research on computers, developing theories that they base on observations made mostly by other Astronomers. Theoretical Astronomers usually create computer models (sets of mathematical equations) which they use to analyze data and interpret observations. Observational Astronomers, or observers, analyze data based on the observations that they gather from telescopes as well as from observations gathered by spacecraft. Observers usually spend several days or weeks at a time making observations. This sometimes involves traveling to research facilities in remote areas, and living and working there for the duration of their observing run.

Astronomers often conduct several projects simultaneously. In addition, they sometimes collaborate on research projects. Most independent researchers are responsible for writing grant proposals and seeking out grants from the federal government and other sources to fund their research projects.

Most Astronomers have teaching, administrative, or other responsibilities in addition to their research work. Many Astronomers are employed as professors in colleges and universities. Their duties include planning and teaching astronomy courses to undergraduate and graduate students. Some professors also teach physics courses. Furthermore, they are responsible for advising students, supervising student research projects, writing scholarly works, performing administrative tasks, and fulfilling community service duties.

Some Astronomers are employed by astronomy observatories and laboratories. They may assist or be in charge of managing and running research facilities. Their responsibilities may include any of the following: maintaining facilities, designing new instrumentation, developing education programs for the public, and writing papers for professional journals. Some Astronomers also have the duty of giving educational presentations to scientific organizations, schools, community organizations, and the general public.

All Astronomers are responsible for keeping up with the technology and developments in their specialties as well as in astronomy in general. Most Astronomers participate in scientific conferences to network with colleagues and to share research information. In addition, Astronomers write scientific papers about their research work and submit the papers to scientific journals for publication.

Salaries

Salaries vary, depending on such factors as experience, employer, and geographical location. According to the Bureau of Labor Statistics, the estimated annual salary in 2001 for most Astronomers ranged between $40,020 and $114,630.

Employment Prospects

Most Astronomers are employed by colleges, universities, government agencies, observatories, and research laboratories. Some Astronomers work in the aerospace or satellite communications industry or other private industry.

Most job opportunities for permanent positions become available as astronomers retire or transfer to other positions. However, the turnover rate is small and the competi-

tion is rather high. According to the American Astronomical Society, there are about 6,000 professional astronomers in North America.

With a degree in astronomy, individuals can follow any number of career paths. For example, they can become telescope operators (for planetariums), observing assistants, optical engineers, planetarium directors, science museum curators, high school science teachers, community college instructors, science educators, science journalists, or computer scientists.

Advancement Prospects

Most Astronomers measure their success in terms of being able to conduct independent research, through making discoveries, and by earning professional recognition.

Astronomers can also pursue management and administrative positions by becoming a project leader, program manager, lab director, or observatory director. As faculty members, Astronomers receive promotional rankings as assistant professors, associate professors, or full professors.

Education and Training

A doctorate in astronomy, astrophysics, or physics is the minimum educational requirement to become an Astronomer. Individuals must first earn a bachelor's degree in physics, astronomy, or other field. They then complete a master's program followed by a doctoral program. As part of their doctoral program, students conduct original research projects.

Experience, Skills, and Personality Traits

Employers generally choose candidates who have related work and research experience. Entry-level applicants may have gained relevant experience through research projects, internships, postdoctoral training, part-time employment, and so on. (Note: It is common for Astronomers to hold several postdoctoral positions before obtaining a permanent position.)

Astronomers must be highly skilled in computers, computer programming, math, and statistics. They also need excellent analytical and problem-solving skills, as well as good observation skills. In addition, they need to have proficient writing, communication, and interpersonal skills for their work.

Being patient, precise, determined, curious, self-motivated, and imaginative are a few personality traits that successful Astronomers have in common.

Unions and Associations

Many Astronomers join professional associations to take advantage of networking opportunities, research data, education programs, and other professional resources and services. The American Astronomical Society is one such professional society. Astronomers may also join science associations such as the American Institute of Physics. In addition, many join associations that serve the interests of academic faculty, such as American Association of University Professors and National Association of Scholars. See Appendix III for contact information.

Tips for Entry

1. If you are in high school, join an amateur astronomy organization to learn more about stars and the universe. For example, you might join a branch of the American Association of Variable Star Observers.
2. Be sure you have a strong foundation in physics, mathematics, and computer science before enrolling in a graduate program.

3. While an undergraduate, get as much experience as you can. You might work as a research assistant for an astronomy professor, or you might volunteer, intern, or work at an astronomy observatory or astronomy laboratory.
4. Having a working knowledge in a foreign language may enhance your employability, particularly if you are proficient in German, Russian, Chinese, or French.
5. Use the Internet to learn more about Astronomers. Some websites you might visit are American Astronomical Society, http://www.aas.org; and The Astronomy Cafe, http://www.theastronomycafe.net.

SPACE PHYSICIST

CAREER PROFILE

Duties: Conduct basic or applied research; design and conduct research projects; may teach college or university students; perform duties as required of position

Alternate Title(s): Astrophysicist; Space Plasma Physicist, or other title that reflects a specialty

Salary Range: $50,000 to $150,000

Employment Prospects: Fair

Advancement Prospects: Good

Prerequisites:

Education or Training—A doctoral degree in space physics or related field

Experience—Work and research experience related to the position one is applying for

Special Skills and Personality Traits—Writing, communication, analytical, problem-solving, interpersonal, and teamwork skills; enthusiastic; honest; curious; persistent; imaginative; creative

Licensure/Certification—None required

CAREER LADDER

```
┌─────────────────────────────────┐
│      Senior Space Physicist      │
└─────────────────────────────────┘

┌─────────────────────────────────┐
│         Space Physicist          │
└─────────────────────────────────┘

┌─────────────────────────────────┐
│  Postdoctoral Research Associate │
└─────────────────────────────────┘
```

Position Description

Space physics is the study of the physical processes of the interplanetary space environment. This discipline deals with the investigation of the charged particles, magnetic fields, and other invisible phenomena that fill the region between the sun and the planets.

Space Physicists are concerned with understanding the relationship between the Sun and the Earth. They also investigate the relationship that the Sun has with the other planets and celestial bodies in the solar system. Because space physics is such a broad field, Space Physicists are involved in one of the discipline's subfields. Some of these specialties are:

- solar physics—the study of the Sun's composition and properties, its activities (such as sun spots and sun flares), and its outer atmosphere (also known as the corona)
- the planetary magnetospheres, which are the magnetic fields that surround magnetic planets (such as the Earth) and protects them from solar activities
- the physics of solar wind, which is composed of streams of particles coming from the Sun and rushing through interplanetary space at very high speeds (imagine 600,000 to 2 million miles per hour)

- the effect of solar wind, sun spots, solar flares, and other activities upon the celestial bodies in the solar system; for example, the phenomena known as the aurora borealis (northern lights) on the Earth is the interaction of the solar wind with particles in the Earth's atmosphere

Many Space Physicists are involved in basic research. They seek to expand knowledge about the phenomena and processes that occur in interplanetary space. They study such questions as: What is space weather? How do sun flares affect the planets in the solar system? How does the Earth's magnetic field protect it? What is the composition of matter in interplanetary space?

Many other Space Physicists are involved in applied research. They apply the findings of basic research to the search for solutions to technological problems caused by solar phenomena. For example, solar activities have caused the destruction of satellites and have interfered with the transmission of communication signals.

Space Physicists obtain data through a variety of tools and instruments that are able to monitor and measure details of the Sun, interplanetary matter, planetary magnetospheres, and so on. Along with supercomputers, they use various specialized telescopes, radar, magnetometers, special cameras, and other instrumentation based in observatories throughout the world. Data is also gathered by instrumentation on board satellites and other spacecraft.

To help them analyze and interpret data, Space Physicists create computer models, which are scientific models based on sets of mathematical equations. Scientists use these models to help them develop theories about what is happening in space. For example, Space Physicists have developed computer models that simulate the theoretical flow of plasma around Mars. In addition, many Space Physicists develop instrumentation and spacecraft that are needed for their research.

Space Physicists are responsible for designing and conducting research projects. Independent researchers choose topics that reflect their interests, while others conduct studies that fulfill their employers' goals and missions. Space Physicists might work on more than one research project at a time, and sometimes collaborate with others on research projects.

Most space physics projects are funded by federal grants or other sources. Thus, many Space Physicists are involved in writing grant proposals and seeking research grants from the federal government and other sources.

Space Physicists typically share information about their research by writing articles (or scientific papers) which they submit to scientific journals for publication. Some of them also make presentations at scientific conferences that are sponsored by professional associations.

Some Space Physicists are employed as professors at colleges and universities. They teach courses in solar physics, as well as in astronomy or physics. Their duties include conducting independent research, preparing courses, teaching classes, advising students, supervising student research projects, writing scholarly works, performing administrative duties, and participating in community service.

Salaries
Salaries vary, depending on such factors as experience, employer, and geographical location. Space Physicists generally earn an annual salary between $50,000 and $150,000 per year.

Employment Prospects
Universities, national laboratories, and aerospace companies are major employers of Space Physicists.

Some experts in the field describe the job market for permanent research positions as being tight, but opportunities are reasonably good for postdoctoral positions. Most job opportunities are created to replace Space Physicists who retire or transfer to other positions.

Advancement Prospects
Space Physicists can advance to supervisory, administrative, and executive-level management positions. Professors can rise through the ranks as assistant professors, associate professors, and full professors.

Education and Training
To conduct independent research, teach in universities and colleges, and hold top management positions, a doctorate is required.

Few institutions currently offer a Ph.D. program in space physics. Many Space Physicists have earned their degrees in astrophysics, astronomy, or physics, with an emphasis in space physics.

Experience, Skills, and Personality Traits
Employers generally choose candidates who have work and research experience related to the position they are applying for. Experience may have been gained through research projects, internships, fellowships, part-time employment, postdoctoral training, and so on.

Space Physicists should have writing, communication, analytical, problem-solving, interpersonal, and teamwork skills. Being enthusiastic, honest, curious, persistent, imaginative, and creative are some personal personality traits that successful Space Physicists share.

Unions and Associations
The American Astronomical Society, Space Physics and Aeronomy Section of AGU (American Geophysical Union), and the International Association of Geomagnetism and Aeronomy are some societies that serve the interests of Space Physicists. Professional associations offer various resources and services such as networking opportunities, education programs, research information, and job listings. (See Appendix III for contact information.)

Space Physicists who teach in academic settings are also eligible to join professional societies for academic faculty, such as the National Association of Scholars and the American Association for Higher Education.

Tips for Entry
1. The U.S. National Aeronautics Space Administration (NASA) offers a variety of programs that allow students to participate in space research. Each NASA field center manages its own programs. For information, contact a NASA office near you, or visit NASA's student opportunities webpage at http://www.nasajobs.nasa.gov/jobs/student_opportunities/student_opportunities.htm.
2. Learn more about space physics on the Internet. One website that offers information is the Space Physics and Aeronomy Section (American Geophysical Union), http://espsun.space.swri.edu/SPA/index.html. For other pertinent websites to read, enter the keyword *space physics* in a search engine.

EARTH SCIENCES

GEOLOGIST

CAREER PROFILE	CAREER LADDER

Duties: Conduct basic or applied research; design and conduct research projects; may perform teaching, consulting, administration, or other major responsibilities, depending on position; research assistants and technicians provide research and administrative support; perform duties as required by position

Alternate Title(s): Geoscientist; Hydrologist, Engineering Geologist, Environmental Geologist, or other title that reflects a specialty

Salary Range: $32,000 to $110,000

Employment Prospects: Good

Advancement Prospects: Good

Prerequisites:

  Education or Training—A bachelor's or advanced degree in geology or related field

  Experience—Work and research experience related to the position one is applying for

  Special Skills and Personality Traits—Computer, observation, analytical, problem-solving, communication, writing, presentation, teamwork, and interpersonal skills; for fieldwork, be physically fit and have physical stamina; flexible; patient; inquisitive; self-motivated; honest; cooperative

  Licensure/Certification—State licensure as Registered Geologist (R.G.) may be required

```
┌──────────────────────────────────┐
│        Senior Geologist           │
└──────────────────────────────────┘

┌──────────────────────────────────┐
│       Research Geologist          │
└──────────────────────────────────┘

┌──────────────────────────────────┐
│    Geologist-in-Training or       │
│  Postdoctoral Research Associate  │
└──────────────────────────────────┘
```

Position Description

Geology is an earth science (or geoscience). It deals with the study of the structure, composition, processes, and history of the Earth.

Geologists estimate that the Earth was formed several billion years ago. They seek to understand how it came into being and how it took shape as well as how it has changed and continues to change today. Geologists examine the materials—rocks, minerals, and soils—that make up the Earth as well as the landforms, such as mountains, volcanoes, valleys, plains, and rivers, on the Earth's surface. Geologists also explore the layers of rock in the Earth's crust and the fossils found there to get an idea on how the Earth has developed over thousands, millions, and billions of years. Further, Geologists study the various processes (such as weather, ero-

sion, earthquakes, and tectonics) that shape Earth and investigate how human activities (such as dredging, mining, and development) affect and change the Earth.

Geologists are also involved in various activities that benefit society. For example, Geologists search for new sources of water, energy, and minerals; they help develop community emergency plans for natural hazards (such as earthquakes, floods, and landslides); and they investigate proposed sites for waste treatment plants, dams, freeways, bridges, harbors, and other structures to make sure they are geologically safe and sound. In addition, Geologists apply their expertise to helping solve problems and issues about the environment, including air quality, water pollution, energy conservation, global warming, endangered species, brownfields, land use, and so on.

Research Geologists work in academic, government, industry, nonprofit, and nongovernmental settings. They conduct basic or applied research. Typically, Geologists focus their studies in one of the many subdisciplines that make up geology. Some of these specialties are:

- mineralogy, the study of minerals such as quartz, gypsum, mercury, borax, and diamonds
- petrology, the study of igneous (volcanic), metamorphic, and sedimentary rocks
- geomorphology, the study of the Earth's surface, the origins of its landforms, and the processes that shape and change landforms
- hydrology, the study of the movement and distribution of water on the Earth's surface as well as beneath it
- oceanography, the investigation of the oceans
- glacial geology, the study of the characteristics and movements of glaciers and how they change the Earth's surface
- geochemistry, the study of the chemical composition of the Earth
- geophysics—the study of the Earth's crust and interior, using the principles of mathematics and physics; also includes the investigation of the Earth's magnetic and electrical properties and the way it transmits energy
- seismology, the study of earthquakes as well as the investigation of the Earth's interior by studying the behavior of seismic waves
- structural geology, the study of how mountains and other features inside the Earth's crusts are formed
- volcanology, the study of volcanoes
- sedimentology, the study of sedimentary rocks, the processes that form these rocks, and they way they are deposited
- stratigraphy, the study of the origin, composition, sequence, and relationship of the layers of rock in the Earth's crust
- geochronology, the study of geological time; determining the geological age of rock layers
- paleontology, the study of animal and plant fossils to understand the evolution of species as well as the geological history of the Earth.
- quaternary geology, the study of geological processes that have occurred over the last two million years

Many Geologists specialize in a particular area in which they apply their geological expertise. Petroleum Geologists are involved in the exploration for oil and natural gas. Economic Geologists study the development of minerals, coal, and other geological materials for profitable uses. Environmental Geologists are concerned with solving human-made problems (such as pollution, waste management, and urban development) and natural hazards (such as flooding, landslides, and coastal erosions). Engineering Geologists provide geological expertise on the design, construction, operation, and maintenance of such structures as dams, bridges, freeways, and skyscrapers.

Geologists are responsible for designing and conducting research projects. In academic settings, Geologists choose research topics that reflect their personal interests while those working in other settings usually conduct research that is determined by their employers' missions. Many Geologists collaborate on projects with geologists from other specialties.

Geologists share information about the results of their research with colleagues. They might write scientific papers which they submit to scientific journals for publication. Some also make presentations at scientific meetings that are sponsored by professional associations.

Geologists spend much of their time working in offices and laboratories. They complete such tasks as designing experiments, conducting library research, developing theoretical models, analyzing and interpreting data, writing reports, and performing administrative tasks.

Many Geologists spend some time conducting research in the field, where they perform such tasks as taking measurements, examining rocks, collecting samples, conducting geological surveys, making field maps, or searching for sites that may potentially hold water, fossils, oil, or mineral deposits. Field research is often conducted in remote areas around the world that can only be reached by walking long distances or by using four-wheel drive vehicles or helicopters. Some conduct research on vessels that sail along coastlines or out at sea. It is not uncommon for Geologists to live and work at field sites for several weeks or months.

Many research scientists are responsible for obtaining grants to fund their research projects. This generally involves writing grant proposals that describe the objectives, methodologies, budgets, and other aspects of their projects, as well as seeking out information about available grants from the federal government and other sources.

Along with their research duties, most Geologists have other major responsibilities. Many teach undergraduate or graduate courses in colleges and universities, while others develop educational programs and materials for the general public. Some Geologists provide consultation services to government agencies, policy makers, industry, and the general public. Others are responsible for the management and administration of laboratories, academic departments, research institutes, companies, and so on.

There are some Geologists whose role is to provide research and administrative support to the research scientists. These Geologists are the research assistants and technicians. Their duties vary, depending on their experience. Some general tasks include collecting data, maintaining computer databases, running experiments, assisting with fieldwork, writing reports, maintaining lab equipment and facilities, performing routine administrative tasks, and so on.

Salaries

Salaries vary, depending on such factors as education, experience, employer, position, and geographical location.

According to the Bureau of Labor Statistics, the estimated annual salary in 2001 for most geoscientists ranged from $33,150 to $109,510, and for most earth science postsecondary instructors, from $32,740 to $105,890.

Employment Prospects
Major employers of Geologists are the oil and mining industries; geological and environmental consulting firms; colleges and universities; and local, state, and federal government agencies (the U.S. Geological Survey is one of the largest employers).

The Bureau of Labor Statistics predicts average growth for employment of geoscientists through 2010. Many opportunities in the coming decade will be created to replace Geologists who retire. The demand for Geologists, particularly hydrologists and engineering geologists, is expected to increase due to the need for companies to comply with environmental laws and regulations, address environmental issues, and assess construction sites for potential geological hazards.

In general, the rise or fall of job opportunities is dependent on such factors as the health of the economy, changes in government policies about the environment or energy, and the availability of federal grants for science research.

With a background in geology, individuals can pursue other career paths. They might become high school science teachers, community college geoscience instructors, science journalists, science librarians, environmental lawyers, land surveyors, cartographers, urban planners, civil engineers, park rangers, conservation scientists, or environmental engineers.

Advancement Prospects
In nonacademic settings, Geologists may be promoted to administrative and management positions such as project leader, program manager, and executive-level administrator. Professors advance in rank (assistant, associate, and full professor). They may also be promoted to department chairs, academic deans, or school administration positions.

Many Geologists measure their success by earning higher salaries, by being able to conduct independent research projects, and through receiving professional recognition.

Education and Training
A bachelor's degree in geology, geophysics, or a related field is the minimum requirement for some entry-level positions in industry or government settings. Many employers prefer or require that candidates hold a master's degree. To teach in universities and colleges, conduct independent research, or hold a top management position, a Ph.D. is generally required.

Experience, Skills, and Personality Traits
Employers typically choose candidates who have work and research experience related to the position for which they are applying. Entry-level scientists may have obtained experience through part-time employment, internships, research projects, postdoctoral training, and so on. Many employers prefer that candidates have field experience. In addition, job candidates should have a basic understanding of the industry, business, or mission in which prospective employers are involved.

Geologists need strong computer skills, and should have some experience with computer modeling, data analysis and integration, geographic information systems (GIS), Global Positioning System (GPS), digital mapping, and remote sensing. In addition, Geologists need strong observation, analytical, and problem-solving skills as well as communication, writing, and presentation skills. They must also have good teamwork and interpersonal skills, as they must be able to work with people of diverse backgrounds and technical abilities. Geologists who are involved in fieldwork must be physically fit and have physical stamina.

Some personality traits that successful Geologists have in common are being flexible, patient, inquisitive, self-motivated, honest, and cooperative.

Special Requirements
Geologists who provide services that involve public health, safety, and welfare may be required to be licensed as registered geologists (R.G.) in the states where they practice. Employers may also require or strongly prefer licensed geologists. Many Geologists obtain licensure on a voluntary basis to enhance their employability. Entry-level applicants may be required to register as a geologist-in-training, which leads to professional registrations.

Licensure requirements vary from state to state. For information, contact the board of geology in the state where you wish to practice. You can also obtain general licensure information from the National Association of State Boards of Geology website, http://www.asbog.org.

Unions and Associations
Most Geologists join professional associations to take advantage of education programs, networking opportunities, and other professional resources and services. The American Geological Institute, the Geological Society of America, the Association for Women Geoscientists, the American Institute of Professional Geologists, and the National Association of Black Geologists and Geophysicists are a few examples of these organizations. Many Geologists also join societies that serve specific interests, such as the American Association of Petroleum Geologists, the Seismological Society of America, the Association of Engineering Geologists, or the Society of Vertebrate Paleontology. (See Appendix III for contact information.)

Professors in geosciences might also join such academic societies as the American Association of University Professors and the American Association for Higher Education.

Tips for Entry

1. While you are a high school student, seek opportunities to go on geological field trips to learn how professionals make observations and describe geological features and processes. Talk to your parents, science teachers, or school librarians for suggestions. Another option is to contact science museums or geology instructors at nearby colleges.

2. The U.S. Geological Survey offers student employment programs for college students in geology, hydrology, administration, and other fields. For more information visit its webpage at http://www.usgs.gov/student.

3. Some sources for job listings include professors, college career centers, professional associations, professional journals, and state employment offices. Also check for job announcements at websites of employers for whom you're interested in working.

4. You can learn more about geology on the Internet. Two websites you might visit are American Geological Institute, http://www.agiweb.org; and U.S. Geological Survey, http://www.usgs.org.

GEOPHYSICIST

CAREER PROFILE

Duties: Conduct basic or applied research; design and conduct research projects; may conduct investigations for natural resources; may teach college or university students; perform duties as required of position

Alternate Title(s): Geoscientist, Geologist; Seismologist, Marine Geophysicist, Mining Geophysicist, or other title that reflects a specialty

Salary Range: $33,000 to $110,000

Employment Prospects: Good

Advancement Prospects: Good

Prerequisites:

Education or Training—A bachelor's or advanced degree in geophysics or related field

Experience—Work and research experience related to the position one is applying for

Special Skills and Personality Traits—Computer, writing, communication, observation, analytical, problem-solving, teamwork, and interpersonal skills; for fieldwork, be physically fit and have physical stamina; flexible; patient; curious; self-motivated

Licensure/Certification—State licensure as Registered Geologist or Registered Geophysicist may be required

CAREER LADDER

```
┌─────────────────────────────────┐
│      Senior Geophysicist         │
└─────────────────────────────────┘

┌─────────────────────────────────┐
│     Research Geophysicist        │
└─────────────────────────────────┘

┌─────────────────────────────────┐
│   Geologist-in-Training or       │
│ Postdoctoral Research Associate  │
└─────────────────────────────────┘
```

Position Description

Geophysics is a branch of geology in which earth scientists study the Earth's interior by applying the principles and methods of physics. Without doing any drilling or excavating, Geophysicists are able to measure the depth of bedrock, locate earthquake faults, map ancient river channels buried beneath the surface, identify soil compositions, evaluate the integrity of man-made structures, search for mineral deposits, and engage in various other research and exploration activities. They use instrumentation that are able to probe far beneath the surface to detect and measure a variety of physical properties—such as magnetism, gravity, and electricity—that humans would not be able to sense.

Many Geophysicists, like other geologists, are involved in basic research. Their particular interests involve learning about the Earth's physical properties and its internal structure, as well as about its earthquake, volcanic, and other internal activities. They also investigate the physical properties of the Earth's atmosphere, oceans, and fresh water systems. Many study plate tectonics, the theory that describes the movements and evolution of the continents and ocean floors and explains the location of earthquakes, volcanoes, and mountain building. Other geologists investigate the physical properties of space and of the other celestial bodies in the solar system to gain an understanding of the Earth's structure and evolution.

Typically, Research Geophysicists specialize in the various subfields of the discipline. For example, Geophysicists might conduct basic or applied research in seismology (the study of earthquakes); geothermal energy; physical oceanography; hydrology (the study of fresh surface water and groundwater); the Earth's gravity field; geodesy (the size and form of the Earth); atmospheric electricity; climate change; or magnetic fields.

Many Geophysicists specialize in exploration geophysics, an applied branch of geophysics. While using geophysical methods, they search for natural resources such as groundwater, oil, or minerals.

Another applied branch is engineering geophysics. Geophysicists in this specialty investigate engineering and environmental problems which affect the safety, health, and welfare of people and other living things. For example, Geophysicists might be asked to identify potential geological hazards at proposed construction sites, or track contaminants in groundwater, or locate sites for underground nuclear waste disposal.

Exploration and engineering Geophysicists often work as part of multidisciplinary teams that usually include geologists from other specialties, engineers, technicians, and scientists from other disciplines. Research Geophysicists also collaborate on research projects with other scientists from time to time.

All Geophysicists make sure that they collect accurate and precise data. They operate ground-based instruments and employ instrumentation installed in planes and satellites to identify various types of rock, obtain measurements, detect variations in gravity, changes in magnetic fields, and so on. To collect their data, Geophysicists use gravitational, electromagnetic, seismic, and other geophysical methods that enable them to detect and measure the diverse properties of the Earth beneath its surface. For example, Geophysicists can measure the speed of sound waves traveling through the Earth's crust by using the seismic method. Seismologists also use this method to investigate earthquakes while Petroleum Geophysicists use it to locate new sources of oil.

Geophysicists perform a variety of tasks that generally include collecting field data, conducting experiments or tests, developing computer models, analyzing and interpreting data, and preparing technical reports. They also have other tasks that are unique to their specializations.

Geologists are responsible for designing and conducting their research projects, in addition to guiding and supervising research assistants and technicians. Many Geophysicists in nonindustry settings are responsible for obtaining research grants from the federal government and other sources to fund their research projects.

Many Geophysicists are faculty members at colleges and universities. Along with conducting research, they are responsible for planning courses, teaching classes, advising students, supervising student research projects, performing administrative tasks, writing scholarly works, and participating in community service.

Geophysicists work in offices and laboratories as well as in the field. Those involved in exploration and engineering projects often work and live in remote areas anywhere in the world, for several weeks or months at a time.

Salaries

Salaries vary, depending on such factors as education, experience, position, employer, and geographical location.

According to a salary survey by the American Geophysical Union, the median starting salary in 2000 for Ph.D.s in industry jobs was $70,000, and between $40,000 to $45,000 for those in government and academic jobs. The Bureau of Labor Statistics reports that the estimated annual salary in 2001 for most geoscientists (including Geophysicists) ranged between $33,150 to $109,510.

Employment Prospects

Major employers of Geophysicists include the petroleum and mining industries, environmental and geotechnical consulting firms, colleges and universities, and government laboratories and agencies.

The competition for jobs is strong. Most opportunities will become available as Geophysicists retire, transfer to other positions, or resign. Some experts in the field expect that opportunities will likely increase in the next several years due to the large number of Geophysicists reaching retirement age.

Advancement Prospects

Geophysicists can advance to management and administrative positions in the various work settings. Professors advance in rank (assistant, associate, and full professor) as well as by obtaining job tenure, which generally assures professors a job until they retire.

Many Geophysicists measure their success by earning higher salaries, by being able to conduct independent research projects, and through receiving professional recognition.

Education and Training

A bachelor's degree in geophysics, geology, or a related field is the minimum requirement to enter this field. Most employers, however, require or prefer that Geophysicist candidates hold a master's degree. A Ph.D. is generally required in order to conduct independent research, teach in four-year colleges or universities, or hold top management positions.

Experience, Skills, and Personality Traits

Candidates should have work and research experience related to the position for which they are applying. Many employers look for candidates who have field experience. Recent graduates may have obtained experience through part-time employment, internships, or research projects. Many employers expect Ph.D. candidates to have completed postdoctoral training. In addition, job candidates should have a basic understanding of the industry, business, or mission in which prospective employers are involved.

Geophysicists need excellent computer, writing, and communication skills. They must also have strong observation, analytical, and problem-solving skills as well as good teamwork and interpersonal skills. In addition, Geophysicists who are involved in extensive fieldwork must be physically fit and have physical stamina.

Some personality traits that successful Geophysicists have in common are being flexible, patient, curious, and self-motivated.

Special Requirements

Geophysicists may be required to be licensed as a Registered Geologist or Registered Geophysicist in the states where they practice. Engineering Geologists may be required to obtain separate licensure. Further, entry-level applicants may be required to register as a Geologist-in-Training, which leads to professional registrations.

Licensure requirements vary from state to state. For information, contact the board of geology in the state where you wish to practice. You can also obtain general licensure information from the National Association of State Boards of Geology website, http://www.asbog.org.

Unions and Associations

Geophysicists can join geological societies to take advantage of various professional services and resources such as education programs, job listings, and networking opportunities. Some associations that serve the various interests of Geophysicists are the American Geophysical Union, the Environmental and Engineering Geophysical Society, the Society of Exploration Geophysicists, and the Seismological Society of America. See Appendix III for contact information.

Tips for Entry

1. Gain experience by seeking internships or summer employment with consulting firms, petroleum companies, or government agencies. Another option is obtaining a research assistant position with a professor who is conducting research in an area in which you are interested.
2. Many positions in industry require travel to other countries; thus, knowledge of a foreign language can be a valuable asset.
3. Many Geophysicists obtain licensure on a voluntary basis to enhance their employability, as many employers prefer to hire licensed Geophysicists, even if states where they practice don't require licensure.
4. Use the Internet to learn more about Geophysicists. A website you might visit is American Geophysical Union, http://www.agu.org. To get a list of other relevant websites to read, enter any of these keywords in a search engine—*geophysics, geophysicists,* or *geophysics resources.*

GEOGRAPHER

CAREER PROFILE

Duties: Conduct basic or applied research; design and conduct research projects; may be engaged in teaching, administration, consulting, or other major responsibilities; perform duties as required of position

Alternate Title(s): Earth Scientist; Physical Scientist; Research Geographer; Economic Geographer, Climatologist, Cartographer or other title that reflects a specialty; GIS Analyst, Urban Planner, Area Specialist or other title that describes a particular occupation

Salary Range: $32,000 to $89,000

Employment Prospects: Good

Advancement Prospects: Good

Prerequisites:

Education or Training—A bachelor's or advanced degree in geography or related field

Experience—Postdoctoral experience may be required for research scientists

Special Skills and Personality Traits—Organization, research, writing, computer, communication, statistics, and math skills; analytical; open-minded; curious; creative

Licensure/Certification—Licensure is required for specific occupations such as high school teachers and surveyors

CAREER LADDER

```
+-----------------------------+
|     Senior Geographer       |
+-----------------------------+

+-----------------------------+
|        Geographer           |
+-----------------------------+

+-----------------------------+
|   Geographer (entry-level)  |
+-----------------------------+
```

Position Description

Geography is the scientific study of the physical processes and human activities that occur on the surface of the Earth. It is an interdisciplinary science that may be classified as a physical (or natural) science or a social science.

Geographers are interested in learning everything there is to know about any particular place on the planet. They study the physical features—landforms, vegetation, soils, water, climates, and so forth—that are found at different locations. They investigate such questions as, How did features form and develop? What changes may be occurring? and Why are they important for being in a particular location?

Geographers also examine the cultural, social, economic, and political activities of people in various locations. Additionally, they investigate how people interact with and affect their environments. Further, Geographers seek to understand how locations differ from each other, as well as understand the relationship between locations. Geographers are also concerned with understanding the natural and human forces that influence the distribution and patterns of physical features and human activities.

Geography is generally divided into branches, with each branch having its own specialties. Physical Geographers make up one branch. They study the physical characteristics (landforms, water, climates, weather, soils, vegetation, and so on) of the Earth and the processes that shape and change them. Many physical Geographers deal with a particular feature. For example, climatologists study climate patterns, geomorphologists examine landforms, and soil scientists investigate the different types of soils.

Human geography is another major branch of geography subdivided into several areas. Social Geographers study the relationships between groups of people, while Cultural Geographers examine how cultural traits (such as beliefs, customs, and values) pass between generations and spread among locations.

Economic Geographers are concerned with the distribution of natural resources and how people use natural resources in various economic activities such as agriculture, forestry, mining, manufacturing, trade, and transportation. Political Geographers study political systems, historical Geographers investigate how places and patterns of human activity have changed over time, and demographers study the patterns of human populations.

Some Geographers specialize in the types of locations they study. Urban Geographers examine how cities develop and grow and are involved in the planning of housing, transportation, industrial sites, and other urban developments. Regional Geographers, on the other hand, focus on a particular area on Earth, such as an island, valley, state, country, continent, or regional area. They are interested in understanding the physical, social, economic, political, and other geographical characteristics of the area.

Many Geographers specialize in the different areas of mapping sciences, which involve the study of maps, their development, and production. Cartographers research geographic information to design and construct maps of locations and to describe human activities. Geographic Information Systems (GIS) specialists are involved in the collection, analysis, and manipulation of geographic data that are stored in computer systems in the form of maps. Some other specialists in this area are surveyors who take measurements of the Earth's surface, and remote-sensing analysts who interpret and analyze aerial and satellite images that are produced by radar.

Geographers work in a wide variety of roles. Many are research scientists who conduct basic or applied research in academic, government, and other settings. Other Geographers are employed as educators, technicians, technologists, engineers, resource specialists, analysts, planners, administrators, and consultants. They apply their geographical expertise in such diverse areas as agriculture, the environment, health care, finance, transportation, and technology. Many hold positions that go by job titles that describe their particular responsibilities. Hence, a Geographer can be a geography teacher, an area specialist, an urban planner, a GIS specialist, a water resources analyst, a forestry technician, an interpretive specialist, a location expert, a surveyor, a health systems planner, a housing specialist, a tourism planner, and so on.

Geographers' duties vary, depending on their specialty and occupation. For example, Geographers employed by universities usually have flexible work schedules, while dividing their time among their teaching, research, writing, consulting, or administrative duties. Some of the general tasks that many Geographers perform on their jobs are:

- developing, planning, and executing projects
- conducting fieldwork that may involve direct observations, conducting interviews, taking measurements, gathering samples, and so on
- collecting, analyzing, and interpreting geographical information such as statistical data, maps, charts, and satellite imagery
- developing computer models or constructing maps to understand patterns and processes
- advising decision makers or policy makers
- writing reports and scientific papers; may write grant proposals
- making presentations at scientific meetings or conferences

Many Geographers work on collaborative projects, which might include team members from the various earth science disciplines such as climatology, geology, geophysics, and oceanography.

Geographers mostly work in offices and laboratories. Geographers who conduct fieldwork may be required to travel to isolated areas and live and work there for several days, weeks, or months.

Salaries

Salaries vary, depending on education, experience, position, geographical location, and other factors. According to the Bureau of Labor Statistics, the estimated annual salary in 2001 for most Geographers ranged from $31,870 to $70,290, and for most postsecondary geography instructors, from $33,090 to $89,380.

Employment Prospects

Geographers work in schools, colleges, universities, research institutions, nonprofit organizations, and nongovernmental organizations. They also are employed by local, state, and federal government agencies (such as planning departments, natural resources departments, geological surveys, and transportation departments). In addition, many Geographers work for various employers in the private sector, including real estate developers, architectural firms, construction companies, engineering companies, satellite companies, utilities, medical services, environmental consulting firms, finance companies, manufacturing firms, publishers, tour companies, and so on.

Opportunities vary among the various types of employers. Currently, the demand for Geographers with cartography and GIS skills is strong and is expected to continue for years to come. In general, opportunities become available as Geographers retire or transfer to other positions.

Advancement Prospects

Geographers can advance in any number of ways, depending on their positions, ambitions, and interests. Those interested in management and administrative work may find opportunities in any work setting. Some Geographers choose to become consultants in their areas of expertise. Academic professors can advance in rank (assistant, associate, and full professor) as well as by obtaining job tenure.

Many Geographers with bachelor's degrees return to school to earn their master's or doctoral degree in order to increase their opportunities for better paying positions.

Education and Training

The minimum requirement for many entry-level positions is a bachelor's degree in geography or a field (such as GIS, hydrology, or planning) that is related to the position being sought. Geographers with advanced degrees can usually expect to be hired for positions with greater responsibilities, including managing projects and supervising other staff. Those wishing to conduct independent research, obtain higher-level administrative positions, or teach in universities must obtain a doctoral degree.

Jobs in these fields generally require knowledge obtained not only in geography but in other disciplines as well—such as economics, political science, environmental science, urban planning, computer science, geology, and landscape architecture.

Experience, Skills, and Personality Traits

Requirements vary for the different positions as well as among the various employers. For entry-level positions, employers generally choose candidates who have related work experience, which may have been gained through research projects, internships, fellowships, part-time employment, and so on. Ph.D. applicants for a research scientist position are usually expected to have a few years of postdoctoral experience.

Strong organizational, research, writing, computer, and communication skills are essential for Geographers to have in their work. In addition, they should be proficient in statistics and math. Some personality traits that successful Geographers share are being analytical, open-minded, curious, and creative.

Special Requirements

Some occupations, such as surveyor and geology teacher, require state licensure. For information about a specific occupation, talk with your college adviser or contact a professional association that serves that profession.

Unions and Associations

Geographers join professional associations to take advantage of services and resources (such as education programs and professional publications) as well as opportunities for networking with colleagues. Many are members of the Association of American Geographers and the American Geographical Society. Geographers also join societies that serve their particular interests. For example, cartographers and GIS professionals might join the American Congress on Surveying and Mapping, while meteorologists and climatologists might join the American Meteorological Society. Many geography professors are members of the American Association of University Professors or other associations that serve the interests of academic faculty. See Appendix III for association contact information.

Tips for Entry

1. To learn about the various career options that are available, talk with several different types of Geographers.
2. Directly contact employers for whom you'd like to work to find out if positions are available or may be opening up.
3. Finding a job can be a job itself. If you need help with your job search skills, visit your college career center. Most centers usually offer job skills workshops on writing résumés, job interviews, and job search strategies.
4. To enhance your employability, learn the skills needed to work with computer cartography and GIS technologies.
5. Learn more about the geography field on the Internet. Some websites you might visit are Association of American Geographers, http://www.aag.org; and National Geographic Society, http://www.nationalgeographic.com.

PALEONTOLOGIST

CAREER PROFILE

Duties: Conduct basic or applied research; may be engaged in teaching, providing educational services, consulting, and other major responsibilities, depending on position; perform duties as required of a position

Alternate Title(s): Research Scientist; Paleontology Professor; Museum Curator; Palynologist, Invertebrate Paleontologist, or other title that reflects a specialty

Salary Range: $33,000 to $110,000

Employment Prospects: Poor

Advancement Prospects: Good

Prerequisites:
Education or Training—A doctoral degree in paleontology or related field
Experience—Lab and field experience required
Special Skills and Personality Traits—Computer, writing, communication, interpersonal, and self-management skills; flexible; patient; persevering; creative; analytical; physically fit; enjoy hiking and being out-of-doors
Licensure/Certification—Licensure as a Registered Geologist (R.G.) may be required

CAREER LADDER

```
┌─────────────────────────────────────┐
│        Senior Paleontologist         │
└─────────────────────────────────────┘

┌─────────────────────────────────────┐
│       Research Paleontologist        │
└─────────────────────────────────────┘

┌─────────────────────────────────────┐
│    Postdoctoral Research Associate   │
└─────────────────────────────────────┘
```

Position Description

Paleontology is the scientific study of the remains (or fossils) of ancient organisms—microbes, plants, and animals—that lived on the Earth over thousands or millions of years ago. Fossils may be bones, shells, leaf impressions, animal footprints, or other things that had been preserved in the sedimentary layers of rock.

Many people confuse archeologists with Paleontologists. However, archeologists do not study fossils; their expertise is in the investigation of artifacts, such as tools and clothing, made by ancient humans. Paleontologists, on the other hand, examine fossils to learn about the structure, evolution, distribution, and environment of ancient life on the Earth. They are trained in geology, biology, chemistry, and physics.

Much of paleontological research is applied in other fields such as archaeology, geology, geography, botany, zoology, forensic science, and environmental science. The study of fossils can provide clues about various facets of the geological past, including prehistoric climates, migration paths of plant and animal life, rates of evolution, the past positions of continents and oceans, and so on. For example, knowledge about the natural changes in prehistoric climates can help environmental scientists who are investigating global warming.

Paleontologists conduct basic or applied research, while specializing in a subfield of paleontology. Some of these specialties are:

- vertebrate paleontology, the study of fossils of animals with backbones (examples: fish, amphibians, mammals and dinosaurs)
- invertebrate paleontology, the study of remains of animals without backbones (examples: corals and mollusks)
- micropaleontology, the study of fossils of very small organisms (such as conodonts) that are found in large numbers in rock
- paleobotany, the study of plant fossils
- palynology, the study of remains of pollen, spores, algae, and other microscopic plant bodies

- biostratigraphy, the study of the distribution of fossils in rock strata (or layers of rock)
- paleoecology, the study of ancient ecosystems and their development

Part of Paleontologists' research involves conducting fieldwork, which may require traveling to remote areas—such as mountains, deserts, or islands—anywhere in the world. They live and work at field sites for extended periods of time. They carefully remove fossils with such tools as brushes, picks, chisels, shovels, and drills.

Back in their laboratories and offices, Paleontologists examine fossils with the aid of such tools as electron microscopes and computers. They compare their discoveries with other paleontological findings as well as with modern life forms to help them understand the fossils. Paleontologists classify their findings according to their age as well as to their botanical or zoological family. In some instances, Paleontologists discover fossils of previously unknown species of animals or plants.

Paleontologists work in a variety of settings. Many Paleontologists are employed as professors in colleges and universities, teaching courses in paleontology, geology, anatomy, biology, and other disciplines. Professors typically divide their time among the following duties: conducting independent research, planning courses, teaching, writing scholarly works, advising students, supervising student research projects, performing administrative tasks, and fulfilling community service obligations.

Many Paleontologists conduct applied research in industry settings (such as oil, coal, and mining companies). They may be employed as staff members or consultants. In general, these Paleontologists study fossils to determine the potential presence of oil, coal, or other materials in particular areas.

Some Paleontologists are hired as museum curators. Some of their duties include conducting basic research, leading field trips, preparing exhibits, developing educational programs, teaching workshops to the general public, writing scientific papers, and managing daily operations of museums or paleontology departments.

Some Paleontologists work for geological surveys, which are federal and state government agencies that conduct geological studies and research. Paleontologists in these work settings might conduct basic or applied research. Some other duties might include providing consulting services to individuals, industry, or legislatures; writing technical reports; developing educational materials; making public presentations; and so on.

Paleontologists typically share information about their research work with colleagues. They might write scientific papers and submit them to scientific journals for publication or make presentations at scientific conferences sponsored by professional associations.

All Paleontologists are responsible for keeping up with technologies and developments in their specialties. They may attend professional conferences, network with colleagues, read professional journals, and so on. Many Paleontologists are responsible for obtaining research grants to fund their projects. They write grant proposals and apply to the federal government and other sources for grants.

Salaries
Salaries vary, depending on factors such as education, experience, position, employer, and geographical location. The Bureau of Labor Statistics reports that the estimated annual salary in 2001 for most geoscientists, including Paleontologists, ranged between $33,150 and $109,510.

Employment Prospects
Paleontologists are mostly employed by colleges, universities, museums, research institutions, and state and federal geological surveys. Many work in the petroleum and other industries.

In general, opportunities for Paleontologists are limited. The turnover rate is quite low, with positions becoming available as Paleontologists retire or transfer to other positions. In addition, the last two decades have seen a slow decrease in the number of permanent jobs, thus the competition for available positions is high.

Advancement Prospects
Most Paleontologists measure their success by being able to conduct independent research, by making discoveries, and through earning professional recognition among their peers.

Management and administrative positions are available in any work setting. For example, depending on their particular circumstances, Paleontologists can become department chairs, administrative deans, museum directors, program directors, or executive officers.

Education and Training
Becoming a Paleontologist generally requires earning a Ph.D. in paleontology, geology, or a related field. Individuals can choose to first pursue a master's degree, followed by doctoral study, or enroll directly into a doctoral program. A Bachelor's degree may be earned in any field, but individuals should obtain a strong foundation in geology, biology, chemistry, physics, and mathematics.

Experience, Skills, and Personality Traits
Job requirements vary for the different positions. Employers generally choose candidates who have related work and research experience, which may have been gained through research projects, internships, fellowships, employment, volunteer fieldwork, postdoctoral training, and so on. They should have lab as well as field experience.

Paleontologists need strong computer, writing, and communication skills for their work. In addition, they should have good interpersonal skills and self-management skills, such as being able to work independently, organize tasks, and handle deadlines. Some personality traits that successful Paleontologists share are being flexible, patient, persevering, creative, and analytical. In addition, Paleontologists must be physically fit and enjoy hiking and being out-of-doors for long periods of time.

Special Requirements

Professional licensure is not required for Paleontologists. However, Paleontologists who provide geological services to the public may be required to be Registered Geologists (R.G.) in the states where they practice.

Unions and Associations

Many Paleontologists are members of professional societies to take advantage of networking opportunities, publications, and other professional resources and services. Some associations that serve this profession are the Paleontological Society, the American Association of Stratigraphic Palynologists, and the Society of Vertebrate Paleontology. See Appendix III for contact information.

Paleontologists are also eligible to join geology societies, such as the American Geological Institute. In addition, they can join academic, museum, or other professional associations that serve the particular areas in which they work.

Tips for Entry

1. Talk with Paleontologists for advice about the best graduate schools for the type of research or area of paleontology that you wish to enter.
2. Being fluent in a modern foreign language (particularly German, French, Russian, or Chinese) may enhance your employability.
3. Learn more about paleontology on the Internet. Two websites that you might visit are Paleontological Society, http://www.paleosoc.org; and the PaleoNet Pages, http://www.ucmp.berkeley.edu/Paleonet.

SEISMOLOGIST

CAREER PROFILE

Duties: Conduct basic or applied research; design and conduct research projects; may teach college or university students; perform duties as required

Alternate Title(s): Geophysicist

Salary Range: $33,000 to $110,000

Employment Prospects: Fair

Advancement Prospects: Fair

Prerequisites:
   Education or Training—A Ph.D. in seismology, geology or related field
   Experience—Postdoctoral experience required
   Special Skills and Personality Traits—Computer, writing, communication, analytical, interpersonal, and teamwork skills; curious; creative; meticulous; detail-oriented; patient; flexible
   Licensure/Certification—None required

CAREER LADDER

```
┌─────────────────────────────────────┐
│        Senior Seismologist           │
└─────────────────────────────────────┘

┌─────────────────────────────────────┐
│           Seismologist               │
└─────────────────────────────────────┘

┌─────────────────────────────────────┐
│   Postdoctoral Research Associate    │
└─────────────────────────────────────┘
```

Position Description

Seismology is the scientific study of earthquakes, the natural phenomena that occur on the fractures, or faults, in the Earth's crust. When the sides of a fault slip against each other and rupture, energy is released in the form of seismic waves that travel in all directions through the crust. Most earthquakes, which occur on a daily basis throughout the world, are mild and not felt at all by people.

The scientists who investigate the nature and behavior of earthquakes are known as Seismologists. They monitor earthquake activity with seismographs that measure and record seismic waves as earthquakes occur. By analyzing and interpreting the data from those instruments, Seismologists can determine on which faults earthquakes took place, their magnitudes, where the epicenters (points of rupture) were, and other characteristics.

Seismologists also conduct research while working in academic, government, industry, and other settings. They apply principles and techniques of geology, physics, and mathematics to understand how and why earthquakes occur. Many study seismic waves to understand the internal structure of the Earth. Some Seismologists investigate the nature and behavior of specific earthquake faults, including those on the ocean floors. Some study strong earthquakes that

occurred hundreds or thousands of years ago to determine whether a fault may still be active. Other Seismologists are concerned with the potential of earthquake hazards and their effects on heavily populated areas such as the San Francisco Bay Area or the Pacific Northwest. (Note: Few Seismologists are involved in research related to earthquake predictions. Most Seismologists believe that predicting earthquakes is not possible.)

Their research sometimes involves designing experiments to simulate processes associated with earthquakes, and comparing their results with the actual events. Some Seismologists develop computer models (sets of mathematical equations) to enable them to create simulations of seismic activities and effects. By changing the variables in the models, Seismologists can change hypothetical conditions and get an idea of what might occur if such conditions were actually created.

As part of their research, many Seismologists conduct field trips to earthquake faults, which are often in remote locations. Their fieldwork might involve examining and measuring the earth's surface after an earthquake occurs, mapping fault lines, searching for hidden fault lines, seeking evidence of seismic activity that occurred hundreds or thousands of years ago, or other tasks.

Many Seismologists are involved in applied research, using seismic technology for specific purposes. For example, some Seismologists are involved in monitoring seismic activity in active volcanoes. A sudden series of earthquakes is one of several clues that helps scientists determine if there is a potential for a volcanic eruption. Other Seismologists, who work for petroleum and mining companies, apply seismic techniques when they study sound waves that are generated by small explosions or mechanical devices to find oil, natural gas, or minerals.

Many Seismologists hold academic positions in colleges and universities. Along with conducting independent research, they teach courses in seismology, geophysics, and other fields. They also advise students and supervise student research projects. Additionally, professors are required to publish scholarly works, perform administrative duties, and participate in community service.

Seismologists perform duties that vary depending on their positions. Some of these duties may include designing research projects, supervising research assistants, performing administrative tasks, writing scientific reports (which may be published in professional journals), attending science conferences, providing consulting services to public officials and authorities, and so on. Some Seismologists are involved in developing educational materials for the public, covering such topics as earthquake hazards and how to prepare for earthquakes and emergency situations.

Seismologists who conduct independent research are usually responsible for obtaining grants to fund their research projects. Their tasks include learning about available grants from the federal government and other sources, getting guidelines, determining budgets for their projects, and writing clear and concise grant proposals.

Salaries

Salaries vary, depending on factors such as employer, education, experience, and geographical location. According to a survey by the Bureau of Labor Statistics, the estimated annual salary in 2001 for most geoscientists, including Seismologists, ranged from $33,150 to $109,510.

Employment Prospects

Seismologists are employed by colleges and universities, government agencies, private industries (especially petroleum and mining industries), and research institutes.

Most opportunities are created to replace individuals who retire, resign, or transfer to other positions. In general, opportunities vary each year as funding of most earthquake research depends on the availability of federal grants.

Advancement Prospects

Seismologists can advance to administrative or management positions, which may require moving to other employers.

Academic professors can advance in rank (assistant, associate, and full professor) as well as by obtaining job tenure.

Education and Training

The minimum qualification for most Seismologist positions is a doctoral degree in seismology, geophysics, geology, or related field. Doctoral degrees are necessary for those wishing to teach in universities and four-year colleges, to conduct independent research, or to pursue administrative positions.

Some industry positions require only a bachelor's degree, though many employers may require or strongly prefer candidates with a master's degree.

Experience, Skills, and Personality Traits

Seismologists generally need work and research experience that is related to the positions for which they are applying. Experience may have been gained through student research projects, internships, fellowships, employment, and so on. Many employers prefer or require that Seismologists have several years of postdoctoral experience.

To do well at their jobs, Seismologists should have excellent computer, writing, communication, and analytical skills. They also must have strong interpersonal and teamwork skills, as they often work with other scientists, technicians, engineers, and others. Some personality traits that successful Seismologists have in common are being curious, creative, meticulous, detail-oriented, patient, and flexible.

Unions and Associations

Many Seismologists join associations to take advantage of professional services and such resources as education programs and networking opportunities. Some professional societies that serve the interests of Seismologists are the Seismological Society of America; the International Association of Seismology and Physics of the Earth's Interior; the American Geophysical Union; and the Geological Society of America. See Appendix III for contact information.

Tips for Entry

1. While you are an undergraduate student, do volunteer work or complete internships at geological surveys, seismic laboratories, or other settings that can provide you with valuable training and experience.
2. If you don't plan to enroll in a graduate program immediately after earning your bachelor's degree, you might gain experience in the field by obtaining a research assistant or technician position at a seismological or geological research facility.
3. Use the Internet to learn more about seismology. Two websites that you might visit are National Earthquake Information Center (U.S. Geological Survey), http://neic.usgs.gov; and Center for Earthquake Research and Information (The University of Memphis), http://www.ceri.memphis.edu/index.shtml.

VOLCANOLOGIST

CAREER PROFILE

Duties: Design and conduct research projects; may teach college or university students; perform duties as required

Alternate Title(s): Geoscientist, Geologist

Salary Range: $33,000 to $110,000

Employment Prospects: Poor

Advancement Prospects: Good

Prerequisites:

Education or Training—A doctoral degree in geophysics or geology with an emphasis in volcanology

Experience—Postdoctoral experience required

Special Skills and Personality Traits—Computer, writing, communication, interpersonal, and self-management skills; be physically fit; creative; persistent; flexible; calm; analytical

Licensure/Certification—None required

CAREER LADDER

```
┌────────────────────────────────┐
│      Senior Volcanologist       │
└────────────────────────────────┘

┌────────────────────────────────┐
│         Volcanologist           │
└────────────────────────────────┘

┌────────────────────────────────┐
│  Postdoctoral Research Associate │
└────────────────────────────────┘
```

Position Description

Volcanology is the study of volcanoes, which are openings in the Earth's surface through which built-up pressures from within the Earth's interior can escape. Volcanic eruptions may be gentle or violent explosions in which lava (superhot melted rock), steam, gasses, and rock spew out of the vents. At least 1,500 volcanoes are known to be active or potentially active throughout the world, including approximately 70 volcanoes in the United States. Most volcanoes are mountains or islands, which are actually the tops of volcanic mountains that formed on the ocean floors.

Volcanologists are the research scientists who seek to understand the nature and causes of volcanic eruptions. They study the actual processes as well as the deposits of volcanic eruptions. Volcano observatories have been built at the rim or slopes of several active volcanoes around the world. There, Volcanologists can monitor volcanic activities on a regular basis. They use seismometers, spectrometers, laser survey instruments, and other equipment to measure changes in:

- seismic activity, as earthquakes normally occur before an eruption
- the shape of the volcano surface
- geophysical properties (such as the magnetic field strength and force of gravity)

- the composition or emission rate of gases
- the temperature, level, flow, and other characteristics of ground water

Volcanologists also make observations at field sites before, during, and after eruptions. They draw detailed geological maps of flow fields, which may require that they hike over young lava flows. They also collect samples of superhot lava to test and analyze later in the labs. In addition, many Volcanologists design experiments that simulate volcanic conditions and activities to test their theories about the phenomena they have directly observed. Some Volcanologists test their understanding of volcanic processes by applying mathematical formulas and developing computer models.

Many Volcanologists focus their work by specializing in a particular area. Some specialize in the study of a specific type of eruption (such as gentle eruptions that form shield mountains) or a particular type of volcanic product such as volcanic ash. Other Volcanologists focus on a specific volcanic activity; for example, certain Volcanologists specifically study seismic activity, geochemistry of volcanoes, or the changing shapes of the volcanic surface.

Many Volcanologists are involved with studying inactive volcanoes, examining the remains of their past eruptions. Some volcanoes are considered to be extinct; that is, they have not been active since the beginning of recorded history. Others have been dormant for a long period of time, but Volcanologists believe they may come alive again. Some Volcanologists specialize in the study of volcanic activities that occur on the ocean floors. Still others study volcanic processes on the moon and other planets in the solar system, using data gathered by spacecraft.

Volcanologists are also concerned with the effects that volcanic eruptions have on life and the environment. Some Volcanologists are involved in educating communities near active volcanoes about the hazards of volcanic eruptions. They also provide warnings to local authorities and leaders about potential hazards and eruptions.

In addition to working in observatories and in the field, Volcanologists work in offices and labs. In general, their duties include designing and conducting research projects; supervising research assistants and technicians; conducting experiments; gathering, analyzing, and interpreting data; writing reports; and performing administrative tasks. Volcanologists also share information about their research work with colleagues by writing scientific papers for publication in scientific journals or making presentations at scientific meetings that are sponsored by professional associations.

Many Volcanologists are faculty members at colleges and universities. In addition to their research work, they are responsible for the following duties: teaching geology, geophysics, volcanology, and other courses; advising students; supervising student research work; performing administrative tasks; writing scholarly works; and fulfilling community service obligations. They are also responsible for obtaining grants from the federal government and other sources for their research projects. Professors typically conduct field research during the summer and other college breaks.

Salaries

Salaries vary, depending on such factors as education, experience, and job duties. According to a salary survey by the Bureau of Labor Statistics, most geoscientists (which would include Volcanologists) in 2001 earned an estimated annual salary that ranged between $33,150 and $109,510.

Employment Prospects

Most Volcanologists work for colleges, universities, government volcanic observatories, or state or federal geological surveys (which are government agencies that conduct geological research).

Volcanology is a young and small discipline. Opportunities are limited, with only a few positions becoming available as Volcanologists retire, resign, or transfer to other positions.

Advancement Prospects

Most Volcanologists measure their success by being able to conduct independent research, by making higher salaries, and through earning professional recognition among their peers.

Education and Training

Becoming a Volcanologist generally requires earning a Ph.D. in geophysics or geology with a specialization in volcanology, or in another related field. Most Volcanologists also have a solid foundation in chemistry, physics, mathematics, and computer science.

Experience, Skills, and Personality Traits

In general, Volcanologists should have related work and research experience, which may have been gained through research projects, internships, fellowships, part-time employment, and so on. Volcanologists typically have several years of postdoctoral experience before obtaining a permanent job.

Volcanologists need strong computer, writing, and communication skills for their work. They should have good interpersonal skills and self-management skills, including the ability to handle stressful situations. In addition, they must be physically fit and enjoy hiking and being outdoors. Being creative, persistent, flexible, calm, and analytical are some personality traits that successful Volcanologists share.

Unions and Associations

Many Volcanologists are members of professional societies in order to take advantage of networking opportunities and other professional resources and services. Some associations that serve the interests of Volcanologists are the American Geophysical Union and the International Association of Volcanology and Chemistry of the Earth's Interior. See Appendix III for contact information.

Tips for Entry

1. Check out various graduate programs to make sure they offer the courses and research areas that interest you.
2. While you are an undergraduate student, do volunteer work or internships at observatories, geological surveys, or other settings that can provide you with valuable training and experience.
3. Many employers advertise job openings in scientific publications and professional journals, as well as on job banks at websites for professional societies.
4. Use the Internet to learn more about volcanology. Here are two websites you might visit: Volcano World, http://volcano.und.nodak.edu, and Volcano Hazards Program (U.S. Geological Survey), http://volcanoes.usgs.gov.

OCEANOGRAPHER

CAREER PROFILE

Duties: Conduct basic or applied research; design and conduct research projects; may teach college or university students; research assistants and technicians provide research and administrative support; perform duties as required of position

Alternate Title(s): Marine Scientist; Marine Biologist, Physical Oceanographer, Ocean Engineer, or other title that reflects a specialty

Salary Range: $33,000 to $110,000

Employment Prospects: Good

Advancement Prospects: Good

Prerequisites:

Education or Training—A bachelor's or advanced degree in oceanography or related field

Experience—Postdoctoral experience may be required for research scientists

Special Skills and Personality Traits—Math, computer, writing, communication, interpersonal, and teamwork skills; sailing, scuba diving, and mechanical skills are desirable; be physically fit; curious; creative; innovative; patient; enthusiastic; flexible

Licensure/Certification—None required

CAREER LADDER

```
┌─────────────────────────────────┐
│      Senior Oceanographer        │
└─────────────────────────────────┘

┌─────────────────────────────────┐
│         Oceanographer            │
└─────────────────────────────────┘

┌─────────────────────────────────┐
│  Postdoctoral Research Associate │
└─────────────────────────────────┘
```

Position Description

Oceanography is the scientific study of the oceans, which cover about 70 percent of the Earth's surface. This discipline integrates the knowledge and applications of geology, geophysics, geography, physics, chemistry, biology, mathematics, and engineering.

Oceanographers seek to understand everything about the ocean and coastal environments. They study the properties of the ocean waters (such as tides, currents, and salt content), the structure and form of the oceans, the composition of sediments on the ocean floors, the various species of sea plants and animals, and the geological history of the oceans. In addition, they seek solutions to such diverse problems as coastal pollution, global warming, the decline of the world's fisheries, the search for oil deposits under the ocean floor, and the effects of human development along coastlines.

Oceanographers usually specialize in one of the discipline's major subfields—biological oceanography, chemical oceanography, physical oceanography, geological oceanography, or ocean engineering. Oceanographers from these diverse disciplines often collaborate on research projects to gain an integrated understanding of the topics or problems they are investigating.

Biological Oceanographers are involved in learning about the species of sea plants and animals. They study the various aspects of biology in regards to sea life, including their anatomy, physiology, genetics, evolution, taxonomy, distribution, and so on. These Oceanographers are also known as marine biologists or fisheries scientists.

Chemical Oceanographers study the chemical composition and properties of the ocean waters. They investigate the various chemical reactions that occur in the ocean and on the sea floor, including interactions with solar energy, atmospheric compounds, sea life, and natural substances (such as minerals and petroleum). These Oceanographers are also known as marine chemists or marine geochemists.

Physical Oceanographers seek to understand how the oceans work. They study the physical properties of ocean water and the relationship of the ocean to the atmosphere which influences weather and climates. They also examine the interaction that the ocean has with coastlines and underwater formations as well as with solar, sound, wind, and other forms of energy.

Geological Oceanographers, or marine geologists, are involved in understanding the Earth's history. Their focus is studying the physical and chemical properties of rock and sediments found at the coastlines and on the ocean floors. Ocean engineers design, build, and maintain the instruments and equipment that scientists need to conduct their field research in, on, and under the ocean waters.

Oceanographers conduct basic and applied research while working in academic, government, industry, nonprofit, and nongovernmental settings. Most Oceanographers conduct field trips along coastlines, in estuaries, or at sea to make observations and collect samples. Their research expeditions sometimes require living and working on ships for several weeks or months. Back at their offices and laboratories, they analyze and interpret data, conduct experiments, develop theoretical models, do library research, write reports, and so on.

Oceanographers' duties vary, depending on their specialty and position. In general, research assistants and laboratory technicians provide scientists with research and academic support. Their tasks may include setting up experiments in the laboratories, collecting samples in the field, analyzing data, repairing instruments, maintaining labs, completing routine administrative tasks, and so on.

Research scientists are responsible for designing and managing research projects. Many of them have other major responsibilities, such as overseeing the daily operations of programs and laboratories, providing consulting services to policy makers, or developing educational materials for the public.

Many Oceanographers hold permanent teaching positions at universities and colleges. In addition to conducting independent research projects, they prepare course syllabuses and lessons, deliver class lectures, advise students about their course work, and supervise student research projects. Furthermore, they are required to publish scholarly works, perform administrative duties, and participate in community services.

Many Oceanographers are responsible for seeking out grants from the federal government and other sources to fund their research projects. This involves writing comprehensive proposals that describe the goals, objectives, methodologies, budget, and other aspects of their projects.

All Oceanographers keep up with developments in their fields by networking with colleagues, attending professional meetings, reading professional journals, and so forth. Most research scientists share information about their research work by writing scientific papers for publication in scientific journals or making presentations at scientific meetings that are sponsored by professional associations.

Salaries
Salaries vary, depending on factors such as education, experience, employer, and job duties. Salaries for research scientists may vary from year to year as their income is tied to the availability of grants and to the amount needed for their research projects. According to a 2001 survey by the Bureau of Labor Statistics, the estimated annual salary for most geoscientists ranged between $33,150 and $109,510.

Employment Prospects
Oceanography is young discipline with new subfields continually emerging. For example, the fields of marine biotechnology and marine molecular biology have emerged in recent years. Some Oceanographers predict the job market to grow in areas that are related to aquaculture, environmental protection, and deep sea geology and exploration.

With a background in oceanography, individuals can pursue careers in other areas such as environmental science, communications, museum science, archeology, recreation and tourism, marine electronics, engineering, and water quality management.

Advancement Prospects
Research scientists can advance to administrative or management positions by becoming project leaders, program managers, laboratory directors, or executive officers. Technicians and research assistants can advance to managerial positions such as laboratory manager or to other nonlaboratory administrative positions. As professors, Oceanographers can advance through the ranks as assistant professors, associate professors, and full professors.

Education and Training
The minimum requirement for research assistant and technician positions is a bachelor's degree in oceanography, earth science, biology, mathematics, or other related field. Some employers prefer or require that candidates hold a master's degree.

Research scientists must have either a master's degree or a Ph.D. A Ph.D. is required in order to teach in universities and four-year colleges, to conduct independent research, or to pursue top management positions.

Experience, Skills, and Personality Traits
Employers generally choose candidates who have related work and research experience, which may have been gained through research projects, internships, fellowships, part-time employment, and so on. Ph.D. applicants for research

scientist positions are usually expected to have several years of related postdoctoral experience.

Oceanographers need strong math and computer skills as well as excellent writing and communication skills. In order to work well with others, they must possess good interpersonal and teamwork skills. Other desirable skills that employers look for are sailing skills, mechanical skills (the ability to fix equipment), and scuba-diving skills. In addition, Oceanographers must be physically fit and have the stamina and strength to work long periods of time on research cruises.

Being curious, creative, innovative, patient, enthusiastic, and flexible are a few personality traits that successful Oceanographers have in common.

Unions and Associations

Most Oceanographers join professional associations to take advantage of networking opportunities, current research information, education programs, and other professional services and resources. Many join societies such as the Oceanography Society, the American Geophysical Union, and the Association for Women Geoscientists. Oceanographers also join societies that serve their particular interests, such as the American Society of Limnology and Oceanography, the Marine Technology Society, or the Oceanic Engineering Society. For contact information see Appendix III.

Most professors join an academic society such as the National Association of Scholars or the American Association of University Professors.

Tips for Entry

1. While you are an undergraduate student (or even a high school student), take the opportunity to get practical experience. You might work as a student research assistant, intern, or volunteer for a professor, science museum, government lab, research institute, or private company.
2. Join a campus or local branch of a professional society and participate in its activities. If possible, attend professional conferences to learn more about the field as well as to network with scientists, administrators, and others.
3. Some experts say that graduates with experience in more than one field of science have better chances of employability, as do those with backgrounds in computer programming or mathematical modeling.
4. Learn more about oceanography on the Internet. Two websites you might visit are Sea Grant, http://www.marinecareers.net/index.htm, and Scripps Institute of Oceanography, http://www.scilib.ucsd.edu/sio/guide/career.html.

OCEAN ENGINEER

CAREER PROFILE

Duties: Research, design, construct, operate, and maintain instrumentation, equipment, vessels, and structures for oceanographic research and work operations; may perform consulting, teaching, or administration duties; perform duties as required of position

Alternate Title(s): Marine Engineer; Coastal Engineer, Civil Engineer, Naval Architect or other title that reflects a specialty or a position

Salary Range: $41,000 to $96,000

Employment Prospects: Good

Advancement Prospects: Good

Prerequisites:

Education or Training—A bachelor's degree in ocean engineering or related field

Experience—Oceanography and/or engineering experience required

Special Skills and Personality Traits—Analysis and design skills; computer, problem-solving, writing, communication, interpersonal, and teamwork skills; creative; adaptive; trustworthy; dedicated; competent; persistent

Licensure/Certification—A Professional Engineer (P.E.) license may be required

CAREER LADDER

```
┌─────────────────────────────┐
│   Senior Ocean Engineer     │
└─────────────────────────────┘

┌─────────────────────────────┐
│       Ocean Engineer        │
└─────────────────────────────┘

┌─────────────────────────────┐
│    Junior Ocean Engineer    │
│   or Engineer-in-Training   │
└─────────────────────────────┘
```

Position Description

Ocean Engineering is an engineering specialty that is part of oceanography, the geoscience that deals with the study of ocean and coastal environments. Ocean Engineers combine their engineering skills and knowledge of oceanography to develop complex engineering systems for oceanographic research, marine transportation, mineral exploration, oil production, commercial fishing, coastline protection, ocean resources management, and other oceanographic operations.

Ocean Engineers design and build various instrumentation, equipment, vessels, and structures that can function in the ocean waters. Their designs must be able to withstand cold temperatures, currents, tides, waves, severe storms, saltwater corrosion, marine fouling (buildup of barnacles or other marine growth on structures), and other conditions of the ocean environment. Some examples of their inventions are computerized buoys; underwater video equipment; seismometers (which record earthquakes under the ocean floors); acoustical devices for detecting objects under the ocean; remote-controlled submersibles; drilling equipment; underwater welding equipment; oil tankers; submarines; navy ships; recreational boats; and platforms for oil exploration and production.

In addition, Ocean Engineers are involved with various types of oceanographic operations, working closely with ocean scientists, technicians, and other engineers. For example, Ocean Engineers might:

• develop new products, such as measuring instrumentation, automatic underwater vehicles, drilling equipment, or stationary platforms for oil exploration
• provide technical support to ocean scientists on research expeditions
• be involved in all phases of oil exploration and production—discovering, producing, and delivering offshore petroleum resources

- develop new methods of oil production that can protect marine wildlife and coastal regions from the undesirable side effects of offshore oil production
- improve the design and construction of oil tankers, recreational boats, submarines, and other ships so that they are safer, faster, sounder, yet less expensive
- design deep water ports, ports, and breakwaters
- design coastal recreational facilities
- solve coastline problems such as natural shoreline erosion or coastal development
- create ways to lessen the impact of storms and other natural shoreline processes
- plan new uses of waterways for marine transportation
- participate in managing ocean resources to ensure the survival of marine species and continuing supplies of food for the world

Many Ocean Engineers work on basic and applied research projects for industry, academic institutions, government agencies, and research institutes. Research scientists might specialize in particular aspects of ocean engineering, such as acoustics, robotics, naval architecture, coastal engineering, chemical engineering, or civil engineering. Typically, academic researchers have the ability to choose topics of interest while Ocean Engineers in other settings conduct research that fits their employers' objectives and missions.

Most Ocean Engineers have a combination of research, consulting, teaching, and/or administration responsibilities. Their duties vary, depending on their specialty, work setting, and position. Those working in nonprofit or academic sectors might be involved with writing grant proposals to fund their research projects. Those working in the private sector might perform various types of services for customers, such as inspecting installations, scouting potential sites for building structures, or making presentations about their employers' products.

Ocean Engineers work in offices and laboratories as well as in the field. Their field assignments may involve traveling to other countries to provide service, train customers, or operate equipment and systems. Research scientists often conduct field expeditions that require working and living on research ships for weeks or months at a time. Some Ocean Engineers go undersea to conduct experiments, install ocean pipes, or perform other tasks.

All Ocean Engineers are expected to keep up with technologies and developments in their specialties. They network with colleagues, read professional journals, attend professional meetings, and so forth.

Salaries
Salaries vary, depending on such factors as education, experience, employer, and job responsibilities. According to the Bureau of Labor Statistics, the estimated annual salary in 2001 for marine engineers and naval architects ranged between $40,780 and $95,780.

Employment Prospects
Ocean Engineers work for businesses, such as ocean engineering firms, and for the oil, shipbuilding, marine transportation, and other industries. They are also employed by research institutes, government agencies, colleges, and universities.

Oceanography is a young discipline with promising prospects for ocean engineers. Job opportunities are expected to grow especially in these areas: aquaculture, environmental protection, and deep sea geology and exploration.

Advancement Prospects
Ocean Engineers advance in any number of ways, depending on their positions, ambitions, and interests. Those interested in management and administrative work may find opportunities in any work setting.

Education and Training
To enter this field requires a bachelor's degree in ocean engineering, oceanography, or another engineering discipline (such as civil engineering or mechanical engineering). A master's degree or a Ph.D. is generally required to conduct research or to advance to top management positions. A Ph.D. is usually required in order to teach in universities and four-year colleges.

Experience, Skills, and Personality Traits
Many Ocean Engineers enter this field with experience as oceanographers, civil engineers, marine environmentalists, naval architects, or marine engineers, or with experience from other marine-related technical fields.

For entry-level positions, employers generally choose candidates who have related work experience, which may have been gained through research projects, internships, employment, postdoctoral training, and so on. They should have developed skills in such areas as analysis and design.

To do well in their jobs, Ocean Engineers need strong computer, problem-solving, writing, and communication skills. Additionally, they need superior interpersonal and teamwork skills, as they work with various people from diverse backgrounds. Some personality traits that successful Ocean Engineers share are being creative, adaptive, trustworthy, dedicated, competent, and persistent.

Special Requirements
Ocean Engineers may by required to have a Professional Engineer (P.E.) license, depending on the employer or position. For example, Ocean Engineers must be licensed P.E.s if they provide consulting services or prepare engineering plans that will be submitted to public authorities for

approval. The minimum requirements for a P.E. license are a bachelor's degree from an institution accredited by the Accreditation Board for Engineering and Technology and four years of qualifying work experience. Other licensure requirements vary from state to state. For more information about the P.E. license, contact the state engineering licensure board in the state where you wish to practice.

Unions and Associations

Ocean Engineers can join professional associations to take advantage of professional services and resources, such as education programs and networking opportunities. Many are members of societies that specifically serve the ocean engineering field, such as the Society of Naval Architects and Marine Engineers, the Oceanic Engineering Society, and the Marine Technology Society. Ocean Engineers are also eligible to join other engineering societies, such as the Institute of Electrical and Electronic Engineers or the American Society of Mechanical Engineers. In addition, Ocean Engineers can join associations that serve all oceanography professionals, such as the Oceanography Society. See Appendix III for contact information.

Tips for Entry

1. While you are an undergraduate student, talk with your professors, college adviser, or college career counselor for suggestions about internships, work experience, or research assistantships that may be available.
2. Contact employers directly to learn about internships and job openings.
3. Learn more about ocean engineering on the Internet. To get a list of relevant websites to read, enter the keywords *ocean engineering* or *ocean engineers* in any search engine.

HYDROLOGIST

CAREER PROFILE

Duties: May perform any of the following—conduct basic or applied research, provide consulting services, teach college or university students, provide education services, manage programs, or other major duty; perform duties as required of position

Alternate Title(s): Hydrogeologist, Water Resource Technician, Water Resources Engineer, Civil Engineer, Geologist

Salary Range: $37,000 to $86,000

Employment Prospects: Good

Advancement Prospects: Good

Prerequisites:

Education or Training—A bachelor's or advanced degree in hydrology or related field

Experience—Fieldwork experience and familiarity with employer's business or industry are desirable

Special Skills and Personality Traits—Computer, writing, communication, interpersonal, and teamwork skills; for fieldwork, good health and physical stamina; self-motivated; imaginative; dedicated; inquisitive; logical; open-minded

Licensure/Certification—State licensure as Hydrologist may be required in Wisconsin; geologists and engineers with Hydrologist duties may be required to have appropriate state licensure.

CAREER LADDER

```
┌─────────────────────────────────────┐
│ Senior Hydrologist or Professional   │
│ Engineer or Registered Geologist     │
└─────────────────────────────────────┘

┌─────────────────────────────────────┐
│ Hydrologist (journey position) or    │
│ Research Hydrologist                 │
└─────────────────────────────────────┘

┌─────────────────────────────────────┐
│ Hydrologist (entry-level) or         │
│ Postdoctoral Research Associate      │
└─────────────────────────────────────┘
```

Position Description

Hydrology is the study of the water cycle, or hydrologic cycle, which is nature's system of circulating water from the atmosphere to the surface of the Earth and back.

Hydrologists are interested in understanding the water cycle on a regional and global basis. The hydrologic cycle consists of several stages and has no beginning or end. The cycle includes the storage and movement of water in its gaseous state in the atmosphere; its change from a gas to precipitation (rain, snow, or ice) which falls to the Earth; the storage of water on the surface as well as beneath it; the various stages in which water moves upon land as it travels toward the seas; and the processes in which water changes into a gas and evaporates into the atmosphere. Hydrologists examine the physical and chemical properties of water; and seek measurable information and knowledge about the occurrence and distribution of water at each phase of the water cycle.

Hydrologists also assist in the search and management of fresh water supplies for public, industrial, agricultural, and other uses. In addition, they address a wide range of such water-related issues and problems as the availability of fresh water sources; water allocation; water quality; water pollution; groundwater contamination; flood control; water conservation; and environmental protection.

Many Hydrologists specialize in a particular area of the hydrologic cycle, and usually hold other job titles. For example, hydrogeologists specialize in the study of groundwater; glaciologists examine glaciers; limnologists study lakes; geochemists investigates the quality of groundwater; and hydrometeorologists investigate water in the atmosphere.

Hydrologists work in academic, government, industry, nonprofit, and nongovernmental settings. Many of them design and conduct basic research projects to further knowledge about the hydrologic cycle. Others are involved in applying findings of basic research to develop useful products or to solve water-related problems. For example, some research scientists are involved in developing tools and systems for making predictions about water availability, flooding, effects of water pollution, or other phenomena. Research Hydrologists often collaborate on projects with scientists from other disciplines (such as meteorology, agriculture, and forestry) where hydrologic issues are also addressed.

Many other Hydrologists work in applied areas, performing roles as researchers, educators, consultants, technicians, engineers, and administrators. They usually work directly with the public, engineers, other scientists, public officials, policy makers, and others. Their duties might include

- designing and conducting technical investigations about specific hydrologic problems
- performing assessments or appraisals on proposed development or construction of bridges, dams, waste treatment centers, or other structures
- providing hydrologic information and technical support to engineers, scientists from other disciplines, policy makers, and/or the general public
- monitoring surface and underground water supplies to ensure that they are in compliance with health standards and environmental laws and regulations
- advising government officials and policy makers about hydrologic issues
- educating the public about water conservation and preservation of water resources
- creating and producing maps, graphs, interpretive reports, computer models, and other products that explain hydrologic information
- managing hydrologic projects or water resource programs

Some Hydrologists are professional engineers (P.E.), registered geologists (R.G.), or engineering hydrologists. They are involved in the planning, designing, control, use, and management of water resources.

Many Hydrologists are adjunct instructors or full-time professors at colleges and universities. They teach hydrology courses to undergraduate and graduate students. Some also teach courses in geology, engineering, geography, or other disciplines. Along with conducting independent research and teaching courses, professors advise students, supervise student research projects, perform administrative tasks, write scholarly works, and participate in community service.

Most Hydrologists spend some time in the field. Their fieldwork might involve such tasks as collecting water samples, measuring rainfall, evaluating groundwater resources, and assessing environmental factors that are affecting the hydrologic cycle in specific locations. Back in their offices and labs, Hydrologists design and conduct experiments or develop computer models to test their theories. They also conduct library research, analyze and interpret data, write technical reports, complete administrative tasks, and so on. Those who conduct independent research are responsible for writing grant proposals and applying for scientific research grants to fund new or ongoing projects.

Salaries

Salaries vary, depending on such factors as education, experience, position, employer, and geographical location. According to the Bureau of Labor Statistics, the estimated annual salary in 2001 for most Hydrologists ranged between $36,870 and $86,250.

Employment Prospects

Hydrologists work for civil engineering and environmental consulting firms; local, state, and federal government agencies; universities and colleges; and nonprofit and nongovernmental organizations.

The Bureau of Labor Statistics reports that opportunities for Hydrologists are expected to increase between 21 and 35 percent through 2010. Much of this will be due to the continuing need for companies and organizations to comply with environmental laws and regulations. In addition, Hydrologists will be needed to address such hydrologic issues as flood control, water pollution, water conservation, waste disposal, and groundwater contamination.

Advancement Prospects

Hydrologists advance in their careers in various ways, depending on their career path, ambitions, and interests. Those interested in management and administrative work can find opportunities in any work setting. Hydrologists with entrepreneurial ambitions can become independent consultants or owners of consulting firms.

Hydrologists with a bachelor's degree in engineering or geology might also pursue advancement by becoming licensed as a professional engineer (P.E.) or registered geologist (R.G.). With licensure, a hydrologist has better chances of commanding higher salaries and receiving more complex assignments.

Education and Training

To enter this field, Hydrologists need at least a bachelor's degree in hydrology, geology, engineering, water resource management, or related discipline. Many employers require or strongly prefer candidates with a master's degree. A Ph.D. is normally required to conduct independent research, teach in four-year colleges and universities, and to hold top management positions.

Experience, Skills, and Personality Traits

Employers generally choose candidates for entry-level positions who have related work and research experience, which may have been gained through research projects, internships, part-time employment, postdoctoral training, and so on. Many employers look for applicants who have fieldwork experience. Employers typically prefer candidates who are familiar with the business or industry in which they are employed.

Hydrologists need strong computer, writing, and communication skills for their jobs. In addition, they should have good interpersonal and teamwork skills as they usually work with others on team projects. Those planning to be involved in fieldwork must be in good health and have physical stamina. Some personality traits that successful Hydrologists share are being self-motivated, imaginative, dedicated, inquisitive, logical, and open-minded.

Special Requirements

As of April, 2002, Wisconsin is the only state known to require Hydrologists to be licensed if they provide services that involve public health, safety, and welfare.

Geologists and engineers who perform hydrology duties may be required to be licensed as a registered geologist (R.G.) or professional engineer (P.E.) in the states where they practice. Individuals take the examination for licensure after they have met the required number of years of work experience as set by their state. (Note: Not all states have licensure for geologists.)

Unions and Associations

Many Hydrologists join professional associations to take advantage of professional resources and services, such as networking opportunities and education programs. The American Institute of Hydrology, the American Water Resources Association, the National Groundwater Association, the American Institute of Professional Geologists, and the American Society of Civil Engineers are some organizations that Hydrologists are eligible to join. See Appendix III for contact information.

Tips for Entry

1. To learn more about the variety of career paths available in this field, talk to various Hydrologists in different settings.
2. Obtaining skills in any of the following areas can enhance your employability: computer programming, computer modeling, remote sensing, geographic information systems (GIS), and the Global Positioning System (GPS).
3. Use the Internet to learn more about hydrology. Some websites you might visit are the Hydrology Web, http://terrassa.pnl.gov:2080/hydroweb.html; Water Resources of the United States (U.S. Geological Survey), http:// water.usgs.gov; or National Groundwater Association, http://www.ngwa.org.

METEOROLOGIST

CAREER PROFILE

Duties: May conduct basic or applied research, forecast weather conditions, or provide consulting services; may teach college or university students; perform duties as required by position

Alternate Title(s): Atmospheric Scientist; Operational Meteorologist, Climatologist, Air Pollution Meteorologist, or other title that reflects a specialty

Salary Range: $31,000 to $106,000

Employment Prospects: Good

Advancement Prospects: Good

Prerequisites:

Education or Training—A bachelor's or advanced degree in atmospheric science or related field

Experience—Requirements vary with the different positions

Special Skills and Personality Traits—Math, computer, communication, writing skills, teamwork, and interpersonal skills; creative; flexible; versatile; analytical; enthusiastic

Licensure/Certification—None required

CAREER LADDER

```
┌─────────────────────────────┐
│    Senior Meteorologist     │
└─────────────────────────────┘

┌─────────────────────────────┐
│       Meteorologist         │
└─────────────────────────────┘

┌─────────────────────────────┐
│ Trainee or Postdoctoral Fellow │
└─────────────────────────────┘
```

Position Description

Meteorology is the study of the Earth's atmosphere, which is a blanket of air that surrounds the Earth. It deals with the study of the structure and composition of the atmosphere as well as the atmospheric conditions (such as wind, temperature, sunlight, and precipitation) that are continually changing to produce weather on Earth. Meteorology also deals with weather forecasting—making predictions about the weather—by applying physical and mathematical principles to atmospheric conditions.

Meteorologists are also known as atmospheric scientists. They typically specialize in one of the different subfields of meteorology. For example, physical Meteorologists investigate electrical and chemical properties of the atmosphere; synoptic Meteorologists study weather forecasting; dynamic Meteorologists examine the movements of weather systems and what controls them; climatologists study long-term weather patterns; and instrumentation specialists are concerned with designing instruments and weather information systems for measuring and recording weather variables.

Many Meteorologists are engaged in research while working in academic, government, military, industry, and other settings. Those who conduct basic research seek further scientific knowledge about the atmosphere, clouds, weather, and climate; causes of hurricanes, flash floods and other events; the effects of long-term droughts; and so on. Other Meteorologists are involved in applied research, addressing meteorological problems and issues in such areas as agriculture, aviation, sea transportation, satellite communication, national defense, and environmental science.

Research meteorologists often collaborate on projects with other Meteorologists specializing in other areas. Some of their research projects may involve working closely with chemists, physicists, geologists, oceanographers, and other scientists. They also work with mathematicians and computer scientists who help them design computer models of atmospheric processes.

The largest group of Meteorologists work in the area of weather forecasting, which is an applied field of meteorology. They are called operational Meteorologists. Broadcast

Meteorologists are probably the most familiar type of weather forecaster. They are employed by television networks, newspapers, radio stations, and Internet weather service providers to forecast the weather and provide weather reports. They may give air quality reports as well. (Note: Not all weather reporters are meteorologists.) Some operational Meteorologists work as private forecasters. They generally provide specialized forecasts to clients in such industries as aviation, shipping, defense, agriculture, fishing, utilities, sports, or securities and commodities.

The majority of operational Meteorologists work in weather stations around the world, collecting and recording atmospheric data several times each day. Their information is transmitted to other operational Meteorologists in world weather centers who produce analyses of global weather forecasts. In the United States, these analyses are sent to regional and local National Weather Service centers where Meteorologists interpret the data and make predictions for their particular regions or local areas. Many operational Meteorologists assist local authorities and the general public to develop emergency plans when hurricanes, blizzards, and other severe and dangerous weather conditions are being predicted.

To make their weather predictions, Meteorologists use a variety of instruments to take measurements of the different atmospheric conditions and to track weather conditions, such as severe storms or tornadoes. Some of these instruments are thermometers, barometers, radar, acoustic sounders (that use sound waves to measure winds), ocean buoys, and weather balloons. Meteorologists also obtain observations from aircraft which are specially equipped with measuring and sampling instruments. In addition, they get observations from weather satellites which use remote-sensing techniques to measure conditions at many levels of the atmosphere.

Computers are also an essential tool in their work. Meteorologists can make long-term predictions with the aid of computer models, which are sets of mathematical equations that represent atmospheric conditions. By changing the variables in the equations, the computer models simulate how weather systems may behave over several days, weeks, and even years.

Meteorologists are also employed as consulting Meteorologists. They provide a wide range of meteorological services to clients in the public and private sectors on a fee basis. For example, a consulting Meteorologist might provide farmers with consultation about climate-related problems; another might help planners find the best location for an airport; and still another might provide expert witness testimony at a court trial about specific weather conditions.

Duties for Meteorologists vary, depending on their specialty, area of work, position, and other factors. For example, some Meteorologists are employed as professors in colleges and universities. They divide their time among

these duties: conducting independent research projects, teaching meteorology or other courses, advising students, supervising student research projects, writing scholarly works for publications, performing administrative duties, and participating in community services.

Research Meteorologists work in offices and laboratories, as well as in the field. Operational Meteorologists mostly work in large field offices located at airports or in urban areas; some work in isolated and remote areas and may work alone. Those working in weather stations may be required to work nights and weekend shifts on a rotating basis.

Salaries
Salaries vary, depending on such factors as job duties, employer, education, experience, and geographical location. According to the Bureau of Labor Statistics, the estimated annual salary in 2001 for most atmospheric scientists ranged from $31,410 to $92,860, and for postsecondary instructors in atmospheric science, $32,740 to $105,890.

Employment Prospects
In the United States, the federal government is the largest employer of Meteorologists, with most federal Meteorologists working for the National Weather Service. Meteorologists also work in private industry as well as for meteorological consulting firms. In addition, Meteorologists are hired by universities, colleges, and research institutions.

According to the Bureau of Labor Statistics, employment for Meteorologists is projected to increase about as fast as the average for all occupations through 2010. However, competition for entry-level Meteorologist positions should be strong if the number of degrees awarded in meteorology remain near current levels. Job prospects are expected to be better in the private sector than in the federal government. For example, opportunities should increase in private weather consulting firms that provide weather services to industries (such as agriculture, utilities, aviation, construction, and transportation) that are dependent on the weather. Keep in mind that growth in the private sector is dependent on the general well-being of the economy.

Advancement Prospects
Meteorologists with management or administrative ambitions can advance to such positions within their specialty. Many Meteorologists pursue advancement by earning higher pay, by being able to conduct independent research projects, and through receiving professional recognition.

Education and Training
Minimally, a bachelor's degree in meteorology or atmospheric science, or in a related field (mathematics or physics, for example) is needed for most entry-level positions.

Entry-level candidates for applied research positions are generally required to possess a master's degrees, while a doctorate is typically required for basic research and university teaching positions.

Experience, Skills, and Personality Traits

Experience and skills requirements vary, depending on the type of position as well as the employer. Entry-level applicants should have related work experience, which may have been gained through internships, research projects, part-time employment, or postdoctoral training.

Meteorologists need to have good math and computer skills. In addition, they need to be able to communicate effectively as well as have excellent writing skills. Further, they should have strong teamwork and interpersonal skills, as they must be able to work well with various people of diverse backgrounds and with different technical levels. Some personality traits that successful Meteorologists share are being creative, flexible, versatile, analytical, and enthusiastic.

Unions and Associations

Many Meteorologists join societies to take advantage of professional services and resources, such as networking opportunities, training programs, and professional certification. Some professional associations are the American Meteorological Society, the National Weather Association (for operational Meteorologists), the National Council of Industrial Meteorologists, the Air Weather Association (for military Meteorologists), and the International Association of Broadcast Meteorologists. See Appendix III for contact information.

Tips for Entry

1. Gain experience in the field by obtaining internships with public or private meteorological employers. Talk with your college adviser or the college placement center for assistance in finding out about relevant internship programs in your area.
2. If you are interested in becoming a broadcasting Meteorologist, take courses in speech, journalism, and other related fields to develop communication skills.
3. To obtain information about Meteorologist jobs with the federal government, contact the United States Office of Personnel Management. Look in your telephone book under U.S. Government for a local phone number. Or visit its website at http://www.usajobs.opm.gov.
4. Use the Internet to learn more about Meteorologists. Here are a few websites that you might visit: University Corporation for Atmospheric Research, http://www.ucar.edu; The American Meteorological Society, http://www.ametsoc.org/AMS; and the National Weather Service, http://www.nws.noaa.gov.

CLIMATOLOGIST

CAREER PROFILE

Duties: Conduct basic or applied research; design and conduct research projects; may provide climate data services; may teach college or university students; perform duties as required by position

Alternate Title(s): Urban Climatologist, Paleoclimatologist, State Climatologist

Salary Range: $31,000 to $93,000

Employment Prospects: Good

Advancement Prospects: Good

Prerequisites:

Education or Training—A master's or doctoral degree in atmospheric science or related field

Experience—Postdoctoral experience may be required for research scientists

Special Skills and Personality Traits—Math, computer, communication, writing, teamwork, and interpersonal skills; enthusiastic; creative; flexible; analytical

Licensure/Certification—None required

CAREER LADDER

```
┌─────────────────────────────────┐
│      Senior Climatologist       │
└─────────────────────────────────┘

┌─────────────────────────────────┐
│         Climatologist           │
└─────────────────────────────────┘

┌─────────────────────────────────┐
│  Postdoctoral Research Associate │
└─────────────────────────────────┘
```

Position Description

Climatology is the scientific study of climate, the pattern of weather that occurs in a place over a period of time. Every location on the Earth has its own unique climate. If a location, for example, is said to have a tropical wet climate, then the weather is generally hot and humid with high temperatures and heavy and frequent rainfall throughout the year. Climates, however, are not constant. They can change over time because of variations that take place in the conditions—such as temperature, precipitation, and air pressure—that shape weather.

Climatologists are concerned with understanding the climates of specific locations (such as towns, cities, states, or countries) as well as the climate on a global basis. They also examine how climates in different locations change over time. Additionally, they investigate how changes in the climate affect the vegetation, soils, and other physical features of a location as well as how such changes affect the way people live and work. Further, Climatologists are involved in predicting long-term changes in climates.

Urban Climatologists specialize in studying climates that occur in and around cities. They address problems such as air pollution, the effects of urban climate on people's health, and how to improve urban climates. Other specialists are Paleoclimatologists who study global and regional climates that occurred over thousands or millions of years ago.

Most Climatologists conduct basic and applied research, while working in academic, government, private sector, and other settings. They often collaborate on projects with colleagues as well as with scientists from other disciplines.

Their research work involves searching for weather data about the location they are investigating. They collect past records of temperature, rainfall, wind speed, and other weather conditions. Many Climatologists also gather information about plant and animal species, as their responses to the weather are clues that climates may be changing. Paleoclimatologists study fossils and rocks to learn about weather conditions that occurred in the past.

To help them analyze and interpret data, Climatologists create computer models, which are mathematical equations that represent the various weather conditions. The models help Climatologists learn how climates have changed in the past as well as predict how climates may change in the future. For example, Climatologists might develop a computer model to help them understand what could happen to the climate if the rate of carbon dioxide in the atmosphere continues to increase at a certain percentage each year.

Climatologists' duties vary, depending on their position and experience. In general, research Climatologists are responsible for designing and conducting research projects. Those who conduct independent research are usually responsible for seeking research grants from the federal government and other sources to fund their projects. This involves preparing a grant proposal that includes the objectives, methodologies, budgets, and other aspects of their projects. Senior researchers and principal investigators usually perform supervisory and management duties.

Most Climatologists share the results of their research with colleagues. They might write articles (scientific papers) which they submit to scientific journals or make presentations at scientific meetings or conferences that are sponsored by professional associations.

Some Climatologists are responsible for providing climate data services to individuals, farmers, businesses, companies, government agencies, and others who use the information to help them make decisions about their personal and economic activities. These Climatologists generally work in climate data centers for government agencies and private firms. Their duties include acquiring, analyzing, and interpreting data for their clients. They also write reports and summaries of climatology information for their clients. In addition, Climatologists are responsible for maintaining and distributing the climatological data of their assigned locations.

Many Climatologists are professors or adjunct instructors in universities and colleges. They teach climatology courses and may teach other courses in geography, atmospheric science (or meteorology), or geoscience. Full-time professors conduct independent research in addition to teaching their courses. Further, they advise students, supervise student research projects, write scholarly works, participate in community service, and perform administrative duties.

All Climatologists are responsible for keeping up with developments in their field as well as with updating their skills. They might enroll in training programs, read professional journals, attend professional conferences, network with colleagues, and so on.

Salaries

Salaries vary, depending on such factors as education, experience, and geographical location. The Bureau of Labor Statistics reports that most atmospheric scientists (which includes Climatologists) in 2001 earned an estimated annual salary between $31,410 and $92,860.

Employment Prospects

Climatologists are employed by government and private climate data centers. Some other employers are government agencies, cooperative extension offices, universities, colleges, research institutes, and meteorology consulting firms.

Climatology is a relatively young and small field. In general, opportunities for Climatologists are expected to grow as technology allows for more detailed data to be gathered and analyzed. According to the 2001 newsletter of the Climate Specialty Group of the Association of American Geographers, opportunities are excellent for Climatologists in the academic, government, and private sectors.

Advancement Prospects

Climatologists can advance to management and administrative positions in any work setting. Academic professors typically advance in terms of rank (assistant, associate, and full professor).

Many Climatologists measure their success by earning higher wages, by conducting independent research, and through gaining professional recognition among their colleagues.

Education and Training

A bachelor's degree in atmospheric science, geography, agronomy, or other related field is the minimum education requirement to enter this field. For most research positions, a master's or doctoral degree in climatology (or another major with an emphasis in this field) is needed. To teach in universities and four-year colleges or to advance to top management positions, a doctoral degree is required.

Experience, Skills, and Personality Traits

Employers generally require that job candidates have related work and research experience. Entry-level applicants may have gained experience through internships, research projects, part-time employment, or volunteer work. Ph.D. candidates for research scientist positions are usually expected to have a few years of postdoctoral experience.

Climatologists must have strong math and computer skills. In addition, they need to be able to communicate effectively as well as have excellent writing skills. Further, they should have strong teamwork and interpersonal skills, as they must be able to work well with various people of diverse backgrounds and with different technical levels. Some personality traits that successful Climatologists share are being enthusiastic, creative, flexible, and analytical.

Unions and Associations

Many Climatologists are members of professional associations which provide networking opportunities and other professional resources and services. Some of the various societies that Climatologists might join are the American Meteorological Society, the Association of American Geographers (Climate Specialty Group), and the American Geological Institute.

Professors might also join such societies as the American Association of University Professors or the National Association of Scholars. See Appendix III for contact information.

Tips for Entry

1. While you are a college student, take advantage of opportunities to gain general experience in climatology or meteorology. For example, you might complete an internship or perform volunteer work at a climate center, weather station, or a consulting firm.

2. Obtain a research assistantship or volunteer to work with a professor who is doing research in areas that interest you.

3. You can learn more about Climatologists on the Internet. One website you might visit is the National Climatic Data Center, http://lwf.ncdc.noaa.gov/oa/ncdc.html. To get a list of other relevant websites, enter one of these keywords in a search engine: *climatology, climatologists,* or *climate science.*

CARTOGRAPHER

CAREER PROFILE

Duties: As mapmakers—design, create, and produce various types of maps; as research scientists—conduct basic or applied research to improve map designs and the mapmaking process; may teach college or university students; perform duties as required of position

Alternate Title(s): Research Scientist, Cartographic Technician, Cartographic Editor, or other title that describes a particular position

Salary Range: $25,000 to $66,000

Employment Prospects: Good

Advancement Prospects: Good

Prerequisites:
   Education or Training—A bachelor's degree or advanced degree in cartography, geography, or related field
   Experience—Requirements vary with the different positions
   Special Skills and Personality Traits—Background in mathematics, computer science, geography, and GIS; interpersonal, organizational analytical, and self-management skills; imaginative; artistic; adaptable; detail-oriented; accurate; precise; patient
   Licensure/Certification—None required

CAREER LADDER

```
┌─────────────────────────────┐
│    Senior Cartographer      │
└─────────────────────────────┘

┌─────────────────────────────┐
│       Cartographer          │
└─────────────────────────────┘

┌─────────────────────────────┐
│  Cartographer (entry-level) │
└─────────────────────────────┘
```

Position Description

Cartography is the scientific discipline that deals with the making of maps, which are visual representations of locations anywhere on the Earth. Maps may be static maps (paper maps or maps bound in atlases) or digital maps that are displayed on computer monitors. Individuals, government officials, businesses, corporations, and others use different types of maps to help them solve problems and make important decisions.

Cartographers make various types of maps. Probably the most familiar types are navigational maps (such as street maps and nautical charts) and topographic maps, which show the physical features of an area. Cartographers also create statistical maps which are based on quantitative data. For example, Cartographers may create several maps of a state in which each map shows a different breakdown (such as age, sex, or ethnic background) of the population of that state. The data for these maps are based on state census

reports. In addition, Cartographers make maps that depict relationships among various levels and layers of geographic information. For example, a Cartographer might make a map that shows the voting precincts of a city, how many voters in each precinct are members of a particular political party, and the income levels of the voters.

As mapmakers, Cartographers work alone or with others to create and produce a map. The map-making process involves several stages. The first phase starts with Cartographers drawing up general guidelines, which may include discussing requirements with those who came up with the original idea. The next stage is conducting research. Cartographers collect, analyze, and interpret geographic data that is to be presented on the maps. They rarely do fieldwork; that is to go and view the places that they map. They gather most of their data from geodetic surveys, aeronautical photographs, statistical reports, existing maps, and other records. In addition, Cartographers obtain data by such automation techniques as GPS (Global Positioning Systems) satellites which can pinpoint any position on Earth, or GIS (geographic information systems) data banks.

Next, Cartographers research the best way to visualize and present the geographic information so that map readers can easily understand how to use the map. Cartographers then develop the graphic design for a map. They make decisions on the scale and size of a map, what the layout should look like, what shapes the symbols should be, what type of lettering should be used, and so forth.

The production phase usually goes through several stages, starting with drawing or revising the base map, then adding the layers of geographic information. Today, most Cartographers create maps on computers with graphics and mapping software. Maps are edited throughout the production phase to ensure that no errors have been made. Cartographers check that maps are drawn accurately, names are typed correctly, symbols are positioned in the right place, and so on. Cartographers who perform the editing function exclusively are sometimes known as cartographic editors or map editors.

Most people think of Cartographers as solely being map makers, but they are also research scientists. Some Cartographers conduct basic research to seek further scientific knowledge about maps and the map-making process. For example, some research Cartographers are interested in understanding the process involved in reading maps. Other research Cartographers are involved in research and development. They apply findings of basic research to create more effective map designs, develop new techniques, or develop new map products.

Some Cartographers are adjunct instructors or full-time professors at colleges and universities. Along with teaching cartography courses, they teach classes in geography or other earth science disciplines. Full-time professors usually divide their time among such activities as conducting independent research projects, planning and teaching courses, advising students, supervising student research projects, performing administrative tasks, writing scholarly works, and participating in community service.

All Cartographers are responsible for keeping up with developments in their field and updating their skills. They read professional journals and books, network with colleagues, attend professional conventions, and so on.

Salaries

Salaries vary, depending on such factors as education, experience, and geographical location. In 2001, the estimated salary for most mapping scientists ranged between $25,060 and $66,030, according to the Bureau of Labor Statistics.

Employment Prospects

Major federal government employers of Cartographers include the U.S. Geological Survey, the National Oceanic and Atmospheric Administration, the Bureau of Land Management, the Army Corps of Engineers, the Forest Service, the National Imagery and Mapping Agency, and the Federal Emergency Management Agency. At the local and state government levels, Cartographers are employed by planning and zoning departments, public works departments, transportation departments, law enforcement agencies, and departments of natural resources. In the private sector, Cartographers find work with engineering firms, construction firms, surveying companies, media companies, mapping companies, utilities, transportation providers, software development companies, and so on. Many Cartographers also work for academic institutions and nonprofit organizations. Some Cartographers are self-employed.

Most opportunities will be created to replace Cartographers who retire, resign, or transfer to other positions.

Advancement Prospects

Mapmakers and research scientists can pursue management and administrative positions, such as becoming project leaders, department or program managers, and executive officers. Professors can advance in rank (assistant, associate, and full professor) as well as by obtaining job tenure.

Education and Training

Traditionally, entrants into this field have been employed as technicians, aides, or trainees and learned on the job, working up to the position of Cartographer. Today, formal training is the more typical path into this field. Many employers require that Cartographers hold a bachelor's or master's degree in cartography, geography, civil engineering, surveying engineering, or a related field. For research positions, a master's or doctoral degree is generally required. A doctoral degree is usually required to teach in four-year colleges and universities, to conduct independent research, and to advance to top management positions.

Experience, Skills, and Personality Traits

Most employers usually require that candidates have work experience related to the position for which they are applying. Candidates for entry-level positions may have acquired their experience through part-time work, internships, research projects, and so forth. Applicants for research scientist and professor positions may be expected to have a few years of postdoctoral experience.

Cartographers need a basic foundation in math, computer science, geography, and GIS (geographic information systems). In addition, they need good interpersonal, organizational, analytical, and self-management skills, such as the ability to prioritize tasks, be able to meet deadlines, and handle stressful situations.

Some personality traits that successful Cartographers share are being imaginative, artistic, adaptable, detail-oriented, accurate, precise, and patient.

Unions and Associations

Most Cartographers join professional societies to take advantage of professional services such as education programs, networking opportunities, and professional publications. Some associations that serve their interests are the Cartography and Geographic Information Society (which is part of the American Congress on Surveying and Mapping), the Association of American Geographers Cartography Specialty Group, and the American Geological Institute. See Appendix III for contact information.

Tips for Entry

1. Talk with various Cartographers to learn about the work they do, how they got to their present position, what types of software they use, and other aspects of their jobs.

2. Some experts report that there will be less of a need for entry-level Cartographers who have only manual mapping and drafting skills. Thus, get as much training as possible (and keep updating your skills) in computer science, GIS, and GPS.

3. Contact local, regional, or state branches of professional associations for information about scholarships, internships, fellowships, and employment.

4. Use the Internet to learn more about cartography. To get a list of relevant websites to read, enter the keyword *cartography* or *cartographers* in any search engine.

MATHEMATICS

MATHEMATICIAN

CAREER PROFILE

Duties: Conduct basic or applied research; design and conduct research projects; may teach college or university students; perform duties as required of position

Alternate Title(s): Theoretical Mathematician, Applied Mathematician, Research Scientist; a title that reflects a specialty such as Operations Research Analyst or Bioinformatician

Salary Range: $27,000 to $110,000

Employment Prospects: Good

Advancement Prospects: Good

Prerequisites:

Education or Training—Master's or doctoral degree in mathematics or related field

Experience—Postdoctoral experience may be required

Special Skills and Personality Traits—Computer programming, problem-solving, writing, communication, interpersonal, and teamwork skills; imaginative; intuitive; curious; persistent; logical; flexible

Licensure/Certification—None required

CAREER LADDER

```
┌─────────────────────────────────┐
│      Senior Mathematician        │
└─────────────────────────────────┘

┌─────────────────────────────────┐
│ Mathematician (Research Scientist)│
└─────────────────────────────────┘

┌─────────────────────────────────┐
│  Postdoctoral Research Associate │
└─────────────────────────────────┘
```

Position Description

Mathematics is a branch of science. It has been described as being one of the oldest and most basic scientific disciplines. Mathematics is the study of measurement, properties (characteristics), and relationships of quantities and sets (collections of items). It is based purely on logic.

Mathematicians are involved in two general areas of study—theoretical mathematics and applied mathematics. Theoretical Mathematicians are engaged in conducting basic research to gain new knowledge and understanding of mathematics. They are interested in exploring axioms and learning what happens when mathematical rules are followed or what happens when they are not followed. They discover new mathematical patterns, reveal unknown relationships, develop new principles of mathematics, and even create new mathematics.

Applied Mathematicians conduct basic and applied research in various other fields—such as physics, aerospace, astronomy, agriculture, biotechnology, computer science, environmental science, medicine, and business. They apply mathematical principles, algorithms, and computational techniques to solve problems in science, health, engineering, economics, finance, and so on. For example, applied Mathematicians might address such questions as: What effects would certain drugs have on curing cancer? What is the most cost-effective way to produce canned vegetables? How many voters might approve a state bond to raise $500 million for new schools? What will the global climate look like in 50 years?

Applied Mathematicians construct mathematical models on computers to help them solve problems. Mathematical models are equations that describe the components of a problem and their relationship to each other. The variables of an equation represent the components in the problem. By assigning different values to the variables, Mathematicians can create simulations to see how alternative solutions might work.

Mathematicians typically specialize in one of the subdisciplines of applied mathematics. The following are a few of the different types of Applied Mathematicians.

• Bioinformaticians manage and analyze biological data stored in computer databases

- Cryptologists analyze and decipher encryption systems that transmit messages in code
- Statisticians analyze and interpret collections of numerical data
- Actuaries examine the financial risk, uncertainties, and probabilities of future events for organizations
- Operations research analysts examine problems related to the allocation of scarce resources (people, equipment, facilities, and money) in organizations

Theoretical and Applied Mathematicians work in offices and laboratories. They perform various duties, which include designing research projects, reviewing scientific literature, analyzing and interpreting data, writing reports, meeting with colleagues, preparing presentations, performing administrative tasks, and so on.

Mathematicians normally work on more than one research project at a time. They often collaborate on projects with other mathematicians as well as with scientists and engineers. Those who conduct independent research are usually responsible for seeking grants from the federal government and other sources to fund their research projects. This involves writing grant proposals that describe goals, methodologies, budgets, and other aspects about their proposed projects.

Most Theoretical Mathematicians and many Applied Mathematicians hold teaching appointments in colleges and universities. They are responsible for teaching courses along with conducting independent research. They also advise students as well as supervise students with their research projects. In addition, faculty perform administrative duties, produce scholarly work, and fulfill community service obligations. In some four-year colleges, professors may be appointed to only teach mathematics courses.

Salaries

Salaries vary, depending on such factors as education, experience, employer, and geographical locations. According to the Bureau of Labor Statistics, the estimated annual salary in 2001 for most Mathematicians ranged between $37,250 and $110,100. The estimated annual salary for most postsecondary mathematics instructors ranged between $27,300 and $88,680.

Employment Prospects

Mathematicians are employed by academic institutions, government agencies, research institutes, and nonprofit organizations. They also work throughout the private sector in such organizations as computer service firms, computer and electronics manufacturers, energy companies, defense contractors, insurance companies, banks, financial services firms, transportation services, aerospace companies, pharmaceutical companies, and engineering research groups.

Competition for Mathematician opportunities is keen. Job openings generally become available as Mathematicians retire or transfer to other positions. (Keep in mind that many Mathematicians in industry and government are known by other job titles, such as operations research analysts, or are hired in related fields such as computer programming.)

With a background in mathematics, individuals can pursue careers as computer scientists, computer programmers, software developers, engineers, school teachers, financial analysts, economists, lawyers, physicians, and so on.

Advancement Prospects

Mathematicians with management and administrative interests can pursue advancement to such positions in any work setting. For example, research scientists in industry or government settings may advance by becoming project leaders, program directors, and executive officers. Professors receive promotional rankings as assistant professors, associate professors, or full professors.

Education and Training

Depending on the employer, Mathematicians must possess either a bachelor's or advanced degree in mathematics or a related field. The minimum requirement for an entry-level position in the federal government is a bachelor's degree. A master's or doctoral degree is required for most research positions in private industry, although employers may hire individuals with a bachelor's degree if they have qualifying work experience. Doctoral degrees are usually required to teach in universities and colleges, to conduct independent research, and to obtain top management positions.

Experience, Skills, and Personality Traits

In general, employers look for applicants who have relevant work experience. Entry-level applicants may have gained experience through research projects, internships, fellowships, part-time employment, and so on. Industry employers prefer candidates who are knowledgeable about related sciences and who have experience working in the employers' particular settings. Many employers prefer or require that Ph.D. applicants for research scientist positions have a few years of postdoctoral experience.

Mathematicians in any setting should be knowledgeable about computer programming and have excellent problem-solving skills. In addition, they should have strong writing, communication, interpersonal, and teamwork skills. Mathematicians must be able to work well with others and present ideas and solutions clearly to colleagues and others.

Being imaginative, intuitive, curious, persistent, logical, and flexible are some personality traits that successful Mathematicians share.

Unions and Associations

Mathematicians can join local, state, and national professional associations to take advantage of an array of services and resources such as education programs and networking opportunities. Some national societies that serve the different interests of Mathematicians are:

- Mathematical Association of America
- American Mathematical Society
- Society for Industrial and Applied Mathematics
- American Statistical Association
- Society of Actuaries
- Association for Women in Mathematics

Faculty members might join societies that serve academic interests such as the National Association of Scholars or the American Association of University Professors. See Appendix III for contact information.

Tips for Entry

1. Talk with college professors, career counselors, and professionals in the various fields to learn about the different career options that are available in applied mathematics.
2. Many employers go to college and university job fairs and career days to recruit for entry-level positions.
3. Most professional societies have career development pages on their websites which may include job listings. Many universities, corporations, research institutes, and other organizations post current vacancies as well as provide information about their application process and working environments.
4. Use the Internet to learn more about Mathematicians. Some websites you might visit are the Young Mathematicians Network, http://www.youngmath.org; American Mathematical Society, http://www.ams.org; and Mathematical Association of America, http://www.maa.org.

STATISTICIAN

CAREER PROFILE

Duties: Conduct basic and applied research; may teach college and university students; applied statisticians collect, organize, analyze, and interpret statistical data and present statistical information to nonstatisticians; perform duties as required of position

Alternate Title(s): Mathematical Statistician; Applied Statistician, Research Analyst; a title that reflects a specialty, such as Biostatistician, Marketing Researcher, or Demographer

Salary Range: $29,000 to $90,000

Employment Prospects: Good

Advancement Prospects: Good

Prerequisites:

Education or Training—Advanced degree in statistics or related field

Experience—Work experience relevant to position one is applying for is required

Special Skills and Personality Traits—Computer programming, communication, interpersonal, teamwork, and writing skills; well-organized; detail-oriented; methodical; practical

Licensure/Certification—None required

CAREER LADDER

```
┌─────────────────────────────────┐
│      Senior Statistician         │
└─────────────────────────────────┘

┌─────────────────────────────────┐
│         Statistician             │
└─────────────────────────────────┘

┌─────────────────────────────────┐
│ Postdoctoral Research Associate or │
│ Applied Statistician (entry-level) │
└─────────────────────────────────┘
```

Position Description

Statistics is a branch of mathematics. It involves the collection, organization, analysis, and interpretation of large masses of numerical, or statistical, data about a particular subject. For example, Statisticians might derive statistical data from reading test scores of all third graders in a state, measurements of the air temperature for a city over a 20-year period, answers from a salary survey of an organization's 5,000 members, or results from experiments done for a geophysics study. Statistical information is used by scientists, engineers, financial analysts, educators, policy makers, and many others for different reasons—to help solve problems, design projects, evaluate programs, make policy decisions, predict future events, and so on.

Statisticians are involved in both basic and applied research. Those Statisticians known as Mathematical Statisticians are engaged in theoretical research. They are interested in gaining new knowledge and understanding of statistics. Many work on developing new analytical methods, sampling techniques, or new computational approaches. Others focus on developing and designing new tools such as software statistical programs.

A large number of Statisticians are applied Statisticians, who conduct basic and applied research in various work settings. They are usually team members of research projects with scientists, engineers, and others. They apply statistical techniques to problems in biology, medicine, agriculture, pharmacology, education, criminal justice, psychology, economics, meteorology, engineering, and other fields. For example, government Statisticians might develop and analyze surveys that measure job growth or public transportation ridership. Statisticians at a pharmaceutical company might evaluate the results of clinical trials to determine if new medications are safe. Statisticians with an environmental group might analyze data about the number of animals in an ecosystem over a certain period of time.

Statisticians' duties include meeting with other team members to learn about their data needs and to determine the most appropriate statistical techniques to use. Statisticians then design the surveys or experiments that will be used to collect the data. Statisticians are also responsible for collecting and processing the data, which may involve supervising assistants and technicians.

Applied Statisticians review and interpret the numerical data. They use computers and statistical software to help them organize and analyze data more efficiently. They sometimes need to develop new statistical computer programs in order to complete their projects.

Applied Statisticians make sure that they produce statistical data that is accurate, unbiased, and trustworthy. Using clear, concrete language that nonstatisticians can understand, Statisticians present the information in written reports, tables, charts, graphics, or other formats.

Many applied Statisticians specialize in a particular field, such as economics, agriculture or biological sciences. Some Statisticians work as consultants. They may provide services to specific industries or specialize in particular statistical methods. In many work settings, applied Statisticians are known by other job titles such as research scientist or research analyst. Some have professional designations that describe the specific area or field in which they work—marketing researcher, biostatistician, demographer, or quality control specialist, for example.

Statisticians in universities and colleges are usually appointed as faculty members. Thus, along with conducting independent research projects, they teach courses to undergraduate and graduate students. They also are responsible for advising students and supervising them with their research projects. In addition, faculty members are required to perform administrative duties, produce scholarly work, and fulfill community service obligations.

All Statisticians are responsible for updating their skills and keeping up with new developments. They attend professional meetings and conferences, enroll in seminars and workshops, read professional literature, network with colleagues, and so forth.

Salaries
Salaries vary, depending on factors such as education, experience, position, employer, and geographical location. The estimated annual salary for most Statisticians in 2001 ranged between $29,400 and $90,010, according to the Bureau of Labor Statistics.

Employment Prospects
Statisticians are mostly employed in government and private industry. Some are employed as academic faculty in universities and colleges.

Job prospects should be good for Statisticians who have additional background or training in another field such as biological science, finance, engineering, or economics. In general, most opportunities become available as Statisticians retire or transfer to other positions.

Many employers in industry hire qualified Statisticians for positions in quality control, systems analysis, business analysis, market research, operations research, software development, and other areas.

Advancement Prospects
Statisticians can advance to supervisory and management positions, as they gain more technical skills and experience. Having advanced degrees may improve chances for advancement opportunities. The top goal for some Statisticians is to become consultants.

Education and Training
For research positions, Statisticians usually need a master's or doctoral degree in statistics, mathematics, or another related field. Many entry-level positions in the federal government require only a bachelor's degree. To teach in four-year colleges and universities, Statisticians must possess a doctoral degree.

Experience, Skills, and Personality Traits
In general, employers look for candidates who have relevant work experience, preferably in their industry or work setting. Entry-level applicants may have gained experience through research projects, internships, fellowships, part-time employment, and so on. In addition, Statisticians need to be familiar with or knowledgeable about the subject matter with which they are working. For example, Statisticians in pharmaceutical firms must be familiar with pharmaceutical terminology and processes in order to handle the data.

Statisticians must have computer programming skills and be familiar with appropriate statistical software. Statisticians need strong communication skills, as they must be able to explain technical information to individuals without statistical backgrounds. In addition, Statisticians need excellent interpersonal and teamwork skills. Further, Statisticians should have good writing skills.

Being well-organized, detail-oriented, methodical, and practical are some personality traits that describe successful Statisticians.

Unions and Associations
Statisticians join professional associations to take advantage of networking opportunities, job listings, education programs, and other professional services and resources. The American Statistical Association, the Institute of Mathematical Statistics, and the Caucus for Women in Statistics are a few societies that serve the interests of Statisticians.

Many Statisticians join associations that serve the general population of mathematicians, such as the Mathematical

Association of America, the American Mathematical Society, or the Society for Industrial and Applied Mathematics. See Appendix III for associations' contact information.

Tips for Entry

1. Are you thinking about a career as an Applied Statistician? To enhance your employability, take some courses in the field—such as biology, economics, or sociology—that interests you. Talk with Statisticians in the field for course recommendations.

2. The U.S. government has been described as being the largest employer of statisticians in this country. You can finding job listings at the U.S. Office of Personnel Management website, http://www.usajobs.opm.gov. Some federal agencies also post employment opportunities, as well as career information at their websites. Some federal agencies you might check out include the U.S. Bureau of the Census, http:www.census.gov; the U.S. Bureau of Labor Statistics, http://www.bls.gov; the U.S. National Institutes of Health, http://www.nih.gov; and the U.S. Bureau of Justice, http://www.ojp.usdoj.gov.

3. Use the Internet to learn more about Statisticians. One website you might visit is American Statistical Association, http://www.amstat.org. To get a list of relevant websites to read, enter the keyword *statisticians* in any search engine.

OPERATIONS RESEARCH ANALYST

CAREER PROFILE

Duties: Apply scientific and mathematical principles and techniques to analyze and solve complex operational problems within organizations; perform duties as required of position

Alternate Title(s): Operations Research Specialist, Management Analyst, Systems Analyst, Systems Engineer

Salary Range: $33,000 to $92,000

Employment Prospects: Good

Advancement Prospects: Good

Prerequisites:

    Education or Training—An advanced degree in operations research or related field

    Experience—Several years of work experience in operations research, systems analysis, or related fields

    Special Skills and Personality Traits—Computer, interpersonal, teamwork, writing, and communication skills; energetic; self-motivated; hardworking; creative; tactful

    Licensure/Certification—None required

CAREER LADDER

```
┌─────────────────────────────────────┐
│  Senior Operations Research Analyst  │
└─────────────────────────────────────┘

┌─────────────────────────────────────┐
│    Operations Research Analyst       │
└─────────────────────────────────────┘

┌─────────────────────────────────────┐
│    Operations Research Analyst       │
│         (entry-level)                │
└─────────────────────────────────────┘
```

Position Description

Operations Research (OR) Analysts are applied mathematicians who study complex problems that are involved with the daily operations of organizations. They provide managers with scientific analyses that managers use to make sound decisions about program planning, scheduling, staffing, job performance measurement, inventory control, pricing, facilities layout, systems design, distribution of goods or services, marketing, and so forth.

Operations research (OR) is an interdisciplinary field that incorporates mathematics, engineering, management, and psychology. The beginning of the OR field goes back to World War II when military planners wanted to base their decisions about military operations on scientific and mathematical principles and techniques. After the war, decision makers in industry found that OR methodologies could be applied to problems in their organizations.

Today OR is also known as management science or decision technology. OR Analysts work in both the public and private sectors. They are involved in diverse areas, including criminal justice, protective service, the environment, health care, social services, transportation, energy policy, defense,

natural resources management, technology, communications, manufacturing, education, meteorology, biological sciences, and so forth.

The procedures that OR Analysts use are basically the same, regardless of their project or work setting. Their projects begin by analyzing the information that managers give them. OR Analysts define the problem in terms of the managers' goals and objectives and identify the details that they need to study. They also break down the problem into components that can be solved mathematically.

Their next step is to collect data. They read relevant materials and literature. They interview people who are involved in or affected by the issues being studied, asking for feedback about the problems as well as for suggestions for ways to solve them. OR Analysts talk to engineers and scientists, to managers and support staff, as well as to vendors and customers.

OR Analysts use various techniques to help them analyze and interpret the data, including statistics, stochastic, queuing theory, network analysis, optimization, and so on. They select the OR methodology that most effectively addresses a problem and helps them find alternative solutions. For example, if an OR Analyst is addressing a question about how to keep lines flowing smoothly in supermarkets, he might use the queuing theory. If a problem involves scheduling bus routes for a city bus system, an OR Analyst might use the mathematical technique called network analysis. Sometimes OR Analysts use a combination of two or more methods to find solutions.

An OR Analyst's work involves constructing mathematical models, or mathematical equations that describe the behavior of the problems being studied. A mathematical equation describes the components of a problem and their relationship to each other. The variables of an equation represent the components in the problem. By assigning different values to the variables, OR Analysts can create simulations to see how alternative solutions might work.

OR Analysts generally use computer programs to create their mathematical models. (They sometimes need to design a new program if one does not exist for their purposes.) With computer models, OR Analysts are able to run the program over and over, changing the values to examine what can happen under different circumstances.

Upon completion of their evaluations, OR Analysts prepare written or oral reports for management. They provide a comprehensive analysis as well as their recommendations for the suitable solutions. They present the information clearly and in language that nontechnical people can understand.

Some OR Analysts are generalists, while others specialize in particular OR methodologies. OR Analysts may work in a central OR department in an organization or be assigned to work in different departments.

OR Analysts work 40 hours a week. Many put in additional hours to meet deadlines.

Salaries

Salaries vary, depending on such factors as qualifications, employer, and geographical location. According to the Bureau of Labor Statistics, the estimated annual salary for most Operations Research Analysts in 2001 ranged from $33,180 to $91,520.

Employment Prospects

OR Analysts work in local, state, and federal government agencies, with the U.S. Armed Forces being the largest employer. In the private sector, OR Analysts find employment in such diverse areas as transportation, telecommunications, healthcare, computer and data processing services, banks, financial services, insurance, energy, manufacturing, retail, health care, and so on. Many are employed by engineering and management services firms as well as research and testing organizations that offer operations research consulting services.

Opportunities for experienced OR Analysts are strong, as managers are continually interested in improving the effectiveness and productivity of their organizations in order to stay competitive in their fields. However, the Bureau of Labor Statistics reports that few of the job openings are expected to have the title of Operations Research Analyst, but rather such titles as management analyst, systems analyst, and operations analyst.

Experienced operations research specialists with advanced degrees should have the best chances of finding employment. Opportunities are expected to be especially good in finance, manufacturing, transportation, telecommunications, and other highly competitive industries.

Advancement Prospects

OR Analysts with management and administrative ambitions can seek such positions in the different work settings. They can advance to top-level positions in the operations research departments as well as in other departments such as marketing. Some OR Analysts aspire to become independent consultants or to own consulting firms.

With additional experience and advanced degrees, OR Analysts can pursue academic careers, by teaching college students and by conducting independent research in operations management.

Education and Training

The minimum requirement for OR Analysts is a bachelor's degree in operations research, science management, mathematics, engineering, or another related field. Most employers prefer that candidates possess a master's or doctoral degree.

OR Analysts are expected to keep up with new developments in operations research and computer science. Many employers provide in-house training for entry-level and experienced OR Analysts. Some employers offer education programs that pay for OR Analysts to enroll in appropriate courses at local colleges or universities.

Experience, Skills, and Personality Traits

In general, applicants should have several years of experience working in operations research, systems analysis, or related areas. In addition, they should have experience working in the industry to which they are applying.

OR Analysts must be computer literate and be able to use various software programs, including database collection and management programs. In addition, OR Analysts must be knowledgeable about computer programming and be able to develop software programs.

OR Analysts need strong interpersonal and teamwork skills, as they must be able to work well with others. In addition, they must have good writing and communication skills in order to present information clearly and persuasively.

Being energetic, self-motivated, hardworking, creative, and tactful are some personality traits that successful OR Analysts have in common.

Unions and Associations

Many OR Analysts belong to professional associations to take advantage of professional services and resources, such as networking opportunities, education programs, and professional publications. At the national level, the Institute for Operations Research and the Management Sciences serves the particular interests of OR Analysts. They are also eligible to join societies for mathematicians such as the Mathematical Association of America, the American Mathematical Society, the Society for Industrial and Applied Mathematics, or the Association for Women in Mathematics. See Appendix III for contact information.

Tips for Entry

1. Talk with OR Analysts in different work settings to get an idea of what areas may interest you. Also ask them to recommend courses in other disciplines that may be useful for an OR career.

2. Take advantage of your college career center. Career counselors can help you find internship and employment opportunities, as well as help you build your job search techniques. College career centers usually offer services to alumni.

3. Learn more about the operations research field on the Internet. One website you might visit is Institute for Operations Research and the Management Sciences, http://www.informs.org. To get a list of other relevant websites, enter the keyword *operations research* in any search engine.

ACTUARY

CAREER PROFILE

Duties: Study the financial risk, uncertainties, and probabilities of future events; perform duties as required of position

Alternate Title(s): Actuarial Assistant, Actuarial Associate, Actuarial Consultant

Salary Range: $39,000 to $133,000

Employment Prospects: Good

Advancement Prospects: Good

Prerequisites:

Education or Training—A bachelor's degree in mathematics, actuarial science, or related field

Experience—Previous work experience may not be necessary for entry-level positions; completion of one or more actuarial examinations is preferred or required

Special Skills and Personality Traits—Project management, problem-solving, teamwork, interpersonal, communication, and computer skills; analytical; flexible; self-motivated; enthusiastic; creative

Licensure/Certification—None required

CAREER LADDER

```
┌─────────────────────────────────────┐
│  Senior Actuary, Department Manager, │
│        or Actuarial Consultant       │
└─────────────────────────────────────┘

┌─────────────────────────────────────┐
│              Actuary                 │
└─────────────────────────────────────┘

┌─────────────────────────────────────┐
│         Actuarial Assistant          │
└─────────────────────────────────────┘
```

Position Description

Actuaries are experts in identifying financial risk, uncertainties, and probabilities that could occur in the future. Most of them work in the fields of insurance, pension plans, and financial investments. Using mathematics, statistics, and financial theory, Actuaries provide their employers with financial strategies and forecasts that can help them make important business decisions. Actuaries also help employers create programs that would be able to handle future financial loss.

Actuaries work on a wide range of different projects, which vary depending on their experience and work setting. For example, they might:

- determine what price or rate at which a product should be sold
- calculate potential profits and losses for a new product or program
- project the cost of a loss over a number of years
- determine the financial risk involved in a business merger or acquisition
- estimate the financial loss for an employer if a natural or man-made disaster should occur

- determine the amount of reserves needed to cover future losses
- appraise the current value of an organization, a particular program, or specific inventory
- design new products or programs
- establish rating guidelines and risk categories
- estimate future cash flows, earnings, taxes, assets, and liabilities
- develop investment strategies
- determine prices for products and services that their employers sell

Actuaries gather, analyze, and interpret data from various sources. They read numerical information, historical data, laws and regulations, trends, and so on. They develop mathematical models to help them analyze problems. Actuaries then discuss their findings with executives, attorneys, marketing staff, and other employees.

Actuaries may provide expert witness testimony at court trials, depositions, administrative hearings, legislative hearings, and alternative dispute resolution hearings. For example, an Actuary might provide testimony about the value of a pension plan in a divorce case, while another Actuary might testify at an administrative hearing about how proposed regulation would affect business.

Actuaries are responsible for keeping up with current legislation, economic and social trends, and developments in their industry.

Actuaries work a standard 40-hour week.

Salaries

Salaries vary, depending on such factors as experience, qualifications, employer, and geographical location. According to the Bureau of Labor Statistics, the estimated annual salary in 2001 for most Actuaries ranged between $38,810 and $132,630.

Employment Prospects

Some employers of Actuaries are insurance companies, banks, financial service firms, health maintenance organizations (HMOs), government agencies, and corporations.

According to the Bureau of Labor Statistics seven out of 10 Actuaries work for insurance companies. (Insurance Actuaries specialize in the different areas of insurance—life, health, property, casualty, or workers' compensation.) The Bureau of Labor Statistics reports that the job growth for Actuaries is slowing in the insurance field. The best opportunities are expected to be found in the computer and data processing services, health services, and management and actuarial consulting industries.

Job opportunities generally become available as Actuaries retire, transfer to other positions, or leave the workforce for various reasons.

Advancement Prospects

Actuaries obtain professional status by passing a series of examinations that are administered by actuary associations. There are two professional levels. The first level is the Associate designation, which takes most Actuaries three to five years to achieve. The higher level is the Fellow designation, which takes a few more years to complete for those who are interested.

Actuaries can advance to supervisory, management, and executive positions, based on their experience, job performance, and professional status (Associate or Fellow). They can also advance by pursuing management positions in other departments of their companies. For example, insurance Actuaries might be appointed to managerial roles in underwriting, accounting, marketing, or other departments. Actuaries can also follow a career path as independent consultants or business owners that provide actuarial services.

Education and Training

Many Employers require or prefer that Actuaries hold a bachelor's degree in mathematics, actuarial science, business, finance, statistics, or another related field. Employers may hire candidates with a non-math degree if they have passed one or more actuarial examinations.

Employers provide on-the-job training for entry-level positions. Many employers have education programs to help Actuaries study for their actuarial examinations.

Experience, Skills, and Personality Traits

Requirements vary from employer to employer for entry-level positions. Employers often hire college graduates with little or no experience, if they can demonstrate strong mathematical and technical aptitudes as well as good business sense. Many employers prefer (or require) that candidates have completed one or more actuarial examinations.

Actuaries must have excellent project management skills. They also need strong problem-solving, teamwork, and interpersonal skills. Having communication skills is important for their job, too. They must be able to explain complex technical concepts in terms that are clearly understood. In addition, Actuaries should have computer skills, with the ability to use such programs as word processing, spreadsheets, statistical analysis, and database manipulation.

Some personality traits that successful Actuaries share are being analytical, flexible, self-motivated, enthusiastic, and creative.

Special Requirements

To gain professional status, an Actuary must obtain the Associate credential. The Casualty Actuarial Society grants the professional credential to those in the property and casualty practices. The Society of Actuaries grants the credential to those who practice in life insurance, health insurance, finance, investments, or pension plans. Professional certifications are obtained on a voluntary basis.

Actuaries who practice in pension plans that are governed by federal laws must be enrolled in the Joint Board for the Enrollment of Actuaries. For further information, write to the Joint Board for the Enrollment of Actuaries, Internal Revenue Service, N:C:SC:DOP, 1111 Constitution Avenue, NW, Washington, D.C. 20224. Or call (202) 694-1891, or fax (202) 694-1876. To access their web site, go to http://www.irs.gov. Click on the *tax professionals* link, and then click on the link for *enrolled actuaries*.

Unions and Associations

Actuaries can join professional associations to take advantage of networking opportunities, education programs, and other services and resources. Some national societies that serve the interests of actuaries include the American Academy of Actuaries, the American Society of Pension Actuaries, the Casualty Actuarial Society, the Conference of

Consulting Actuaries, and the Society of Actuaries. See Appendix III for contact information.

Tips for Entry

1. As a college student, obtain internships to see if the actuarial field is right for you. Visit your college career center for help in finding internships.

2. You can enhance your employability for entry-level positions by passing one or more actuarial examinations while still in college.

3. Learn more about Actuary careers on the Internet. Two websites to visit are Actuary.com, http://www.actuary.com; and Be an Actuary, http://www.BeAnActuary.com.

COMPUTER SCIENCE

COMPUTER SCIENTIST

CAREER PROFILE

Duties: Conduct basic or applied research; design and conduct research projects; may teach college or university students; perform duties as required of position

Alternate Title(s): Research Scientist; a title that reflects a specialty such as Artificial Intelligence Scientist

Salary Range: $29,000 to $119,000

Employment Prospects: Good

Advancement Prospects: Good

Prerequisites:

Education or Training—A master's or doctoral degree in computer science or a related field

Experience—Previous work and research experience related to the position being applied for

Special Skills and Personality Traits—Communication, writing, analytical, interpersonal, and self-management skills; analytical; detail-oriented; persistent; creative; innovative

Licensure/Certification—None required

CAREER LADDER

```
┌─────────────────────────────┐
│   Senior Computer Scientist  │
└─────────────────────────────┘

┌─────────────────────────────┐
│      Computer Scientist      │
└─────────────────────────────┘

┌─────────────────────────────┐
│ Postdoctoral Research Associate │
└─────────────────────────────┘
```

Position Description

Computer Scientists are researchers and inventors. They are involved in the study and design of computers and computational processes. They are interested in understanding the foundations (algorithms and theories) upon which the operation and design of computers and computer systems are based. They are also concerned with understanding the computational processes for handling and managing large masses of information. Furthermore, they create computer hardware, software, and information technologies that are used in medicine, science, biotechnology, agriculture, education, law, space travel, energy, protective services, business, finance, and other areas.

Computer Scientists conduct basic and applied research in academic, government, and industrial settings. Their work involves developing mathematical models as well as building computational artifacts (such as computer chips, operating systems, computing programs, and robots) to analyze and test their theories. Those who are involved in basic research pursue new knowledge and understanding of computing processes and computer systems. Applied researchers, on the other hand, are engaged in the research and development of new and improved computer products that solve specific problems in computer science and in other disciplines.

Although it is a relatively young discipline, computer science has been evolving rapidly since its beginnings in the 1940s. As new computer technologies are discovered, new subdisciplines emerge. Research Computer Scientists typically focus their studies in one or more areas. Some subdisciplines include computer theory and algorithms, numerical analysis, learning theory, computer architecture, programming languages, software engineering, operating systems, communications and networking, data mining, database systems, information management, computer security, cryptography, artificial intelligence, robotics, human and computer interaction, computational biology, computer graphics, mobile computing, and electronic commerce. In addition, Computer Scientists conduct studies that are connected to research in other disciplines such as biology, economics, mechanics, physics, art, and medicine.

Academic researchers typically choose the types of projects that they wish to explore while government and industrial researchers generally conduct research that meets the missions of their employers. Many Computer Scientists work on team projects, collaborating with other Computer Scientists who are experts in their particular subdisciplines. They also work with other scientists, engineers, technologists, and technicians. Senior research scientists may be involved in leading team projects or research divisions.

Computer Scientists work in offices and laboratories. They perform a wide range of tasks that vary each day. For example, they design research projects, gather research data, read research studies, conduct experiments or develop models, analyze and interpret data, write reports, attend meetings, provide consulting services, and perform administrative tasks. Independent researchers are usually responsible for writing grant proposals and seeking out grants to fund their research projects.

Computer Scientists are expected to share the results of their research with their colleagues. They may write scientific papers or make presentations at scientific meetings. Some scientists develop websites to disseminate their research data. Further, Computer Scientists are responsible for keeping up with new technologies and developments. They read professional journals and books, enroll in workshops and seminars, attend professional conferences, network with colleagues, and so on.

Some Computer Scientists teach academic courses in computer science, electrical engineering, or other areas. They may be hired as adjunct (part-time) instructors or full-time professors. In addition to their research and teaching duties, full-time faculty members are responsible for producing scholarly work and performing administrative and community service duties.

Computer Scientists occasionally work long hours, including weekends, to compete various tasks and to meet deadlines.

Salaries
Salaries vary, depending on education, experience, employer, geographical location, and other factors. In 2001, the estimated annual salary for most research Computer Scientists ranged between $42,590 and $119,150 according to the Bureau of Labor Statistics.

The 2000–01 Taulbee survey, completed by the Computing Research Association, reports that the annual salary for faculty who are new doctorate holders ranged from $28,500 to $108,000. Respondents included postdoctoral fellows, tenured faculty, and nontenured faculty.

Employment Prospects
Computer Scientists find employment in a variety of settings in the private and public sectors. Opportunities become available each year as Computer Scientists retire, advance to higher positions, or transfer to other occupations. In addition, new positions are created each year to meet the growing needs of employers.

Advancement Prospects
Computer Scientists can advance to administrative and management positions as project leaders, program managers, and research division directors. Professors receive promotional rankings as assistant professors, associate professors, or full professors.

Computer Scientists with entrepreneurial ambitions may become independent consultants or owners of start-up companies that offer consulting or other computing services, produce computer hardware or software, or sell computer products.

Education and Training
Computer Scientists generally hold a master's or doctoral degree in computer science, computer engineering, or a related field. Industrial employers may hire candidates with only a bachelor's degree if they have several years of extensive experience. To teach in colleges and universities, conduct independent research, or to advance to top-level management positions, a doctoral degree is usually required.

Computer science students are trained in the basic concepts and techniques of computing, algorithms, and computer design. Doctorate programs in computer science normally take between four and six years to complete, which includes completing an independent research project.

Experience, Skills, and Personality Traits
Employers generally choose candidates who have previous work experience and have completed relevant research studies. Entry-level applicants may have gained experience through research projects, internships, part-time employment, and so on. Employers may require that candidates have completed a few years of postdoctoral training. Candidates for industry positions should have some related industry experience or a background in business or economics.

Computer Scientists have strong communication and writing skills as well as excellent analytical and interpersonal skills. In addition, they have good self-management skills—the ability to organize and prioritize tasks, meet deadlines, work independently, work well with others, and so on. Being analytical, detail-oriented, persistent, creative, and innovative are some personality traits that successful Computer Scientists share.

Unions and Associations
Various local, state, and national societies serve the different professional interests of Computer Scientists. They offer networking opportunities, education programs, certification programs, job listings, and other professional services and resources. Some professional associations that serve the general interests of Computer Scientists include the Association for Computing Machinery, the IEEE Computer Society, and the Association for Women in Computing. (See Appendix III for contact information.)

Academic Computer Scientists might also join societies that serve academic interests such as the National Association of Scholars or the American Association for Higher Education.

Tips for Entry

1. Take advantage of internship or work-study programs at your college. Ask your college adviser, professors, college career counselors, and others about available internship programs. Also contact companies or government agencies that you're interesting in working for to learn about available programs.

2. Many employers recruit prospective candidates at college job fairs. Bring copies of your résumé, and be ready to handle job interviews. Also be sure to get business cards of recruiters so that you can contact them later for further information.

3. Learn more about the research world of Computer Scientists on the Internet. Here are some websites that you might visit: Computing Research Association, http://www.cra.org; Association for Computing Machinery, http://www.acm.org; and IEEE Computer Society, http://www.computer.org.

SOFTWARE ENGINEER

Duties: Conduct basic or applied research; develop and design software products; may maintain software systems; may teach college and university students; perform duties as required of position

Alternate Title(s): Software Developer, Research Software Engineer

Salary Range: $44,000 to $119,000

Employment Prospects: Good

Advancement Prospects: Good

Prerequisites:

Education or Training—A bachelor's or advanced degree in software engineering

Experience—Previous experience, including experience with appropriate programming languages and operating systems

Special Skills and Personality Traits—Communication, interpersonal, teamwork, analytical, problem-solving, writing, and self-management skills; creative; persistent; goal-oriented; enthusiastic; self-motivated

Licensure/Certification—Professional Engineer (P.E.) licensure may be required

```
┌─────────────────────────────────┐
│    Senior Software Engineer     │
└─────────────────────────────────┘

┌─────────────────────────────────┐
│       Software Engineer         │
└─────────────────────────────────┘

┌─────────────────────────────────┐
│  Software Engineer (entry-level) │
└─────────────────────────────────┘
```

Position Description

Software Engineers are involved in the research, production, and maintenance of computer software products. These products provide the instructions that allow computers to operate automatically as well as to perform the various tasks (such as word processing) required by computer users. Software Engineers are responsible for creating software products that are of high quality and are cost-effective. They ensure that software products are reliable and make computers perform predictably, efficiently, and safely.

Applying principles and techniques of computer science, engineering, and mathematics, Software Engineers are involved in the development of different types of software products for personal computers, mainframe computers, supercomputers, and embedded computers. They create software for computer operating systems, which instruct computers to perform basic functions, such as starting up and shutting down, using the keyboard or other input tools, and transferring data from memory to the hard drive.

Software Engineers also develop application software which allows users to perform specific activities on their computers such as create pictures and designs, do word processing or complex calculations, make spreadsheets, access the Internet, create websites, organize and manage data, and so on.

Software Engineers design application software that includes single programs (such as a font management program) as well as software packages that are a small collection of programs that work together to accomplish a particular task (such as a photo-editing system). They also create software suites which are comprised of several independent programs and software packages that share a common use or data format. For example, Software Engineers might develop a design suite that integrates drawing, graphics design, photo-editing, web development, text-editing, and other programs.

In addition, Software Engineers are involved with designing software for the various computer systems used in scientific research, businesses, government operations, protective services, legal systems, education, banking and financial services, medical care and medical systems, utilities, telecommunications, transportation, space exploration, manufacturing, and other areas. For example, Software Engineers might develop a software system for a law firm that can be used for accounting, payroll, legal, and other independent applications.

Software Engineers generally work as part of a software development team that may include computer engineers, marketing specialists, manufacturing personnel, graphic designers, and others. Software development, whether for software or software systems, is comprised of several stages—product research and development, software design, programming, and quality assurance and testing. Software Engineers may be involved in the whole life cycle of the development of a product or with only certain aspects of the cycle. They may also be involved in creating documentation (such as operating manuals and help screens) that aids users in the operation of software products.

Software Engineers are sometimes confused with computer programmers. Software programs are lines of codes that are written in special programming languages, such as C++ and Java. Computer programmers are responsible for writing these codes, following the specifications created by Software Engineers. Software Engineers possess programming skills and may do programming as part of their duties.

Many Software Engineers are involved with project management, which includes such duties as planning projects, writing proposals, administering budgets, and coordinating schedules. Project managers also provide training and supervision for computer programmers, technicians, and other staff members.

Some Software Engineers, called system Software Engineers, work in organizations. Along with designing software systems for their employers, they may be responsible for maintaining the software systems. They coordinate the specific software needs of different departments, revise and enhance software systems, plan for future software system needs, troubleshoot problems, and so forth.

Some Software Engineers are involved in basic research, working in academic, government, and industrial research laboratories. Their primary purpose is to understand the fundamental mechanisms in the development of software. Basic researchers contribute new theories, methodologies, and tools to the field.

Research Software Engineers perform a wide range of tasks that vary each day. For example, they plan and coordinate research projects, gather research data, review research literature, conduct experiments or develop models, analyze and interpret data, write reports, attend meetings, provide consulting services, perform administrative tasks, and so forth. Many Research Software Engineers collaborate on projects with other computer scientists and scientists from other disciplines. They may be involved in studies within

computer science, biotechnology, medicine, astrophysics, geology, or any other discipline.

Some Software Engineers are adjunct (part-time) instructors or full-time professors who teach software engineering courses to undergraduate, graduate, and continuing education students. Full-time faculty are typically involved in conducting independent research studies as well. In addition to their research and teaching duties, full-time faculty members are responsible for producing scholarly work, fulfilling community service obligations, and performing administrative duties.

Salaries

Salaries vary, depending on such factors as education, experience, employer, position, and geographical location. According the Bureau of Labor Statistics, the range of estimated annual salaries in 2001 is as follows:

- for most Software Engineers who develop systems software, $45,820 to $110,750
- for most Software Engineers who develop software applications, $44,380 to $109,170
- for most research computer scientists, including those who do software engineering research, $42,590 to $119,150

Employment Prospects

The largest employer of Software Engineers is the computer and data processing services industry, which includes software companies and consulting firms. Software Engineers are also employed in such other industries as banking, financial services, insurance, aerospace, transportation, communication, medicine, health care, law, education, agriculture, biotechnology, energy, utilities, and manufacturing. Software Engineers also find employment with engineering firms. Many Software Engineers are employed as faculty members in colleges and universities. Further, many Software Engineers are independent consultants.

The Bureau of Labor Statistics reports that computer Software Engineer is expected to be among the fastest growing occupations through 2010.

The demand for qualified Software Engineers to develop and design software systems and applications for new technologies should continue to create new positions with various employers. Opportunities shall also become available to replace workers who retire, advance to higher positions, or transfer to other occupations.

Advancement Prospects

Software Engineers can advance to administrative and management positions as project managers, division directors, and executive officers. Those with entrepreneurial ambitions can become independent consultants or company owners.

Education and Training

Educational requirements vary with different software engineering positions. The minimum requirement for many jobs is a bachelor's degree in software engineering, computer science, or computer engineering with an emphasis in software engineering. An advanced degree is typically required for positions in academic, government, and industrial research laboratories. To conduct independent research, advance to high-level administrative positions, or teach in academic institutions, a doctoral degree is typically required.

Many universities and colleges offer software engineering certification programs, which are usually aimed at computer programmers and other computer specialists who wish to gain knowledge and skills to switch into the software engineering field.

Throughout their careers, Software Engineers enroll in training and continuing education programs to update their skills and keep up with advancements in their field. They may complete courses, seminars, or workshops that are offered by employers, vendors, academic institutions, and professional computing societies.

Experience, Skills, and Personality Traits

In general, employers hire candidates who have experience related to the positions for which they are applying. Entry-level candidates should have about one year of qualifying work experience, which may have been gained through part-time employment, research assistantships, internships, student research projects, and so on. Additionally, candidates should be familiar with appropriate programming languages and operating systems. Employers in the private sector typically expect candidates to have experience working in their industry.

Software Engineers need strong communication, interpersonal, and teamwork skills to work well with others from different backgrounds. Additionally, they possess excellent analytical, problem-solving, and writing skills. Software Engineers also have good self-management skills, including the ability to organize and prioritize tasks, meet deadlines, work independently, and handle stressful situations.

Some personality traits that successful Software Engineers share are being creative, persistent, goal-oriented, enthusiastic, and self-motivated.

Special Requirements

There has been ongoing debate among professional societies and state engineering license boards about whether Software Engineers should be licensed or certified if they are developing critical software that affects public safety and welfare. As of April 2002, Texas requires certain Software Engineers to be licensed.

Software Engineers may obtain Professional Engineer (P.E.) licensure on a voluntary basis. Those who offer their services directly to the public may be required to be licensed. For specific licensure information, contact the board of examiners for professional engineers in the state (or Washington, D.C., or American territory) where you wish to practice.

Unions and Associations

Many Software Engineers join professional associations to take advantage of education programs, professional certification, job listings, networking opportunities, and other professional resources and services. Societies are available at the local, state, and national levels. Two national societies are the Technical Council on Software Engineering (part of IEEE Computer Society) and the Association for Computing Machinery Special Interest Group in Software Engineering. See Appendix III for contact information.

Tips for Entry

1. Join student software engineering clubs while in college. Also take advantage of student memberships with professional societies. You can begin building a network of contacts from your membership in student and professional organizations.

2. Are you interested in a career in research? Gain experience by obtaining research assistantships with professors in areas that interest you. You might also seek internships with research laboratories in government agencies or private companies.

3. Be aware that many employers use programmer, programmer/analyst, software specialist, and similar job titles for positions which entail the duties of a Software Engineer. Read job ads and listings carefully.

4. Learn more about software engineering on the Internet. Here are two websites you might visit: Software Engineering Resources (by R. S. Pressman and Associates, Inc.), http://www.rspa.com/spi; and SE Web: Software Engineering Resources from the IEEE Computer Society, http://www.computer.org/SEweb. To find other relevant websites, enter the keyword *software engineering* in any search engine.

COMPUTER HARDWARE ENGINEER

CAREER PROFILE

Duties: Conduct basic or applied research; develop and design computers and computer-related equipment; may teach college and university students; perform duties as required

Alternate Title(s): Computer Engineer, Electrical Engineer; title that reflects a specialty such as Research Engineer, Product Development Engineer, or Computer Chip Designer

Salary Range: $46,000 to $113,000

Employment Prospects: Good

Advancement Prospects: Good

Prerequisites:

Education or Training—A bachelor's or advanced degree in electrical or computer engineering

Experience—One or more years of work experience related to position applying for

Special Skills and Personality Traits—Programming, analytical, writing, communication, interpersonal, and teamwork skills; innovative; creative; detail-oriented; focused

Licensure/Certification—Professional Engineer (P.E.) licensure may be required

CAREER LADDER

```
┌─────────────────────────────────────┐
│  Senior Computer Hardware Engineer   │
└─────────────────────────────────────┘

┌─────────────────────────────────────┐
│    Computer Hardware Engineer        │
└─────────────────────────────────────┘

┌─────────────────────────────────────┐
│    Computer Hardware Engineer        │
│          (entry-level)               │
└─────────────────────────────────────┘
```

Position Description

Computer Hardware Engineers are involved in incorporating new technology to design and construct improved computers that can perform tasks more efficiently and quickly. They create different types of computers, from hand-held computers to powerful supercomputers. They also design the various parts that make up computers, such as circuit boards, processors, computer chips, networking boards, audio boards, and input tools (i.e., the mouse and keyboard). They construct monitors, printers, modems, scanners, storage units, and other computer accessories. Computer Hardware Engineers also work on embedded computers that are part of the devices which they control. Embedded computers are found in watches, cameras, electronics, appliances, medical diagnostic tools, vehicles, aircraft, spacecraft, automation systems, and communication networks.

The work of Computer Hardware Engineers involves the application of principles and techniques of engineering, computer science, and mathematics. Like other engineers, Computer Hardware Engineers are involved in one or more areas of the development and manufacture of computers and computer-related products. For example, they might:

- conduct research—applying fundamental theories and techniques to solve technical problems or develop products
- develop and design products, which involves determining the functions of proposed products, developing designs, building and testing prototypes, and so forth
- supervise the production process in the manufacturing of products
- be involved with quality assurance, which involves testing and evaluating the production process for flaws
- manage projects—planning projects, administering budgets, monitoring work schedules, supervising staff, and performing other administrative and management duties

Computer Hardware Engineers normally work as part of a team, collaborating with engineers, computer scientists, computer specialists (such as systems analysts), marketing specialists, and others. They may hold titles that describe their particular role. For instance, those involved in manufacturing may be known as production engineers while those working solely in developing new products may be called product development engineers.

Some Computer Hardware Engineers are involved with conducting basic scientific research. They are interested in adding new knowledge to the computer engineering field. They seek to develop new theories, methodologies, and technologies as well as to find practical uses for computers in medicine, biotechnology, astrophysics, and other scientific disciplines. In general, research computer engineers build chips, circuit boards, computers, and other computational artifacts to observe and test in order to understand how they work and behave. Additionally, they evaluate the effectiveness of their artifacts to solve the problems that they are studying.

Some Computer Hardware Engineers teach academic courses in computer engineering, electrical engineering, or computer science. They may be hired on a part-time or full-time basis. Most full-time faculty are responsible for designing and conducting research projects. Additionally, they advise students, supervise student research projects, produce scholarly works, fulfill community service obligations, and perform administrative duties.

Salaries
Salaries vary, depending on such factors as education, experience, employer, and geographical location. According to the Bureau of Labor Statistics, the estimated annual salary in 2001 for most Computer Hardware Engineers ranged between $45,760 and $112,830.

Employment Prospects
Computer Hardware Engineers work for computer companies as well as for businesses and firms in other industries (such as aerospace) that build or use computer systems. They are also employed by academic institutions; government agencies; and engineering, consulting, and design firms. Some Computer Hardware Engineers might be independent consultants.

The Bureau of Labor Statistics reports that job prospects are expected to be favorable for Hardware Engineers through 2010. Job growth is projected to increase by 21 to 35 percent, particularly in the computer and office equipment industries. Most job openings will become available to replace engineers who advance, transfer to other positions, retire, or leave the job force for other reasons.

Advancement Prospects
Typically, engineers with administrative and management ambitions advance to such positions as project manager, division director, and executive officer. Computer Hardware Engineers with entrepreneurial goals aim to become independent consultants or company owners.

Education and Training
Employers generally hire Computer Hardware Engineers who possess a bachelor's degree in electrical engineering or computer engineering. (Computer engineering programs include integrated course work in the foundations of electrical engineering and computer science.) Employers may hire candidates who hold a degree in computer science if they have completed appropriate course work in electrical engineering or have qualifying experience.

Many employers require an advanced degree for research positions. A doctoral degree is typically required to teach in colleges and universities, advance to high-level management positions, or conduct independent research.

Computer Hardware Engineers are expected to keep up with technological advancements and periodically update their skills. They enroll in training and continuing education programs offered by employers, vendors, academic institutions, and professional computing societies.

Experience, Skills, and Personality Traits
Requirements vary with the different positions. Job applicants must be able to demonstrate that they have work experience that is relevant to the positions for which they are applying. Candidates for industrial positions should have related industry experience or a background in business or economics. Entry-level applicants may have gained experience through research projects, internships, part-time employment, postdoctoral training, and so on.

In order to do their work well, Computer Hardware Engineers need competent programming skills, analytical skills, writing skills, and communication skills. Further, they should have strong interpersonal and teamwork skills, as they must be able to work well with professionals, technicians, managers, and others from different backgrounds. Being innovative, creative, detail-oriented, and focused are some personality traits that successful Computer Hardware Engineers have in common.

Special Requirements
Computer Hardware Engineers may be required by their employers to be licensed as Professional Engineers (P.E.) where they practice. In addition, engineers who offer their services directly to the public are required to be licensed. For specific licensure information, contact the state board of examiner for professional engineers where you wish to practice.

Many computer engineers obtain P.E. licenses voluntarily so as to enhance their employability. Entry-level engineers may apply for the Engineer-in-Training licensure.

Unions and Associations

The Association for Computing Machinery and the IEEE (Institute of Electrical and Electronics Engineers) Computer Society are two professional associations at the national level that many Computer Hardware Engineers join. Societies that serve the interests of computer engineers are also available at the local and state levels. By joining professional associations, engineers can take advantage of networking opportunities, education programs, professional publications, and other professional services and resources.

Professional engineers might join the National Society of Professional Engineers. Academic faculty members might join the National Association of Scholars, the American Association for Higher Education, or other academic societies. For contact information, see Appendix III.

Tips for Entry

1. Take advantage of internship or work-study programs that place students in computer companies or computer divisions of noncomputer firms. If a company likes your work, it may offer you a full-time position after graduation. To learn about such programs, talk with your college adviser or college career counselor. You can also ask college professors and fellow students about opportunities or contact personnel offices at companies for whom you would like to work.

2. Do some research about a company before applying or interviewing for a job there. Find out how it ranks in its industry and how well it is doing financially. Many computer and business journals and books are available to provide you with pertinent information. You can find many of these resources at your school or public library. Additionally, you can see if a company has a website on the Internet.

3. Use the Internet to learn more about computer engineering. To get a list of relevant websites to read, enter either of these keywords in a search engine: *computer hardware engineers* or *computer engineering.*

ARTIFICIAL INTELLIGENCE (AI) SCIENTIST

CAREER PROFILE

Duties: Conduct basic or applied research in artificial intelligence; may teach undergraduate or graduate students; perform duties as required

Alternate Title(s): Computer Scientist, Artificial Intelligence Researcher

Salary Range: $26,000 to $119,000

Employment Prospects: Good

Advancement Prospects: Good

Prerequisites:

Education or Training—Advanced degree in computer science or related field

Experience—One or more years of work experience, completion of research studies in the specialized areas of prospective employers

Special Skills and Personality Traits—Computer programming, writing, problem-solving, analytical, communication, interpersonal, and teamwork skills; imaginative; creative; curious; persistent; flexible; self-motivated

Licensure/Certification—None required

CAREER LADDER

```
┌─────────────────────────────────────────┐
│   Senior Artificial Intelligence Scientist │
└─────────────────────────────────────────┘

┌─────────────────────────────────────────┐
│      Artificial Intelligence Scientist    │
└─────────────────────────────────────────┘

┌─────────────────────────────────────────┐
│      Postdoctoral Research Associate       │
└─────────────────────────────────────────┘
```

Position Description

Artificial intelligence (or AI) is the scientific study of computational models that describe human thinking processes. It is a young discipline that began during the 1950s. From the start, AI Scientists believed that it would be possible for computers to one day think and behave like human beings. Several decades later, man-made creatures with humanlike minds have not yet been invented. However, much of AI research has resulted in many practical applications that people use for work and pleasure. Some examples are word processing applications, operating systems software, computer games, automation systems in factories, voice-mail systems, Internet search engines, and e-mail filtering. Other examples are computer programs that allow cameras, kitchen appliances, medical diagnostic tools, vehicles, aircraft, robotic rovers, spacecraft, and other objects to perform tasks automatically.

Artificial intelligence is a multidisciplinary endeavor that combines knowledge from computer science, mathematics, electrical engineering, logic, neuroscience, biology, philosophy, linguistics, psychology, cognitive science, physics, and other disciplines. AI Scientists develop algorithms (or mathematical equations) that explain specific characteristics of human intelligence, such as applying rules to make decisions, recognizing patterns, doing steps in logical order, or assessing how to improve task performance. Using a programming language, AI Scientists translate the algorithms into code that becomes the instructions (or programs) that control computers. For example, an AI Scientist might develop algorithms that instruct a mobile robot to recognize obstacles in its path and go around them.

AI Scientists are engaged in research in academic, government, and industrial settings. Those who conduct basic research are interested in adding to the body of knowledge about artificial intelligence, which includes understanding how human intelligence works. They contribute new principles and methodologies as well as new technologies. Typically, basic AI Scientists construct artifacts—computer models and computer systems—to test the validity of their theories. To conduct their studies, they sometimes need to create new programming languages, software tools, standard designs, and methodologies.

Many AI Scientists are involved in applied research in which they seek practical uses for basic AI research. They are usually part of research and development teams that create new or improved commercial products. Examples of such products include software packages, kitchen appliances, medical devices, animated films, service robots, and vehicles. Applied researchers typically specialize in a particular field or industry, such as biology, geology, nuclear physics, medicine, pharmaceuticals, agriculture, robotics, electronics, software engineering, architecture, manufacturing, military, aviation, aerospace, law, law enforcement, education, or entertainment.

AI Scientists generally work on several projects at a time. They work on solo projects as well as collaborate with others. Team projects may involve working with scientists and engineers from other disciplines.

Tasks for AI Scientists are varied each day. For example, they may read scientific literature; conduct experiments; meet with colleagues to discuss research projects; keep up with correspondence, phone messages, and e-mail; and work on scholarly articles or presentations. Senior researchers are involved in writing grant proposals, administering budgets, supervising research staff, and so on.

Many AI Scientists hold full-time teaching appointments at research universities. They are responsible for handling a variety of tasks involved with teaching, student advising, and research. In addition, they perform administrative and community service duties, as well as produce scholarly works for publication. Further, they are usually responsible for seeking out research grants to fund their current and proposed projects.

AI Scientists are expected to keep up with developments in their fields, as well as to update their skills as needed. They enroll in training and continuing education programs, read professional publications, attend professional conferences, and network with colleagues.

Salary

Salaries vary, depending on education, experience, employer, geographical location, and other factors. According to the Bureau of Labor Statistics, the estimated annual salary in 2001 for most computer research scientists (including AI Scientists), ranged between $42,590 and $119,150. The 2001 estimated annual salary for most computer science instructors in postsecondary institutions ranged between $26,020 and $90,290.

Employment Prospects

Many AI Scientists work for academic and government laboratories. Some are employed by large computer and robotics companies that have strong research and development departments.

As automation and robotics technologies are increasingly used in practical applications, opportunities for AI Scientists will grow accordingly. In general, most opportunities will become available as AI Scientists retire or transfer to other positions. Employers may create additional positions as their needs grow and funding is available.

With a background in artificial intelligence, individuals can pursue other career opportunities in the field, such as becoming an AI engineer, programmer, project manager, marketing specialist, or sales representative.

Advancement Prospects

AI Scientists may advance to management and administrative positions as project leaders, program directors, and executive officers. Professors receive promotional rankings as assistant professor, associate professor, or full professor.

Education and Training

Advanced degrees are usually required for individuals to become AI Scientists. Most AI Scientists have earned a master's or doctorate in computer science, mathematics, or another related field. A Doctoral degree is required to teach in academic institutions, conduct independent research, or advance to high-level management positions.

To broaden their background, many AI Scientists have taken courses in cognitive psychology, linguistics, philosophy, neurobiology, anthropology, and other disciplines.

Experience, Skills, and Personality Traits

AI Scientists are expected to have one or more years of work experience, depending on the positions for which they are applying. In addition, they are expected to have completed research studies in the areas in which research labs specialize. Entry-level applicants may have gained experience through research projects, internships, part-time employment, teaching assistantships, and so on. Many employers expect candidates to have completed a few years of postdoctoral training.

AI Scientists need adequate computer programming and writing skills along with excellent problem-solving and analytical skills. They also should have strong communication, interpersonal, and teamwork skills, as they must be able to work well with others and present ideas clearly to colleagues and others. Some personality traits that successful. AI Scientists share are being imaginative, creative, curious, persistent, flexible, and self-motivated.

Unions and Associations

Many AI Scientists join local, state, and national professional associations to take advantage of networking opportunities, education programs, professional publications, and other professional resources and services. Two national societies that serve the interests of AI Scientists are the American Association for Artificial Intelligence and the

Association for Computing Machinery Special-Interest Group for Artificial Intelligence. See Appendix III for contact information.

Tips for Entry

1. Not all graduate computer science departments have strong AI programs, nor are all AI programs alike. Do your research. Choose a program that offers the type of courses and the areas of research in which you are interested.

2. Gain experience by obtaining internships or research assistantships. You can learn about opportunities from your college adviser, professors, career college center, and professional societies.

3. Use the Internet to learn more about the field of artificial intelligence. One website you might visit is AI Topics (by American Association for Artificial Intelligence), http://www.aaai.org/AITopics/aitopics.html. To find other pertinent websites, enter the keyword *artificial intelligence* in a search engine.

ROBOTICS RESEARCHER

CAREER PROFILE

Duties: Conduct basic or applied research; develop and design robots and robotic systems; may teach college students; perform duties as required

Alternate Title(s): Robotics Research Scientist, Robotics Engineer, Computer Scientist, Mechanics Engineer, Electrical Engineer, Automation Engineer

Salary Range: $26,000 to $119,000

Employment Prospects: Good

Advancement Prospects: Good

Prerequisites:

    Education or Training—Advanced degree in robotics, computer science, or related field

    Experience—Previous work and research experience related to a position is required

    Special Skills and Personality Traits—Analytical, problem-solving, writing, programming, communication, interpersonal, and teamwork skills; creative; imaginative; innovative; curious; persistent

    Licensure/Certification—None required

CAREER LADDER

```
┌─────────────────────────────────┐
│    Senior Robotics Researcher    │
└─────────────────────────────────┘

┌─────────────────────────────────┐
│       Robotics Researcher        │
└─────────────────────────────────┘

┌─────────────────────────────────┐
│   Research Associate or Robotics │
│      Researcher (entry-level)    │
└─────────────────────────────────┘
```

Position Description

Robotics Researchers are involved in the scientific study and practical application of robots. These are man-made machines that can move automatically and perform human tasks. Most robots have three main components—a computer that functions as a brain, a body made up of mechanical parts and devices, and sensors which give robots the ability to "see," "hear," "touch," "move," and so forth. Robots come in different shapes and forms. For example, some robots are box-shaped with moveable arms or other attachments, while other robots resemble insects, four-legged animals, and the human form. In recent years, researchers have been developing microscopic robots called nanobots.

Robotics Researchers study how robots work and how robots may be used. For the last several decades, Robotics Researchers have created increasingly more complex robots that have been used for various applications in many fields. Different types of robots are used to perform repetitive tasks, such as painting, welding parts, or assembling parts in factories. Robots also have been programmed to perform extremely difficult and dangerous tasks—such as exploring space, ocean floors, and volcanoes; locating and disposing of bombs; examining extremely toxic environments; and performing routine inspections in such hard-to-reach places as heating ducts, pipes, and sewers. In addition, robots are being used to help surgeons perform certain medical operations.

Robotics Researchers are involved in basic or applied research in academic, government, and industrial laboratories. Basic researchers conduct studies to learn more about robots and robotic systems. They are interested in understanding the principles upon which robots and robotic systems work. They conduct studies without any specific purpose other than to learn and to add new knowledge to the robotics field. They develop new principles, new methodologies, and new technologies. Applied researchers use the results of basic research to solve practical problems. They invent new types of robots and robotic systems as well as improve existing ones. The kinds of research that applied researchers conduct are usually defined by their employers.

Robotics Researchers are responsible for designing and conducting research projects. Their research involves applying principles and techniques from computer science, engineering, and mathematics. They sometimes build computer models—also known as algorithms (or mathematical equations)—to describe specific movements that researchers want robots to make. By changing the values in the equations, they can predict how robots might behave.

Some Robotics Researchers apply artificial intelligence technologies to their projects, using software programs that instruct robots or robotic systems to use human thinking processes to solve problems. For example, a robot might be programmed to recognize certain patterns around it or to automatically improve how well it performs its tasks by evaluating how well it had previously performed them.

Robotics Researchers typically collaborate with other scientists and engineers on research projects. Robotics Researchers also share the results of their research by writing scientific papers and making presentations at scientific conferences.

Researchers perform a variety of tasks each day, which might include reading research literature, analyzing and interpreting data, building computer models, writing reports, supervising assistants and technicians, performing administrative tasks, and so on. Many Robotics Researchers are responsible for obtaining research grants to fund their projects. This involves learning about available grants from the federal government and other sources and writing grant proposals that describe the objectives, methodologies, budgets, and other aspects of their projects.

Robotics Researchers may be appointed as full-time faculty members in computer science or engineering departments at research universities. In addition to conducting independent research, they teach courses to undergraduate and graduate students. They also perform other duties that include advising students, supervising student research projects, writing scholarly works, fulfilling administrative tasks, and participating in community service.

Salaries

Salaries vary, depending on education, experience, employer, geographical location, and other factors. In general, Robotics Researchers receive similar earnings as research computer scientists. In 2001, the estimated annual salary for most research computer scientists ranged between $42,590 and $119,150, according to the Bureau of Labor Statistics. This U.S. agency also reports that the 2001 estimated annual salary for most postsecondary computer science instructors ranged between $26,020 to $90,290; for most postsecondary engineering instructors, between $36,090 to $111,960.

Employment Prospects

Robotics Researchers are employed by academic and government research laboratories. Many researchers, particularly robotics engineers, find employment in the robotics industry (which manufactures and sells robots) as well as in other areas, such as the automotive, medicine, electronics manufacturing and assembly, military, and service industries.

Most research opportunities become available as Robotics Researchers retire, advance to higher positions, or transfer to other positions.

Advancement Prospects

Robotics Researchers measure their success in various ways—through new discoveries and inventions, by earning higher pay, by gaining professional recognition, and so on.

Researchers with administrative and management ambitions can advance to higher positions such as team leader, project manager, division director, and executive officer. Those with entrepreneurial ambitions can become an independent consultants or company owner.

Education and Training

Robotics Researchers hold a master's or doctoral degree in robotics, computer science, mechanical engineering, or another related field.

A Ph.D. is usually required to teach in academic institutions, to conduct independent research, or to advance to high-level management positions.

Experience, Skills, and Personality Traits

Employers generally choose candidates who have previous work experience and have completed relevant research studies related to the positions for which they are applying. Entry-level applicants may have gained experience through research projects, internships, part-time employment, and so on. Employers may require that candidates have completed a few years of postdoctoral training. Candidates for industry positions should have related industry experience or background in business or economics.

Robotics Researchers need strong analytical, problem-solving, and writing skills to do their work effectively. Having adequate skills in programming is also important. In addition, they must have excellent communication, interpersonal, and teamwork skills, as they must be able to work well with colleagues and others. Being creative, imaginative, innovative, curious, and persistent are some personality traits that successful Robotics Researchers share.

Unions and Associations

Robotics Researchers join local, state, and national professional associations to take advantage of professional services and resources such as networking opportunities, education programs, and professional publications. Two professional societies at the national level that serve the interests of Robotics Researchers are the IEEE Robotics and Automation Society and the American Society of Mechanical Engineers. See Appendix III for contact information.

Tips for Entry

1. In middle school or high school, you can start preparing for a career in robotics by reading about robotics and taking courses in science and mathematics. Get hands-on learning by examining mechanical and electronic devices to see how and why they operate. For example, you might build your own robots from kits. Also consider joining a science club, hobby club, or a youth group (such as 4-H) that provides opportunities for tinkering with mechanical and electronics devices.

2. As an undergraduate student, you might seek out internship opportunities in academic, government, or industrial research laboratories to gain experience. You might also ask professors, whose research work interests you, about research assistantships.

3. Learn more about robotics on the Internet. Here are some websites you might visit: IEEE Robotics and Automation Society, http://www.ncsu.edu/IEEE-RAS; RobotCafe.com, http://www.robotcafe.com; and Robot Information Central (by Arrick Robotics), http://www.robots.com/robots.html. For information about industrial applications of robots, check out Robotics Industries Association, http://www.robotics.org.

AGRICULTURAL SCIENCE AND FOOD SCIENCE

HORTICULTURAL SCIENTIST

CAREER PROFILE

Duties: Conduct basic or applied research; design and conduct research projects; may teach college or university students; as research assistants and technicians, provide research and administrative support; perform duties as required of position

Alternate Title(s): Research Horticulturist, Research Scientist; Research Assistant

Salary Range: $29,000 to $99,000

Employment Prospects: Good

Advancement Prospects: Good

Prerequisites:

Education or Training—A bachelor's or advanced degree in horticulture or a related field

Experience—Previous work and research experience required

Special Skills and Personality Traits—Computer, communication, writing, interpersonal, and self-management skills; creative; enthusiastic; persistent; flexible

Licensure/Certification—No licensure required

CAREER LADDER

```
┌─────────────────────────────────────┐
│   Senior Horticultural Scientist     │
└─────────────────────────────────────┘

┌─────────────────────────────────────┐
│     Horticultural Scientist          │
└─────────────────────────────────────┘

┌─────────────────────────────────────┐
│   Postdoctoral Research Associate    │
└─────────────────────────────────────┘
```

Position Description

Horticulture, a branch of agriculture, is the science of growing edible and ornamental plants for gardens and landscaping. These include vegetables, fruits, herbs, spices, flowers, potted plants, shrubs, trees, ground covers, and turfgrass. Most horticultural crops are grown commercially in greenhouses and nurseries, as well as on farms and in orchards.

Many technical and professional occupations are available in the field of horticulture. Those who are involved in conducting research are Horticultural Scientists. They understand how plants grow and know the most effective methods for growing them. They are trained in botany, genetics, biochemistry, plant pathology, plant physiology, soil science, entomology, and other biological and physical science disciplines. In addition, Horticultural Scientists have an understanding of the commercial value of horticultural crops and are knowledgeable about federal and state regulations related to horticultural matters.

Horticulture is divided into different specialties. Horticultural Scientists might specialize in one or more of the following areas:

- olericulture—the study of cultivating vegetable crops
- pomology—the growth and production of fruit crops (nuts and fruits)
- viticulture—the science of growing grape vines
- floriculture—the production and use of flowers and foliage plants
- ornamental horticulture—the use and management of trees, shrubs, and other plants grown for decorative purposes
- turfgrass science—the study of grasses for functional, recreational, and ornamental purposes

Horticultural Scientists work in academic, industrial, government, and nongovernmental settings. Some Horticultural Scientists conduct basic research for the sole purpose of adding new knowledge and understanding to their fields. Others are involved in applied research, addressing specific problems or issues which are usually determined by their employers. Applied researchers also are part of research teams engaged in the development of new commercial products or services.

Basic or applied researchers are engaged in a variety of projects. They study ways to improve the nutritional value, quality, or crop yield of different plants. They develop new plant varieties through the use of seeds, tissue cultures, grafting, and other scientific methods. They seek out new or improved techniques for producing, harvesting, processing, storing, or marketing horticultural crops. Further, they seek solutions to manage pests, control weeds, treat plant diseases, and protect the environment.

Most academic scientists are employed as faculty at colleges and universities. Along with conducting research, they are responsible for teaching courses to undergraduate and graduate students. Most professors are required to perform administrative duties and community service as well as produce scholarly works.

At land-grant universities, some Horticultural Scientists receive appointments from Cooperative Extension Service offices. (Those offices provide free educational programs in agriculture, economic development, and other topics to local communities.) These Horticultural Scientists conduct independent research studies as well as applied research projects on topics that concern local industry. In addition, they provide public service to farmers, growers, local industry, professional horticulturists, and amateur gardeners. For example, they perform such activities as providing technical information and advice, conducting educational programs, and publishing technical bulletins.

Many Horticultural Scientists in the research arena are research assistants and technicians. They provide scientists with research and administrative support. They perform a variety of tasks that may include conducting experiments and tests, analyzing data, writing reports, handling and caring for greenhouse plants, maintaining laboratory equipment and facilities, performing routine administrative tasks, and so on.

Horticultural Scientists perform their studies in offices, laboratories, and greenhouses. They also conduct field work in test fields and gardens, which are usually part of research facilities. Their work occasionally exposes them to fertilizers, pesticides, and other chemicals that may be harmful.

Salaries

Salaries vary, depending on such factors as education, experience, employer, and geographical location. According to the Bureau of Labor Statistics, the estimated annual salary in 2001 for most agricultural scientists (including Horticultural Scientists) ranged between $28,690 and $85,350. The estimated annual salary for most college and university faculty ranged between $34,010 and $99,140.

Employment Prospects

Horticultural Scientists are employed by colleges and universities, the U.S. Department of Agriculture, state agricultural experimental stations, and state extension offices. They also find employment with botanical gardens, zoos, arboretums, parks, private industry, and nongovernmental organizations.

In general, horticulture is described as one of the fastest growing industries in the United States. Retail garden and lawn sales continue to grow steadily, as more and more people take up gardening for pleasure or hire experts to improve and maintain their private yards.

Opportunities for research Horticulturists usually become available as individuals retire, transfer to other positions, or enter other professions.

Research Horticulturists can seek other occupations in which to use their training, such as vocational horticultural instructor, extension educator, nursery manager, plant breeder, vineyard manager, landscape designer, floral arts designer, golf course superintendent, plant inspector, environmentalist, arborist, seed company sales representative, botanical illustrator, and horticultural therapist.

Advancement Prospects

Experienced researchers become team leaders and project managers as well as specialists in their areas of interest. They can also advance to such administrative and management positions as department administrator, program manager, and executive officer. Professors receive promotional rankings as assistant professors, associate professors, or full professors.

Those with entrepreneurial ambitions strive to become independent consultants and owners of consulting firms, nurseries, seed companies, landscaping firms, or other horticulture-related business.

Education and Training

A bachelor's degree in horticulture, agricultural science, or a related field is the minimum requirement for research assistant and technician positions; but many employers prefer candidates with a master's degree. Horticultural Scientist positions in industry or government usually require a master's or doctoral degree.

A Ph.D. is generally required for Horticultural Scientists to teach in universities and four-year colleges, to obtain top management positions, or to conduct independent research.

Experience, Skills, and Personality Traits

Employers typically choose candidates for entry-level positions who have related work and research experience, which may have been gained through student research projects, internships, fellowships, part-time employment, and so on. Ph.D. candidates for research scientist positions are usually expected to have a few years of postdoctoral experience.

Horticulturists need basic computer skills for their work. They also need excellent communication, writing, and interpersonal skills to do their work effectively. They should have strong self-management skills such as being able to work independently, organize and prioritize tasks, and meet deadlines. Being creative, enthusiastic, persistent, and flexible are a few personality traits that research Horticulturists share.

Unions and Associations

Many Horticultural Scientists join local, state, and national professional associations to take advantage of education programs, professional certification, networking opportunities, and other professional services and resources. Some national societies include the American Society for Horticultural Science, the Botanical Society of America, and the American Society of Agronomy. See Appendix III for contact information.

Tips for Entry

1. If you are a middle school or high school student, start gaining knowledge and experience in horticulture. For example, you might read books and magazines about plants; raise a vegetable or flower garden; join a garden club or horticultural society; get a part-time job with a local nursery, garden center, seed company, landscaping firm, or gardening service; or volunteer in the gardening or landscaping department of a public park, zoo, or botanical garden.

2. While in college, take advantage of research assistant opportunities at your college or apply for internships with government agencies and private employers. You can learn about positions from your college career center as well as from your academic adviser and professors.

3. Contact employers with whom you would like to work to find out about current and future job vacancies. A few days after submitting a résumé or job application, contact the prospective employer and ask when you could come in for a job or information interview.

4. You can learn more about horticulture on the Internet. One website you might visit is American Society for Horticultural Science, http://www.ashs.org. To find additional websites, enter the keyword *horticulture* in a search engine.

CROP SCIENTIST

CAREER PROFILE

Duties: Conduct basic or applied research; design and conduct research projects; may teach college or university students; perform duties as required of position

Alternate Title(s): Agronomist, Research Scientist, Crop Specialist

Salary Range: $29,000 to $99,000

Employment Prospects: Good

Advancement Prospects: Good

Prerequisites:

Education or Training—A master's or doctoral degree in crop science or a related field

Experience—Work and research experience related to positions applying for is required

Special Skills and Personality Traits—Organizational, writing, communication, teamwork, interpersonal, and self-management skills; enthusiastic; objective; inquisitive; open-minded; adaptable

Licensure/Certification—No licensure required

CAREER LADDER

```
┌─────────────────────────────┐
│    Senior Crop Scientist    │
└─────────────────────────────┘

┌─────────────────────────────┐
│        Crop Scientist       │
└─────────────────────────────┘

┌─────────────────────────────┐
│      Research Associate      │
└─────────────────────────────┘
```

Position Description

Crop Scientists study the growth and management of field crops—corn, wheat, barley, rice, millet, potatoes, dry beans, legumes, alfalfa, vetch, sunflowers, flax, cotton, sugarcane, turfgrass, and so on. The different field crops are grown to produce food for people all over the world. Field crops are also grown for a variety of nonfood uses, including fibers, feed for livestock, and ground cover for roadsides, parks, athletic fields, golf courses, and home lawns. Some field crops (such as corn) are grown to produce alternative sources of energy. Many field crops are used as raw materials in various industrial applications such as paints, solvents, adhesives, lubricants, cosmetics, dyes, pharmaceuticals, packaging materials, and building materials.

Crop science, also called agronomy, is a branch of agricultural science. Crop Scientists are concerned with conducting studies that help farmers and growers produce high-quality crops more efficiently and economically. Crop Scientists are also interested in helping farmers make decisions that not only serve to increase the yields of their crops but also conserve natural resources and protect the environment.

Crop Scientists conduct basic and applied research in such areas as crop production, crop yield, genetics, breeding, physiology, plant disease, weed control, and pest control. They develop new crop varieties that are more suitable for particular locations, study new uses for specific crops, and investigate the feasibility of introducing alternative crops to an area. Additionally, Crop Scientists develop new principles, methods, and technologies that are relevant to crop systems for small and large farms. Further, they are involved with studying environmental issues that are related to crop production, such as soil erosion, pesticide contamination of water sources, damaged ecosystems, and conservation of natural resources.

Their research is highly scientific and technical. They apply principles of biological sciences, chemistry, and physics to their quest for knowledge and solutions to problems. They have a fundamental understanding of soils, climates, and plant science, which includes genetics, plant breeding, cell biology, and plant physiology. Many Crop Scientists are also skilled in biotechnology, which are techniques that use cells or tissues to create new or improved products. Crop Scientists also use such research tools as computers, satellites, electron microscopes, geographic information systems (GIS) technology, geographical positioning systems (GPS) technology, and remote sensing equipment.

Crop Scientists often work on projects with soil scientists, microbiologists, entomologists, geneticists, meteorologists, agricultural engineers, and other scientists. They sometimes collaborate on projects with Crop Scientists from other countries.

Crop Scientists' work involves designing and managing research projects. They perform various tasks, such as conducting experiments, interpreting and analyzing data, preparing reports, and performing administrative tasks. They conduct research in laboratories and greenhouses, as well as outdoors in experimental fields.

Along with conducting research, many Crop Scientists perform duties in education. For example, some Crop Scientists teach agricultural courses in colleges and universities, while others coordinate and teach education programs in Cooperative Extension Service offices. (These offices provide free educational programs in agriculture, economic development, and other topics to local communities.) Many Crop Scientists also provide consulting and technical support services to farmers, growers, agribusinesses, government agencies, and so forth.

Crop Scientists are expected to share research results with colleagues, farmers, professional societies, and others. They write articles, or scientific papers, which are published in scientific journals. Some make presentations at scientific meetings that are sponsored by professional associations. Others build websites to disseminate their research data as well as to provide practical information related to the production, handling, and marketing of crops.

Crop Scientists who conduct independent research are usually responsible for obtaining research grants from the federal government and other sources to fund their projects.

All Crop Scientists are responsible for keeping up with new developments in their field. They attend professional meetings and conferences, read professional journals and books, network with colleagues, and so on.

Traveling to other states and countries may be required of those who offer consulting services. Crop Scientists might also travel out-of-state or abroad to attend professional conferences and meetings.

Salaries

Salaries vary, depending on such factors as education, experience, and geographical location. According to the Bureau of Labor Statistics, the estimated annual salary for most agricultural scientists (including Crop Scientists) in 2001 ranged between $28,690 and $85,350. The estimated annual salary for most postsecondary agricultural science instructors ranged between $34,010 and $99,140.

Entry-level research scientists at the Agricultural Research Service, part of the U.S. Department of Agricul-

ture, usually start at the GS-11 or GS-12 level. (GS stands for General Schedule, the pay schedule for most federal employees.) In 2002, the annual basic pay ranged from $41,684 to $64,944. Earnings may be greater in locations where the cost of living is higher.

Employment Prospects

Crop Scientists are employed by government agencies, agricultural research stations, universities, and nongovernmental organizations. They also work for agribusinesses, agrochemical companies, seed companies, agricultural consulting firms, and other private companies. Some Crop Scientists are independent consultants.

In general, most opportunities become available as Crop Scientists retire, transfer to other positions, or leave the job market entirely. Employers create additional positions to meet their growing needs.

With a background in crop science, individuals can pursue other careers, including commodity broker, crop chemist, climatologist, environmental specialist, farmer, farm manager, agricultural lawyer, plant breeder, agricultural teacher, or extension agent.

Advancement Prospects

Crop Scientists with administrative or management ambitions can advance to such positions as project leader, program manager, laboratory director, or executive officer.

Education and Training

Employers generally require that Crop Scientists hold a master's or doctoral degree in crop science, agronomy, or another related field. Employers may hire candidates with a bachelor's degree if they have extensive qualifying experience.

A doctoral degree is usually required to teach in universities and four-year colleges, conduct independent research, or obtain top management positions.

Experience, Skills, and Personality Traits

Employers generally choose candidates who have a few years of related work and research experience. Entry-level applicants may have gained experience through research projects, internships, postdoctoral training, employment, and so on. Hands-on farm experience is not generally necessary, but having such experience can be an advantage.

Crop Scientists need strong organizational, writing, and communication skills to do their work effectively. They must also have teamwork and interpersonal skills, along with self-management skills, such as being able to work independently, organize and prioritize work, and handle stressful situations.

Being enthusiastic, objective, inquisitive, open-minded, and adaptable are a few personality traits that successful Crop Scientists share.

Unions and Associations

The American Society of Agronomy and the Crop Science Society of America are two national societies that serve the particular interests of Crop Scientists. They offer networking opportunities, professional certification, education programs, and other professional services and resources. See Appendix III for contact information.

Tips for Entry

1. Before enrolling in a crop science program, be sure that its mission and philosophy are compatible with yours. Also check that they offer courses which interest you and that there are professors with whom you would like to study and possibly do research projects. In addition, find out what kinds of opportunities for practical training are available.

2. Some experts report that scientific and technological advancements are rapidly changing farming practices and crop production. Thus Crop Scientists who have expertise in biotechnology and information technology can expect to have better chances of obtaining jobs.

3. Use the Internet to learn more about crop science. To get a list of relevant websites enter one of these keywords in a search engine: *crop science, crop scientists,* or *agronomy.*

SOIL SCIENTIST

CAREER PROFILE

Duties: Conduct basic or applied research; design and conduct research projects; may perform education, consulting, or technical service duties; perform duties as required of position

Alternate Title(s): Agronomist, Pedologist, Research Scientist

Salary Range: $29,000 to $99,000

Employment Prospects: Good

Advancement Prospects: Good

Prerequisites:

Education or Training—A bachelor's or advanced degree in soil science or related field required for many research positions

Experience—Previous work and research experience required

Special Skills and Personality Traits—Analytical, problem-solving, communication, writing, teamwork, and interpersonal skills; enthusiastic; persistent; detail-oriented; self-motivated

Licensure/Certification—State licensure or certification may be required

CAREER LADDER

```
┌─────────────────────────────────────┐
│  Senior Soil Scientist or Consultant │
└─────────────────────────────────────┘

┌─────────────────────────────────────┐
│            Soil Scientist            │
└─────────────────────────────────────┘

┌─────────────────────────────────────┐
│       Soil Scientist (entry-level)   │
└─────────────────────────────────────┘
```

Position Description

About 25 percent of the Earth's surface is made up of dry land, and only about half of that holds soil suitable for food production. Thus, soil is an essential—and precious—natural resource, which takes thousands of years to form from rock through wind and water erosion.

Soil Scientists specialize in the study of soils and soil environments. They are experts in understanding the biology, microbiology, morphology, classification, chemistry, and physics of different soils. Soil Scientists work with crop scientists and other agricultural scientists to seek ways to increase crop production while still conserving natural resources and protecting the environment.

Most Soil Scientists are involved in research work in academic, government, and industrial settings. They cover such diverse topics as soil decomposition, soil fertility, water erosion, pesticides, the effects of tillage or crop rotation, water management, and waste management. Basic researchers conduct studies that are aimed at gaining new understanding and knowledge about the properties and behaviors of the various soils, soil conservation, and soil management. Applied researchers, on the other hand, work on solving specific issues. For example, they might find ways to repair contaminated soil or to improve the quality of soil in a particular location. Applied researchers also develop new technologies and management practices that can improve crop yields, conserve natural resources, or protect the environment.

Soil Scientists perform their research in offices and laboratories as well as in the field. Increasingly Soil Scientists are integrating electronic and information technologies—such as remote sensing, geographic positioning systems (GPS), and geographical information systems (GIS)—into their work. Many Soil Scientists also work with computer models to analyze and interpret data.

Soil Scientists typically work on several projects at a time, and often collaborate on projects with fellow Soil Scientists and other scientists and engineers. Their research work involves conducting experiments and tests, analyzing and interpreting research data, reading scientific literature, writing reports, and so on. Soil Scientists who conduct independent research are usually responsible for obtaining research grants from the federal government and other sources.

Soil Scientists share information about their research with colleagues and others by writing scientific papers for professional journals, making presentations at professional meetings, or building websites to disseminate research data.

Some Soil Scientists offer consulting and technical services to farmers, engineers, landscape designers, land developers, environmentalists, government agencies, and others. They provide decision makers with information about the suitability of soils in a location for particular uses or about the impact of specific activities on the land—including agricultural production, landscape design, erosion control, forest products, mine reclamation, and site restorations. Soil Scientists might provide these services as independent consultants or as staff employees.

Many Soil Scientists are employed as full-time professors or adjunct instructors by colleges and universities. They teach courses about soil classification, soil mapping, soil biophysics, water management, agricultural ecology, and so forth. Depending on the institution, soil science faculty may teach in agriculture, botany, geography, geology, engineering, and other departments. Full-time faculty are responsible for conducting independent research projects, advising students, producing scholarly work, and performing community service and administrative duties.

Soil Scientists who work in government settings may perform educational duties along with research and technical service duties. For example, they might conduct workshops for farmers or develop educational materials about management practices suitable for their locations.

Soil Scientists often work long days in order to complete their tasks or meet deadlines. Many travel frequently to other cities, states, or countries.

Salaries

Salaries vary, depending on such factors as education, experience, and geographical location. According to the Bureau of Labor Statistics, the estimated annual salary in 2001 for most agricultural scientists (including Soil Scientists) ranged between $28,690 and $85,350; for most postsecondary agricultural instructors, between $34,010 and $99,140.

Entry-level research scientists at the Agricultural Research Service, which is part of the U.S. Department of Agriculture, usually start at the GS-11 or GS-12 level. (GS stands for General Schedule, the pay schedule for most federal employees.) In 2002, the annual basic pay ranged from $41,684 to $64,944. Earnings may be greater in locations where the cost of living is higher.

Employment Prospects

Government agencies, academic institutions, agricultural research stations, and nonprofit organizations are all employers of Soil Scientists. In addition, Soil Scientists are employed by commercial farms and land appraisal firms, as well as by various private businesses and companies in agribusiness, chemicals fertilizer, petroleum, and other industries. Soil Scientists also work for consulting firms in such areas as agriculture, environmental science, and engineering. Many Soil Scientists work as full-time or part-time independent consultants. Opportunities for Soil Scientists are also available with international organizations.

In general, most job openings become available as scientists retire, transfer to other positions, or leave the workforce for other reasons.

With a background in soil science, individuals can pursue other careers, such as becoming soil surveyors, farmers, farm managers, extension agents, park rangers, foresters, geologists, and environmental specialists.

Advancement Prospects

Soil Scientists advance in their careers in various ways, depending on their career path, ambitions, and interests. Those interested in management and administrative work can find opportunities in any work setting. Those with entrepreneurial ambitions can become independent consultants or owners of consulting firms.

Education and Training

To enter this field, Soil Scientists need at least a bachelor's degree in soil science, agronomy, natural resources management, environmental studies, earth science, or related field. Many employers require, or strongly prefer, that candidates have a master's degree. A Ph.D. is usually required to teach in four-year colleges and universities, conduct independent research, or hold top management positions.

Entry-level Soil Scientists typically work under the training and supervision of experienced Soil Scientists for the first few years of their careers.

Experience, Skills, and Personality Traits

Employers generally choose candidates for entry-level positions who have related work and research experience, which may have been gained through research projects, internships, part-time employment, or postdoctoral training. Many employers look for applicants who have field experience. Employers typically prefer candidates who are familiar with their business or industry.

In order to do their work effectively, Soil Scientists must have excellent analytical and problem-solving skills. They also need strong communication and writing skills, as well as teamwork and interpersonal skills. Being enthusiastic, persistent, detail-oriented, and self-motivated are a few personality traits that successful Soil Scientists have in common.

Special Requirements

Soil Scientists who provide services that involve the health, safety, and welfare of the general public may be required to be licensed or certified as Professional Soil Scientists. Employers may also require or strongly prefer licensed professionals. Many Soil Scientists obtain licensure on a voluntary basis to enhance their employability. Further, entry-level applicants may be required to register as Soil Scientists-in-Training, which leads to professional registration.

Licensure requirements vary from state to state. For information, contact the appropriate board of professional licensure where you wish to practice.

Unions and Associations

Many Soil Scientists join local, state, or national societies to take advantage of professional services and resources such as education programs, professional certification, and networking opportunities. The Soil Science Society of America, the Association of Women Soil Scientists, the National Society of Consulting Soil Scientists, and the American Society of Agronomy are some national societies that serve the interests of Soil Scientists. See Appendix III for contact information.

Tips for Entry

1. As a college student, gain experience by obtaining an internship or work-study position, or by becoming a research assistant with a professor whose work interests you.

2. Many trade and professional associations post listings for local, state, and nation-wide job openings on their websites. Be sure to check out agricultural, geology, and environmental science associations as well as those specifically organized for Soil Scientists.

3. Use the Internet to learn more Soil Scientists. Two websites you might visit are Association for Women Soil Scientists, http://awss.homestead.com; and Soil Science Society of America, http://www.soils.org.

ANIMAL SCIENTIST

CAREER PROFILE

Duties: Conduct basic or applied research; design and conduct research projects; may teach college or university students; as research assistants and technicians, provide research and administrative support; perform duties as required of position

Alternate Title(s): Title that reflects a particular specialty, such as Dairy Scientist or Poultry Scientist

Salary Range: $29,000 to $99,000

Employment Prospects: Good

Advancement Prospects: Good

Prerequisites:

    Education or Training—A bachelor's or advanced degree in animal science

    Experience—Related work and research experience required

    Special Skills and Personality Traits—Computer, writing, communication, teamwork, interpersonal, and self-management skills; curious; creative; persistent; analytical; flexible

    Licensure/Certification—No licensure required

CAREER LADDER

```
┌─────────────────────────────────┐
│     Senior Animal Scientist      │
└─────────────────────────────────┘

┌─────────────────────────────────┐
│        Animal Scientist          │
└─────────────────────────────────┘

┌─────────────────────────────────┐
│  Postdoctoral Research Associate │
└─────────────────────────────────┘
```

Position Description

Animal science, an applied science, is a branch of agriculture. It is the study of animals that are used as sources of food and fiber as well as of animals that are used for work, play, or companionship. Traditionally, animal science is known as the study of livestock animals—beef cattle, dairy cows, poultry, sheep, swine, and horses. (In some locales, this discipline is still known as animal husbandry.) However, today this discipline includes the study of goats, buffalo, emus, ostriches, llamas, and other exotic species. It also includes the study of aquaculture, or fish and shellfish—such as trout, salmon, catfish, tilapia, shrimp, and oysters—that are farmed in natural and controlled environments. Further, animal science includes the study of dogs, cats, reptiles, aquarium fish, rodents, and other small animals that serve as household pets.

Animal Scientists are interested in two broad areas of research. One area is the study of the animals themselves. Animal Scientists are interested in the welfare and well-being of the animals. These scientists investigate topics that concern the reproduction; growth and development; genetics; nutrition; care; and management of animals.

The other general area of study is food and fiber production. Animal Scientists are engaged in studies that help provide high-quality products—such as meat, eggs, dairy products, and wool—at affordable prices to consumers. Animal Scientists research topics involving food or fiber production, processing, handling, and quality control.

Animal Scientists apply principles of the biological, physical, and social sciences to their research studies. They conduct research in academic, government, and industry settings. Some Animal Scientists are involved in basic research. They conduct research for the sole purpose of adding new knowledge—theories and technologies—to their discipline. Other Animal Scientists conduct applied research. They apply the findings of basic research to develop useful products or find solutions to problems in animal production, animal management, or food processing.

Animal Scientists sometimes collaborate on projects with colleagues in their field as well as with other scientists, such as physiologists and geneticists. Animal Scientists might also work with agricultural engineers, technicians, managers, and other professionals.

Animal Scientists' research involves designing and overseeing research projects. They perform various tasks, such as conducting experiments, interpreting and analyzing data, preparing reports, and doing administrative tasks. Senior researchers and principal investigators may perform supervisory and management duties. Animal Scientists who conduct independent research are usually responsible for obtaining research grants from the federal government and other sources to fund their projects.

Typically, Animal Scientists exchange research information with their colleagues. They might write articles, or scientific papers, which are published in scientific journals. Some might make presentations at scientific meetings that are sponsored by professional associations.

Some Animal Scientists are employed as university and college professors. Along with teaching courses in animal science, they may teach classes in other disciplines in which they specialize, such as nutrition, physiology, or genetics. Academic Animal Scientists juggle various tasks each day. Their duties include conducting independent research, preparing for and teaching courses, advising students, supervising student research projects, producing scholarly works, performing administrative duties, and participating in community service.

Animal Scientists are also employed as technicians and research assistants. They provide research scientists with research and administrative support. Their tasks include conducting experiments, making observations, analyzing data, writing reports, handling and caring for lab animals, maintaining laboratory equipment and facilities, completing routine administrative tasks, and so on.

All Animal Scientists are responsible for keeping up with new developments. They attend professional meetings and conferences, read professional journals and books, network with colleagues, and so on.

Animal Scientists work in offices and laboratories. In addition, they may spend some of their time conducting research in feedlots, dairies, barns, or other animal facilities.

Salaries

Salaries vary, depending on such factors as education, experience, employer, and geographical location. According to the Bureau of Labor Statistics, the estimated annual salary for most agricultural scientists (including Animal Scientists) in 2001 ranged between $28,690 and $85,350. The estimated annual salary for most postsecondary agricultural science instructors ranged between $34,010 and $99,140.

Entry-level research scientists at the Agricultural Research Service, part of the U.S. Department of Agriculture, usually start at the GS-11 or GS-12 level. (GS stands for General Schedule, the pay schedule for most federal employees.) In 2003, the annual basic pay ranged from $42,976 to $66,961. Earnings may be greater in locations where the cost of living is higher.

Employment Prospects

Animal Scientists are employed by colleges and universities; government agencies and laboratories; agricultural research stations; food and meat processing companies; biotechnology firms; agribusinesses; and so on.

The Bureau of Labor Statistics anticipates little growth through 2010 for the employment of agricultural scientists, which includes Animal Scientists. In general, most opportunities become available as Animal Scientists retire, transfer to other positions, or leave the job market entirely.

With a background in animal science, individuals can qualify for positions in a number of areas. For example, they can become extension agents, farm managers, livestock producers, aquaculturists, feedlot operators, animal breeders, meat inspectors, horse trainers, dog trainers, animal caretakers, veterinary assistants, and market forecasters. They can also find employment in such positions as quality control specialist, sales representative, manager, and public relations specialist with food processing companies, feed manufacturers, animal breed companies, pharmaceutical companies, trade associations, and other organizations. With additional training and education, individuals can become vocational agricultural teachers, veterinarians, animal behaviorists, or medical doctors.

Advancement Prospects

Research scientists can advance to administrative and management positions, by becoming project leaders, program managers, laboratory directors, executive officers, and so on. Professors receive promotional rankings as assistant professor, associate professor, or full professor.

Education and Training

A bachelor's degree in animal science or a related field is the usual minimum requirement for research assistant and technician positions. Some employers require (or strongly prefer) that candidates hold a master's degree. Research scientists must possess a master's degree or a Ph.D. A Ph.D. is required to teach in universities and four-year colleges, conduct independent research, or obtain top management positions.

Experience, Skills, and Personality Traits

Requirements vary for the different positions as well as among various employers. For entry-level positions, employers generally choose candidates who have related work and research experience. This may have been gained through research projects, internships, fellowships, part-time employment, and so on. Ph.D. candidates for research scientist positions may be required to have a few years of postdoctoral experience.

Animal Scientists need adequate computer, writing, and communication skills to do their work effectively. They should also have strong teamwork and interpersonal skills along with excellent self-management skills, such as being able to work independently, organize and prioritize work, and handle stressful situations.

Some personality traits that successful Animal Scientists share are being curious, creative, persistent, analytical, and flexible.

Unions and Associations

Many Animal Scientists join professional associations at the local, state, and national levels. These societies offer a variety of services and resources, such as professional certification, education programs, and networking opportunities, to help Animal Scientists with their professional development. Some national professional societies that serve the interests of different Animal Scientists are the American Society of Animal Science, the American Dairy Science Association, the American Meat Science Association, and the Poultry Science Association. See Appendix III for contact information.

Tips for Entry

1. As a middle school or high school student, start learning about animal science. Read books about different livestock animals. You might check out local 4-H clubs or other youth groups to see what they might offer. You might visit dairy farms, poultry farms, cattle ranches, petting zoos, and so on. If possible, raise a domestic animal.

2. If you are a college student, gain valuable experience, working as an intern in several settings or become a research assistant with a professor in whose work you are interested.

3. Professional journals, such as the *Journal of Animal Science,* usually carry advertisements for internship and employment opportunities.

4. Learn more about Animal Scientists on the Internet. Here are a few websites to visit: American Society of Animal Science, http://www.asas.org; Animal and Plant Health Inspection Service (part of the U.S. Department of Agriculture), http://www.aphis.usda.gov; and Virtual Livestock Library (Oklahoma State University), http://www.ansi.okstate.edu/library.

FOOD SCIENTIST

CAREER PROFILE

Duties: Conduct basic or applied research; manage and conduct research projects; may teach college or university students; food technologists research, develop, and produce new and improved food products; perform other duties as required of position

Alternate Title(s): Research Scientist, Food Technologist; title that reflects a specialty, such as Food Chemist or Food Microbiologist; title that reflects a specific occupation such as Quality Assurance Specialist or Product Development Scientist

Salary Range: $29,000 to $99,000

Employment Prospects: Good

Advancement Prospects: Good

Prerequisites:

Education or Training—A bachelor's or advanced degree in food science or related field

Experience—Requirements vary for the different positions

Special Skills and Personality Traits—Communication, problem-solving, critical thinking, writing, computer skills, and interpersonal skills; creative, curious, outgoing, tenacious, instinctive, and self-motivated

Licensure/Certification—None required

CAREER LADDER

```
┌─────────────────────────────────┐
│   Senior Food Scientist or      │
│   Senior Food Technologist      │
└─────────────────────────────────┘

┌─────────────────────────────────┐
│  Food Scientist or Food Technologist │
└─────────────────────────────────┘

┌─────────────────────────────────┐
│ Postdoctoral Research Associate or │
│ Food Technologist (entry-level)  │
└─────────────────────────────────┘
```

Position Description

Food Scientists are involved in the research, development, and production of packaged, canned, and frozen food products. Their role is to make sure that these products are healthy, safe, tasty, and attractive. Food Scientists, however, are not chefs, nutritionists, home economists, or food service professionals. They are trained scientists in food science, a branch of agriculture. They apply the principles and techniques of chemistry, microbiology, physics, engineering, and other scientific disciplines to study the nature of foods as well as to develop and produce new food products that meet the needs and desires of consumers.

Many Food Scientists work in academic and government settings, where they conduct basic research to gain new knowledge and understanding about the composition and properties of different foods—meats, fish, dairy products, grains, vegetables, and fruits. They also study ingredients, such as food additives, alternative sweeteners, and fat substitutes, that are added to food products.

Food Scientists examine how foods behave under certain conditions, such as when they are being preserved, frozen, or cooked over high heat. They also investigate why and how different foods decompose and spoil. In addition, they study how the quality, wholesomeness, and safety of foods may be improved for consumption.

Many academic Food Scientists hold appointments as full-time faculty members. In addition to doing research, they teach courses to undergraduate and graduate students. They also advise students, supervise student research projects, perform administrative duties, produce scholarly work, and fulfill community service obligations.

Food Scientists who work in the food industry are usually known as food technologists. They apply the findings of basic research to the creation, preservation, processing, packaging, storage, and distribution of safe and nutritious food products. Some food technologists work for food processing companies that make various types of food products—beverages, soups, breads, baked goods, frozen dinners, lunch meats, canned fruits and vegetables, packaged salads, cheeses, ice cream, candies, cakes, sauces, condiments, and so on. Other food technologists work for food ingredient companies which make spices, flavors, stabilizers, thickeners, preservatives, and other key ingredients needed for food products.

Industrial Food Scientists specialize in the different areas of product development and production. Those who are responsible for creating new or improved products are called product development scientists. Their role is to develop formulas (or recipes) that preserve the flavor, appearance, texture, and nutritional value of the ingredients in the food products.

Many industrial Food Scientists are employed as quality assurance specialists or quality control scientists. They are responsible for determining the quality of ingredients and food products. They check raw foods to make sure they are fresh and conform to specifications. These scientists also monitor production lines to ensure that the regulations and standards set by the government, by the food industry, and by employers are being followed. Other food technologists specialize in package development, production management, safety, marketing, technical sales, or management.

All Food Scientists are expected to keep up with constantly changing developments and new technologies. They might read scientific journals and books, attend professional conferences and meetings, network with colleagues, enroll in continuing education programs, and so forth.

Food Scientists conduct their work in test kitchens or laboratories that are set up like kitchens. They use ovens, microwaves, blenders, hand food processors, and other cooking equipment.

Salaries

Salaries vary, depending on education, experience, geographical location, and other factors. The Bureau of Labor Statistics reports that the estimated annual salary in 2001 for most Food Scientists ranged between $28,690 and $85,350. The estimated annual salary for most college and university faculty members ranged between $34,010 and $99,140.

According to the American Chemical Society, the median annual salary for Food Scientists is about $50,000. The median annual salary for scientists with a bachelor's degree is about $47,000; with a master's degree, about $51,000; and with a doctorate, about $65,000.

Employment Prospects

Most research Food Scientists work for academic institutions, state and federal government agencies and laboratories, and independent research institutes. Some researchers are employed by international organizations and work in other nations. Food technologists are employed by food processors, food ingredient companies, food equipment manufacturers, food store chains, and so forth.

The food industry is one of the largest industries in the world and continues to expand as the population grows. Each year over thousands of new food products are introduced into the market, although only a very small percentage of these products become established. Opportunities for Food Scientists are expected to continue growing throughout the decade to keep pace with consumer demands for safe, healthy, and convenient food products.

Advancement Prospects

Food Scientists can advance in any number of ways, depending on their interests. Those with administrative and management ambitions can advance to such positions as program manager, research director, department administrator, or executive officer. Professors receive promotional rankings as assistant professor, associate professor, or full professor. Food Scientists can also become independent consultants or business owners.

Many Food Scientists pursue advancement by earning higher pay; receiving higher-level responsibilities; conducting independent research projects; and receiving professional recognition.

Education and Training

Food Scientists possess a bachelor's or advanced degree in food science, food chemistry, or another related field.

Specific educational requirements vary with different positions. A bachelor's degree is the minimum requirement for most industrial positions. At many companies, the minimum requirement for their research and development positions is a master's degree. A doctorate is typically needed in order to conduct independent research teach in universities and colleges, or advance to high-level positions.

Experience, Skills, and Personality Traits

Requirements vary among employers. In general, candidates must have relevant work experience and be able to demonstrate that they have the appropriate knowledge and experience for the jobs in which they are applying. Entry-level applicants may have gained experience through internships, research assistantships, fellowships, and part-time employment.

For industrial positions, candidates should have a basic understanding of business principles as well as an awareness of consumer demands.

To perform well in their work, Food Scientists need strong communication, problem-solving, and critical thinking skills. They must also have good writing and computer skills. In addition, they need excellent interpersonal skills in order to work well with scientists, engineers, managers, technicians, and others.

Some personality traits that successful Food Scientists share are being creative, curious, outgoing, tenacious, instinctive, and self-motivated.

Unions and Associations

Many Food Scientists join local, state, or national societies to take advantage of networking opportunities and other professional services and resources. Some professional associations that serve the interests of Food Scientists are the Institute of Food Technologists, the Society of Flavor Chemists, and the American Chemical Society. See Appendix III for contact information.

Tips for Entry

1. As a high school and college student, gain experience in food research or technology by obtaining part-time employment, internships, research assistantships, or work-study positions in academic, government, or industrial settings.

2. In general, larger companies hire entry-level candidates with advanced degrees for product development positions. Smaller companies will hire candidates with bachelor's degrees if they have sufficient qualifying experience.

3. The Agricultural Research Service, part of the United States Department of Agriculture (USDA), posts job openings and information about working with the service at their website, http://www.ars.usda.gov. You can also get information by writing USDA Agricultural Research Service, Recruitment Office, 5601 Sunnysite Avenue, Mail Stop 5144, Beltsville, Md. 20705. You can phone (301) 504-1709 or fax (301) 504-1740.

4. Learn more about food science on the Internet. Two websites you might visit are Institute of Food Technologists, http://www.ift.org; and Center for Food Safety and Applied Nutrition, http://www.cfsan.fda.gov. To get a list of other websites, enter the key word *food science* in any search engine.

AGRICULTURAL ENGINEER

CAREER PROFILE

Duties: Design solutions for agriculture, food systems, and other biological systems; perform duties as required of position

Alternate Title(s): A title such as Food Engineer or Environmental Engineer that reflects a specialty

Salary Range: $33,000 to $86,000

Employment Prospects: Good

Advancement Prospects: Good

Prerequisites:

    Education or Training—A bachelor's degree in agricultural engineering or a related field

    Experience—One or more years of work experience related to the position one is applying for

    Special Skills and Personality Traits—Analytical, problem-solving, interpersonal, communication, writing, and computer skills; creative; enthusiastic; precise; clever

    Licensure/Certification—Professional Engineer (P.E.) licensure may be required

CAREER LADDER

```
┌─────────────────────────────────────┐
│   Supervising or Project Engineer    │
└─────────────────────────────────────┘

┌─────────────────────────────────────┐
│        Agricultural Engineer         │
└─────────────────────────────────────┘

┌─────────────────────────────────────┐
│   Agricultural Engineer (entry-level)│
└─────────────────────────────────────┘
```

Position Description

Agricultural Engineers apply principles and techniques of biological and physical sciences and engineering to resolve problems in agriculture, food systems, and related biological systems. They develop practical, safe, and sound economical solutions as well as ways to conserve natural resources (air, soil, water, and energy) and protect the environment.

Agricultural Engineers are involved in a wide range of projects that help farmers, agribusinesses, food processing companies, horticulturists, groundskeepers, landscapers, homeowners, conservation organizations, and others. For example, Agricultural Engineers might

- develop machinery and equipment for various purposes, such as crop processing and handling; horticulture production; feed processing and handling of livestock; lawn and ground care; and recreation
- design and install mechanical systems to improve the production, processing, handling, storage, and distribution of food, fiber, or pharmaceutical products
- design and construct commercial buildings, food mills, farm structures, livestock facilities, greenhouses, storage bins, and other buildings required for the production, processing, and storage of food, plants, crops, or livestock
- develop heat, air, and other systems needed for controlled environments such as greenhouses, livestock facilities, and storage structures
- design systems for farming and food processing operations that integrate electronic and information technologies, such as computers, automation systems, and geographical information systems (GIS)
- design and build irrigation and drainage systems that reduce soil erosion
- design waste treatment systems that protect the environment

Agricultural Engineers usually specialize in a particular area of agricultural engineering, such as food engineering, machinery systems engineering, soil and water engineering, environmental engineering, and so on. They may be involved in one or more of the following areas: research and design, testing, production, maintenance, sales, technical support, or project management.

Some Agricultural Engineers work as independent consultants or as staff members in consulting firms, where they provide expertise in one or more specialties. They offer their services to farmers, growers, private citizens and to small businesses without engineering staff. They also give support to engineering departments in governmental agencies and large companies. Consultants may be hired to assist with product development, project management, safety evaluation, systems analysis, and so on. Some consultants offer technical analysis and expert witness services to law firms, financial services, government boards, and other organizations.

Agricultural Engineers usually work on several projects at a time, each at different stages. They plan projects, conduct research, create designs, oversee construction, and so forth. Their duties are varied, depending on their positions as well as the type of projects on which they work.

All Agricultural Engineers are responsible for keeping up with developments in their field. Their activities might include reading professional journals and books, networking with peers, enrolling in continuing education courses, and attending professional conferences.

Agricultural Engineers may be required to work more than 40 hours a week to complete tasks or meet pressing deadlines. Their projects may involve traveling and staying several nights or weeks away from home.

Salaries

Salaries vary, depending on education, experience, geographical location, and other factors. For example, Agricultural Engineers with a master's degree earn more than those with a bachelor's degree.

In general, the average annual salary for entry-level Agricultural Engineers is about $33,000. The Bureau of Labor Statistics reports that the estimated annual salary for most Agricultural Engineers ranged between $32,920 and $86,470 in 2001.

Employment Prospects

Some major employers of Agricultural Engineers are government agencies, agricultural companies, and food products companies. Many Agricultural Engineers are employed by engineering and management firms that provide consulting services to farmers and agricultural industries. In addition, many Agricultural Engineers are independent consultants. Some Agricultural Engineers are employed as faculty in academic institutions.

In the United States, agricultural engineering is a small field compared to other engineering disciplines. However, the field is expected to grow due to the continuing global demand for food supplies at affordable prices. Advancements in biotechnology as well as concerns over environmental protection and natural resources conservation should also contribute to job growth. Currently, most opportunities become available as Agricultural Engineers transfer to other positions, retire, or leave the job force for various reasons.

Advancement Prospects

As Agricultural Engineers gain experience, they can become technical specialists in such areas as agricultural waste management, project management, or wetland regulations. Those with administrative or management ambitions can pursue positions such as project manager, program director, and executive officer. Some Agricultural Engineers become independent consultants or owners of consulting firms.

Education and Training

The minimum requirement needed to become an Agricultural Engineer is a bachelor's degree in agricultural engineering, agricultural systems management, or another engineering discipline. Some employers require or strongly prefer candidates with an advanced degree.

Agricultural engineering programs are generally offered at state universities that are designated as U.S. land-grant schools. Agricultural engineering programs vary with each institution. Students take a combination of basic courses in engineering and biological systems along with agricultural engineering courses in their areas of interest.

Entry-level engineers are given on-the-job training. Many employers also provide some type of classroom training.

Experience, Skills, and Personality Traits

Generally, candidates should be knowledgeable about the principles and methodologies of agricultural engineering related to the particular area (such as food engineering) in which they would be working. Employers typically prefer that candidates have one or more years of work experience related to the position for which they are applying. Entry-level candidates may have gained experience through internships, work-study programs, summer employment, research projects, and so on.

Agricultural Engineers need excellent analytical and problem-solving abilities as well as strong interpersonal and communication skills for their jobs. Good writing and computer skills are also important for this line of work. Being creative, enthusiastic, precise, and clever are a few personality traits that successful Agricultural Engineers share.

Special Requirements

Agricultural Engineers must be licensed as Professional Engineers (P.E.) if they offer their services directly to the public. Some employers require or strongly prefer that candidates also possess P.E. licensure. Many Agricultural Engineers obtain P.E. licenses voluntarily so as to enhance their employability. Entry-level engineers may apply for the Engineer-in-Training licensure.

The P.E. licensing process consists of two stages. Engineers who successfully pass the first examination become licensed as Engineers-in-Training. After working several years under the supervision of licensed engineers, they become eligible to take the second examination for the professional engineer licensure.

Requirements for P.E. licensure vary with each state, territory, and Washington, D.C. For specific information, contact the board of examiners for professional engineers where you wish to practice.

Unions and Associations

Most Agricultural Engineers join professional societies to take advantage of professional services and resources such as education programs, publications, and networking opportunities. Professional associations are available at the local, state, and national levels.

The American Society of Agricultural Engineers (ASAE) is a national association that many Agricultural Engineers join. The Professional Engineering Institute, an ASAE division, serves the particular interests of consultants. Agricultural Engineers with P.E. licensure are eligible to join the National Society of Professional Engineers. See Appendix III for contact information.

Tips for Entry

1. If you are a middle school or high school student, join 4-H and get involved with science and technology programs. You might also contact an engineering program at a nearby college or university to see if it offers internship or mentoring programs for middle and high school students.

2. While you are in college, participate in agricultural engineering clubs that are available on your campus. Begin building a network of associates whom you can contact for future job searches as well as for professional advice.

3. Participate in internship and cooperative education (work-study) programs to obtain valuable hands-on training and experience. Many employers offer interns and work-study students permanent positions upon graduation.

4. Use the Internet to learn more about agricultural engineering. To get a list of relevant websites, enter the keyword *agricultural engineering* or *agricultural engineers* in any search engine.

MEDICAL SCIENCE

MEDICAL SCIENTIST

CAREER PROFILE

Duties: Conduct basic, translational, clinical, or other type of biomedical research; design and conduct research projects; may teach college or medical students; perform duties as required of position

Alternate Title(s): Physician-Scientist, Medical Research Scientist, Clinical Investigator; a title that reflects a field of study or medical specialty, such as Geneticist, Epidemiologist, Pharmacologist, Medical Oncologist, or Cardiovascular Surgeon

Salary Range: $30,000 to $112,000

Employment Prospects: Good

Advancement Prospects: Good

Prerequisites:

Education or Training—Ph.D. in a biological science discipline; M.D. or D.O. degree required for clinical research positions

Experience—Previous work and research experience required; several years of postdoctoral work

Special Skills and Personality Traits—Writing, communication, interpersonal, teamwork, self-management, and problem-solving skills; persistent; independent; curious; flexible; enthusiastic

Licensure/Certification—Physician-scientists must be licensed; board certification in medical specialty or subspecialty may be required

CAREER LADDER

```
┌─────────────────────────────────┐
│     Senior Medical Scientist     │
└─────────────────────────────────┘

┌─────────────────────────────────┐
│        Medical Scientist         │
└─────────────────────────────────┘

┌─────────────────────────────────┐
│  Postdoctoral Research Associate │
└─────────────────────────────────┘
```

Position Description

Medical Scientists are biomedical researchers. They engage in research that advances medicine and benefits human health. Their research has resulted in medical tests, techniques, methodologies, therapies, devices, and equipment that medical doctors and specialists use to diagnose, treat, and cure their patients. In addition, Medical Scientists have conducted research that has produced general guidelines for leading healthy lives from infancy to old age. Further, Medical Scientists have provided policy makers with the necessary information to make laws and public policies that ensure the safety and quality of health and health services.

Medical Scientists work in academic, government, industrial, and nongovernmental settings. Many biomedical researchers are Ph.D. scientists with specialties in different biological disciplines. They are molecular biologists, biophysicists, biochemists, physiologists, microbiologists, geneticists, anatomists, ecologists, and so on. Some Medical Scientists are medical doctors, dentists, and veterinarians, or medical specialists, such as dermatologists, ophthalmologists, pediatricians, medical oncologists, urologists, gynecologists, endocrinologists, surgeons, anesthesiologists, and psychiatrists. These Medical Scientists are sometimes known as physician-scientists.

Medical scientists perform their work in laboratories and offices, as well as clinical settings such as hospitals. Depending on their research, they may be involved in examining cells, tissues, or organs; manipulating genetic matter;

creating computer models; or conducting interviews or surveys. They also devise experiments or tests that may use greenhouse plants, lab animals, or human subjects.

Medical Scientists are engaged in various areas of biomedical research. Some Medical Scientists conduct basic laboratory research. They do not direct their studies toward finding specific solutions to biomedical problems. Their concern is to advance knowledge and understanding of biological systems and diseases. They study such questions as: How do genes function? How do cells and tissues in a life system work together? How does an infectious agent, such as a virus, affect living organisms? How do cancer cells grow? What may cause cells to resist disease?

Some Medical Scientists are involved in translational research, or applied research. They specifically conduct studies that translate knowledge gained through basic research, and sometimes from clinical research. Their objectives are to discover medical solutions for the diagnosis, prevention, or treatment of diseases. They work on the development of new and improved vaccines, medicines, medical devices, diagnostic tools, methodologies, medical procedures, instrumentation, and so on. Further, they seek ways to improve the quality of health and health services.

Other Medical Scientists are involved in clinical research. These researchers test the safety and effectiveness of vaccines, therapies, new combinations of drugs, medical devices, surgical procedures, and so forth on volunteer patients. The tests, or clinical trials, are done in three phases, in which Medical Scientists gather information about whether a treatment, methodology, or other variable will work, and about the risks that may be involved. The clinical trials take place in hospitals or other clinical settings. Because the research is patient-oriented, most Medical Scientists in these studies are physicians. Those clinical researchers who are not physicians collaborate with medical doctors who deal directly with the patients.

Medical Scientists also conduct other types of biomedical research. Some are engaged in prevention research, in which they examine how people may avoid contracting a particular disease. Some Medical Scientists are involved in outcomes research. They study the results that particular medical interventions or health-care practices have upon patients' lives. Other Medical Scientists are interested in health services research, in which they cover topics related to the delivery of health-care services.

Medical Scientists are usually involved with more than one study at any given time. They often collaborate on projects with other medical scientists, biological scientists, engineers, and other science professionals.

Medical Scientists fulfill a variety of duties each day. They perform such tasks as designing research projects, conducting experiments, recording experimental data, reviewing research literature, analyzing and interpreting data, writing reports, meeting with colleagues, and performing adminis-

trative tasks. Many Medical Scientists, particularly senior scientists, are responsible for supervising and training clerical staff, research assistants, and lab technicians.

In addition, Medical Scientists present the results of their research work to the scientific community. Most of them write articles which they submit to scientific journals. Some of them make presentations at scientific conferences. Their research findings may also be posted on the Internet, on their personal website, or on websites developed by academic institutions, professional societies, government agencies, and other organizations.

Independent researchers are responsible for seeking grants to fund new research projects as well as for raising funds to continue current studies. They prepare proposals that describe their purposes, goals, methodologies, budgets, and other aspects of their proposed studies.

Many Medical Scientists teach in colleges, universities, and medical schools. They may be employed as adjunct (part-time) instructors or be appointed to full-time positions. Along with their research and teaching duties, full-time faculty in research institutions are responsible for advising students, supervising students with their research projects, performing administrative duties, fulfilling community service obligations, and producing scholarly work.

Medical Scientists occasionally work evenings and on weekends to perform their experiments, write reports, complete administrative tasks, attend meetings, and so on.

Salaries

Salaries vary, depending on such factors as experience, employer, and geographical location. According to the Bureau of Labor Statistics, the estimated annual salary in 2001 for most medical scientists ranged from $29,570 to $111,750.

Employment Prospects

Medical Scientists are employed by colleges and universities as well as by medical schools, teaching hospitals, and medical centers. Medical Scientists also find employment in the military, in government agencies, and at research institutes. In addition, Medical Scientists work in private industries, such as the biotechnology and pharmaceutical industries.

The Bureau of Labor Statistics reports that the job growth for medical scientists is predicted to be between 21 and 35 percent through 2010; however, the competition for positions is strong. Most job openings become available to replace Medical Scientists who have retired or transferred to other positions. Employers create new positions to meet growing needs, as long as funding is available.

Opportunities for experienced physician-scientists are particularly good. The demand should grow in the coming years, as many experts report that the number of newly-trained physician-scientists has been decreasing in recent years.

Advancement Prospects

Medical Scientists can advance to supervisory, managerial, or administrative positions in any work setting. For example, they can become a project leader, program manager, division director, or executive officer. Those with entrepreneurial ambitions can become independent consultants or owners of companies that provide medical services—such as research and testing—or that develop and produce medical products.

Education and Training

Employers require that Medical Scientists have a doctoral degree (Ph.D.), doctor of medicine degree (M.D.), or a doctor of osteopathy degree (D.O.). Medical Scientists who perform clinical research, which deals directly with patients, are usually required to have an M.D. or D.O.

Most Medical Scientists earn their doctoral degrees in biological science disciplines (such as anatomy or microbiology) or subfields (such as comparative anatomy or medical microbiology). Other disciplines in which Medical Scientists obtain their doctoral degrees are biomedical engineering, epidemiology, public health, mathematics, psychology, and organic chemistry.

Several years of intensive study are required of students who aim to become Medical Scientists. Anyone interested in earning only a Ph.D. should first complete a bachelor's degree program (about four to five years) and then a master's degree program (about one to two years). A Ph.D. program (about five to eight years) includes advanced classroom studies and lab research training as well as completion of a dissertation that involves original research. Ph.D. graduates typically complete several years of postdoctoral training to gain further research experience in their fields.

The educational path for physician-scientists varies. One path is the completion of a dual degree (M.D./Ph.D.) program, which is offered at many medical schools. (Students usually enter medical school after completion of bachelor's degrees in premedicine or a science field.) M.D./Ph.D. programs normally take between seven to nine years. In general, students first complete the first two years of clinical study. During the next three to five (or more years), they do their graduate work in their chosen fields. After they have completed their dissertations, they then finish the last two years of medical school.

Those aspiring to work in clinical research complete three or more years of graduate medical education, more commonly known as residency, in a medical specialty such as internal medicine. If they wish to specialize in a subspecialty, such as cardiovascular disease or medical oncology in internal medicine, they complete another one to three more years of training.

Experience, Skills, and Personality Traits

Medical Scientists typically have previous work and research experience related to the positions for which they are applying. Many employers prefer that Medical Scientists have several years of postdoctoral experience in their research areas.

Medical Scientists must be able to express themselves clearly and succinctly to different groups of people from diverse backgrounds and with various levels of technical expertise. Therefore, they need excellent writing, communication, interpersonal, and teamwork skills. In addition, having strong self-management and problem-solving skills are important to accomplishing their objectives.

Successful Medical Scientists have several personality traits in common, such as being persistent, independent, curious, flexible, and enthusiastic.

Special Requirements

Professional licensure is not required for individuals to become Medical Scientists. Physician-scientists, however, are licensed physicians in the states where they practice. Licensure requirements vary from state to state. For specific information, contact the medical licensing board in the state where you wish to practice.

Most physician-scientists become board-certified in a specialty, such as obstetrics and gynecology, internal medicine, or surgery. Some also obtain board certification in a subspecialty. For example, internal medicine specialists can also become board-certified in such subspecialties as cardiovascular disease, hematology, infectious diseases, or medical oncology. Board certification is usually through one of the 24 member boards that are recognized by the American Board of Medical Specialties and the American Medical Association.

Unions and Associations

Many Medical Scientists belong to professional associations that serve their particular professions as microbiologists, pathologists, epidemiologists, cardiovascular surgeons, medical oncologists, pediatricians, and so on. Physician-scientists may join medical societies such as the American Medical Association. Professional associations provide Medical Scientists with networking opportunities, education programs, certification programs, professional publications, and other professional services and resources. See Appendix III for contact information.

Tips for Entry

1. As a middle school or high school student, start learning about biomedical research and researchers. For example, you might read science, medical, and health books and periodicals. Talk or correspond with professionals. Check out relevant websites, such as those for biomedical research institutes.

2. If you are interested in working for the federal government, contact the U.S. Office of Personnel Management (OPM). You may find a local office through

your telephone directory. Or go to the OPM website, http://www.usajobs.opm.gov.

3. Find out whether the medical schools in which you are interested offer the Medical Scientist Training Program (MSTP). This a combined M.D./Ph.D. program, which is sponsored by the federal government. It pays tuition costs for accepted students and provides them with annual stipends. You may find further information at this National Institutes of Health webpage: http://www.nih.gov/nigms/funding/trngmech.html#ee.

4. Use the Internet to learn more about biomedical researchers. One website you might visit is National Institutes of Health, http://www.nih.gov. To get a list of other relevant websites, enter one of these keywords in any search engine: *medical scientists, physician scientists,* or *biomedical research.*

PATHOLOGIST

CAREER PROFILE

Duties: Conduct basic or applied research studies; design and conduct research projects; may teach medical students and residents; may perform diagnostic duties; perform other duties as required

Alternate Title(s): Clinical Pathologist, Forensic Pathologist, Pediatric Pathologist, or other title that reflects a specialty

Salary Range: $30,000 to $112,000

Employment Prospects: Good

Advancement Prospects: Good

Prerequisites:
  Education or Training—An M.D. or D.O.
  Experience—Requirements vary for the different positions
  Special Skills and Personality Traits—Diagnostic, investigative, communication, writing, interpersonal, and self-management skills; detail-oriented; analytical; creative; honest
  Licensure/Certification—Physician licensure; board certification in specialty and subspecialty may be required

CAREER LADDER

```
┌─────────────────────────────────┐
│       Senior Pathologist        │
└─────────────────────────────────┘

┌─────────────────────────────────┐
│          Pathologist            │
└─────────────────────────────────┘

┌─────────────────────────────────┐
│     Pathology Resident or       │
│ Postdoctoral Research Associate │
└─────────────────────────────────┘
```

Position Description

Pathologists are medical doctors, trained in the science and practice of pathology. Pathology is the scientific study of how cells and tissues become altered by disease. It is also the practice of laboratory medicine. The pathology lab provides physicians with diagnostic information about their patients' illnesses and diseases.

Unlike other physicians, Pathologists do not examine patients, but rather analyze specimens (or samples) of patients' cells, tissue, and bodily fluids. Pathologists use principles and techniques from anatomy, biochemistry, physiology, microbiology, biophysics, molecular genetics, and other biological sciences to study and diagnose disease.

The study and practice of pathology is generally divided into two specialties. One specialty is called anatomical pathology. Pathologists make diagnoses that are based on analyzing cells and tissues through microscopic examination or by gross examination, which is what Pathologists can see, feel, and measure. The other specialty is called clinical pathology, which focuses on the analysis of blood and other bodily fluids. Pathologists perform various chemical and bio-

logical lab tests, interpreting the results to diagnose signs of disease. Most Pathologists are trained in both specialties.

Many Pathologists also specialize in one of its many subspecialties. They may specialize by studying diseases within a particular population or by studying diseases that affect specific organs or life systems. For example, some subspecialties include pediatric pathology (childhood diseases), ocular pathology (eye diseases), dermatopathology (skin diseases), neuropathology (diseases of the nervous system), and hematopathology (bone marrow and clotting disorders such as leukemia and anemia).

Other pathology subspecialties pertain to the type of diagnostic examinations or activities that are performed. Some areas in which Pathologists focus their studies are:

- surgical pathology—the analysis and diagnosis of specimens, which usually contain tumors, that have been removed in surgery
- cytopathology—the examination of bodily fluids or samples of cells, which have been scraped from tissues or collected with a fine needle, to detect early signs of disease

- autopsy pathology—the internal and external examination of dead bodies to determine the cause of death
- forensic pathology—the medico-legal investigation into the cause and manner of death of individuals who are connected to criminal cases
- chemistry pathology—the biochemical analysis of substances, such as hormones, enzymes, antibodies, proteins, and vitamins, in samples of bodily fluids
- hematology—the analysis of blood cells and bone marrow to determine the morphology (structure) of blood cells, how well blood may be clotting, and if there are any abnormalities in blood cell counts
- microbiology—the examination of specimens to identify microorganisms (such as bacteria, viruses, and parasites) that can cause infections as well as to determine the most effective drugs to treat infections
- molecular pathology—the use of DNA sequences and other tools of molecular biology to diagnose and monitor the spread of disease
- immunology—the analysis of the amount of antibodies being made by the body to fight infections or diseases
- blood banking, or transfusion medicine—the collection, storage, processing, and testing of blood and blood products, which have been donated by people
- medical informatics—the development and maintenance of information systems to manage large volumes of data (laboratory tests and other medical information) in the laboratory

Research Pathologists work in academic, government, industrial, and other settings. Many are involved with conducting basic research to gain new knowledge and understanding about the pathology of different diseases. They are interested in learning about the nature of different diseases, their causes, how they develop and progress, and how diseases affect the human body. Research Pathologists are also engaged in applied research. They apply the findings of basic research to develop new and improved diagnostic techniques and tests for the different diseases.

Research Pathologists typically collaborate on projects with other Pathologists and scientists. Principal investigators are usually responsible for seeking grants to fund new research projects as well as for raising funds to continue current studies.

Research Pathologists perform a variety of duties each day. Some tasks might include planning research projects, conducting experiments, analyzing and interpreting data, writing reports, reading literature, meeting with colleagues, preparing articles or presentations about research, performing administrative tasks, and so on. Pathologists use a variety of sophisticated tools and methods in their work. These include electron microscopy, computer models, biochemical analysis, cell culture, molecular genetic techniques, and experimental animals.

Academic researchers normally hold faculty appointments in medical schools. In addition to doing research, academic Pathologists teach courses in their specialties to medical students and train pathology residents. Their duties also include producing scholarly works for publication, performing administrative duties, and fulfilling community service obligations. In addition, many academic Pathologists continue to provide pathology services to physicians. Pathologists analyze and interpret various diagnostic tests to identify the cause of patients' illnesses or to determine if patients have diseases or early signs of diseases. They may perform tests and examinations directly or supervise technologists or residents in these tasks. The Pathologists are responsible for making the diagnoses and summarizing the results in pathology reports, which they give to the medical doctors. Physicians sometimes consult with Pathologists for advice and suggestions for treating diseases.

Pathologists are responsible for keeping up with new developments in their specialties as well as in the field of pathology in general. They attend professional meetings and conferences at the local, state, national, and international levels. They also read professional books and journals, enroll in workshops and seminars, and network with colleagues.

Salaries
Salaries vary, depending on such factors as experience, employer, and geographical location. According to the Bureau of Labor Statistics, the estimated annual salary in 2001 for most medical scientists, including Pathologists, ranged between $29,570 and $111,750.

Employment Prospects
Pathologists are employed by hospitals, clinics, and other medical facilities. Research Pathologists are find employment in medical schools, government agencies (such as Food and Drug Administration and National Institutes of Health), the military, biotechnology firms, pharmaceutical companies, and research institutes.

In general, opportunities for Pathologists become available as individuals retire or transfer to other positions. Employers will create additional positions to meet growing needs, as long as funding is available.

Advancement Prospects
Pathologists can advance to administrative and management positions in medical laboratories, research organizations, medical schools, and professional societies.

Education and Training
To become a Pathologist, medical training is necessary. Students first complete four years of medical training to earn either a doctor of medicine degree (M.D.) or doctor of

osteopathy degree (D.O.). This is followed by four to five years of graduate medical education (more commonly known as residency) to gain practical experience in the practice of pathology. Pathology residents do their training in anatomic pathology and/or clinical pathology. Those wishing to practice in a subspecialty of pathology, such as forensic pathology or pediatric pathology, complete an additional one to two years of training in the subspecialty.

Many research Pathologists have earned a doctoral degree in pathology, in a biomedical science, or in another related field. Some schools offer dual-degree programs that allow students to earn both an M.D. and a Ph.D.

Experience, Skills, and Personality Traits

Job requirements vary with the different employers. In general, they look for Pathologists with previous work experience that is pertinent to the positions for which they are applying. They may have gained experience through employment, residencies, or postdoctoral training.

Research Pathologists are expected to have excellent diagnostic and investigative skills as well as strong communication and writing skills so they can present information clearly. They should also have good interpersonal skills as they will work and deal with various people from diverse professions and backgrounds. Additionally, Pathologists must have adequate self-management skills, including the ability to handle stressful situations, meet deadlines, organize and prioritize multiple tasks, and work independently. Being detail-oriented, analytical, creative, and honest are some personality traits that successful Pathologists share.

Special Requirements

Pathologists must be licensed to practice medicine in the United States, its territories, or District of Columbia where they wish to practice. Employers may require that Pathologists be board-certified by the American Board of Pathology or the American Osteopathic Board of Pathology. Many Pathologists apply for board certification on a voluntary basis.

Unions and Associations

Many Pathologists are members of local, state, regional, and national societies that serve their particular interests.

These organizations offer various professional services and resources such as education programs, professional publications, current research information, and networking opportunities. Some professional associations at the national level are:

- American Society for Clinical Pathology
- American Society for Investigative Pathology
- Association for Molecular Pathology
- Association for Pathology Informatics
- College of American Pathologists
- Society for Cardiovascular Pathology
- Society for Pediatric Pathology
- United States and Canadian Academy of Pathology

In addition, Pathologists may join the American Medical Association and other professional associations that serve the general interests of physicians. For contact information for any of these organizations, please see Appendix III

Tips for Entry

1. Talk with Pathologists to learn more about their jobs as well as about their education and training. As a high school student or undergraduate, you might get a part-time job or internship at a clinical laboratory to get an idea of the work that is done there.
2. To learn about fellowships and permanent positions, contact professional societies. Many societies have websites where they post information about fellowships they sponsor as well as links to other organizations. Many also post job listings on their websites.
3. Use the Internet to learn more about human pathology and medical Pathologists. Visit websites of related organizations, such as College of American Pathologists, http://www.cap.org; American Society for Clinical Pathology, http://www.ascp.org; American Society for Investigative Pathology, http://www.asip.org; and Intersociety Committee on Pathology Information, http://www.pathologytraining.org.

PHARMACOLOGIST

CAREER PROFILE

Duties: Conduct basic, applied, or clinical research; design and conduct research projects; may teach courses in college, university, or medical school; perform tasks as required of position

Alternate Title(s): Medical Scientist, Research Associate; Clinical Pharmacologist or other title that reflects a specialty

Salary Range: $30,000 to $112,000

Employment Prospects: Good

Advancement Prospects: Good

Prerequisites:

　Education or Training—Ph.D. required for research scientist positions; an M.D. degree may be required for clinical research positions

　Experience—Previous work and research experience related to the position one is applying for

　Special Skills and Personality Traits—Analytical, writing, communication, teamwork, interpersonal, mathematics, and statistics skills; enthusiastic; organized; flexible; diligent; creative

　Licensure/Certification—Physician licensure and board-certification may be required for clinical research positions

CAREER LADDER

```
┌─────────────────────────────────┐
│      Senior Pharmacologist      │
└─────────────────────────────────┘

┌─────────────────────────────────┐
│          Pharmacologist         │
└─────────────────────────────────┘

┌─────────────────────────────────┐
│  Postdoctoral Research Associate │
└─────────────────────────────────┘
```

Position Description

Pharmacologists are involved in the scientific study of drugs and how they can best treat or prevent disease and illness. They investigate such questions as: How do drugs alter the processes of cells? How can a certain disease be managed with drugs? What side effects can occur when taking a particular drug?

These scientists study the properties of various drugs, both beneficial and harmful. They investigate drug actions—the mechanisms that cause drugs to work in biological systems—and they examine how biological systems handle drugs. Furthermore, Pharmacologists are involved in developing new or improved synthetic drugs for therapeutic purposes.

Pharmacologists are often confused with pharmacists. However, pharmacology and pharmacy are two separate and distinct disciplines within the pharmaceutical sciences. Pharmacologists are scientific investigators who work in academic, government, or industrial research laboratories, while pharmacists prepare and dispense medicines to physicians and patients in health-care facilities and pharmacies. Pharmacologists supply the information that pharmacists use to provide physicians and patients advice about the selection and use of drugs.

Pharmacology is a multidisciplinary field, in which Pharmacologists apply principles and techniques of analytical chemistry, biochemistry, cellular biology, molecular biology, genetics, immunology, medicinal chemistry, microbiology, pathology, and physiology. Pharmacology is generally divided into two areas of study. Some Pharmacologists are involved in pharmacodynamics, which examines how drugs work in and affect biological systems. Other Pharmacologists do research in pharmacokinetics, which studies how the body handles drugs and chemicals.

Many Pharmacologists also specialize in one of the subdisciplines of pharmacology, such as:

- cardiovascular pharmacology—the heart, the vascular system, and other life systems that regulate the cardiovascular function
- neuropharmacology—the brain and nervous system
- psychopharmacology—the effect of drugs on mood and human behavior
- molecular pharmacology—the application of molecular biology to study how drugs work at the cellular and molecular levels
- chemotherapeutics—the development of chemical agents that can destroy or inhibit the growth of parasites or diseased cells without seriously hurting the host cells
- clinical pharmacology—the study of therapeutic and toxic actions of drugs in humans

Pharmacologists are engaged in different types of research. Those who conduct basic research are interested in gaining new knowledge and understanding about the properties of drugs and their interactions in biological systems. Other Pharmacologists apply the findings of basic research to find practical solutions to drug, chemical, and hormone-related problems that affect human health. These applied researchers typically work on the development of new or improved drug therapies and medicinal products.

Some Pharmacologists specialize in clinical research, which involves the final stages of development of new drugs or new uses for existing drugs. They study the effectiveness of experimental therapies on human subjects, who are volunteer patients. Because drugs are administered to patients, clinical Pharmacologists are either medical doctors or they collaborate with physicians who work directly with patients.

Pharmacologists usually work on more than one research project at a time, and often collaborate on projects with other Pharmacologists and scientists from other disciplines. Pharmacologists share information about their research by writing articles (or scientific papers) for scientific journals or by giving presentations at scientific conferences.

Pharmacologists work in laboratories and offices, while performing a variety of tasks each day. Some of their duties might include designing research projects; formulating hypotheses; conducting experiments; developing computer models to test theories; studying scientific literature; analyzing and interpreting data; writing reports; meeting with colleagues; and performing administrative tasks. Senior researchers or principal investigators typically perform supervisory and management tasks. In addition, principal investigators are usually responsible for obtaining research grants to fund their new and ongoing research projects.

Many Pharmacologists hold academic appointments at colleges and universities. They may teach undergraduate, graduate, medical, nursing, dental, or pharmacy courses. In addition to research and teaching duties, professors are responsible for advising students, supervising student research projects, and performing administrative tasks. They are also required to publish scholarly work and fulfill community service obligations.

Salaries
Salaries vary, depending on experience, employer, geographical location, and other factors. According to the Bureau of Labor Statistics, the estimated annual salary in 2001 for most medical scientists (including Pharmacologists) ranged between $29,570 and $111,750.

Employment Prospects
Pharmacologists are employed by government agencies, research institutes, academic institutions, pharmaceutical firms, biotechnology companies, and hospitals.

Employment opportunities are good for highly trained and experienced Pharmacologists. Most job openings become available as Pharmacologists transfer to other positions or retire. Employers create additional positions to meet growing needs, as long as funding is available.

Advancement Prospects
Pharmacologists with management or administrative ambitions can advance to such positions in any work setting. Professors receive promotional rankings as assistant professor, associate professor or full professor.

Education and Training
A master's degree in pharmacology, toxicology, biology, chemistry, or other related field, is the minimum requirement for applicants to qualify for research assistant and associate positions. A doctoral degree is usually required to conduct independent research, direct research laboratories, or to teach in colleges and universities. Some employers require that Pharmacologists possess medical doctor degrees to perform clinical research or teach in medical schools.

Ph.D. graduates normally complete one or more years of postdoctoral training before obtaining permanent positions.

Some schools offer dual-degree programs in which students can earn an M.D. and a Ph.D. in pharmacology or a related field.

Experience, Skills, and Personality Traits
Employers generally choose candidates who have previous work and research experience related to the jobs for which they are applying. Entry-level applicants may have gained experience through research projects, internships, fellowships, or part-time employment. Many employers require that Ph.D. applicants have a few years of postdoctoral experience.

Pharmacologists need strong analytical, writing, and communication skills to succeed at their work. They must have excellent teamwork and interpersonal skills, as they must be able to work well with scientists, technicians, administrators, patients, and others. Mathematics and statistics skills are also helpful. Being enthusiastic, organized, flexible, diligent, and creative are some personality traits that successful Pharmacologists share.

Special Requirements

Clinical Pharmacologists may be required to be licensed physicians as well as board-certified by the American Board of Clinical Pharmacology.

Unions and Associations

Many Pharmacologists join professional associations to take advantage of professional services and resources such as education programs, certification programs, and networking opportunities. Some national societies that serve the different interests of Pharmacologists include the American Society for Pharmacology and Experimental Therapeutics; the American College of Clinical Pharmacology; the American Society for Clinical Pharmacology and Therapeutics; the American Association of Pharmaceutical Scientists; and the American Psychological Association Division of Psychopharmacology and Substance Abuse. For contact information, please see Appendix III.

Tips for Entry

1. Gain experience during your undergraduate years by obtaining an internship or research assistantship.
2. Check with professional associations, government agencies, research institutes, companies, universities, and so forth for job listings. They may provide job hot lines or have postings on their websites.
3. Learn more about Pharmacologists on the Internet. Check out websites for the American Society for Pharmacology and Experimental Therapeutics, http://www.aspet.org; and the National Institute of General Medical Sciences's Medicines by Design: The Biological Revolution in Pharmacology, http://www.nigms.nih.gov/news/science_ed/medbydes.html.

EPIDEMIOLOGIST

CAREER PROFILE

Duties: Plan and conduct research studies on human health and disease; perform duties as required of position

Alternate Title(s): Environment Epidemiologist, Cancer Epidemiologist, or other title that reflect a specialized area; Public Health Epidemiologist, Disease Intervention Specialist, Medical Epidemiologist, or other title that reflects a particular position

Salary Range: $36,000 to $79,000

Employment Prospects: Good

Advancement Prospects: Good

Prerequisites:

Education or Training—Advanced degree in epidemiology, public health, or related field; M.D. or D.O. may be required

Experience—Previous work experience related to position normally required

Special Skills and Personality Traits—Organizational, reasoning, writing, communication, interpersonal, and teamwork skills; curious; flexible; logical; innovative; patient

Licensure/Certification—Physician or registered nurse (R.N.) licensure may be required

CAREER LADDER

```
┌─────────────────────────────┐
│    Senior Epidemiologist    │
└─────────────────────────────┘

┌─────────────────────────────┐
│       Epidemiologist        │
└─────────────────────────────┘

┌─────────────────────────────┐
│    Epidemiologist Trainee   │
└─────────────────────────────┘
```

Position Description

Epidemiology is the scientific study of human health and disease. Often known as "disease detectives," Epidemiologists identify health problems and health hazards in communities, nationwide, and throughout the world. They study the patterns and causes of diseases that occur within certain populations of people, communities, or geographical regions. They examine what causes a disease to occur within a location or a population of people, why some people contracted the disease, and why others did not. Epidemiologists also recommend solutions for preventing the disease and controlling it from spreading further.

Epidemiologists investigate sudden outbreaks of infectious diseases as well as examine the risk factors that lead to chronic diseases, such as cancer, arthritis, or HIV/AIDS. Epidemiologists also conduct research on a wide range of health issues such as birth defects, developmental disabilities, infant mortality, teenage suicides, violent behavior, injury control, occupational health, and environmental hazards. For example, Epidemiologists might seek answers to questions such as these: What is causing workers at a workplace to become ill with the same symptoms? What caused so many guests at a wedding reception to get *E. coli* food poisoning? What are the risk factors for cardiovascular disease among women between the ages of 40 and 65? What are the reasons for the increasing number of obese children in the United States?

Epidemiologists also conduct prevention research, in which they study ways to prevent people from contracting a certain injury, illness, or chronic disease. Epidemiologists also perform outcomes research, in which they examine the patterns and delivery of treatments for a particular disease and the effects of these treatments on the patients.

The results of epidemiological studies help public health authorities, government officials, and lawmakers develop policies, strategies, and interventions that prevent or control disease. Further, they help other public health specialists develop general guidelines that promote good mental and physical health practices for people of all ages and backgrounds.

Epidemiologists usually specialize in one or more areas of research. The list is long and varied and new specialties are continually being added. Some specialties are cardiovascular epidemiology, cancer prevention epidemiology, infectious disease epidemiology, molecular epidemiology, reproductive epidemiology, psychiatric epidemiology, and environmental epidemiology. Some Epidemiologists focus their research work on developing new epidemiological methodologies.

Epidemiologists may work on studies alone or collaborate with colleagues, scientists, and public health specialists. Many Epidemiologists work closely with the news media in order to inform the general public of critical health news.

Epidemiologists conduct their studies by gathering information from a sampling of people who are part of the population whom they are studying. The most common methodology is collecting data through surveys and interviews with people. Another methodology is observing people over a period of time to gather pertinent information. Some researchers choose to conduct experiments in which they provide or withhold substances from people to determine the toxic or beneficial effects of the substances. Some Epidemiologists work in the laboratory, examining blood samples for viruses or bacteria.

Epidemiologists' duties vary, depending on their position and experience. For example, senior Epidemiologists are usually responsible for designing, planning, and managing research projects. Many Epidemiologists hold full-time faculty positions in colleges, universities, and medical schools. Along with conducting epidemiological studies, they teach and advise students and perform other duties that are required of their academic appointments.

Some general tasks that Epidemiologists perform include

- recruiting people for project surveys and interviews
- analyzing and interpreting research data
- reviewing and analyzing medical and scientific reports
- preparing written or oral presentations about research projects and results
- providing consultative services to policy makers, educators, health-care providers, the general public, and public health specialists
- developing informational materials related to the prevention and control of disease
- attending meetings and conferences
- performing administrative tasks, such as writing correspondence and reports

Many Epidemiologists travel to other cities, states, and countries to gather research data, attend professional meetings, make presentations, and so forth. Their work may require them to spend several days or weeks at a location.

Salaries

Salaries vary, depending on such factors as education, experience, employer, and geographical location. According to the Bureau of Labor Statistics, the estimated annual salary for most Epidemiologists in 2001 ranged from $36,380 to $79,470.

Employment Prospects

Epidemiologists are employed by local and state public health departments, government agencies, colleges and universities, medical schools, research institutes, health organizations, HMOs, pharmaceutical companies, and biotechnology firms.

Most opportunities become available as Epidemiologists advance or transfer to other positions or retire. Employers create additional staff positions to meet their growing needs, as funding becomes available.

Advancement Prospects

Administrative and management positions are available to Epidemiologists in any work setting. They can advance to such positions by becoming a project coordinator, program manager, director, or executive officer.

Education and Training

Educational requirements vary for different positions. In general, Epidemiologists are required to possess either a master's or doctoral degree in epidemiology, public health, or another related field. Some employers hire candidates with a bachelor's degree in biological sciences, health sciences, social sciences, or other discipline, if they have qualifying work experience.

Those interested in becoming Medical Epidemiologists need a medical degree (M.D.) or doctor of osteopathy degree (D.O.) in addition to a master's degree in public health with an emphasis in epidemiology. A doctorate is the usual requirement for teaching in academic institutions, advancing to high-level management positions, and conducting independent research.

Many students entering graduate programs in epidemiology have a bachelor's degree in the biological sciences. Others hold an undergraduate degree in sociology, psychology, or other discipline.

Experience, Skills, and Personality Traits

In general, employers look for candidates who have previous work experience that is relevant to the positions for which they are applying. Entry-level candidates should have at least one year of qualifying work experience, which may have been gained through internships, work-study programs, summer employment, or postdoctoral training.

Having strong organizational, reasoning, writing, and communication skills are essential for Epidemiologists to perform their work well. In addition, they need excellent interpersonal and teamwork skills, as they must be able to handle working with people from different backgrounds. Being curious, flexible, logical, innovative, and patient are a few personality traits that successful Epidemiologists have in common.

Special Requirements

Some Epidemiologist positions require valid physician or registered nurse (R.N.) licensure.

Unions and Associations

Various local, state, regional, and national societies serve the diverse interests of Epidemiologists. These organizations offer Epidemiologists many professional resources and services such as networking opportunities, job listings, education programs, and professional publications. A few of the many professional associations at the national level are:

- American Academy of Pediatrics—Epidemiology Section
- American College of Epidemiology
- American College of Preventative Medicine
- American Epidemiology Society
- American Public Health Association—Epidemiology Section

- Association for Professionals in Infection Control and Epidemiology, Inc.
- Society for Epidemiological Research

For contact information see Appendix III.

Tips for Entry

1. As a middle or high school student, start exploring the different career options available to Epidemiologists. For example, you might contact different professional societies for information, read about the various subfields, talk with Epidemiologists, or visit the epidemiology lab at a nearby university.
2. Contact professional associations for information about internship, fellowship, and other training programs that they might sponsor.
3. Gain work experience by doing internships in different work settings and/or volunteering to work on research projects with professors.
4. Use the Internet to learn more about the field of epidemiology. Check out the Centers for Disease Control and Prevention, website http://www.cdc.gov. To get a list of other relevant websites, enter the keyword *epidemiology* or *epidemiologists* in a search engine.

BIOMEDICAL ENGINEER

CAREER PROFILE

Duties: Conduct basic or applied research; design or develop medical technology that improves human health; perform duties as required of position

Alternate Title(s): A title that reflects a specialized area, such as Biomaterials Engineer, Rehabilitation Engineer, or Clinical Engineer

Salary Range: $38,000 to $94,000

Employment Prospects: Good

Advancement Prospects: Good

Prerequisites:

Education or Training—A bachelor's degree in biomedical engineering

Experience—Previous work experience related to position required

Special Skills and Personality Traits—Foundation in mechanical engineering or other basic engineering discipline; problem-solving, writing, communication, presentation, teamwork, and interpersonal skills; open-minded; determined; inquisitive; analytical; creative

Licensure/Certification—Professional Engineer (P.E.) licensure may be required

CAREER LADDER

```
┌─────────────────────────────────────┐
│     Senior Biomedical Engineer       │
└─────────────────────────────────────┘

┌─────────────────────────────────────┐
│        Biomedical Engineer           │
└─────────────────────────────────────┘

┌─────────────────────────────────────┐
│    Biomedical Engineer (Trainee)     │
└─────────────────────────────────────┘
```

Position Description

Biomedical engineering, or bioengineering, is an applied science that integrates the principles of physical sciences, mathematics, and engineering with the study of biological systems, medicine, and health. The engineers in this field are called Biomedical Engineers. They work closely with physicians and other health-care providers as well as scientists and other engineers to develop medical technology that improves human health.

Biomedical Engineers invent medical devices, health-care products, and information systems that are used for diagnosing, treating, curing, and rehabilitating patients. For example, Biomedical Engineers have developed and designed medical instruments, robotic tools for surgery, imaging systems, heart-assist pumps, dialysis machines, diagnostic equipment, artificial organs, implants, prosthetics, wheelchairs, and computer systems for critical care units. Biomedical Engineers also work with doctors and surgeons to develop new or improved surgery, treatment, and other medical procedures.

Many Biomedical Engineers are involved in conducting studies in academic, government, industrial, or other research laboratories. They direct independent research projects as well as participate on research teams composed of Biomedical Engineers and other scientists and engineers.

Some Biomedical Engineers perform basic research related to biology and medicine in which they seek to gain further knowledge and understanding of biological systems. Others perform applied research, seeking solutions to specific medical and health-care problems. Still others are involved in the research, development, and design of new medical devices and instrumentation for commercial purposes.

Biomedical engineering is comprised of many specialties, and new areas are continually emerging as technology advances. Typically, Biomedical Engineers utilize basic knowledge from the different specialties to conduct their basic or applied research. Listed below are some areas in which Biomedical Engineers specialize:

- Biomaterials—the development and selection of materials such as metal alloys, ceramics, polymers, and composites that will be placed inside the human body to aid in healing bones or to help patients move better.
- Biomechanics—the application of the principles of mechanics (how forces affect matter) to biological or medical problems, such as injuries or problems with the flow of bodily fluids. Biomechanical research has led to the development of artificial organs and limbs, defibrillators, and cardiac pacemakers.
- Systems physiology—the use of mathematical and computer models to examine life processes such as metabolism. The results of these studies help other Biomedical Engineers develop products and methods for solving various medical problems. For example, musculoskeletal studies might lead to new applications in physical therapy for physically disabled individuals.
- Bioinstrumentation—the application of electronics and measurement principles and techniques to develop medical devices that diagnose, treat, and monitor patients. Some examples are X rays, laser systems for eye surgery, and computer systems to monitor patients during surgery.
- Biotechnology—the use of living cells or their materials in the development of pharmaceutical, diagnostic, and other medical products.
- Tissue engineering—the design of artificial tissues to repair or replace human tissues that have been damaged by disease or trauma.
- Rehabilitation engineering—the development of devices and procedures that help persons with physical impairments to be able to move around more easily as well as to live more independently. Rehabilitation engineers sometimes work directly with disabled persons.
- Bioinformatics—the scientific management of biological information that is stored in computer databases. Biological information may include genetic data, information about whole organisms, or data from clinical trials.
- Clinical engineering—the application of technology in hospitals and other clinical settings to support patient care. Biomedical Engineers, or more specifically clinical engineers, in this field usually work in clinical settings to design, modify, and analyze medical devices and information systems that meet the particular needs of physicians, surgeons, and other health-care practitioners.

Biomedical Engineers from the different specialties often work together or consult with each other on their projects.

Many Biomedical Engineers hold part-time (adjunct) or full-time teaching positions in colleges, universities, and medical schools. They may teach students in biological sciences, engineering, nursing, medicine, or other disciplines. Full-time instructors may be appointed to tenure- or nontenure- track faculty positions. In addition to conducting research and teaching, full-time faculty are expected to produce scholarly works, advise students, fulfill community services, and perform administrative duties.

All Biomedical Engineers are responsible for keeping up with trends and technology within their specialties. They enroll in training workshops and educational seminars, read professional books and journals, attend professional meetings and conferences, network with colleagues, and so on.

Salaries
Salaries vary, depending on such factors as education, experience, employer, and geographical location. According to the Bureau of Labor Statistics, the estimated annual salary in 2001 for most Biomedical Engineers ranged from $38,050 to $94,040.

Employment Prospects
Some employers of Biomedical Engineers are hospitals, medical centers, academic institutions, research institutes, and government agencies. Many Biomedical Engineers are employed in private industries that manufacture drugs, medical devices, and medical supplies. Some Biomedical Engineers are independent consultants.

Job opportunities for Biomedical Engineers are predicted to increase between 21 and 35 percent through 2010, according to the Bureau of Labor Statistics. Such factors as the growing elderly population and the increasing number of people concerned with health should contribute to the demand for medical devices and health-care products. In addition, technology continues to play an increased role in medicine, while providing health-care practitioners with newer and better tools and procedures for diagnosing, treating, and curing their patients.

Advancement Prospects
Biomedical Engineers with management and administrative ambitions can become project leaders, program managers, directors, and executive officers. Those with entrepreneurial interests can become independent consultants or owners of start-up companies that manufacture medical devices or health-care products.

Education and Training
Minimally, Biomedical Engineers need a bachelor's degree in biomedical engineering or other engineering field with a concentration in biomedical engineering. Many employers require that candidates have a master's degree. To teach in colleges or universities, conduct independent research, or obtain high-level administrative positions, candidates are usually required to have a master's degree or a Ph.D.

Biomedical Engineers might pursue advance training in biomedical engineering, by earning either a master's degree or doctorate in biomedical engineering. Others might obtain medical training and earn a medical degree, or complete dual degree programs in which they earn an M.D. and a Ph.D. in biomedical engineering.

Experience, Skills, and Personality Traits

Employers hire candidates who have previous work experience that is related to the positions for which they are applying. Entry-level applicants may have gained experience through internships, work-study positions, summer employment, research assistantships, fellowships, and so forth.

Along with their bioengineering training, Biomedical Engineers are expected to have a strong foundation in mechanical engineering, electronics engineering, or other basic engineering disciplines.

To do their work effectively, Biomedical Engineers are expected to have excellent problem-solving, writing, communication, and presentation skills. They also need good teamwork and interpersonal skills, as they must be able to work well with colleagues, medical doctors, scientists, technicians, and others. Some personality traits that successful Biomedical Engineers share are being open-minded, determined, inquisitive, analytical, and creative.

Special Requirements

Biomedical Engineers may be required to hold Professional Engineer (P.E.) licensure, particularly if they offer services directly to the general public. For specific information about P.E. licensure, contact the licensing board for engineers in the state where you wish to practice.

Unions and Associations

Many Biomedical Engineers are members of professional associations so that they can take advantage of professional resources and services such as education programs, certification programs, professional publications, and networking opportunities. Some societies that serve the various interests of Biomedical Engineers are:

- American Association for the Advancement of Science
- American College of Clinical Engineering
- American Institute for Medical and Biological Engineering
- American Institute of Chemical Engineers
- American Society of Biomechanics
- Biomedical Engineering Society
- IEEE Engineering in Medicine and Biology Society
- National Society of Professional Engineers
- Rehabilitation Engineering and Assistive Technology Society of North America
- Tissue Engineering Society International

For contact information, please see Appendix III.

Tips for Entry

1. As a college undergraduate, gain experience by taking advantage of internship or work-study programs.
2. Fellowships and research assistantships are available to support students as they pursue graduate studies. For example, three organizations that provide fellowships are the National Science Foundation, the Whitaker Foundation, and Tau Beta Pi. To learn about other programs, talk with your college adviser and college professors. Also contact your career college center or professional societies for information.
3. Learn more about biomedical engineering on the Internet. Some helpful websites include the Biomedical Engineering Network, http://www.bmenet.org; The Whitaker Foundation, http://www.whitaker.org; and National Institute of Biomedical Imaging and Bioengineering, http://www.nibib1.nih.gov.

MEDICAL PHYSICIST

CAREER PROFILE

Duties: Conduct scientific research; may provide clinical services and consultation; may teach students, residents, and others; perform duties as required of position

Alternate Title(s): Medical Radiation Physicist or other title that reflects a specialty

Salary Range: $49,000 to $123,000

Employment Prospects: Good

Advancement Prospects: Good

Prerequisites:

Education or Training—A master's or doctoral degree in medical physics or a related field, medical physicist residency may be required

Experience—Previous work experience related to position applying for is required

Special Skills and Personality Traits—Communication, interpersonal, teamwork, analytical, and self-management skills; flexible; adaptable; logical; inquisitive

Licensure/Certification—State licensure and/or board certification for clinical Medical Physicists may be required

CAREER LADDER

```
┌─────────────────────────────────────┐
│       Senior Medical Physicist        │
└─────────────────────────────────────┘

┌─────────────────────────────────────┐
│          Medical Physicist            │
└─────────────────────────────────────┘

┌─────────────────────────────────────┐
│       Research Associate or           │
│     Medical Physicist Resident        │
└─────────────────────────────────────┘
```

Position Description

Medical Physics, a branch of applied physics, is devoted to solving biomedical problems. It involves the application of physical tools (such as radiation, ultrasound, heat, lasers, and magnetic fields) to the diagnosis and treatment of human diseases and health problems. Medical Physicists are generally engaged in three activities: scientific research, clinical practice, and teaching.

Medical physics is made up of several specialties, which include:

- radiation therapy physics—the application of radiation to treat diseases such as cancer
- diagnostic imaging physics—the use of medical imaging systems (such as X rays, ultrasonic radiation, magnetic resonance imaging, and computerized tomography scans) to diagnose illnesses and injuries inside the body
- medical nuclear physics (or nuclear medicine)—the use of radioactive isotopes for diagnosing and treating patients

- medical health physics—the safe and proper application of radiation for diagnosis or treatment purposes

In their capacities as research scientists, Medical Physicists conduct studies in academic, government, industrial, and nongovernmental laboratories. They often collaborate on projects with medical doctors, scientists, engineers, and others.

Medical Physicists engage in various types of research. Some of them conduct basic research to gain further knowledge and understanding in medical physics. They develop new theories relevant to biomedical processes, diagnostic techniques, radiation delivery systems, radiation therapy, and so on. Like other physicists, Medical Physicists may emphasize a theoretical or experimental approach in their studies. Theoretical researchers create computer models to analyze whether the results of experiments (which may be done by other physicists) fulfill the predictions of physics theories. Experimental Medical Physicists design and run experiments and make careful observations and measurements to explain what happened in the experiments.

Some Medical Physicists are involved in applied research or translational research. By using the results of basic medical physics research, they develop new or improved tools, methodologies, and approaches for more accurate, precise, and safe diagnostic and therapeutic uses. For example, Medical Physicists might develop new techniques for imaging internal organs or participate in the design of improved radiotherapy treatment. Still other Medical Physicists participate in clinical research. They study the results of experimental techniques and therapies that are tested on human subjects, who are volunteer patients.

Many Medical Physicists are involved in the practice of medical physics. They provide clinical services and consultation in hospitals, medical clinics, and other health-care facilities. As health-care practitioners, Medical Physicists work closely with physicians, nurses, radiologists, and other technical staff. They collaborate in the planning and delivery of radiation treatments for patients. They also monitor procedures and equipment to ensure that the proper and safe dosages of radiation are delivered appropriately to patients.

Medical Physicists also provide consultation for the optimal use of the various diagnostic imaging systems. They make sure that equipment is properly installed and in working order, and that it meets government regulations and standards. They also develop accurate, safe, and proper diagnostic and treatment procedures and protocols. Furthermore, they provide essential education to medical staff, patients, and the general public on radiation safety. Medical Physicists may be involved in performing other services or supervising other staff members.

Most Medical Physicists are involved in teaching. Some are adjunct (part-time) instructors or full-time professors in colleges and universities, teaching physics and medical physics courses in undergraduate and graduate programs. Others hold teaching appointments in medical schools and teaching hospitals where they train medical students, medical residents, and medical technologists (such as radiology and nuclear medicine technologists) in the proper use of radiation for the diagnosis and treatment of patients.

In general, Medical Physicists divide their time among research, clinical service, and teaching. Their involvement in each area varies, depending on their education, interests, workplace, and other factors. For example, Medical Physicists who work in academic institutions mostly do research and teaching activities, while those working in nonteaching hospitals and medical clinics are more involved in clinical practice.

Salaries

Salaries vary, depending on the type of position, experience, education, geographical location, and other factors. Most physicists, including Medical Physicists, earned an estimated annual salary in 2001 that ranged between $49,320 and $123,220, according to the Bureau of Labor Statistics.

Employment Prospects

Medical Physicists work in hospitals, cancer treatment centers, and other medical care facilities. They also are employed by government agencies, industry, research institutes, academic institutions, and consulting firms.

Most job opportunities open up to replace Medical Physicists who are retiring or transferring to other positions.

Advancement Prospects

Administrative and management positions are available for Medical Physicists in any work setting. Those with entrepreneurial ambitions can become independent consultants as well as owners of consulting firms or companies that provide clinical services to health-care practitioners and medical-care facilities.

Education and Training

Most employers require that Medical Physicists hold a master's or doctoral degree in medical physics, physics, radiation biology, or another related field. Doctoral degrees are usually required for Medical Physicists to conduct independent research, teach in universities and colleges, or advance to executive level positions.

Upon earning their academic degrees, graduates usually obtain medical physics residencies to gain practical experience in clinical service.

Those interested in a research career usually work one or more years in postdoctoral positions to get additional training in their research areas.

Experience, Skills, and Personality Traits

Job requirements vary with the different employers. They generally hire candidates who have work experience related to the positions for which they are applying. Entry-level applicants may have gained experience through internships, research assistantships, residency programs, postdoctoral training, and so on.

Because Medical Physicists work with medical doctors, scientists, engineers, patients, and others, they must have excellent communication, interpersonal, and teamwork skills. In addition, they should have strong analytical and self-management skills. Being flexible, adaptable, logical, and inquisitive are some personality traits that successful Medical Physicists share.

Special Requirements

Some states require that clinical Medical Physicists hold valid licensure to practice. For specific information, contact the professional licensing agency in the state where you wish to practice.

Hospital, clinics, and medical centers may require that clinical Medical Physicists be board-certified by a recognized organization such as the American Board of Medical Physics or the American Board of Radiology.

Unions and Associations

Many Medical Physicists join one or more professional associations to take advantage of networking opportunities, professional certification, education programs, and other professional services and resources. Professional associations are available at the local, state, national, and international level. Some national societies that serve the different interests of Medical Physicists include the American College of Medical Physics; the American Association of Physicists in Medicine; the American College of Radiology; the Society of Nuclear Medicine; the Health Physics Society; the Biophysical Society; and the American Physical Society. See Appendix III for contact information.

Tips for Entry

1. As an undergraduate, gain experience through internships or work-study programs. You might also volunteer to work with a professor who is conducting research that interests you.
2. When you are doing a job search, remember to contact professors, colleagues, college career counselors, medical practitioners, scientists, and others whom you know for job leads.
3. Learn more about Medical Physicists on the Internet. You can start by visiting the American Association of Physicists in Medicine, http://www.aapm.org; or the American College for Medical Physics, http://www.acmp.org.

ENVIRONMENTAL PROTECTION AND CONSERVATION

ENVIRONMENTAL SCIENTIST

CAREER PROFILE

Duties: Primary responsibilities vary according to the position: conduct research, perform regulatory duties, manage environmental programs, or conduct environmental assessments; perform duties as required of position

Alternate Title(s): Environmental Consultant, Environmental Analyst, Environmental Specialist, Environmental Technician; a title that reflects a specialty or occupation such as Environmental Chemist, Hydrologist, or Fisheries Conservationist

Salary Range: $30,000 to $96,000

Employment Prospects: Good

Advancement Prospects: Good

Prerequisites:

Education or Training—A bachelor's or advanced degree in environmental science or a related field

Experience—Previous work and research experience; postdoctoral experience may be required for research scientists

Special Skills and Personality Traits—Technical, interpersonal, teamwork, communication, technical writing, and problem-solving skills; creative; positive; energetic; dedicated; flexible; detail-oriented

Licensure/Certification—Completion of a certification program may be required for certain jobs

CAREER LADDER

```
┌─────────────────────────────────────┐
│ Senior Environmental Scientist or    │
│ Environmental Consultant             │
└─────────────────────────────────────┘

┌─────────────────────────────────────┐
│ Environmental Scientist              │
└─────────────────────────────────────┘

┌─────────────────────────────────────┐
│ Postdoctoral Research Associate or   │
│ Environmental Scientist (entry-level)│
└─────────────────────────────────────┘
```

Position Description

Environmental Scientists are involved with the protection of the environment and the conservation of air, water, land, and other natural resources. They study how human activities affect the health of the environment and humans. They investigate and monitor such environmental problems as air pollution, water pollution, toxic waste sites, contamination of water supplies, global climate changes, destruction of ecosystems, population growth, endangerment of plant and animal species, depletion of natural resources, and public health and safety. In addition, Environmental Scientists develop solutions and manage programs that help prevent, control, or treat environmental problems at local, regional, and global levels.

Environmental science is a multidisciplinary field that integrates principles and techniques from the biological, physical, and earth sciences (or geosciences). Environmental Scientists therefore include biologists, oceanographers, botanists, health scientists, chemists, geologists, geographers, hydrologists, ecologists, foresters, agronomists, soil scientists, and other scientists.

Since environmental science is such a broad field, many Environmental Scientists specialize in a particular area. Some specialties are air quality management, groundwater protection, hazardous waste management, solid waste management, wetlands protection, energy, industrial hygiene, land conservation, and fishery and wildlife management.

Environmental Scientists work in academic, government, industrial, nonprofit, and nongovernmental settings. They hold different types of positions. Many of them are environmental researchers. They conduct basic research to gain new knowledge and understanding about air, water, and soil environments as well as about the impact of human activities on the natural environment and the various environmental conditions. Basic environmental research also contributes to the creation of effective environmental laws and policies.

Other Environmental Scientists are involved in applied research. They use the findings of basic research to develop practical solutions to specific environmental problems. They design new or improved technologies and practices that can help with the prevention or remediation of environmental problems as well as with the management of natural resources. For example, Environmental Scientists might develop conservation practices to protect drinking water supplies, design innovative technologies to reduce pollution emissions in refineries, or devise new methods to clean up contaminated sites.

In industrial research labs, many Environmental Scientists are involved in the development of new products, by studying ways to create products that are less harmful to the environment. Other researchers are concerned with improving production processes and investigate ways to reduce the amount of waste that enters the environment.

Environmental Scientists are also employed in various nonresearch positions, as environmental managers, technicians, and specialists. These professionals might perform such duties as:

- performing lab analyses of water, soil, and air samples to identify sources of pollutants or contaminants
- designing and managing programs and systems for the protection or restoration of air quality, water supplies, and land areas
- conducting assessments of proposed projects—such as construction sites, housing developments, stream alterations, offshore drilling, pesticide use, or the installation of underground storage tanks—to determine their impact on the environment
- monitoring the toxicity of air, water, and soil at specific sites, in communities, or in regional areas
- performing resource surveys of specific plant or animal species in wetlands, forests, and other ecosystems
- enforcing local, state, and federal regulations pertaining to air pollution, surface water, drinking and ground water, hazardous waste, solid waste, and infectious waste
- inspecting environmental systems and facilities to ensure that companies, businesses, agencies, and organizations are compliant with local, state, and federal laws
- responding to emergency spills of hazardous wastes and oversee the cleaning up of hazardous sites
- conducting investigations into environmental violations, which includes such tasks as gathering and preparing evidence and providing testimony as expert witnesses
- performing project management duties, which includes planning and overseeing projects, coordinating schedules, making technical presentations, and so forth

Many Environmental Scientists are consultants who offer environmental services to government agencies, businesses, manufacturers, farmers, developers, hospitals, and others. Consultants may be independent contractors or employees of environmental consulting firms. They are hired by clients to perform specific jobs, such as conducting environmental assessments of proposed construction projects, overseeing the cleanup of toxic sites, or making sure that clients are in compliance with environmental regulations. Environmental consultants are expected to continually generate new business for their firms.

Many Environmental Scientists are involved in environmental education, as employees of government agencies. Some Environmental Scientists develop and coordinate public educational outreach programs. Some of them provide technical assistance to companies, hospitals, manufacturers, and others to help them generate less waste and prevent pollution.

Additionally, many Environmental Scientists are adjunct (part-time) instructors and full-time professors at colleges and universities. Many full-time faculty members are responsible for conducting research projects along with teaching courses, advising students, and performing other required duties. They are also expected to produce scholarly works about their research projects.

Environmental Scientists work in offices, laboratories, and in the field. Their field work may be performed at lakes or rivers, by coastlines, on mountains, or in forests. Depending on the nature of their project, they may be required to be away from home for several days or weeks at a time.

Many Environmental Scientists are frequently exposed to toxic chemicals, thus they follow certain procedures to keep health and safety hazards to a minimum. Certain tasks may require them to wear special clothing, respiratory protection masks, or other safety equipment.

Salaries

Salaries vary, depending on such factors as education, experience, occupation, employer, and geographical location. According to the Bureau of Labor Statistics, the estimated annual salary in 2001 for most Environmental Scientists ranged between $29,660 and $78,320; and for most environmental science post-secondary instructors, between $32,760 and $95,940.

Employment Prospects

Job opportunities for Environmental Scientists exist at local, state, national, and international levels. However, the job market for Environmental Scientists is sensitive to changes in environmental policies. For example, job opportunities can be expected to shrink when environmental regulations are loosened or repealed.

The Bureau of Labor Statistics reports that the employment of Environmental Scientists is expected to grow between 21 to 35 percent through 2010. This will be partly due to the large number of Environmental Scientists reaching retirement age in the coming years. In addition, the need to address environmental problems and comply with environmental laws and regulations should contribute to a growing demand for Environmental Scientists.

With their backgrounds, Environmental Scientists can pursue other careers in the environmental field. For example, they can become high school teachers, environmental policy analysts, lobbyists, environmental advocates, landscape architects, surveyors, park rangers, environmental journalists, and environmental health specialists.

Advancement Prospects

Environmental Scientists can advance to management and administrative positions, by becoming a project leader, program manager, director, or executive officer. The highest ambition for some Environmental Scientists is to become an independent consultant or owner of an environmental consulting firm or other environmental-related business.

Education and Training

A bachelor's degree is usually required of candidates applying for such positions as environmental regulatory specialists, environmental technicians, and research associates. Some employers require, or strongly prefer, that candidates have a master's degree. A master's or doctoral degree is normally required for anyone interested in research, consulting, and management positions. For a candidate to teach in universities and colleges, advance to top management positions, or conduct independent research, a doctorate is the typical requirement.

A bachelor's and advanced degree may be earned in environmental science or a related discipline in the biological sciences, physical sciences, or geosciences. For example, many Environmental Scientists hold a degree in ecology, biology, chemistry, geology, geography, meteorology, hydrology, agronomy, soil science, or another science discipline. Some Environmental Scientists have earned their undergraduate degree in science or nonscience disciplines, then obtained an advanced degree in environmental science.

Experience, Skills, and Personality Traits

Employers typically hire candidates who have previous work experience related to the positions for which they are applying. Entry-level applicants may have gained experience through research projects, internships, fellowships, or part-time employment. Many employers expect Ph.D. applicants to have worked one or more years in postdoctoral positions. Environmental consultants are typically midlevel and senior level scientists in their field, which includes experience in research, project management, and technical leadership.

Prospective Environmental Scientists should have strong technical skills, including some experience with data analysis, computer modeling, remote sensing, geographical information systems (GIS), and Global Positioning System (GPS) technology. In addition, they need excellent interpersonal, teamwork, and communication skills as well as strong technical writing and problem-solving skills.

Being creative, positive, energetic, dedicated, flexible, and detail-oriented are some personality traits that successful Environmental Scientists share.

Special Requirements

Federal or state laws may require that employees complete appropriate certification programs if they perform certain types of lab analyses, such as wastewater analysis or hazardous materials analysis. To learn about certification for specific occupations, contact the U.S. Environmental Protection Agency or the state department of health or state department of natural resources in the state where you plan to work.

Unions and Associations

Professional associations for Environmental Scientists are available at local, state, national, and international levels. They offer their members the opportunity to network with colleagues as well as provide various professional services and resources such as education programs, professional certification, job listings, professional publications, and current research data. Some societies that serve the different interests of Environmental Scientists include:

- National Association of Environmental Professionals
- Air and Waste Management Association
- Soil and Water Conservation Society
- Water Environment Federation
- National Association of Local Government Environmental Professionals

Environmental Scientists also join societies that serve their particular disciplines, such as the American Institute of Biological Sciences, the Society of Wetland Scientists, the American Chemical Society, the Geological Society of America, the American Society of Agronomy, or the Society of American Foresters. See Appendix III for contact information.

Tips for Entry

1. While you are an undergraduate, seek out internships or work-study positions with environmental consulting firms, government agencies, conservation groups, and other organizations. If you are interested in a research career, you can also gain experience through research assistantship positions.

2. Some sources of environmental job listings are professional associations, environmental organizations, college career centers, and environmental publications. Many groups have phone job banks or post job vacancies at their websites.

3. Keep in mind that job ads for Environmental Scientist may reflect the type of specialists that employers want, such as environmental chemist, soil scientist, or hydrologist. Also be aware that a job title can refer to different positions. Therefore, carefully read job descriptions to make sure they are positions that you qualify for as well as jobs that you want.

4. Use the Internet to learn more about the environmental field. Some websites you might visit are U.S. Environmental Protection Agency, http://www.epa.gov; Environmental Careers Organization, http://www.eco.org; ECO World: Global Environmental Community, http://www.ecoworld.com; and the Environmental Education Directory, http://www.enviroeducation.com.

ENVIRONMENTAL CHEMIST

CAREER PROFILE

Duties: Provide lab analyses support; perform basic or applied research, perform other duties as required

Alternate Title(s): Industrial Chemist, Air Quality Chemist, or other title that reflects a specific position

Salary Range: $30,000 to $89,000

Employment Prospects: Good

Advancement Prospects: Good

Prerequisites:

Education or Training—A bachelor's or advanced degree in chemistry

Experience—One or more years of work experience performing chemical analyses

Special Skills and Personality Traits—Communication, interpersonal, teamwork, analytical, and organizational skills; curious; patient; persistent; flexible; creative; detail-oriented

Licensure/Certification—Certification may be required for certain jobs

CAREER LADDER

```
┌─────────────────────────────────┐
│  Senior Environmental Chemist    │
└─────────────────────────────────┘

┌─────────────────────────────────┐
│     Environmental Chemist        │
└─────────────────────────────────┘

┌─────────────────────────────────┐
│ Environmental Chemist (entry-level) │
└─────────────────────────────────┘
```

Position Description

Environmental Chemists play an important role in the protection of the environment and in the conservation of natural resources. They study and seek solutions to a wide range of environmental problems, such as air pollution, water pollution, hazardous waste disposal, contaminated groundwater, and damaged ecosystems.

Environmental Chemists use the principles and techniques of chemistry, biochemistry, and other related sciences to examine the chemical compounds of pollutants and contaminants found in the air, water, and soil. They study the composition and reactions of toxic substances, as well as study the fates of those substances—where they end up in the environment—and how they are transported there. In addition, Environmental Chemists examine how toxic substances affect the air, water, and soil environments.

Environmental Chemists work in public and private settings. Many of them are responsible for providing lab analyses to public works (such as wastewater treatment plants), regulatory agencies, refineries, chemical plants, industrial plants, research labs, and so forth. Their primary duty is to analyze soil, water, and air samples from industrial sites, waste treatment centers, water supplies, contaminated sites, and so forth. They may be asked to:

- identify and measure the amount of contaminants within samples
- estimate the exposure and effects of environmental contamination on humans and other living organisms
- assess the potential risk of pollution or contamination to the environment and public health
- monitor industrial processes or wastewater and, if necessary, incorporate appropriate chemical treatments to correct any problems
- test air, water, and soil samples to make sure that operations or processes are in compliance with local, state, and federal environmental laws and regulations

Many Environmental Chemists are members of teams that respond to emergencies such as oil spills or sudden discharges of toxic substances into water supplies. Some government-employed Environmental Chemists assist in collecting evidence to prosecute violators of environmental regulations. Government employees also might develop safety regulations or provide technical advice to companies, the general public, and others regarding hazardous waste disposal and treatment methods.

Many Environmental Chemists are involved in conducting research in academic, government, industrial, and other private research labs. Some conduct basic research to gain new knowledge and understanding about toxic chemicals, the effects of pollutants on the environment and on human health, the way human activities affect the chemistry of the biosphere, and so on. They study such questions as: What happens to certain toxic compounds when they dissolve in water? How does the atmosphere carry pollutants? What is the rate of global oxygen depletion? What happens to pesticides in the environment?

The results of basic research often lead to the development of practical applications for solving environmental problems. For example, Environmental Chemists might discover new industrial processes that reduce pollutants, invent new recycling technologies, develop ways to decontaminate toxic waste sites, or create better methods of treating and storing hazardous wastes.

Research Environmental Chemists conduct studies in various areas, such as toxicology, hydrogeology, oceanography, and health and safety. They often collaborate on projects with environmental engineers, environmental scientists, and scientists from other disciplines. Researchers also develop new technologies and methods for detecting, measuring, and analyzing pollutants and toxic substances.

Environmental Chemists are involved in a variety of tasks, which vary each day. They perform such tasks as collecting samples in the field, setting up tests or experiments, recording data, developing computer models to analyze and interpret data, writing reports, attending meetings, and performing administrative tasks. Senior chemists may also perform supervisory and managerial duties.

Many Environmental Chemists teach courses in chemistry or environmental studies in colleges and universities, as adjunct (part-time) lecturers or as full-time faculty members. Full-time professors juggle research, teaching, and other responsibilities each day. In addition, they are required to produce scholarly works on a regular basis.

Environmental Chemists perform controlled tests and experiments in the laboratory as well as conduct studies in the field. Their fieldwork may involve traveling to isolated areas, such as forests and wilderness areas.

They follow specific safety procedures while handling chemicals to keep health and safety hazards to a minimum. They may be required to wear protective clothing, respiratory masks, and other safety equipment.

Salaries

Salaries vary, depending on such factors as education, experience, employer, and geographical location. The starting salaries for Environmental Chemists with a doctoral degree is typically higher than for those with a master's or bachelor's degree.

The estimated annual salary in 2001 for most chemists, including Environmental Chemists, ranged between $30,450 and $89,830, according to the Bureau of Labor Statistics.

Employment Prospects

Environmental Chemists work for government agencies and laboratories, colleges and universities, and nonprofit and nongovernmental research institutes. They also find employment in various industries, such as the chemical, pharmaceutical, mining, and pulp and paper industries. Many Environmental Chemists are independent consultants or are employed by environmental consulting firms.

In general, the job market for Environmental Chemists is expected to grow in the coming years, due to the need for businesses and organizations to comply with environmental laws and regulations. In addition, more companies are placing emphasis on modifying their production processes to reduce pollutants.

Advancement Prospects

Many Environmental Chemists measure their success by being able to conduct independent research, by making discoveries or inventions, by earning higher incomes, and through gaining professional recognition. Those with managerial ambitions can pursue such positions as project leader, program manager, and program director.

Education and Training

Employers normally require that Environmental Chemists hold a bachelor's or advanced degree in chemistry. Employers sometimes accept degrees in other disciplines, if candidates have a minimum number of hours of course work in chemistry as well as qualifying experience.

To teach at the university level, conduct independent research, or advance to top management posts, a doctorate is generally required.

Employers usually provide formal and/or on-the-job training to new employees.

Experience, Skills, and Personality Traits

Job applicants generally need one or more years of work experience performing chemical analyses. Recent graduates may have gained experience through internships, work-study programs, part-time or summer employment, or research assistantships. In addition, applicants should have experience with or be knowledgeable about the environmental issues with which they will be working. They should be able to understand and use the terminology of biology, geology, ecology, mineralogy, genetics, water chemistry, and other disciplines.

To do their work effectively, Environmental Chemists need strong communication, interpersonal, and teamwork skills. They should also have excellent analytical and organizational skills. Being curious, patient, persistent, flexible, creative, and detail-oriented are some personality traits that successful Environmental Chemists share.

Special Requirements

Federal or state laws may require that employees complete appropriate certification programs, if they are to perform certain types of lab analyses, such as wastewater analysis or hazardous materials analysis. To learn about certification for specific occupations, contact the U.S. Environmental Protection Agency or the state department of health or state department of natural resources in the state where you plan to work.

Unions and Associations

Environmental Chemists can join local, state, or national societies to take advantage of professional services and resources such as education programs, professional certification, job listings, and networking opportunities. Many of them join the Division of Environmental Chemistry, part of the American Chemical Society. They also become members of societies that serve the general interests of chemists, such as the American Institute of Chemists and the American Association for the Advancement of Science.

In addition, Environmental Chemists are eligible to join professional associations that serve the interests of professionals working in a particular field. For example, the National Ground Water Association, the Water Environment Federation, and the Air and Waste Management Association are some such societies. See Appendix III for contact information.

Tips for Entry

1. As a college student, gain experience by obtaining internship(s) with government agencies or private employers and by doing volunteer work with environmental organizations.
2. To enhance their employability, as well as to gain training and background in the field, many chemistry students take some courses in environmental science.
3. Use the Internet to learn more about environmental chemistry. To get a list of relevant websites, enter the keywords *environmental chemistry* or *environmental chemists* in a search engine.

ENVIRONMENTAL ENGINEER

CAREER PROFILE

Duties: Design solutions to prevent, control, and fix problems related to air quality, water quality, hazardous waste management, and other environmental issues; perform duties as required

Alternate Title(s): Hazardous Waste Engineer, Water Resources Engineer, or other title that reflects a specialty; Civil Engineer, Mechanical Engineer, or Chemical Engineer

Salary Range: $38,000 to $90,000

Employment Prospects: Good

Advancement Prospects: Good

Prerequisites:

Education or Training—A bachelor's degree in environmental engineering or a related field; a master's degree may be preferred

Experience—Previous experience required or preferred; must be knowledgeable about environmental laws and safety

Special Skills and Personality Traits—Communication, interpersonal, teamwork, and writing skills; creative; curious; analytical; detail-oriented

Licensure/Certification—Professional Engineer (P.E.) licensure may be required

CAREER LADDER

```
┌─────────────────────────────────┐
│  Senior Environmental Engineer or│
│         Project Engineer         │
└─────────────────────────────────┘

┌─────────────────────────────────┐
│      Environmental Engineer      │
└─────────────────────────────────┘

┌─────────────────────────────────┐
│ Environmental Engineer-in-Training│
└─────────────────────────────────┘
```

Position Description

Environmental Engineers apply principles of biology, chemistry, engineering, and mathematics toward protecting the environment and conserving natural resources. They address a wide range of environmental issues, including air quality management, water quality management, solid waste management, storm water management, toxic waste disposal, recycling, public health, land management, wildlife management, and so on.

Environmental Engineers work for private companies, government agencies, and other organizations, either full time or as consultants. Some Environmental Engineers are civil engineers, mechanical engineers, or chemical engineers who specialize in environmental engineering.

Environmental Engineers are responsible for finding solutions that prevent, control, or fix environmental problems at local, regional, and worldwide levels. They invent devices and develop systems that reduce the release of pollutants and wastes into the environment and protect public health. For example, Environmental Engineers might build a pollution control system to reduce pollutant emissions at a refinery.

Environmental Engineers also plan, design, and construct such facilities as wastewater treatment plants, landfills, and recycling centers. Some of them are in charge of the operation and maintenance of such facilities. In addition, Environmental Engineers participate in the cleanup of contaminated sites and the restoration of damaged ecosystems (such as wetlands). Furthermore, they respond to such environmental emergencies as oil spills, industrial accidents, and poisoned water supplies.

Environmental Engineers usually work on projects with other engineers and scientists, technicians, and project managers. They typically work on several projects at a time, with their responsibilities varying from one project to the next. For example, they might perform any of the following duties:

- identify the specific problems or issues to be addressed in a project
- conduct assessments to determine the extent of contamination at a site
- determine the impact that a prospective construction project may have on the environment
- develop risk management or prevention plans for environmental systems, processes, or facilities
- oversee the construction of facilities or the implementation of treatment systems, production processes, and so forth
- evaluate environmental data about particular problems and recommend solutions to employers or clients
- prepare bid proposals, evaluations, or other reports on which employers or clients base their decisions
- complete permit applications and other paperwork required by government agencies
- ensure that employers or clients are in compliance with all necessary local, state, and federal environmental regulations

Environmental Engineers also perform other types of work. Some are employed as regulatory specialists by government agencies. They enforce environmental regulations, monitor activities of companies and organizations, and develop environmental policies.

Some Environmental Engineers conduct basic research in academic or government settings. They add new theories that lead to practical applications, as well as invent new technologies and practices to address various environmental issues. In addition, some Environmental Engineers teach engineering courses at colleges and universities. Full-time professors are responsible for conducting independent research, teaching courses, and advising students.

All Environmental Engineers are responsible for keeping up with technologies and developments in environmental engineering as well as with environmental issues.

Environmental Engineers work in offices and in the field. Consultants often travel to other cities, states, and countries to perform work at clients' sites.

Salaries
Salaries vary, depending on education, experience, employer, geographical location, and other factors. The estimated annual salary for most Environmental Engineers in 2001 ranged from $38,470 to $90,390, according to the Bureau of Labor Statistics.

Employment Prospects
Most Environmental Engineers find employment with government agencies, engineering and management firms that provide consulting services, or manufacturers in various industries. Some Environmental Engineers are employed by public-interest organizations that are involved in environmental issues. Others are employed as academic faculty in colleges and universities. In addition, some Environmental Engineers are independent consultants.

Job opportunities for Environmental Engineers are expected to grow by 36 percent or more through 2010, according to the U.S. Bureau of Labor Statistics. However, the job outlook may be affected by downturns in the economy. A change in government policies and priorities can also effect job opportunities. For example, when policy makers enact looser environmental regulations, fewer job opportunities become available.

Advancement Prospects
As Environmental Engineers gain experience, they can become technical specialists and project managers. Other management and administrative opportunities are available as well. Those with entrepreneurial ambitions can become independent consultants or owners of consulting firms.

Many Environmental Engineers pursue advancement by earning higher salaries, by being assigned to more difficult projects, and by receiving professional recognition.

Education and Training
Most employers require that candidates for Environmental Engineer positions possess, at the minimum, a bachelor's degree in environmental engineering, civil engineering, mechanical engineering, chemical engineering, environmental science, physical science, mathematics, geology, or another related discipline. Many employers prefer candidates who have a master's degree. Doctoral degrees are usually required of candidates to teach in colleges and universities or conduct independent research.

Entry-level engineers are given on-the-job training. Many employers also provide some type of classroom training.

Experience, Skills, and Personality Traits
Employers usually prefer that candidates have one or more years of related work experience. They should also be knowledgeable about environmental laws and safety. Entry-level candidates may have gained experience through internship, work study programs, summer employment, or research projects.

Environmental Engineers are expected to have strong communication, interpersonal, and teamwork skills in order to work effectively with people from diverse backgrounds. In addition, they must have excellent writing skills, as preparing reports is an important part of their work.

Being creative, curious, analytical, and detail-oriented are some personality traits that successful Environmental Engineers have in common.

Special Requirements
Environmental Engineers must be licensed as Professional Engineers (P.E.) if they perform work that affects the life,

health, or property of the public or if they offer their engineering services directly to the public. This licensing process consists of two stages. Engineers who successfully pass the first examination become licensed as Engineers-in-Training. After working several years under the supervision of licensed engineers, they become eligible to take the second examination for the Professional Engineer licensure.

Requirements for P.E. licensure vary among states, territories, and Washington, D.C. For specific information, contact the state board of examiners for professional engineers where you wish to practice.

Unions and Associations

Professional associations for Environmental Engineers are available at the local, state, and national levels. These organizations provide networking opportunities, education programs, job listings, professional certification, and other professional services and resources. Some national societies are the American Academy of Environmental Engineers, the Air and Waste Management Association, and American Water Works Association.

Environmental Engineers are also eligible to join other engineering societies, such as the American Institute of Chemical Engineers, American Society of Civil Engineers, and the American Society of Mechanical Engineers. In addition, professional engineers can join the National Society of Professional Engineers. See Appendix III for contact information.

Tips for Entry

1. Talk with professionals in environmental engineering for advice about courses that you might take in engineering and in other disciplines.
2. To learn about current vacancies for specific employers, contact their human resource offices.
3. Many employers post job listings and information about their recruiting or application process at their websites.
4. Use the Internet to learn more about the field of environmental engineering. To get a list of relevant websites, enter the keywords *environmental engineers* or *environmental engineering* in a search engine.

ENVIRONMENTAL PLANNER

CAREER PROFILE

Duties: Evaluate the environmental impact of current and proposed uses for land areas; recommend solutions to environmental problems; formulate plans for environmental programs; perform duties as required

Alternate Title(s): Urban Planner, Regional Planner, Watershed Planner, Transportation Planner or other title that reflects a specialty

Salary Range: $30,000 to $74,000

Employment Prospects: Good

Advancement Prospects: Fair

Prerequisites:
   Education or Training—A bachelor's or master's degree in planning, environmental studies, or related field
   Experience—Planning experience required; knowledgeable about environmental issues and environmental laws and regulations
   Special Skills and Personality Traits—Computer, GIS, analytical, communication, writing, research, presentation, interpersonal, and teamwork skills; energetic; innovative; creative; pragmatic; flexible
   Licensure/Certification—None required

CAREER LADDER

```
┌────────────────────────────────────┐
│     Senior Environmental Planner     │
└────────────────────────────────────┘

┌────────────────────────────────────┐
│        Environmental Planner         │
└────────────────────────────────────┘

┌────────────────────────────────────┐
│   Environmental Planner (entry-level)│
└────────────────────────────────────┘
```

Position Description

Environmental Planners contribute to the process of developing land-use plans for communities, companies, organizations, and individuals. These plans are formal documents that outline how areas of land, such as a city, region, or park would be used and developed through the years. The plans provide goals, objectives, and strategies for various purposes, such as public works, transportation, housing, commercial sites, industry, agriculture, recreation, and open space. Environmental Planners, along with other professional planners, help decision-makers adopt land-use plans that offer economic and social benefits for people as well as preserve natural environments.

The Environmental Planner's role is to provide environmental analyses of existing conditions and future trends for land areas. In other words, they evaluate the environmental impact of current and proposed uses of land areas. They address such environmental issues as air pollution, water quality management, solid waste management, toxic waste disposal, traffic congestion, urban sprawl, and habitat conservation.

Their investigations involve collecting, organizing, and analyzing information about natural resources and land-use patterns. (This consists of all the uses—such as housing, agriculture, or open space—for a specific area of land.) Environmental Planners analyze and interpret statistical data about physical, social, and economic factors. They also seek feedback from land developers, conservationists, property owners, special-interest groups, local residents, and other interested parties.

Environmental Planners review alternative solutions to environmental problems and make recommendations. They prepare reports and present them to decision makers, who may decide to adopt or modify the solutions. These solutions then become the environmental plans, which may be integrated with comprehensive land-use plans.

Environmental Planners also assist in the implementation of land-use plans by developing environmental programs that meet planning objectives. For example, municipal Environmental Planners might formulate plans that include cleaning up brownfields (abandoned and contaminated properties), building a new sewage treatment facility, and planting more trees in neighborhoods. Environmental Planners submit reports to decision makers about their proposed programs. Furthermore, Environmental Planners develop strategies to make sure their programs can be realized. For example, Environmental Planners help city officials write policies that would clean up brownfields in their community.

Environmental planning is a complicated and multifaceted process. Some Environmental Planners are involved with all aspects of environmental planning. Others focus on working in a particular service such as conducting environmental impact studies or developing environmental programs and policies. Some Environmental Planners specialize in planning for a specific geographical area—a town, region, or watershed, for example. Other planners prefer to work on particular issues such as public transportation, hazardous waste management, flood management, or water quality management

Environmental Planners apply principles of environmental science, economics, and other social sciences to their work. In addition, they follow standard planning processes. They are also familiar with local, state, and federal environmental laws, and are responsible for making their plans compliant with appropriate regulations. In addition, Environmental Planners are expected to keep up to date with new and proposed legislation.

Environmental Planners usually work a 40-hour week. Many work evenings and on weekends to attend meetings or public hearings. Environmental Planners spend some time in the field to inspect and document land conditions.

Salaries

Salaries vary, depending on such factors as education, experience, employer, and geographical location. According to the U.S. Bureau of Labor Statistics, the estimated salary range in 2001 for most urban and regional planners was between $30,940 and $74,240.

Employment Prospects

Environmental Planners are employed by local, state, and federal government agencies. Some other employers include planning and design firms, real estate development companies, and environmental law firms. Environmental Planners may also find employment with companies and organizations that own and manage land.

Professional planners, in general, will continually be needed to address transportation, land use, development, environmental issues, and other problems that come with the growth of communities and regions. Most job openings are expected to be created to replace planners who retire, transfer to other positions, or leave the job force entirely. Employers will create additional positions to meet growing needs, as long as resources are available.

Advancement Prospects

Managerial and administrative positions available to Environmental Planners include project leader, planning supervisor, planning manager, and program director. An advanced degree is usually required for candidates to obtain management positions.

Many Environmental Planners pursue advancement by receiving greater responsibilities, being assigned complex projects, earning higher pay, and gaining professional recognition.

Education and Training

Minimally, Environmental Planners must possess a bachelor's degree in environmental studies, planning, business, public administration, or a related field. Some employers require that Environmental Planners hold a master's degree in planning, with emphasis in environmental planning, land use planning, landscape architecture, or another related field.

Experience, Skills, and Personality Traits

Employers typically seek candidates who have work experience relevant to the positions for which they are applying. Many employers require that entry-level applicants have at least one year of planning experience, which may have been gained through internships, summer employment, work-study programs, and so on. Candidates should be knowledgeable about the environmental issues that they would be addressing. They should also be familiar with environmental laws and regulations and be able to interpret and apply regulations accordingly.

Environmental Planners should have strong computer skills, and familiarity with geographical information systems (GIS) is highly desirable. Also essential for their line of work are analytical, communication, writing, research, and presentation skills. Having excellent interpersonal and teamwork skills is also important, as they must be able to work well with people from diverse backgrounds.

Some personality traits that successful Environmental Planners share are being energetic, innovative, creative, pragmatic, and flexible. They are also visionaries.

Unions and Associations

Many Environmental Planners join local, regional, and national professional associations to take advantage of networking opportunities, training programs, and other professional services and resources. Two national societies that serve the interests of Environmental Planners are the American Planning Association and the National Association of Environmental Professionals.

Tips for Entry

1. As a high school student, you can start gaining practical experience by volunteering or working part-time with environmental organizations.

2. Gain valuable work experience by obtaining an internship with a local government planning office or planning firm.

3. For some government positions, candidates must pass some or all of the following steps of an agency's selection process: job application, written exam, interview, medical examination, drug testing, and background investigation. To qualify for many federal positions, applicants must be U.S. citizens.

4. Use the Internet to learn more about the planning field. Two websites you might visit are Cyburbia: The Urban Planning Portal, http://www.cyburbia.org; and Planetizen: The Planning and Development Network, http://www.planetizen.com. To get a list of websites pertaining to environmental planning, enter the keywords *environmental planning* or *environmental planners* in a search engine.

FORESTER

CAREER PROFILE

Duties: Primary responsibilities vary according to position: manage forest lands, conduct research, provide consulting services, teach, or provide educational outreach; perform duties as required of position

Alternate Title(s): Professional Forester, Forest Scientist; Procurement Forester, Service Forester, Urban Forester, Extension Forester, or other title that reflects a specific position

Salary Range: $29,000 to $69,000

Employment Prospects: Fair to Good

Advancement Prospects: Good

Prerequisites:

Education or Training—A bachelor's degree in forestry, biology, or related field; an advanced degree is usually required for researchers

Experience—Forest management experience required; an understanding of forestry-related policy issues and environmental laws and regulations

Special Skills and Personality Traits—Communication, interpersonal, teamwork, conflict management, writing, computer, presentation, and self-management skills; diplomatic; honest; flexible; ethical; innovative; energetic; self-motivated

Licensure/Certification—Professional licensure or registration may be required

CAREER LADDER

```
┌─────────────────────────────┐
│   Senior Forester or         │
│   Supervisory Forester       │
└─────────────────────────────┘

┌─────────────────────────────┐
│   Professional Forester      │
└─────────────────────────────┘

┌─────────────────────────────┐
│   Forester Trainee           │
└─────────────────────────────┘
```

Position Description

Foresters are involved in the science, art, and practice of conserving and managing forest lands and all the natural resources contained in those wooded areas. They oversee public forest lands as well as forested properties owned by companies, organizations, and individuals. Forest lands are used for various purposes, such as:

- timber production for wood, paper, and other forest products
- the protection of watersheds that supply water to communities
- the protection of endangered plant and animal species
- hiking, camping, hunting, fishing, and other recreational activities
- cattle grazelands
- natural beauty, or aesthetic purposes

Applying scientific, economic, and social principles and techniques to the care and control of forest lands, Foresters perform a variety of different roles. They are managers, advisers, consultants, researchers, and educators.

A large number of Foresters, also known as professional foresters, are involved in the management of public and private forest lands. They develop management plans, or long-term strategies, for achieving the land-use objectives of public agencies or private owners. Some Professional Foresters focus on the management of specific natural resources, such as wildlife management or watershed management.

Professional Foresters also perform a variety of duties that are specific to their positions. Some duties might include conducting forest inventory, appraising timber, designing reforestation (planting and growing of trees) operations, developing harvest plans, supervising logging operations, surveying wildlife populations, designing forest roads, and protecting forests from fire, disease, and insect infestations.

Public forest lands may be under municipal, state, or federal jurisdiction. (Foresters who manage forest ecosystems within metropolitan environments are often known as urban foresters). Along with forest management, most government Foresters perform such duties as planning and overseeing special forest programs or projects, developing forest policies and regulations, enforcing natural resources ordinances, designing recreational areas, and providing technical support to the general public.

Some state government Foresters are service foresters. Their role is to provide forestry assistance to private landowners within the counties that they are assigned to cover. They give out technical information about silviculture (the development and care of trees), cutting practices, state forestry laws and regulations, and other topics. Service foresters may conduct general assessments of private properties to give owners an idea of the potential uses for their land. In addition, service foresters inform landowners about forestry programs and forest management practices that may fit their particular needs. Service foresters also recommend consulting Foresters and other natural resource professionals who can help landowners develop management plans.

Industrial foresters are responsible for managing timberlands owned by sawmills, pulp mills, and other private companies in the forest industry. In addition, they make sure that all state and federal government laws, regulations, and specifications are being followed.

Other industrial Foresters, called procurement foresters, are responsible for purchasing timber from private landowners and overseeing the process of removing timber from their lands. Procurement foresters perform such duties as taking inventory of the timber on the property, appraising the value of the timber, negotiating purchasing contracts with landowners, and working with subcontractors to remove timber.

Many Foresters are private consulting Foresters who offer any number of services to private landowners. For example, they may develop forest management plans, administer timber sales for landowners, supervise the harvesting of timber, oversee reforestation, conduct forest inventory, and provide assessments of damaged property.

Research Foresters, or forest scientists, conduct research in government and academic settings. Some of them perform basic studies to advance knowledge and understanding about forests, forest ecosystems, and forest management. Other researchers conduct applied research to find solutions to particular problems, such as prevention of forest fires or the maintenance of urban forests. Researchers also develop new forest management practices and technologies. Research Foresters work in laboratories as well as in the field, including in experimental forests.

Many forest scientists are adjunct instructors or full-time professors in forestry programs at colleges and universities. Full-time professors juggle research and teaching responsibilities with administrative and community service duties. They are also expected to produce scholarly works about their research projects.

Some Foresters, known as extension foresters, work for state cooperative extension programs at land-grant universities. These foresters provide technical advice and educational outreach programs to local forest landowners. They provide landowners, the forestry community, and the general public with new technical information from university forestry departments as well as from research and experiment stations run by the USDA Forest Service. (USDA is the U.S. Department of Agriculture.)

Depending on their projects, Foresters may work alone or as part of teams which may include other Foresters, forestry technicians, natural resources professionals (such as ecologists, hydrologists, geologists, and soil scientists), landscape architects, engineers, and others. Their work also requires them to meet and deal regularly with landowners, loggers, government officials, conservation groups, and the general public.

Foresters take advantage of developing technologies to assist them with their jobs. They use computers extensively, both in the field and in the office. Special software, such as geographical information systems (GIS) software, helps them gather, analyze, store, and retrieve information they need for their work. They also use photogrammetry and remote sensing for mapping large forest areas and for detecting widespread trends regarding forest and land use.

Most Foresters spend time working outdoors in all seasons and weather conditions. (As Foresters gain experience and hold more administrative responsibilities, they spend less time working outdoors.) Their work can also be physically demanding and dangerous; for example, many Foresters assist with fighting fires. In addition, Foresters sometimes work in isolated areas, which may require walking long distances through wetlands and wildernesses.

Foresters sometimes work during evenings and on weekends to complete tasks, attend meetings and conferences, and participate in other work-related activities and programs.

Salaries

Salaries vary, depending on such factors as education, experience, type of employer, and geographical location. According to the Bureau of Labor Statistics, the estimated annual salary in 2001 for most Foresters ranged from $29,000 to $60,710.

Employment Prospects

The federal government is the largest employer of Foresters. Many of them are employed by the USDA Forest Service, the Bureau of Land Management, the National Park Service, and the military. Some other employers of Foresters include municipal and state government agencies, forest products manufacturing companies, forestry consulting firms, academic institutions, and conservation organizations. Many Foresters are self-employed as independent consultants.

Foresters are concentrated in the western and southeastern regions of the U.S. where most forests are found, but opportunities are available throughout the country. Competition for both entry-level and experienced positions is high. Most job opportunities are created to replace Foresters who retire or transfer to other positions. Some experts predict an increased demand for professional Foresters in the coming years, as a large number of Foresters start reaching retirement age. In general, though, the job market for Foresters is dependent on economic conditions. For example, when the economy is on a downturn, fewer jobs become available.

Depending on their backgrounds, training, and interests, Foresters can also seek employment as park rangers, environmental educators, wildlife managers, landscape gardeners, environmental analysts, hydrologists, timber sales administrators, science writers, and lobbyists.

Advancement Prospects

Foresters with administrative and management ambitions can pursue supervisory, managerial, and executive-level positions in government agencies, corporations, and conservation organizations. The highest ambition for some Foresters is to become a self-employed consultant or business owner. Many Foresters realize advancement through job satisfaction, higher pay, assignments of choice, and professional recognition.

Education and Training

A bachelor's degree in forestry, natural resource management, biology, or another related field is the minimum requirement for a candidate to become a professional Forester. A master's or doctoral degree may be required for one to become a forest scientist. To teach in colleges and universities and to conduct independent research, a candidate should have a doctorate degree.

Many employers require or prefer that candidates hold a forestry degree from a forestry school, accredited by the Society of American Foresters, which is the governing authority for curricula standards in forestry.

Experience, Skills, and Personality Traits

Job requirements differ for the various types of positions that are available to Foresters. In general, employers look for candidates who have previous forest management experience related to the position for which they are applying. Recent college graduates may have gained experience through summer employment, volunteer work, internships, research assistantships, and so on. Candidates should also have a strong understanding of forestry-related policy issues and local, state, and federal environmental laws and regulations.

Because Foresters must be able to work well with diverse types of people, they should have effective communication, interpersonal, and teamwork skills. Adequate conflict management skills are also helpful. In addition, Foresters need adequate writing, computer, and presentation skills, as well as strong self-management skills, such as being able to organize and prioritize tasks, work under limited supervision, and handle stressful situations.

Some personality traits that successful Foresters share are being diplomatic, honest, flexible, ethical, innovative, energetic, and self-motivated.

Special Requirements

Some states require that Foresters be licensed or registered to practice their profession. Licensure or registration requirements vary from state to state. For specific information, contact the professional licensure board in the state where you would like to practice.

Unions and Associations

Foresters might join local, state, and national professional associations to take advantage of networking opportunities, professional certification education programs, and other professional services and resources. Some societies available at the national level are the Society of American Foresters, the Association of Consulting Foresters of America, and the Forest Stewards Guild. See Appendix III for contact information.

Tips for Entry

1. While you are still in high school and college, gain experience working in forestry or conservation during summer breaks. Apply for jobs with parks, government agencies, private companies, or conservation groups. Contact employers in early spring about summer employment opportunities. Also take advantage of your school career center to help you to find summer jobs.
2. Many government agencies, such as the USDA Forest Service, offer several student programs (internship and work-study programs) to college students. To find out if a local, state, or federal agency has such programs, contact it directly or visit its website on the Internet.

3. Enhance your employability by learning how to use geographical information systems (GIS) technology, as more employers are looking for GIS skills in entry-level candidates.

4. To improve your opportunities, be willing to relocate to other states or regions.

5. Private-sector employers generally look for candidates who are knowledgeable about economics and business.

6. Learn more about Foresters on the Internet. Some websites you might visit are USDA Forest Service, http://www.fs.fed.us; Society of American Foresters, http://www.safnet.org; and the National Association of State Foresters, http://www.stateforesters.org.

RANGE SCIENTIST

CAREER PROFILE

Duties: Study, manage, conserve, and protect rangelands; as range manager, develop and administer range management plans; as researcher, conduct research projects; may teach or coordinate educational outreach programs; perform duties as required of position

Alternate Title(s): Range Manager, Range Conservationist, Range Management Specialist, Range Ecologist, Restoration Ecologist

Salary Range: $31,000 to $70,000

Employment Prospects: Fair to Good

Advancement Prospects: Good

Prerequisites:

    Education or Training—A bachelor's degree in range science, biology, or related field; an advanced degree for research positions

    Experience—Previous work experience required; be knowledgeable about rangeland ecosystems

    Special Skills and Personality Traits—Interpersonal, teamwork, communication, writing, and self-management skills; creative; inquisitive; observant; adaptable; detail-oriented; analytical

    Licensure/Certification—None required

CAREER LADDER

```
┌─────────────────────────────┐
│  Senior Range Scientist or  │
│      Program Manager        │
└─────────────────────────────┘

┌─────────────────────────────┐
│       Range Scientist       │
└─────────────────────────────┘

┌─────────────────────────────┐
│  Range Scientist (entry-level)  │
└─────────────────────────────┘
```

Position Description

Range Scientists are involved in the study, management, conservation, and protection of rangelands and the natural resources found on them. Rangelands are ecological systems dominated by grasses, shrubs, and other natural vegetation. In the United States, millions of acres of rangelands cover the country as grasslands (such as prairies), savannas, shrub lands, tundra, alpine meadows, wetlands, and deserts. These rangelands are owned by the public as well as by private individuals and companies. (Public rangelands may be under the jurisdiction of municipal, state, or federal government agencies.)

Rangelands are used for a variety of purposes. They produce forage for grazing by cattle and other livestock animals and provide browsing for wildlife. Rangelands also supply humans with water, minerals, energy resources, and other precious natural resources. In addition, rangelands are natural systems that produce oxygen for all living things as well as reduce carbon dioxide in the air. Rangelands are home to diverse wildlife habitats, including those of threatened and endangered species. Further, rangelands provide open space and places for hiking, camping, fishing, hunting, and other recreational activities.

A large number of Range Scientists, usually known as range managers, are involved in the practice of range management. They develop and administer management plans that outline how rangelands are to be used, improved, and maintained. These plans meet the specific goals of public agencies or private owners. Range managers try to get the maximum use out of rangelands without harming them. For example, a management plan might define grazing seasons, the number of animals allowed to forage in certain range areas, types of vegetation to plant for foraging, methods for controlling toxic plants, practices for protecting land from fires and pest damages, and strategies to restore damaged lands.

Range managers are also responsible for overseeing and monitoring the progress of all conservation, restoration, and construction projects on the lands they manage. They make sure that management practices comply with all appropriate laws and regulations. In addition, they conduct investigations to define and solve problems as they arise. Many range managers help with fighting fires on range lands and provide emergency help after floods, mudslides, and tropical storms.

Responsibilities vary with the different range managers. Some work for government agencies. Their duties include:

- administering grazing and cropland leases for use of public lands
- monitoring the activities of landowners to ensure they are complying with appropriate laws and regulations
- providing technical assistance to landowners
- coordinating outreach educational programs that offer the latest information about range management practices and technologies
- reviewing proposed legislation
- explaining their agency's policies, rules, and regulations to the public, legislators, and special-interest groups
- conducting hearings or meetings regarding disputes affecting public lands

Many Range Scientists are involved in conducting research in academic and government settings. Some of them conduct basic research to gain additional knowledge and understanding of the structure and processes of rangeland ecosystems as well as the different natural resources found on rangelands. Other Range Scientists conduct applied studies to develop new management practices and technologies for reducing soil erosion, improving water quality, enhancing wildlife habitats, restoring damaged ecosystems, and so forth.

As researchers, Range Scientists' duties include designing research projects, designing and conducting experiments, gathering data, reviewing other research studies, analyzing and interpreting data, writing reports, meeting with colleagues, and performing administrative duties. They also share the results of their research through articles published in professional journals and presentations given at professional conferences.

Some researchers are responsible for obtaining grants to fund their new or ongoing projects. This includes preparing budgets and grant proposals, as well as seeking appropriate grants for which to apply.

Many academic researchers are full-time professors. In addition to their research duties, they are responsible for teaching undergraduate or graduate courses, advising students, and supervising student research projects. They are also expected to produce scholarly works on a regular basis as well as perform administrative duties and community service.

Range Scientists work from time to time with other scientists (such as foresters, hydrologists, and soil scientists),

administrators, and technicians. Many Range Scientists must deal with government officials, special-interest groups, the general public, and others on a regular basis.

Range Scientists work in offices as well as in the field. Researchers also spend part of their time working in laboratories. Range Scientists typically spend more hours working outdoors during the early years of their careers.

Fieldwork is done in all types of weather, and sometimes Range Scientists are required to work in isolated areas.

Salaries

Salaries vary, depending on such factors as education, experience, employer, and geographical location. The Bureau of Labor Statistics reports that most conservation scientists, including Range Scientists, earned an estimated annual salary between $30,560 and $69,870 in 2001.

Employment Prospects

Range Scientists are employed by government agencies at the federal, state, and local levels. Most federal Range Scientists are employed in the various agencies of the U.S. Department of Agriculture and the U.S. Department of the Interior. Range Scientists also find employment with ranches, preserves, environmental consulting firms, forestry-related companies, and academic institutions. Some Range Scientists are self-employed as independent consultants.

Job opportunities generally become available as Range Scientists retire or leave their positions for other reasons. Employers create additional positions to meet growing needs. New opportunities in the public sector depend on available funding.

With their backgrounds, Range Scientists can also qualify for other occupations, such as ranch manager, park ranger, natural resources specialist, watershed manager, forester, agronomist, environmental educator, science writer, lobbyist, and conservation activist.

Advancement Prospects

Range Scientists can advance to administrative and management positions, such as program manager and director. In general, Range Scientists measure their success in individual terms. For example, they may realize advancement through pay increases, by receiving choice assignments, or by earning professional recognition from their peers.

Education and Training

A bachelor's degree in range science, range management, biology, ecology, or another related discipline is the minimum requirement needed to become a Range Scientist. A master's or doctoral degree is usually required for research positions. To teach in universities and colleges, conduct independent research, or hold top management positions, a doctoral degree is generally required.

Range Scientists continue developing their own professional growth through independent study, enrollment in education and training programs, and networking with colleagues.

Experience, Skills, and Personality Traits

Employers typically choose candidates who have work experience related to the position for which they are applying. Entry-level candidates may have obtained experience through part-time employment, internships, research projects, or postdoctoral training. Candidates are expected to be knowledgeable about rangeland ecosystems.

In general, Range Scientists need strong interpersonal, teamwork, communication, and writing skills. They should also have excellent self-management skills, including the ability to organize and prioritize tasks, handle stressful situations, and work independently. Being creative, inquisitive, observant, adaptable, detail-oriented, and analytical are a few personality traits that successful Range Scientists share.

Unions and Associations

Most Range Scientists join local, state, or national societies to take advantage of professional services and resources such as education programs, professional certification, and networking opportunities. One national association that serves rangeland professionals is the Society for Range Management. Other national societies that many Range Scientists join are the American Forage and Grassland Council, the American Society of Agronomy, and the Ecological Society of America. See Appendix III for contact information.

Tips for Entry

1. As a college student, gain experience through internship, work-study, or summer employment programs that offer placements with private or public sector employers. Talk with your college adviser or a college career counselor for assistance in finding such programs.

2. Check out the websites of state and federal agencies where you might be interested in working. Along with learning about an agency's activities, you may find job listings as well as information about recruitment and application processes.

3. Use the Internet to learn more about the range management field. Two websites you might visit for more information are Rangelands of the Western U.S., http://ag.arizona.edu/agnic; and USDA Forest Service Rangelands, http://www.fs.fed.us/rangelands/index.html.

FORENSIC SCIENCE

FORENSIC SCIENTIST

CAREER PROFILE

Duties: Provide expert evaluation and opinions about scientific or technical issues related to legal and regulatory matters; perform duties as required of position

Alternate Title(s): Forensic Consultant, Forensic Examiner; a title that reflects a specialty such as Criminalist, Forensic Accountant, or Forensic Dentist

Salary Range: Salaries vary for the different occupations

Employment Prospects: Good

Advancement Prospects: Limited

Prerequisites:

    Education or Training—Bachelor's or advanced degree

    Experience—Previous work experience in field; consultants must have several years of experience

    Special Skills and Personality Traits—Interpersonal, communication, writing, presentation, and self-management skills; credible; unbiased; objective; fair; analytical; detail-oriented

    Licensure/Certification—Professional licensure or certification may be required

CAREER LADDER

```
┌─────────────────────────────────┐
│   Senior Forensic Scientist or   │
│       Forensic Consultant        │
└─────────────────────────────────┘

┌─────────────────────────────────┐
│        Forensic Scientist        │
└─────────────────────────────────┘

┌─────────────────────────────────┐
│     Forensic Scientist Trainee   │
└─────────────────────────────────┘
```

Position Description

Forensic Scientists provide expert evaluations and opinions about scientific and technical issues related to legal and regulatory matters. They are hired by law enforcement agencies, attorneys, courts, government agencies, insurance companies, and others. They assist in criminal investigations and civil litigation, as well as in administrative cases that involve violations of government regulations.

Forensic Scientists specialize in various types of forensic activities. For example, some Forensic Scientists analyze blood, DNA, bullet markings, tire tracks, soil samples, documents, computer files, accounting records, or other types of physical evidence. Other Forensic Scientists reconstruct accidents to determine what caused them, assess the behavior or mental conditions of individuals, or give clinical interpretations of X rays or patient records. Often times, therefore, several Forensic Scientists are called upon to address specific issues in litigation or regulatory cases.

Forensic Scientists are expected to perform unbiased and objective forensic investigations. They use scientific methods to analyze and interpret physical, medical, or other types of evidence. Upon completion of their evaluations, Forensic Scientists prepare comprehensive reports about their findings and conclusions. They present technical information in language that can be understood by law enforcement officers, lawyers, judges, juries, and others.

Forensic Scientists may be called upon to testify at depositions or court trials as expert witnesses. They address only those issues for which the courts have determined them to be qualified to answer. As expert witnesses, Forensic Scientists are used for two general purposes. One purpose is to give their opinions on evidence they have examined. The other purpose is to provide technical information so that the judges and juries can better understand the particular issues in a case. Expert witnesses are expected to explain technical concepts and details in terms that are easy to understand.

Forensic Scientists may also be called on to provide expert testimony at administrative hearings, alternative conflict resolution conferences, legislative hearings, and other types of legal hearings.

Forensic science is a broad field that encompasses specialists from the various disciplines of science, mathematics, engineering, medicine, and social science. With the advancement of technology, new forensic specialties will continue to emerge. The following are just some of the different Forensic Scientists and the types of forensic investigations that they do:

- Criminalists analyze, identify, and evaluate physical evidence—hair, blood, fingerprints, and so forth—that are found at crime scenes. (They work in law enforcement and private crime labs.)
- Forensic pathologists perform autopsies to determine the causes of death and the manner in which individuals died. (Many of them work in medical examiners' or coroners' offices.)
- Forensic toxicologists evaluate analytical, clinical, and environmental data to verify that drugs or poisonous substances led or contributed to the death or intoxication of individuals.
- Forensic anthropologists apply anthropology principles and techniques to help law enforcement officers identify bodies that are beyond recognition as well as recover buried bodies and solve crime.
- Forensic dentists, or forensic odontologists, examine dental evidence to identify unknown human remains or to determine the presence and extent of dental injuries or physical neglect in cases of abuse.
- Forensic geologists evaluate the composition of geological materials or building materials to find facts that may support criminal, civil, or regulatory matters.
- Forensic engineers examine machines, products, and structures to determine how accidents or catastrophes occurred.
- Forensic computer specialists examine computers to discover and recover electronic data that may be potential evidence in criminal investigations.
- Questioned document examiners analyze documents to determine if they are authentic, counterfeit, or forgeries.
- Forensic accountants apply accounting, auditing, and investigative techniques to analyze and interpret financial evidence.
- Forensic psychologists and forensic psychiatrists provide expert evaluations of and opinions about the mental conditions of criminal defendants or individuals involved in civil disputes. They also examine correctional issues as well as issues related to juvenile and family court matters.
- Forensic nurses assist in criminal and civil matters that involve abuse, violence, traumatic accidents, or criminal activities.
- Forensic wildlife scientists analyze physical evidence connected to criminal investigations involving victims that are protected and endangered animals.

A large number of Forensic Scientists are consultants, who offer forensic consulting and expert witness services on a contractual basis to attorneys, courts, and others. They may be self-employed or work with forensic consulting firms. These professionals are also known as forensic consultants or forensic examiners.

Many independent consultants hold full-time positions as professors at colleges, universities, or medical schools. They teach in general forensic science programs as well as in their particular disciplines, such as forensic psychiatry or forensic anthropology. They offer their forensic services part-time, and sometimes do cases on a pro bono basis.

Many Forensic Scientists are involved in independent research studies. They might conduct basic research to gain further knowledge and understanding about their subject areas. For example, a forensic psychiatrist might do basic research on juvenile violence, a forensic geologist might examine the characteristics of soil in a particular region, or a Forensic Scientist might study the reliability of using tape recordings to identify criminal suspects. In addition, Forensic Scientists continually develop new methods and technologies for their particular areas of forensic investigations.

Many Forensic Scientists write articles and books about their studies and practices. They also give presentations as well as conduct seminars and training workshops at professional conferences and meetings.

Forensic Scientists may work in offices, laboratories, or morgues. Many of them travel to sites where events, such as criminal activities and accidents, occurred, to help collect evidence or to put the facts they have uncovered into context.

Salaries

Earnings vary for the different types of Forensic Scientists. Criminalists, for example, generally earn between $30,000 and $60,000, while forensic psychiatrists earn between $50,000 and $100,000 or more. Salaries also vary within the different specialties, depending on such factors as education, experience, employer, and geographical location.

Forensic consultants typically charge clients an hourly rate for their services. The fees vary, depending on a number of factors—an individual's credentials, the area of expertise, type of services being offered, the demand for such services in a consultant's location, and so on. In general, fees range from about $100 to about $2,000 or more per hour. Consultants may bill clients for out-of-pocket expenses such as photocopying expenses, telephone calls, and travel costs. Most consultants charge additional fees for time spent waiting and appearing at a trial, deposition, or alternative dispute hearing.

Employment Prospects

Forensic Scientists are employed by law enforcement agencies, medical examiners' or coroners' offices, government agencies, private laboratories, and others. Most forensic consultants are self-employed or owners of forensic consulting firms.

In general, job openings for staff positions become available as Forensic Scientists retire or transfer to other positions. Opportunities for forensic consultants depend on the demand by lawyers and others for their particular area of expertise, and on the number of similar consultants in their geographical area.

Advancement Prospects

Forensic Scientists in staff positions can advance to administrative and managerial positions by becoming a unit supervisor, program manager, or lab director. Those with entrepreneurial ambitions can become self-employed or a business owner.

Forensic consultants determine their own measurements of success. For example, some consultants may realize advancement by earning higher incomes, through earning professional awards for their work, or by being sought out to provide expertise for very complex or publicized cases.

Education and Training

Forensic Scientists hold a bachelor's or advanced degree in their fields. A doctoral degree is normally required to teach in colleges and universities, to advance to top management positions, or to conduct independent research.

Most Forensic Scientists enroll in continuing education and training programs throughout their careers to develop and maintain their professional skills and expertise.

Experience, Skills, and Personality Traits

Employers typically hire Forensic Scientists who have previous work experience. Entry-level candidates may have gained experience through internships, part-time employment, research assistantships, or other related positions. Some employers allow candidates to substitute an advanced degree for one or more years of work experience. Forensic consultants are expected to be highly-skilled and experienced professionals in their fields.

As they must be able to work well with various different people, Forensic Scientists must have excellent interpersonal and communication skills. They also need superior writing and presentation skills. In addition, they should have strong self-management skills, such as the ability to organize and prioritize several tasks, work independently, and handle stressful situations. Being credible, unbiased, objective, fair, analytical, and detail-oriented are a few personality traits that successful Forensic Scientists share.

Special Requirements

Forensic Scientists hold the appropriate professional licensure or certification that is required by their states for their occupations. For example, forensic engineers may be required to possess Professional Engineer (P.E.) licensure in the states where they practice.

Unions and Associations

Most Forensic Scientists join local, state, regional, and national associations that serve their particular fields (such as forensic accounting, criminalistics, and forensic psychiatry). Many also join societies that serve the interests of forensic scientists in general, such as the American Academy of Forensic Sciences or the American College of Forensic Examiners. By joining professional societies, they can take advantage of professional services and resources such as education programs, professional certification, publications, and networking opportunities. For contact information, please see Appendix III.

Tips for Entry

1. As a high school student, start learning about the different types of Forensic Scientists to find out which occupations interest you. Along with reading books and other materials, talk with different professionals.
2. Contact human resources departments or visit websites of employers to learn about available internship programs or job vacancies.
3. Take one or more courses in small business skills, if you plan to become a self-employed consultant.
4. You can learn more about the field of forensic science on the internet. Some websites you might visit are Reddy's Forensic Page, http://www.forensicpage.com; National Center for Forensic Science (hosted by the University of Central Florida), http://ncfs.ucf.edu; and American Academy of Forensic Sciences, http://www.aafs.org.

CRIMINALIST

CAREER PROFILE

Duties: To analyze, identify, and interpret physical evidence collected at crime scenes; prepare formal reports about findings and opinions; provide expert witness testimony; perform duties as required

Alternate Title(s): Forensic Scientist, Crime Laboratory Analyst; a title that reflects a specialty such as Forensic Chemist, DNA Specialist, Toolmark Examiner, or Questioned Document Examiner

Salary Range: About $30,000 to $60,000 or more

Employment Prospects: Good

Advancement Prospects: Good

Prerequisites:

Education or Training—A bachelor's degree in chemistry, biology, forensic science, or a related field

Experience—One or more years of crime lab or related experience; knowledgeable about lab procedures and lab instruments and equipment; knowledgeable about proper procedures for handling and processing physical evidence

Special Skills and Personality Traits—Mathematical, computer, problem-solving, writing, communication, presentation, interpersonal, teamwork, and self-management skills; honest; patient; detail-oriented; objective; diligent

Licensure/Certification—None required

CAREER LADDER

```
Team Leader or Unit Supervisor
```

```
Criminalist
```

```
Criminalist Trainee
```

Position Description

Criminalists are forensic scientists who help law enforcement officers solve crimes. Their job is to analyze, identify, and interpret physical evidence that has been collected at crime scenes. Using scientific methods and principles, Criminalists attempt to prove that crimes have taken place, to reconstruct what occurred at the crime scene, and to identify crime suspects and victims.

Criminalists are often confused with criminologists. Both professions are part of the same field—criminology, or the study of the causes of crime. However, Criminalists work in forensic or crime labs performing lab analyses on physical evidence. Criminologists, on the other hand, usually work in academic settings, conducting research about crime and criminal behavior.

Criminalists examine a wide range of materials gathered from crime scenes. They conduct chemical, microscopic,

comparative, and other types of analyses on evidence, depending on the type of evidence. They may examine and identify blood stains, hair, fibers, drugs, paint, glass fragments, soil, tire tracks, fingerprints, flammable gases, documents, computer files, and so on.

In large crime labs, Criminalists usually specialize in one or more types of evidence testing. Some of these areas include:

- forensic biology—the examination of physiological fluids and dried stains, including blood, saliva, bodily fluids, and DNA
- latent prints—the identification and comparison of hidden impressions from fingers, palms, feet, shoes, tire treads, and other sources
- drug chemistry—the analysis of blood and other body fluids and tissues for the presence of controlled substances (alcohol and drugs)

- toxicology—the analysis of blood and other body fluids and tissues for the presence of poisons
- microscopy—the examination of hairs, fibers, soils, glass fragments, and other small particles of physical evidence (or trace evidence)
- firearms and toolmarks—the examination of firearms and tools to determine if they may have been used in crimes
- questioned documents—the examination of wills, checks, invoices, currency, correspondence, and other documents to determine if they are counterfeit or forgeries or if any alterations have been made to the documents
- polygraph examination—the use of polygraph machines to determine if suspects or witnesses are being truthful or deceptive about issues related to crimes
- computer forensics—the recovery and analysis of data in computers

Before performing any tests on an item, Criminalists first find out what needs to be known about the evidence and get an idea of the significance of the item. They sometimes visit crime scenes to get a better sense of what they are dealing with. Criminalists can then determine what type of data they need to obtain and the best methods to use.

Criminalists next perform their tests. They sort, compare, or identify the evidence, developing useful information for the investigation or trial. They analyze and interpret the test results. They then prepare formal reports that describe in detail their findings and that explain the methods they used to obtain the results. Their reports need to be clear, concise, and easily understood by law enforcement officers, attorneys, judges, and juries.

If needed, Criminalists also provide expert witness testimony at depositions and trials. They may appear as witnesses for the prosecution or for the defense. They answer legal issues related to their particular examinations on physical evidence or on crime lab techniques.

Criminalists are expected to perform their duties accurately and correctly. They follow strict procedures at all times to maintain the chain of custody for all physical evidence that they handle. This includes writing about everything that they do to physical evidence so as to ensure that it has not been tampered with or contaminated. If the chain of custody is broken for a piece of physical evidence, it will usually not be admitted as testimony in court trials.

Criminalists are responsible for keeping up with current information and updating their skills as new technologies and methodologies emerge. Many Criminalists are involved in developing new or improved methodologies and techniques for their areas of forensic investigations.

To ensure their safety, Criminalists follow strict lab procedures for operating lab equipment, handling chemicals, and performing tests. They also wear protective clothing to protect themselves from exposure to disease, odors, fumes, and chemicals.

Criminalists work a regular 40 hour week. Many of them rotate on an on-call schedule, being available for work 24 hours a day.

Salaries

Annual salaries vary, depending on such factors as experience, education, employer, size of lab, and geographical location. Entry-level Criminalists generally begin in the low- to mid-$30,000 range. Senior Criminalists may earn up to $60,000 or more, while salaries for lab directors may range up to $100,000 or more.

Employment Prospects

Most Criminalists are employed by crime labs which are part of local, state, or federal law enforcement agencies. Other Criminalists work in private laboratories as well as in academic laboratories that offer services to law enforcement agencies on a contractual basis.

The competition for jobs is keen, but qualified Criminalists should be able to find positions readily. Most opportunities become available as Criminalists retire or transfer to other positions. Many experts expect the job market to increase due to backlogs in evidence analysis and to the advancements in technology. Opportunities should especially grow in the area of DNA analysis.

Applicants for positions in government agencies must pass a selection process that includes any of the following steps: written exam, interview, medical exam, drug test, background investigation, and polygraph examination. Many agencies, particularly at the federal level, require that employees be U.S. citizens.

Advancement Prospects

Criminalists can pursue managerial and administrative positions by becoming a unit supervisor, assistant lab director, or lab director. Criminalists can also specialize in a particular area, such as drug analysis or firearms examination.

Education and Training

Criminalists hold a bachelor's degree in chemistry, biology, forensic science, or a related field. In addition, many Criminalists hold a master's degree in forensic science, biochemistry, biology, chemistry, or a related field.

To pursue top-level administrative positions, such as a lab directorship, Criminalists may need an advanced degree.

Throughout their careers, many Criminalists enroll in education programs, training seminars, conference workshops, and so on, to increase their knowledge and update their skills. In addition, employers typically provide in-service training programs for their employees.

Experience, Special Skills, and Personality Traits

Most crime labs typically choose candidates who have previous work experience. Entry-level candidates may have gained experience through internships, part-time employment, research assistantships, or other positions in analytical, research, or crime laboratories. Employers may allow candidates to substitute advanced degrees for at least one year of work experience. Successful candidates are able to demonstrate their knowledge about appropriate lab procedures and handling of lab instruments and equipment, as well as their knowledge about proper procedures for handling and processing physical evidence.

In general, Criminalists need good mathematical and computer skills. To do their various duties (such as interpreting tests, preparing reports, and testifying as expert witnesses), Criminalists must have excellent skills in problem-solving, writing, communication, and presentation. Having interpersonal and teamwork skills are also essential. Further, Criminalists need strong self-management skills, including the ability to work independently, handle stressful situations, meet deadlines, and organize and prioritize tasks.

Some personality traits that successful Criminalists share are being honest, patient, detail-oriented, objective, and diligent.

Unions and Associations

Many Criminalists are members of professional societies at the local, state, regional, national, and international levels that serve their particular interests. These societies offer various professional services and resources such as education programs, professional certification, publications, job listings, and networking opportunities. Some professional associations include:

- American Academy of Forensic Sciences
- International Association of Bloodstain Pattern Analysts
- American Society of Questioned Document Examiners
- Association of Firearm and Toolmark Examiners
- Society of Forensic Toxicologists.
- For contact information, please see Appendix III.

Tips for Entry

1. In high school or college, get an idea if becoming a Criminalist is right for you. Read books and articles about the criminalistic field. Contact professional societies for more information. Tour a local crime lab. Attend court trials to listen to Criminalists give expert witness testimony. Talk with Criminalists about their work.

2. While in college, you can gain experience working in crime labs through internship or work-study programs. Contact crime labs directly about available opportunities for students.

3. Increasingly, crime labs are preferring to hire candidates with a master's degree. Many Criminalists pursue advanced degrees while working or after several years on the job.

4. Research a prospective employer before going to a job interview. (Many crime labs have websites.) Then think about how you might fit in with that organization, why you would be an asset to the employer, what professional goals you hope to achieve by working there, and so on. Practice answering the usual job interview questions with those ideas in mind.

5. Learn more about the criminalistics field on the Internet. Two websites you might visit are American Academy of Forensic Sciences, http://www.aafs.org; and Zeno's Forensic Site, http://forensic.to/forensic.html. To find websites for a specific occupation, use the plural version of the title as a keyword. For example, *forensic chemists, questioned document examiners,* or *DNA analysts.*

FORENSIC ENGINEER

CAREER PROFILE

Duties: Provide expert evaluations and opinions on engineering issues; conduct forensic investigations into the causes of accidents and catastrophes; provide expert witness testimony; prepare reports; may provide litigation consulting services; perform duties as required

Alternate Title(s): Forensic Consultant, a title that reflects an engineering specialty, such as Mechanical Engineer or Civil Engineer

Salary Range: about $100 to $200 or more per hour, for independent consultants

Employment Prospects: Good

Advancement Prospects: Good

Prerequisites:

    Education or Training—A bachelor's or advanced degree in an engineering discipline

    Experience—Several years of work experience in specialty

    Special Skills and Personality Traits—Communication, writing, presentation, and self-management skills; business skills for entrepreneurs; competent, unbiased, ethical, honest

    Licensure/Certification—Professional Engineer (P.E.) licensure

CAREER LADDER

```
┌─────────────────────────────┐
│   Senior Forensic Engineer   │
└─────────────────────────────┘

┌─────────────────────────────┐
│      Forensic Engineer       │
└─────────────────────────────┘

┌─────────────────────────────┐
│          Engineer            │
└─────────────────────────────┘
```

Position Description

Forensic Engineers offer expert evaluations and opinions on engineering issues related to legal and regulatory matters. They are experienced in such engineering fields as civil, mechanical, chemical, materials, electrical, computer hardware, biomedical, aerospace, agricultural, petroleum, environmental, structural, transportation, and fire protection engineering.

Forensic Engineers analyze physical evidence to determine the causes of accidents and catastrophes. For example, they might be asked to investigate such questions as these: What was the cause of a store fire? What caused a plane to crash? Why did a new skyscraper collapse during an earthquake? What caused workers to fall on a construction site? Was a person's injury caused by a defect in an artificial limb? Did a lawn mower explode because it failed to work properly? What caused toxic waste to leak into a community's water supply?

Most Forensic Engineers are independent consultants or staff consultants with engineering firms that offer forensic engineering services. Many focus their work in a few areas such as agricultural accidents, industrial accidents, amusement ride accidents, vehicle accidents, airplane accidents, fire cause and origin, mechanical failures, electrical failures, product design failures, industrial equipment damage, or chemical failures.

Forensic Engineers are hired by lawyers to help them prepare for civil and criminal litigation, administrative hearings, alternative dispute resolution conferences, and other legal hearings. They are also retained by insurance companies to help investigate insurance claims for personal injuries, property damages, or property losses.

Forensic Engineers conduct forensic investigations with scientific precision. They review police reports, eyewitness statements, expert reports, and other materials for background information. They inspect sites where accidents, catastrophes, or losses occurred and examine all available physical evidence. They may reproduce accidents in laboratory settings to discover what happened. They may perform standardized tests on products to evaluate them for failure or defects. Forensic Engineers document every step of their inspections with written notes, photographs, and videotapes.

Forensic Engineers analyze and interpret their data, sometimes with the help of computer models, to show sequence of events or contributing factors that may have led to an accident. They are expected to come up with objective conclusions that sometimes may not be favorable for their clients.

Forensic Engineers prepare reports of their findings and conclusions. Their reports are organized clearly and concisely, yet comprehensively, as they may be used for pretrial proceedings, trials, and settlement negotiations. Consequently, they present information in simplified terms so that nontechnical individuals can understand technical and scientific concepts.

Many Forensic Engineers also offer expert witness services. They provide expert testimony in depositions and trials. They may be asked to provide scientific or technical explanations to help judges and juries understand specific issues in a civil or criminal trial. They may be asked for their expert opinions about their specific analyses of the events that took place.

Many Forensic Engineers also offer litigation consulting services to attorneys. Some of their services may include:

- educating lawyers about the subject matter so they can fully understand the issues of a case
- evaluating a case to identify technical issues and facts of a case
- finding appropriate expert witnesses
- helping lawyers develop effective strategies for a case
- formulating a list of questions that lawyers would ask witnesses of the opposing party during depositions or trials
- preparing demonstrative evidence (such as diagrams, models, or computer animation)

Forensic Engineers are responsible for keeping abreast of the latest forensic research, techniques, and technologies in their areas of expertise.

Forensic Engineers generally work a 40-hour week. They sometimes work additional hours during evenings and on weekends to complete tasks and meet deadlines. They may travel to different cities and states to meet with clients, survey traffic scenes, or testify in court.

Salaries

Earnings for self-employed Forensic Engineers are based on fees, which generally range from $100 to $200 per hour or more, depending on the service that they offer. Independent consultants usually charge additional fees for out-of-pocket expenses, such as phone calls and travel costs. Most consultants also charge for time spent waiting and appearing at a trial, deposition, or alternative dispute hearing.

Forensic Engineers who are employed by consulting firms earn salaries which vary, depending on their experience, geographical location, and other factors. According to a 2001 salary survey by the National Society of Professional Engineers, the median annual salary for staff Forensic Engineers was $143,500.

Employment Prospects

Most Forensic Engineers are either self-employed consultants or work for forensic engineering firms. Some engineers and college professors from the different engineering fields may offer forensic consulting services on a part-time basis.

Experienced and credible Forensic Engineers are always in demand by lawyers, courts, and corporations to explain technical matters related to legal cases.

Advancement Prospects

As staff members, Forensic Engineers can advance through the ranks as junior consultants, consultants, senior consultants, and principal consultants. Opportunities to advance to supervisory and management positions are also available. Some Forensic Engineers pursue their ambitions of becoming successful independent consultants or owners of consulting firms.

Education and Training

Forensic Engineers hold at least a bachelor's degree in an engineering disciplines. Many Forensic Engineers also hold a master's or doctoral degree in their field.

Forensic engineering is not a separate discipline but rather a specialized practice of the engineering sciences; therefore, few universities offer courses in forensic engineering. Forensic Engineers are responsible for their own professional development, which they may gain through self-study, hands-on experience, continuing education programs, and training workshops sponsored by professional associations.

Experience, Skills, and Personality Traits

In order to qualify as a litigation consultant or expert witness, Forensic Engineers must demonstrate to clients (or courts) that they have sufficient experience and skills in their engineering specialty. Generally, they have worked several years in their field prior to entering the practice of forensic engineering consulting. Forensic Engineers must have technical competency in their specialties, as well as knowledge about legal procedures.

Forensic Engineers need the ability to present technical concepts in clear language, both orally and in written form;

therefore they must have excellent communication and writing skills. In addition, having strong presentation and self-management skills is important for their work. Independent consultants and business owners should have adequate business skills in order to succeed. Being competent, unbiased, ethical, and honest are some personality traits that successful Forensic Engineers share.

Special Requirements

Forensic Engineers are required to obtain Professional Engineer (P.E.) licensure in the states where they practice. P.E. licensure is also required in the District of Columbia and the U.S. territories.

General requirements for P.E. licensure include graduating from an engineering program accredited by the American Board of Engineering and Technology, having four years of relevant work experience, and passing a state examination. For further licensure information, contact the engineering licensure office in the state where you wish to practice.

Unions and Associations

Various professional societies are available at the local, state, and national levels for Forensic Engineers. They offer professional services and resources such as networking opportunities, education programs, professional certification, and publications. Some national associations are:

• National Academy of Forensic Engineers
• National Society of Professional Engineers
• American Society of Safety Engineers
• American Academy of Forensic Sciences
• American College of Forensic Examiners

For contact information, please see Appendix III.

Tips for Entry

1. For staff positions, candidates may be allowed to substitute an advanced degree for one or more years of practical experience.
2. If you plan on starting your own business, consider taking a few small business courses at a local community college or other academic institution.
3. Learn more about forensic engineering on the Internet. One website that you might visit is National Academy of Forensic Engineers, http://www.nafe.org. To find other relevant websites enter the keywords *forensic engineering* or *forensic engineers* in a search engine.

FORENSIC ANTHROPOLOGIST

CAREER PROFILE

Duties: Apply anthropology principles and techniques to make positive identification of human remains, to recover hidden or buried bodies, or to help determine cause and manner of death; provide expert witness testimony; perform other duties as required

Alternate Title(s): Physical Anthropologist; Forensic Scientist; Forensic Examiner

Salary Range: $100 to $200 or more per hour

Employment Prospects: Poor

Advancement Prospects: Fair

Prerequisites:

Education or Training—An advanced degree in physical anthropology, forensic anthropology, or a related field

Experience—Several years of experience, leading to recognition as expert in field; knowledgeable of procedures for handling and processing physical evidence

Special Skills and Personality Traits—Analytical, critical thinking, writing, communication, self-management skills; detail-oriented; level-headed; flexible; unbiased; honest; fair

Licensure/Certification—None required

CAREER LADDER

```
┌─────────────────────────────────┐
│  Senior Forensic Anthropologist  │
└─────────────────────────────────┘

┌─────────────────────────────────┐
│ Forensic Anthropology Consultant │
└─────────────────────────────────┘

┌─────────────────────────────────┐
│ Physical Anthropology Professor  │
└─────────────────────────────────┘
```

Position Description

Forensic Anthropologists are physical anthropologists who specialize in providing expert evaluation and opinion to criminal and other forensic investigations. They assist law enforcement agencies and medical examiners' (or coroners') offices with cases which involve skeletons, decomposed corpses, burned bodies, or partial remains of victims. The deaths of victims may have been the results of suicide, homicide, explosions, natural disasters, or other tragedies.

Forensic Anthropologists generally perform forensic work in three areas. One area is the analysis of skeletal remains to help law enforcement officers establish positive human identification. Through their examinations, Forensic Anthropologists can ascertain the sex, age, ancestry, stature, body build, and health status of victims. In addition, they can find clues about victims' behavioral patterns—their physical habits, what kind of work they did, what sports they played, and so on.

Forensic Anthropologists provide as much data about unidentified bodies as they can to law enforcement officers.

The officers then try to seek matches with information about missing persons in their area as well as nationwide. (Officers use aids such as the National Crime Information Center database of missing persons.)

Forensic Anthropologists can often make a positive identification by superimposing a video shot of a missing person's photograph upon skeletal remains.

In some cases, matches with missing person information cannot be made. Law enforcement officers may call upon the help of Forensic Anthropologists who have skills in facial reproduction. These forensic examiners can make models of human skulls and show how the faces of victims may have appeared in life. Law enforcement officers take photographs of the facial reproductions and send them to other law enforcement agencies as well as to the media.

The recovery of buried, hidden, or scattered human remains is another area in which Forensic Anthropologists assist law enforcement officers. Using archeology principles and techniques, Forensic Anthropologists can conduct controlled excavations of remains in different types of terrain, including deserts, forests, riverbeds, wetlands, urban areas, and so on. They may also help with the collection and processing of entomological, botanical, and geological evidence for analysis by other forensic experts, such as forensic entomologists and forensic geologists. Additionally, Forensic Anthropologists can verify if recovered bones are human or animal. They can also determine whether human skeletons are of recent or ancient origin. If they are ancient remains, Forensic Anthropologists usually contact appropriate authorities, such as state archeologists.

Assisting forensic pathologists (also known as medical examiners) is another area in which Forensic Anthropologists work. They help forensic pathologists establish the cause and manner of death of decomposed corpses and human remains. Through analysis of bones and soft tissues, Forensic Anthropologists can estimate how much time has elapsed since victims died. They can also identify traumatic injuries to skeletons, and whether injuries occurred before death, at the time of death, or after death. Further, Forensic Anthropologists can provide such information as the original positions of bodies when victims died, the type of tools that were used to bury victims or to dismember them, and any environmental forces that altered human remains after death.

Forensic Anthropologists may be called upon to provide expert witness testimony in depositions and court trials. They provide expert opinions only on issues related to forensic anthropology, and present information in terms that can be easily understood by judges and juries.

Most Forensic Anthropologists are independent consultants who offer forensic services on a part-time basis. A large majority of them hold full-time faculty positions in colleges and universities, teaching in anthropology departments as well as in biology, anatomy, sociology, and other departments.

In addition, most professors are involved in conducting independent research in forensic anthropology and other areas of anthropology. They conduct studies to gain new understanding and knowledge about human skeletons and skeletal biology. They also conduct research that leads to the development of new methodologies and technologies for making human identifications and conducting forensic investigations.

Salaries
Independent Forensic Anthropologists charge clients an hourly rate which normally ranges from about $100 to $200 or more. They may charge additional fees for expenses such as telephone calls and travel costs.

According to the Bureau of Labor Statistics, most anthropologists earned an estimated annual salary that ranged between $23,260 and $66,670 in 2001. The estimated annual salary for most postsecondary anthropology instructors ranged between $32,990 and $93,320. Their salaries vary, depending on their experience, education, position, geographical location, and other factors.

Employment Prospects
Forensic anthropology is still a young and small field, but opportunities in general are growing. According to Dr. Sharon Neely, from the Department of Anthropology, Northern Kentucky University, the field is currently made up of less than 200 Forensic Anthropologists. However, only a small number of them work in the field on a full-time basis.

Most Forensic Anthropologists are employed as physical anthropology professors or museum curators who provide forensic services on a part-time basis. State and federal law enforcement agencies, medical examiners' offices, and the military employ a few Forensic Anthropologists as forensic analysts. They conduct other types of forensic analyses in addition to performing forensic anthropology services.

Advancement Prospects
Administrative and management opportunities vary with the different work settings. For example, in forensic labs, individuals can become a team leader, unit supervisor, or lab director, while in academic settings, professors can advance to become department chair, school dean, or administrative dean.

Education and Training
Forensic Anthropologists hold a master's or doctoral degree in physical anthropology, forensic anthropology, or another related area. They must possess a doctorate in order to teach in universities and colleges. Their graduate training includes course work in human skeletal biology, osteology, pathology, forensic science, microscopy, criminal law, archaeological field methods, and other related subjects.

Experience, Skills, and Personality Traits
Forensic Anthropologists usually have several years of experience and are recognized as experts in their fields. Law enforcement agencies, medical examiners' officers, and attorneys expect consultants to be knowledgeable about the proper procedures for handling and processing physical evidence in criminal cases. To be qualified to give expert witness testimony, Forensic Anthropologists must be able to demonstrate to the courts that they have sufficient knowledge, skills, or practical experience to address specific issues related to legal cases.

Forensic Anthropologists need strong analytical, critical thinking, writing, and communication skills for their work. In addition, they must have excellent self-management skills, such as the ability to handle stressful situations, work independently, organize and perform multiple tasks, and meet deadlines. Being detail-oriented, level-headed, flexible, unbiased, honest, and fair are some personality traits that successful Forensic Anthropologists have in common.

Unions and Associations
Many Forensic Anthropologists join local, state, or national associations to take advantage of professional services and

resources, including networking opportunities, education programs, professional certification, research collections, and so on. Some national societies that serve the interests of this profession are the American Association of Physical Anthropology, the American Anthropological Association, the Society for Applied Anthropology, and the American Academy of Forensic Sciences. For contact information, please see Appendix III.

Tips for Entry

1. Learn more about this field by reading books and articles about forensic anthropology and talking with several Forensic Anthropologists.
2. While in college, gain as much practical experience as you can in the fields of anthropology and forensic science. For example, you might do an internship in a crime lab, volunteer for a fieldwork project, and/or obtain a research assistantship with a professor whose primary field is forensic anthropology.
3. Join professional associations for anthropologists as well as for forensic scientists.
4. Making presentations at professional conferences, conducting training workshops in forensic anthropology methods, and becoming published are some ways which help Forensic Anthropologists become well known.
5. Use the Internet to learn more about Forensic Anthropologists. One website you might visit is ForensicAnthro.com, http://www.forensicanthro.com To get a list of other relevant websites to read, enter the keywords *forensic anthropology* or *forensic anthropologists* in any search engine.

FORENSIC PSYCHIATRIST

CAREER PROFILE

Duties: Provide expert opinion on mental health issues related to legal matters; provide expert witness services; provide litigation consulting services; perform duties as required

Alternate Title(s): Psychiatrist; Forensic Psychiatrist Consultant

Salary Range: $59,000 to $146,000

Employment Prospects: Good

Advancement Prospects: Fair

Prerequisites:

Education or Training—A medical degree

Experience—Several years of clinical experience; familiarity with laws relating to cases they are consulting on or testifying about

Special Skills and Personality Traits—Communication, presentation, writing, analytical, critical thinking, and self-management skills; humble; patient; flexible; prepared; honest; unbiased

Licensure/Certification—Hold valid physician licensure; be a board certified Forensic Psychologist

CAREER LADDER

```
┌─────────────────────────────────┐
│      Forensic Psychiatrist       │
└─────────────────────────────────┘

┌─────────────────────────────────┐
│   Forensic Psychiatrist Trainee  │
└─────────────────────────────────┘

┌─────────────────────────────────┐
│      Psychiatrist Resident       │
└─────────────────────────────────┘

┌─────────────────────────────────┐
│        Medical Student           │
└─────────────────────────────────┘
```

Position Description

Forensic Psychiatrists help lawyers and courts understand mental disorders that are related to criminal and civil matters. These forensic experts are trained medical doctors who specialize in a specialty of psychiatry, the medical discipline that diagnoses and treats patients with mental problems. However, Forensic Psychiatrists do not act in the capacity of clinical psychiatrists. That is, they do not provide therapy to help individuals become healthy. Instead, Forensic Psychiatrists perform psychiatric evaluations of individuals in the context of legal issues and provide lawyers and courts with their expert opinions. Their evaluations are based on scientific research and clinical expertise.

Forensic Psychiatrists offer expert witness services to lawyers, courts, and others, as independent contractors. These services include performing evaluations, writing evaluation reports, and providing expert testimony at depositions and trials. As expert witnesses, Forensic Psychiatrists provide expert opinions only on issues for which courts have qualified them. They are expected to explain medical concepts in terms that judges and juries can understand.

In criminal cases, Forensic Psychiatrists conduct evaluations on adult and juvenile defendants and offer opinions about whether such defendants are mentally competent to stand trial, to waive legal representation, to be sentenced, or to be executed. They also may be asked to give expert testimony on the current mental conditions of defendants as well as about their mental state at the time the crime took place.

In civil litigation, Forensic Psychiatrists are often retained to provide expert evaluations and opinions on the mental competence of individuals to be able to do certain things, such as get married, make a will, sign a contract, take care of children, or refuse medical treatment. Forensic Psychiatrists are also brought in by attorneys to address mental health issues in civil lawsuits involving personal injury, product liability, sexual harassment, workers' compensation, job discrimination, malpractice, and so on.

Forensic Psychiatrists also provide expert witness services for other types of legal hearings—including juvenile court hearings, family court hearings, administrative hearings, alternative conflict resolution conferences, and legislative hearings.

Although Forensic Psychiatrists conduct assessments for legal matters, they are still obligated to maintain confidentiality about the information that individuals give them. They make sure that confidential information is not given to unauthorized persons.

Most Forensic Psychiatrists also offer attorneys litigation consulting services to help them prepare their cases for trial. Some of these services include:

- evaluating the merits of a case to help lawyers determine whether a civil suit should be filed or a criminal case be brought to trial
- reviewing a case to help lawyers identify the issues and facts of a case
- educating lawyers about mental disorders and mental health issues related to a case
- identifying and recruiting expert witnesses who would be appropriate for testifying about specific issues of a case
- helping lawyers develop effective strategies for presenting clear and convincing testimony
- formulating a list of questions that lawyers would ask witnesses for the opposing party
- assisting lawyers in preparing witnesses for depositions and trials
- advising lawyers on jury selection, by providing them with immediate feedback about potential jurors

Forensic Psychiatrists are ethically bound to provide only litigation consulting or expert witness services for a case. This is to prevent any conflict of interest, as well as to ensure that their expert witness testimony is objective and unbiased.

Many Forensic Psychiatrists maintain their private practices. Some of them perform clinical work with parolees, probationers, and crime victims. Other Forensic Psychiatrists are employed in prisons and forensic hospitals where their patients are prisoners.

Many other Forensic Psychiatrists hold faculty appointments in universities and medical schools where they teach courses in forensics and psychiatry. In addition, they conduct independent research studies, produce scholarly works about their research, and perform other duties as required of their position as full-time professor.

Forensic Psychiatrists have flexible work hours. They sometimes travel to other cities and states for their work.

Salaries

Forensic Psychiatrists' income may be based on salaries, professional fees, or a combination of both. Their salaries and fees vary, depending on such factors as experience, subspecialties, and geographical location. Independent consultants charge hourly fees for their services, which typically range from $150 to $500 per hour. The estimated annual salary for most psychiatrists, in general, ranged between $58,900 and $126,460 in 2001, according to the Bureau of Labor Statistics.

Employment Prospects

Many Forensic Psychiatrists either have their own practices or are part of group practices. Some find employment with federal prisons, hospitals, law enforcement agencies, prosecutors' offices, and other organizations.

Staff positions usually become available as Forensic Psychiatrists transfer to other positions or retire. New opportunities may be created to meet growing needs if funding is available.

Highly-qualified Forensic Psychiatrists are always in demand by attorneys to provide them with consulting and expert witness services.

Advancement Prospects

Staff psychiatrists can advance to become program manager, department administrator, or top-level executive officer of their organization. Those in private practice measure success in various ways, such as by being professionally recognized for their work and by earning higher income.

Education and Training

Medical training is required to become a Forensic Psychiatrist. Students first complete four years of medical training to earn either a doctor of medicine degree or doctor of osteopathic degree. This is followed by three to four years of graduate medical education (more commonly known as residency) to gain practical experience in the practice of psychiatry. They receive training in such areas as inpatient and outpatient treatment, medication management, crisis evaluations, and other areas. After completing their psychiatry residency, psychiatrists take an additional one or two years to complete a fellowship in forensic psychiatry.

Experience, Skills, and Personality Traits

To be expert witnesses, Forensic Psychiatrist normally need several years of clinical experience in the issues (such as workers' compensation, violence, or personal injury) that they would be addressing. In addition, Forensic Psychiatrists are expected to be familiar with the state and federal laws that apply to the cases in which they are consulting. (Federal and state courts specify the types of psychiatric issues that may be addressed in civil or criminal litigation, as well as have their own set of criteria that they use to decide psychiatric issues.)

In general, Forensic Psychiatrists need excellent communication and presentation skills, and must be able to present information clearly and logically in terms that attorneys, judges, and juries can comprehend. Forensic Psychiatrists also need strong writing, analytical, critical thinking, and self-management skills. Being humble, patient, flexible, prepared, honest, and unbiased are some personality traits that successful Forensic Psychiatrists share.

Special Requirements

All states, U.S. territories, and the District of Columbia require that all physicians—including Forensic Psychiatrists, hold valid licensure to practice. For specific information, contact the medical licensing board where you wish to practice.

Forensic Psychiatrists can apply for board certification by the American Board of Psychiatry and Neurology (ABPN), which demonstrates that they have completed training in their specialty. This requires first earning the Board Certified Psychiatrist designation from the ABPN. For more information, visit the American Board of Psychiatry and Neurology website at http://www.abpn.com.

Unions and Associations

Many Forensic Psychiatrists join professional associations to take advantage of networking opportunities and other professional resources and services. Two societies that serve the interests of Forensic Psychiatrists are the American Psychiatric Association and the American Academy of Psychiatry and the Law. Forensic Psychiatrists may also join the American Medical Association. For contact information, please see Appendix III.

Tips for Entry

1. Find out if the forensic psychiatry field is right for you. Read about forensic psychiatry. Talk with Forensic Psychiatrists about their professional career as well as their medical and psychiatric training.
2. Getting into medical school is competitive. Apply to several schools, especially ones that offer psychiatry as a clinical specialty.
3. Learn about job vacancies in professional journals, from professional societies, and through professional contacts.
4. Learn more about forensic psychiatry on the Internet. To get a list of relevant websites, enter the keywords *forensic psychiatry* or *forensic psychiatrists* in any search engine.

WILDLIFE FORENSIC SCIENTIST

CAREER PROFILE

Duties: Provide expert evaluation and opinion about physical evidence in criminal investigations involving animal victims; examine animal bodies, parts, and products to identify species and find proof that crimes have been committed; perform duties as required

Alternate Title(s): Wildlife Forensic Analyst, Wildlife Forensic Specialist, Wildlife Forensic Biologist

Salary Range: $29,000 to $80,000

Employment Prospects: Poor

Advancement Prospects: Fair

Prerequisites:
  Education or Training—A bachelor's degree in biology, chemistry, or related field
  Experience—Previous work experience in crime or wildlife-related labs generally required
  Special Skills and Personality Traits—Analytical, writing, communication, and self-management skills; patient; observant; unbiased; objective
  Licensure/Certification—None required

CAREER LADDER

```
┌────────────────────────────────────────┐
│   Senior Wildlife Forensic Scientist    │
└────────────────────────────────────────┘

┌────────────────────────────────────────┐
│      Wildlife Forensic Scientist        │
└────────────────────────────────────────┘

┌────────────────────────────────────────┐
│  Wildlife Forensic Scientist Trainee or │
│               Criminalist               │
└────────────────────────────────────────┘
```

Position Description

Wildlife Forensic Scientists assist law enforcement agencies with criminal investigations which involve protected and endangered animal species. State and federal laws, as well as international treaties, have been established to protect mammals, birds, reptiles, amphibians, and other wildlife in the United States as well as throughout the world. Yet many people continue to hunt protected species for fun or for financial gain. In fact, several billion dollars in illegal trade of wildlife and wildlife parts occur each year worldwide. Tusks, internal organs, fur, and other wildlife parts, for example, have been sold and used to make leather goods, garments, jewelry, artwork, food, medicinal cures, and other products.

Wildlife Forensic Scientists are responsible for examining physical evidence—which may be animal bodies, parts, or products—and finding proof that crimes have been committed. They work in forensic labs that are set up and equipped like any other crime lab. They apply similar forensic methods and techniques that criminalists use to examine physical evidence in human crimes.

Identifying the species of the animal victim is crucial as it determines whether wildlife laws have been broken. Wildlife Forensic Scientists use a variety of methods to identify species, including chemical, DNA, blood testing, and physical comparison techniques. Essentially, they examine evidence samples and match them with known samples. For example, a forensic examiner may have a feather as physical evidence, and would try to identify the species by matching it to a sample from a reference library of bird feathers.

Wildlife Forensic Scientists perform autopsies on animal carcasses to determine the cause of the victims' death. The forensic examiners confirm whether victims may have died from natural causes, which includes being killed by other animals for food or for territory. If they died by unnatural causes, forensic scientists determine how they were killed, such as by gunshot wounds, pesticide poisoning, environmental pollution, trap wounds, or other forms of trauma.

Wildlife Forensic Scientists examine stomach contents, bullets, shot pellets, poisons, pesticides, soil samples, and trace evidence to find a connection with the victims, criminal suspects, and crime scenes. In small labs, samples of physical evidence may be sent to other crime labs to perform tests, such as DNA analysis, which cannot be done in their labs.

Wildlife Forensic Scientists also examine confiscated products that are suspected of having originated from protected or endangered species. For example, they examine fresh, frozen, or smoked meats; fur coats; reptile leather products such as shoes and purses; loose feathers and down; carved ivory objects; turtle shell jewelry; cosmetics; pharmaceuticals; and so on. Wildlife Forensic Scientists try to determine whether suspected products have characteristics that define them as being certain species.

When these forensic examiners complete their evaluations, they prepare comprehensive reports of their findings and conclusions. They attach photographs, drawings, and other documentation to support their opinions. They are responsible for writing reports that are clear, concise, and easy to understand by investigators, attorneys, and courts. Wildlife Forensic Scientists are sometimes called upon to provide expert witness testimony about their evaluations at court depositions and trials.

Wildlife Forensic Scientists also perform a variety of other duties. For example, they might:

- assist in the development of a lab database or library of visual clues of animal species and individual animals; for example, a lab might build a collection of tissue and blood samples from various types of reptiles
- conduct basic research studies on individual animal species to gain knowledge and understanding of the species
- perform analytical work related to wildlife management (for example, determine the age of elk)
- develop new techniques for identifying various animal species through examination of eggs, animal parts, blood, cooked meats, oils, or cosmetics
- conduct or assist investigators with crime scene investigations
- conduct training workshops for game wardens, park rangers, and others in wildlife crime scene investigations, interpreting physical evidence, and other topics
- occasionally act as department liaison with law enforcement agencies, and other governmental agencies as well as with the general public

Wildlife Forensic Scientists work in wildlife forensic labs that are part of game and wildlife agencies, law enforcement crime labs, private labs, or research labs in academic institutions. Many Wildlife Forensic Scientists perform wildlife forensic examinations as part of their duties as criminalists.

Wildlife Forensic Scientists work odd hours and occasionally travel. They may be on call 24 hours a day.

Salaries
Salaries vary, depending on such factors as education, experience, job responsibilities, and geographical location.

Federal Wildlife Forensic Scientists receive a salary based on a pay schedule called the General Schedule, or GS. Entry-level positions usually start at the GS-7 level and can advance up to the GS-12 level. Senior scientists earn salaries at the GS-13 level. In 2003, the basic pay from GS-7 to GS-13 levels ranged from \$29,037 to \$79,629.

Employment Prospects
Wildlife forensics is a new and small field. Opportunities are expected to grow, but most positions will become available as Wildlife Forensic Scientists retire or transfer to other positions. Most full-time Wildlife Forensic Scientists are hired by the National Fish and Wildlife Forensics Laboratory, part of the U.S. Wildlife Service, in Ashland, Oregon. Wildlife Forensic Scientists are also employed with state wildlife forensic labs to perform full-time or part-time duties. Forensic specialists in marine life work at the Marine Forensics Branch in Charleston, South Carolina.

Applicants for positions in government agencies must pass a selection process that includes any of the following steps: written exam, interview, medical exam, drug test, background investigation, and polygraph examination. Federal government agencies require that employees be U.S. citizens.

Advancement Prospects
Many Wildlife Forensic Scientists pursue advancement by earning higher salaries, by being assigned more complex responsibilities, through gaining professional recognition, and by other individual measurements.

Education and Training
Minimally, Wildlife Forensic Scientists possess a bachelor's degree in biology, chemistry, biochemistry, forensic science, or another related discipline. For individuals to advance to senior and management positions, a master's or doctoral degree may be required or strongly preferred.

Experience, Skills, and Personality Traits
Most labs typically choose candidates who have previous work experience in crime labs or in wildlife-related laboratories. Entry-level candidates may have gained experience through internships, part-time employment, research assistantships, or other positions in analytical, research, or crime laboratories. Candidates should be able to demonstrate their knowledge about proper lab procedures, handling of lab instruments and equipment, and procedures for handling and processing physical evidence. Employers may allow candidates to substitute advanced degrees for at least one year of work experience.

Wildlife Forensic Scientists need strong analytical, writing, and communication skills to do their work effectively. They also should have good self-management skills, such as the ability to organize and prioritize tasks, handle stressful situations, and work independently. Being patient, observant, unbiased, and objective are a few personality traits that successful Wildlife Forensic Scientists share.

Unions and Associations

Many Wildlife Forensic Scientists join the American Academy of Forensic Sciences as well as professional societies that are devoted to specific fields (such as chemistry, herpetology, and ornithology). By joining professional associations, they can take advantage of networking opportunities and other professional services and resources. For contact information, please see Appendix III.

Tips for Entry

1. Talk with professionals to learn more about the job.
2. While in college, seek volunteer, internship or work-study positions with crime labs or research labs that perform wildlife forensics services to wildlife agencies.
3. Learn more about wildlife forensics on the Internet. You might start by visiting the National Fish and Wildlife Forensics Laboratory website at http://www.laboratory.fws.gov. To find other relevant websites, enter the keywords *wildlife forensics* in any search engine.

INDUSTRY

INDUSTRIAL RESEARCH SCIENTIST

CAREER PROFILE	CAREER LADDER

Duties: Apply scientific principles to the development of new products or the improvement of existing ones; plan, conduct, and evaluate experiments, perform duties as required

Alternate Title(s): Research and Development (R&D) Scientist, Bench Scientist; a title that reflects a specialty such as Microbiologist, Biochemist, Food Scientist, or Agricultural Scientist

Salary Range: $65,000 to $100,000+

Employment Prospects: Good

Advancement Prospects: Good

Prerequisites:

Education/Training—A doctoral degree in a scientific discipline

Experience—Work and research experience related to the position being applied for is required

Special Skills and Personality Traits—Leadership, teamwork, interpersonal, writing, communication, presentation, and self-management skills; enthusiastic; creative; dedicated; analytical; flexible

Licensure/Certification—None required

```
┌─────────────────────────────────┐
│   Senior Research Scientist or   │
│      Principal Investigator      │
└─────────────────────────────────┘

┌─────────────────────────────────┐
│        Research Scientist        │
└─────────────────────────────────┘

┌─────────────────────────────────┐
│        Research Associate        │
└─────────────────────────────────┘
```

Position Description

Industrial Research Scientists are biologists, molecular biologists, geneticists, chemists, biochemists, physicists, geologists, agricultural scientists, food scientists, materials scientists, and so on. They are involved with the research and development of products for commercial purposes. These scientists work for small start-up companies as well as for established corporations in the various industries—such as the pharmaceuticals, biotechnology, agriculture, food processing, chemicals, paints, fabric, computer hardware, electronics, energy, aviation, aerospace, and telecommunications industries

The process of developing new products or improving existing ones is called product development. Research Scientists usually work on product development as members of multidisciplinary teams. These project teams are composed of scientists from different disciplines in addition to project managers, engineers, technicians, and others.

Research Scientists are sometimes called bench scientists as they spend much of their time working in the laboratory. They perform a variety of duties, such as:

- planning and organizing their work schedules
- designing and conducting experiments
- analyzing and interpreting data
- reading scientific journals and other research literature
- meeting with colleagues to discuss projects
- providing written or oral updates of studies at project meetings
- arranging for quality testings of raw materials and products to verify that they are in compliance with regulations
- preparing written reports
- operating scientific instrumentation
- supervising research assistants and technicians, who provide administrative and research support

Research Scientists are required to follow standard company procedures and industry protocols. Furthermore, they are required to write detailed notes about the work they perform. Their information is usually submitted with applications for licenses, permits, patents, regulatory approval, and for other business and legal documentation.

Research Scientists keep up with developments and technologies in their scientific disciplines. They read professional journals and books, attend professional conferences, network with colleagues, and enroll in continuing education programs.

Salaries

Salaries vary, depending on education, experience, scientific discipline, industry, geographical location, and other factors. Wetfeet.com reports that Research Scientists in the pharmaceutical and biotechnology industries earn between $65,000 and $100,000.

The Bureau of Labor Statistics reports these estimated salary ranges in 2001 for the following scientists:

- agricultural and food scientists, $28,690 to $85,350
- biochemists, $33,930 to $97,710
- chemists, $30,450 to $89,830
- computer scientists, $42,590 to $119,150
- geologists, $33,150 to $109,510
- materials scientists, $32,630 to $103,980
- microbiologists, $30,740 to $87,220
- physicists, $49,320 to $123,220

Employment Prospects

Opportunities vary with the different industries, with biotechnology offering the best job outlook for the coming years.

Most job openings are created to replace individuals who retire, transfer to other positions, or resign. Employers will create additional positions to fit growing needs for their companies.

The job market for Research Scientists usually falls and rises with the economy. During healthy periods, more jobs are generally available. Companies may reduce or shut down research operations when they are experiencing funding problems.

With their experience and training, industrial Research Scientists can also seek such nonresearch positions as a quality professional, regulatory affairs specialist, patent agent, technical writer, sales representative, or market research analyst.

Advancement Prospects

Those interested in pursuing managerial and administrative positions can become a principal investigator, program manager, laboratory director, department manager, or executive officer. Doctoral degrees may be required for them to obtain top management positions.

Education and Training

Most industrial Research Scientists possess a doctorate in their scientific discipline—i.e., microbiology, molecular biol-

ogy, biochemistry, organic chemistry, toxicology, physics, geology, and so on.

Some employers hire Research Scientists with a master's degree, as long as they have qualifying experience.

Experience, Skills, and Personality Traits

Employers normally hire candidates who have work and research experience related to the positions for which they are applying. Experience may have been gained through student research projects, internships, fellowships, part-time employment, and so on. Ph.D. candidates for research scientist positions may be required to have several years of postdoctoral experience.

Industrial Research Scientists are expected to have excellent leadership, teamwork, and interpersonal skills, as they must be able to work well with people from various backgrounds. In addition, Research Scientists have good writing, communication, and presentation skills. They also have strong self-management skills, including the ability to follow directions, work efficiently and independently, organize and prioritize tasks, meet deadlines, and so on.

Being enthusiastic, creative, dedicated, analytical, and flexible are some personality traits that industrial Research Scientists have in common.

Unions and Associations

Many Research Scientists belong to professional associations that serve the interests of their particular disciplines. By joining these societies, they can take advantage of such professional services and resources as networking opportunities, continuing education programs, professional certification, and publications.

Tips for Entry

1. Gain research experience during your undergraduate years by obtaining a research assistantship or by volunteering to work on a professor's research project. Also gain industrial experience. Many companies offer internship or work-study programs to college students. Contact companies with whom you would like to work to find out about such opportunities.
2. Attend career fairs sponsored by colleges or community organizations. Along with learning about job openings, take advantage of learning more about companies from their representatives.
3. Are your job skills lacking? Get help from your college career center. Counselors are available to help you fill out applications and prepare résumés more effectively. They can also help you prepare for job interviews and offer other resources for your use.
4. Use the Internet to learn more about companies where you would like to work. To see if a company has a website, enter its name in any search engine.

SCIENCE TECHNICIAN

CAREER PROFILE

Duties: Provide laboratory and technical support to scientists, engineers, and others; may work in research and development, quality control, production, or other area; perform duties as required

Alternate Title(s): Laboratory Technician, Laboratory Assistant; a title that reflects a specialty, such as Chemical Technician or Agriculture Technician, or a specific job, such as Quality Control Technician or Plant Breeding Technician

Salary Range: $17,000 to $65,000

Employment Prospects: Good

Advancement Prospects: Limited

Prerequisites:

Education/Training—A high school diploma; an associate or bachelor's degree in a science discipline usually required

Experience—Laboratory experience preferred

Special Skills and Personality Traits—Organizational, analytical, observation, computer, writing, communication, interpersonal, and teamwork skills; adaptable; self-motivated; reliable; accurate; detail-oriented; curious; creative

Licensure/Certification—None required

CAREER LADDER

```
┌─────────────────────────────────┐
│     Senior Science Technician    │
└─────────────────────────────────┘

┌─────────────────────────────────┐
│        Science Technician        │
└─────────────────────────────────┘

┌─────────────────────────────────┐
│       Laboratory Assistant or    │
│     Science Technician Trainee   │
└─────────────────────────────────┘
```

Position Description

In industry, Science Technicians play an important role in developing and producing products and services that meet customers' satisfaction. They provide laboratory and technical support to scientists and engineers in research and development, quality control, manufacturing, packaging, and other areas.

Like scientists, Science Technicians specialize in different scientific disciplines. For example, biological technicians assist biological science and medical science researchers. Chemical technicians work with chemical scientists and chemical engineers. Agricultural technicians provide assistance to agricultural scientists and food science technicians work with food scientists and food technologists.

Science Technicians' responsibilities vary, depending on the area in which they work. Research technicians assist scientists in the research and development of new or improved products (or services). Under the guidance of scientists,

technicians perform a variety of laboratory tasks as well as experiments. They also assist with the development and improvement of laboratory procedures, in the interpretation of research data, and with finding solutions to problems.

Many Science Technicians are involved in the manufacturing of new and existing products. They monitor production processes to ensure that products are being manufactured according to product specifications, company procedures, and industry standards. Additionally, Science Technicians verify the quality of raw materials, products, and processes. They also make sure that raw materials and production processes comply with all governmental laws and regulations that govern their particular industries. Some Science Technicians provide support in their companies' waste management operations and other activities related to environmental regulatory compliance.

Science Technicians perform a number of tasks, which vary each day. Many of their duties are specific to their specialty and work setting. They also perform many of the same general tasks, such as:

- setting up, operating, and adjusting laboratory instruments
- collecting data, such as samples for testing
- preparing chemical solutions, cultures, or samples
- monitoring tests or experiments
- verifying information and checking calculations
- analyzing and interpreting data on tests or experiments
- keeping detailed records of work activities
- writing technical summaries and reports
- maintaining inventory of laboratory supplies
- cleaning and maintaining laboratory instruments and equipment

Entry-level technicians typically perform basic routine tasks, and work under the close supervision of scientists, technologists, or senior technicians. As they gain experience, they are assigned increasingly complicated duties. For example, experienced Science Technicians sometimes conduct experiments or tests independently, and provide scientists with reports of their results to review.

Most industrial Science Technicians work in laboratories. Some of them, such as agricultural, geological, petroleum, and environmental technicians, perform much of their work outdoors. Some of them often travel to remote locations.

Science Technicians may be exposed to dust, noise, toxic chemicals, infectious agents, extremes in temperature, or other hazards. To prevent risks, technicians are required to follow safety procedures, such as wearing respiratory masks while handling toxic chemicals.

Science Technicians work a standard 40-hour week. In some companies, production technicians work day, evening, or night shifts.

Salaries

Salaries vary, depending on education, experience, industry, and geographical location. According to the Bureau of Labor Statistics, the estimated annual salary in 2001 for most of the following Science Technicians ranged as follows:

- Biological technicians—$20,410 to $51,160
- Agricultural and food science technicians—$16,810 to $46,460
- Chemical technicians—$22,190 to $56,450
- Geological and petroleum technicians—$19,340 to $64,350
- Environmental science technicians—$21,020 to $55,520

Employment Prospects

Science Technicians are employed in research and development, quality control, and manufacturing in many industries, including biotechnology, biomedicine, agriculture, food processing, chemicals, petroleum, energy, aerospace, communications, and so on.

Opportunities for experienced Science Technicians should be available for years to come, particularly in the biotechnology and pharmaceutical industries and in research and testing services. However, the job market typically reflects the health of the economy. Fewer job openings and more layoffs for Science Technicians can be expected during economic downturns.

Advancement Prospects

Advancement opportunities for Science Technicians are limited to supervisory positions.

For a technician to advance to positions with higher pay and more responsibility, additional education is required. Many employers offer tuition programs to help Science Technicians who would like to continue their formal education and obtain higher degrees. With a bachelor's or master's degree in science, Science Technicians can qualify for research associate, research assistant, and technologist positions.

Education and Training

Requirements vary with the different employers. Science Technicians need at least a high school diploma or a general equivalency diploma. In addition, many employers require that Science Technicians possess an associate degree in an applied science or science-related technology, or have at least two years of specialized training. Some employers may require that Science Technicians have a bachelor's degree in an appropriate science discipline. For example, chemical technicians may be required to possess bachelor's degrees in chemistry or biochemistry.

Many technical and community colleges offer certificate and associate degree programs which combine instruction in scientific principles and theory with practical applications in laboratory settings. Most associate degrees are designed to fulfill general education requirements for four-year colleges and universities. Thus, students are able to transfer easily to a four-year college or university.

Employers typically provide entry-level Science Technicians with on-the-job training. Many Science Technicians enroll in training programs and continuing education courses throughout their careers in order to maintain and update their knowledge and skills.

Experience, Skills, and Personality Traits

Employers typically prefer that candidates for entry-level positions have laboratory experience, which may have been gained through training programs, internships, or part-time employment.

To do well in their work, Science Technicians need strong organizational, analytical, and observation skills. Having good computer, writing, and communication skills is also essential. In addition, they need effective interpersonal and teamwork skills, as they must be able to work well with scientists and others. Being adaptable, self-motivated, reliable, accurate, detail-oriented, curious, and creative are some personality traits that successful Science Technicians have in common.

Unions and Associations

Science Technicians are eligible to join science societies that serve their particular disciplines. For example, chemical technicians may join the American Chemical Society and food science technicians may belong to the Institute of Food Technologists. By joining professional associations, they can take advantage of networking opportunities, education programs, and other professional resources and services. For contact information for these associations, please see Appendix III.

Tips for Entry

1. In high school, take as many science and mathematics courses as you can.

2. Some two-year colleges offer internship and work-study programs which place students at local companies. Check with your college career center to see what is available.

3. To enhance your employability and advancement prospects, continue to update your technical skills.

4. Contact employers directly about permanent and temporary job openings. Also learn about jobs through your college career center as well as your state employment office.

5. Use the Internet to learn more about Science Technicians. To get a list of relevant websites, enter the keyword *science technician* in a search engine. To learn about specific occupations, enter their job titles, such as *chemical technicians, agricultural technicians,* or *biotechnology technicians.*

PROJECT MANAGER

CAREER PROFILE

Duties: Plan, direct, and coordinate the activities of company projects; perform duties as required

Alternate Title(s): Project Director, Project Manager/Consultant

Salary Range: $44,000 to $139,000

Employment Prospects: Good

Advancement Prospects: Good

Prerequisites:

    Education or Training—A bachelor's degree in a technical or scientific discipline

    Experience—Several years of experience in the scientific discipline and industry in which one would be working

    Special Skills and Personality Traits—Leadership, teambuilding, interpersonal, communication organizational, analytical, problem-solving, writing, self-management, and computer skills; energetic; enthusiastic; honest; dependable; flexible; creative

    Licensure/Certification—Professional certification may be required or preferred

CAREER LADDER

```
┌─────────────────────────────────┐
│      Senior Project Manager      │
└─────────────────────────────────┘

┌─────────────────────────────────┐
│         Project Manager          │
└─────────────────────────────────┘

┌─────────────────────────────────┐
│     Assistant Project Manager    │
└─────────────────────────────────┘

┌─────────────────────────────────┐
│      Project Coordinator or      │
│        Project Scheduler         │
└─────────────────────────────────┘
```

Position Description

Project Managers plan, administer, and coordinate projects that companies initiate for various purposes. This includes developing new products or services; improving existing products; conducting basic or applied research for new ventures; launching the sale of new products; improving organizational structure, systems, or processes; constructing buildings; and so on. Project Managers are responsible for the success or failure of projects that they direct.

Project Managers are usually assigned to oversee projects from beginning to end. They work closely with scientists or engineers as well as with business managers to plan the direction of the project. This involves defining the project goals, which integrate scientific or technical goals with company strategic and business objectives. It also includes establishing administrative policies and procedures as well as determining the resources—money, staff, equipment, materials, and so on—that would be needed for the projects. Project Managers also identify potential risks that may occur during the various project stages.

Project Managers act as liaisons between project members and the senior, or higher-level, management of their companies. However, most Project Managers have no authority to make any decisions regarding the scientific or technical direction of the projects. Their role is to control the cost, time, and quality of the projects.

Project Managers develop project schedules that outline the required sequences of steps for completing the projects. In addition, they are in charge of allocating resources. For example, they coordinate all the purchasing or leasing of machinery and equipment, interface with vendors to make sure their materials conform to industrial standards, oversee the contracting of outside professional services, and supervise the hiring and training of new or temporary employees for the projects.

Project Managers perform various duties to assure that projects run smoothly, by applying project management methods and technologies as well as by meeting deadlines and staying within budget constraints. Some of their tasks include:

- coordinating work schedules of team members
- monitoring the progress of individual team members to ensure they are meeting project goals

- evaluating project-related issues and providing recommendations for solving problems
- confirming that projects are in compliance with appropriate procedures, protocol, and regulations
- providing progress reports to team members and senior managers
- scheduling, directing, and leading project team meetings
- meeting with contractors, subcontractors, vendors, and material suppliers
- preparing required forms, reports, and paperwork

Most Project Managers are involved in two or more projects at a time. They may run a project alone or lead a project management team, which would entail delegating tasks to assistants such as coordinators, schedulers, and assistant project managers. Project Managers report to technical project sponsors, who are usually the scientists or engineers that conceptualized the projects.

Project Managers work mostly in offices. Some may work in laboratories or in industrial plants, depending on the nature of the projects.

Project Managers often work evenings and on weekends to complete tasks and meet project deadlines. Many Project Managers feel stressed as they are expected to complete projects with short deadlines or within tight budgets. Some Project Managers are required to be available 24 hours a day.

Salaries

Salaries vary, depending on various factors, including education, experience, level of responsibility, industry, employer, and geographical location. In addition, many companies reward Project Mangers with bonuses for their job performance.

The Bureau of Labor Statistics reports that the estimated annual salary in 2001 for most natural science managers ranged between $44,460 and $139,420, and for most engineering managers, between $55,700 and $135,680. According to a 2000 survey by the Project Management Institute, the average salary for Project Managers was $83,390 per year.

Employment Prospects

Project Managers are employed in various industries, including the biotechnology, pharmaceuticals, biomedicine, computer and data processing, information technology, construction, agriculture, automotive, aerospace, aviation, and telecommunications industries. Many Project Managers work as consultants, either as self-employed or for firms that provide project management services.

Job opportunities for experienced Project Managers should continue to be good for years to come, as companies continually need personnel to manage new projects. However, most openings become available as Project Managers transfer to other positions, retire, or leave the workforce.

The demand for Project Managers vary with the different industries. Job opportunities should be better in those areas that are experiencing growth, such as biotechnology and biomedicine. However, the job market generally goes up and down with the economy. When the economy is healthy, for example, more opportunities are available. When the economy is on a downturn, companies tend to put projects on hold and lay off workers or hire fewer people.

Advancement Prospects

Advancement opportunities are limited for Project Managers. They generally realize advancement by earning higher salaries and through job satisfaction. In large companies, Project Managers may be promoted to senior project management positions. Many Project Managers become consultants.

Another career option for Project Managers is to pursue managerial positions in nontechnical areas such as sales, marketing, or human resources. Additional experience or training may be needed.

Education and Training

The minimum educational requirement for Project Managers is a bachelor's degree in a technical or scientific discipline related to the type of projects they would be managing. For example, Project Managers in technology usually hold a degree in computer science, electrical engineering, or other related fields. Some employers prefer to hire Project Managers with an advanced degree.

Many employers also hire Project Mangers who have a bachelor's or master's degree in business administration.

Most companies provide training to new Project Managers.

Experience, Skills, and Personality Traits

Employers typically hire Project Managers who have experience or are familiar with the industry and discipline in which they would be working. Project Managers also have an understanding of business and financial principles. Most Project Managers in scientific and engineering fields have several years of work experience as scientists, engineers, technologists, technicians, or in other positions. They also have a few years of experience working on technical projects.

Project Managers must have excellent leadership, teambuilding, interpersonal, and communication skills, as they must be able to inspire people to work well together and focus on completing projects. Additionally, Project Managers need effective organizational, analytical, problem-solving, and writing skills. They also need strong self-management skills, such as the ability to prioritize and perform multiple tasks, work independently, handle stressful situations, and meet deadlines. Further, Project Managers have computer skills and experience working with word processing, spreadsheet, project management, and other software.

Being energetic, enthusiastic, honest, dependable, flexible, and creative are some personality traits that successful Project Managers share.

Unions and Associations

Project Managers can join professional associations to take advantage of professional resources and services, such as training programs, publications, research, and networking opportunities. Many Project Managers belong to the Project Management Institute, a national society. (For contact information, please see Appendix III.) Additionally, local or regional societies that serve the interests of Project Managers are available in many areas.

Tips for Entry

1. As a college student, you might gain experience by obtaining an internship or work-study position in project management. Talk with your adviser or a college career counselor for assistance in finding such positions.

2. Early in your career, let your supervisor know about your interest in project management. Together, discuss your career goals and how you can gain experience to become a Project Manager.

3. To enhance your employability, you might complete a project management certificate program through a college or university continuing education program.

4. Many Project Managers have gained experience through support project management roles, such as by being a project coordinator, project scheduler, or assistant project manager.

5. Use the Internet to learn more about project management. Some websites you might visit are Project Management Institute, http://www.pmi.org; Project Management.com, http://www.projectmanagement.com; and ALLPM: The Project Managers Homepage, http://www.allpm.com.

QUALITY PROFESSIONAL

CAREER PROFILE

Duties: Inspect, test, and audit raw materials, manufacturing processes, and products for quality requirements; responsibilities vary with the different positions; perform duties as required of position

Alternate Title(s): Quality Control Technician, Quality Control Engineer, Quality Control Analyst, Quality Assurance Manager, Quality Control Auditor, or other title that reflects a specific position

Salary Range: $25,000 to $100,000

Employment Prospects: Good

Advancement Prospects: Good

Prerequisites:

    Education or Training—A bachelor's degree in engineering or a scientific discipline for most positions

    Experience—Experience in quality control preferred; previous experience related to position

    Special Skills and Personality Traits—Math, writing, communication, computer, interpersonal, teamwork, and self-management skills; flexible; meticulous; detail-oriented; observant

    Licensure/Certification—Professional certification may be required

CAREER LADDER

```
┌─────────────────────────────────┐
│   Quality Assurance Manager      │
└─────────────────────────────────┘

┌─────────────────────────────────┐
│  Quality Control Manager or      │
│  Quality Assurance Engineer      │
└─────────────────────────────────┘

┌─────────────────────────────────┐
│   Quality Control Engineer       │
└─────────────────────────────────┘

┌─────────────────────────────────┐
│   Quality Control Technician     │
└─────────────────────────────────┘
```

Position Description

The term *quality* in manufacturing means that products have all the characteristics required to meet customer satisfaction and that they are free of any defects or deficiencies. Manufacturing companies employ various Quality Professionals to ensure that quality is being monitored throughout all product development and manufacturing phases. Quality Professionals also guarantee that the quality of the products, the raw materials used for making them, and the manufacturing processes all comply with company and industrial standards, or technical specifications. In addition, some Quality Professionals are involved with monitoring the quality of other aspects of a company's performance such as employee training programs, customer service, and information systems.

Quality operations are generally divided into two units—quality assurance and quality control. The quality assurance staff is responsible for developing policies, procedures, and product assurance programs which ensure that the require-

ments of quality are being fulfilled. Some of them are involved with monitoring quality programs and making sure that requirements have been met.

The quality control staff, on the other hand, is responsible for the day-to-day inspections of raw materials, packaging, and products during production processes. They check for unsatisfactory performance and can request that work be redone, materials or products be thrown out, or even stop production until corrections have been made.

Most manufacturers employ various types of Quality Professionals—technicians, specialists, engineers, and managers. They may work in either the quality control or quality assurance units. Quality technicians are usually entry-level personnel. Quality control technicians are responsible for inspecting and testing raw materials, samples, parts, or finished products. Quality assurance technicians conduct audits on products to make sure they meet appropriate levels of quality. All technicians keep accurate records of their test or audit data. They are also responsible for evaluating the data and preparing reports of their findings.

Quality control analysts are responsible for the inspection of raw materials (such as food ingredients, chemicals for drugs, plastics, or packaging materials) before they can be used. Following standard operating procedures, they perform lab analyses on raw materials, and report any abnormalities. Quality control analysts are responsible for documenting their tests and evaluations.

Quality engineers are responsible for ensuring the quality standards during the production process. They often work closely with manufacturing engineers and technicians. Their duties vary, depending on their experience, position, and other factors. Some duties that quality engineers might perform include:

- inspecting and testing products during the production processes
- performing quality audits on finished products
- applying quality control standards
- inspecting, testing, and evaluating the precision and accuracy of production equipment and quality testing and inspection tools
- developing quality control standards for processing raw materials into products
- conducting audits to confirm that processes are in compliance with company specifications and industrial standards
- preparing documentation

Quality assurance auditors are responsible for auditing the activities of production and quality control departments. They assure that these departments are in compliance with in-house and industrial standards. They may also be responsible for confirming that their companies are meeting regulatory requirements for standard manufacturing practices.

Quality managers are responsible for planning, developing, and implementing quality activities and programs. They are also responsible for supervising quality technicians, engineers, specialists, and others. Some quality managers are in charge of particular units. For example, quality control managers are responsible for product quality on their shifts, while quality assurance managers are responsible for overseeing the full life cycle of a specific product line. Other quality managers are in charge of quality departments, being responsible for planning, directing, and administering all quality programs. These managers, sometimes known as directors of quality operations, are usually members of company management teams which develop and implement company policies and operating procedures.

Depending on their positions, Quality Professionals may work in offices, in laboratories, or at production sites. Quality Professionals generally work a 40-hour week. Many of them work evening or night shifts.

Salaries

Salaries vary, depending on such factors as education, experience, position, employer, and geographical location. Quality control engineers and managers typically make higher earnings than technicians. According to Wetfeet.com, annual salaries for quality control and quality assurance professionals range from $25,000 to $100,000.

Employment Prospects

Quality Professionals are employed in practically all industries, such as the automotive, aviation, defense, medical devices, pharmaceuticals, biotechnology, chemicals, petroleum, telecommunications, computer hardware, computer software, environmental, energy, and food processing industries.

Most openings become available as Quality Professionals transfer to other positions or retire. Employers will create additional jobs to fit growing needs as long as resources are available. During economic downturns, fewer jobs and more layoffs can be expected.

Advancement Prospects

Quality Professionals with managerial and administrative aspirations can rise through the ranks as team leaders, project leaders, supervisors, managers, and executives.

Options vary for the different Quality Professionals. For example, quality technicians can usually rise to the supervisor level. With further education, they can become quality engineers.

Education and Training

Educational requirements vary with the different positions. Some employers prefer that candidates for quality assurance positions hold a master's degree in engineering or business administration, with a concentration in quality management. A bachelor's degree in engineering or science discipline is the minimum requirement for quality engineers, analysts, auditors, and managers. Many employers require or strongly prefer to hire candidates with an advanced degree.

The minimum requirement for quality technicians varies with the different employers. Some employers hire qualified candidates with high school diplomas or general equivalency diplomas. Others require candidates to have an associate's or bachelor's degree.

Employers typically provide training for new employees.

Experience, Skills, and Personality Traits

Requirements vary with the different positions. Usually the higher the position, the more years of experience are needed. For example, a biotechnology firm may require two to five years of experience for quality control analyst positions.

Many Employers prefer to hire candidates who have one or more years of experience in quality control. They also look for applicants who have work experience related to the positions for which they are applying.

In general, Quality Professionals should have strong math, writing, and communication skills. Having adequate computer skills is also essential. In addition, they need excellent interpersonal and teamwork skills as well as self-management skills, such as the ability to organize and prioritize tasks, handle stressful situations, and work independently. Being flexible, meticulous, detail-oriented, and observant are some personality traits that Quality Professionals share.

Unions and Associations

Many Quality Professionals are members of the American Society for Quality and other local, state, or national professional associations. (For contact information, please see Appendix III.) By joining these societies, they can take advantage of training programs, professional certification, current research data, networking opportunities, and other professional services and resources.

Tips for Entry

1. Gain experience by obtaining a part-time job, summer job, or internship in quality control.
2. Read job descriptions carefully, as job titles differ from one company to the next.
3. Take advantage of resources such as state employment offices, career centers, professional associations, and Internet job banks to learn about job openings for Quality Professionals.
4. Before taking a job offer, be sure you understand how the quality department is structured and what kind of career advancement opportunities are available to you. Be sure to ask a prospective employer before taking any job offer.
5. Use the Internet to learn more about the quality control/assurance field. One website where you might start is American Society for Quality, http://www.asq.org.

REGULATORY AFFAIRS SPECIALIST (HEALTH CARE PRODUCTS)

CAREER PROFILE

Duties: Confirm that companies in the health-care product industry are in compliance with all appropriate laws and regulations; assist companies with obtaining permits, licenses, approvals, and so on for marketing new products; perform duties as required

Alternate Title(s): Regulatory Affairs Associate, Regulatory Affairs Manager

Salary Range: $35,000 to $90,000

Employment Prospects: Good

Advancement Prospects: Good

Prerequisites:

Education or Training—A bachelor's degree in a science or health field usually preferred

Experience—Previous industry work experience; experience or familiarity with regulatory affairs preferred

Special Skills and Personality Traits—Negotiation, organizational, writing, computer, statistical, communication, presentation, interpersonal, and teamwork skills; inquisitive; tactful; friendly; detail-oriented; diligent; pragmatic

Licensure/Certification—None required

CAREER LADDER

```
┌─────────────────────────────────┐
│          Director,              │
│  Regulatory Affairs Operations  │
└─────────────────────────────────┘

┌─────────────────────────────────┐
│   Regulatory Affairs Manager    │
└─────────────────────────────────┘

┌─────────────────────────────────┐
│ Senior Regulatory Affairs Specialist │
└─────────────────────────────────┘

┌─────────────────────────────────┐
│   Regulatory Affairs Specialist │
│        (or Associate)           │
└─────────────────────────────────┘
```

Position Description

Regulatory Affairs (RA) Specialists play an important role in bringing safe and effective health care products to domestic as well as international consumers. Health care products include pharmaceuticals, medical devices, in vitro diagnostics, biologic products (such as plasma and tissue products), biotechnology products, nutritional supplements, cosmetics, and veterinary products. RA Specialists are responsible for making sure that companies comply with the wide array of laws and regulations that govern the development, manufacturing, processing, and marketing of the different types of health care products.

In the pharmaceutical, biotechnology, and biomedical device industries, RA Specialists are also involved in obtaining product approval for new products. In the United States—as well as in other countries—all products that would be used for treating medical conditions or diseases must first be approved by regulatory agencies before they

can be sold. For example, companies must obtain approval from the U.S. Food and Drug Administration (FDA) for new medicines, treatments, biologic products, medical devices, and other products they want to sell nationwide.

RA Specialists also help their companies seek FDA approval for performing clinical studies on health care products. These studies involve testing the products on human subjects to further study their safety and effectiveness. The results from these studies would be presented to the FDA to obtain approval for marketing their products.

RA Specialists work under the guidance and supervision of RA managers. In some companies, RA Specialists are known as regulatory affairs associates.

RA Specialists act as regulatory resources for their companies. They are usually assigned to provide support to several projects at a time. They are responsible for understanding, interpreting, and applying laws, regulations, guidelines, and guidance from different regulatory agencies. They advise scientists, engineers, project managers, and others about pertinent requirements which need to be followed. RA Specialists are also responsible for tracking and documenting changes in regulations and guidelines that relate to their assigned projects. They inform appropriate personnel who have the authority to make the changes needed for companies to be in compliance.

RA Specialists may be involved with certain phases or the whole life cycle of a project—from product development to the marketing of the final product. They interact with the different departments, such as the research and development, manufacturing, quality control, packaging, and advertising departments. For example, RA Specialists might work with quality professionals to verify that manufacturing processes are in compliance with regulations.

Regulatory Affairs Specialists perform a wide range of duties, which vary according to their skill levels and experience. Some of their duties may include:

- preparing and filing applications for licenses, permits, and product registrations required for commercial distribution of products
- gathering and assembling information for regulatory submissions
- reviewing technical documents for regulatory submissions
- acting as company liaison with regulatory affairs personnel in other countries
- negotiating submission issues with FDA reviewers for product approvals
- preparing regulatory reports
- assisting with inspections and audits from the FDA and other regulatory agencies
- helping to establish and maintain standard procedures and polices to assure continued compliance in all work areas
- training new company employees about regulatory requirements as well as industrial standards and protocols

Some RA Specialists also perform the role of quality professional in their company.

Regulatory Affairs Specialists generally work a 40-hour week. Some may be required to travel to other countries to meet with regulatory agencies.

Salaries

Salaries vary, depending on such factors as experience, education, job duties, employer, and geographical location. Wetfeet.com reports that annual salaries for RA Specialists in biotechnology and pharmaceutical companies range between $35,000 and $90,000.

Regulatory affairs managers and directors can expect to earn up to $100,000 or more.

Employment Prospects

Health Care Regulatory Affairs Specialists are employed in the biotechnology, pharmaceutical, and biomedical device industries. They may also find employment with companies that manufacture cosmetics, nutritional products, and veterinary products. Many also work as consultants for firms that offer regulatory affairs services.

Experts in the field report that qualified regulatory affairs professionals are in demand, particularly in biotechnology, and opportunities should continue to increase for years to come. Most opportunities become available as individuals retire, transfer to other positions, or leave the workforce. Additional openings are created by employers as their needs grow.

Advancement Prospects

RA Specialists can rise through the ranks as senior specialist, manager, and director. Moving from one company to the next may be required in order for a specialist to obtain higher level positions. In large companies, they can become promoted to vice president of regulatory affairs operations or other executive offices. Those with entrepreneurial ambitions can start up their own consulting firms.

A master's or doctoral degree may be required for higher-level positions.

Education and Training

In general, Regulatory Affairs Specialists must possess a bachelor's degree, preferably in the science or health care field. A bachelor's degree in engineering is also acceptable for positions in the medical devices industry. Some employers may require that Specialists hold an advanced degree in the sciences or in regulatory affairs.

Entry-level Specialists receive on-the-job training. Many also receive formal instruction through outside sources, such as training seminars sponsored by RA organizations or continuing education RA programs.

Throughout their careers, RA professionals enroll in training and educational programs to keep up with new developments in their areas as well as to update their skills.

Experience, Skills, and Personality Traits

Employers generally prefer to hire RA professionals who have industry experience as research scientists, clinical researchers, quality professionals, production scientists, and so on. Candidates for entry-level RA associate positions should have at least one year of work experience within the industry to which they are applying. Employers also prefer that entry-level candidates have experience in or are familiar with regulatory affairs.

RA Specialists need excellent negotiation, organizational, and writing skills as well as proficient computer and statistical skills. Having excellent communication, presentation, interpersonal, and teamwork skills is also important for their work.

Being inquisitive, tactful, friendly, detail-oriented, diligent, and pragmatic are some personality traits that successful RA Specialists share.

Unions and Associations

Many RA Specialists belong to the Regulatory Affairs Professionals Society, a national association that provides networking opportunities, training programs, professional certification and other professional services and resources. For contact information, please see Appendix III.

Tips for Entry

1. Early in your career, let your supervisor know about your interest in regulatory affairs. Together, discuss your career goals and how you can gain experience to eventually enter this field.

2. To enhance your employability, take courses in regulatory affairs offered by colleges and universities, or by professional associations.

3. Use the Internet to learn about job vacancies for regulatory affairs positions. For example, you can access online job banks, such as "Medzilla.com," http://www.medzilla.com; "Monsters.com," http://www.monsters.com; and "America's Job Bank," (http://www.ajb.org). Also check out job listings at professional associations. In addition, many companies have websites on which they post current job vacancies as well as other recruitment information.

4. Learn more about the field of regulatory affairs on the Internet. Some websites you might visit are Regulatory Affairs Professionals Society, http://www.raps.org; U.S. Food and Drug Administration (FDA), http://www.fda.gov; and Office of Regulatory Affairs, FDA, http://www.fda.gov/ora.

PATENT AGENT

CAREER PROFILE

Duties: Prepare patent applications; prosecute patents in the U.S. Patent and Trademark Office (USPTO); perform other duties as required

Alternate Title(s): Patent Analyst, Patent Prosecutor Specialist

Salary Range: $50,000 to $100,000 or more

Employment Prospects: Good

Advancement Prospects: Fair

Prerequisites:

Education or Training—A bachelor's degree in engineering or a science discipline; advanced degree usually preferred

Experience—Have work experience in science or technical field; experience in or familiarity with patent law

Special Skills and Personality Traits—Writing, analytical, communication, and interpersonal skills; curious; detail-oriented; organized; flexible

Licensure/Certification—Must be registered with the USPTO to practice patent law before this office

CAREER LADDER

```
┌─────────────────────────────┐
│  Supervisory Patent Agent or │
│       Patent Attorney        │
└─────────────────────────────┘

┌─────────────────────────────┐
│         Patent Agent         │
└─────────────────────────────┘

┌─────────────────────────────┐
│       Technical Adviser      │
└─────────────────────────────┘

┌─────────────────────────────┐
│     Scientist or Engineer    │
└─────────────────────────────┘
```

Position Description

Patent Agents help companies obtain patents for new inventions that they own, such as medicines, computer hardware, devices, equipment, chemical processes, plant varieties, shoe designs, and compositions of matter. Patents are legal documents that protect the property rights of invention owners. Patent holders are able to sell their patented inventions exclusively. That means that no one else may make, use, sell, or import such inventions unless the patent holders first give their permission. In the United States, the U.S. Patent and Trademark Office (USPTO) has the authority to issue U.S. patents, which are usually granted for a term of 20 years.

Patent Agents are involved with the preparation of patent applications, upon which the granting of patents is based. A patent application consists of a detailed description—including drawings—of an invention that describes how the invention is made and used. The application also includes the set of claims to the invention, which defines the territory of use that belongs exclusively to the inventors. Patent Agents work closely with inventors to draft the patent application so that they are technically and legally clear. In companies, Patent Agents work with the research scientists who made the inventions.

Patent Agents who are registered to practice patent law before the USPTO may provide another service to companies. They can represent companies in the patent application process. (This is also known as the prosecution of patents.) As registered Patent Agents, they can file patent applications, respond to formal correspondence (called office actions) from the USPTO, meet with examiners to discuss the merits of their clients' inventions, make sure all deadlines are met, and so forth. Patent Agents also counsel their clients on the progress of their applications.

Although registered Patent Agents can practice law before the USPTO, they are not lawyers. They cannot represent clients or practice patent law in federal or state courts. It is also unlawful for Patent Agents to provide any legal services other than the prosecution of patents with the USPTO. For example, Patent Agents cannot provide legal advice, negotiate licenses to use patented inventions, represent clients in court litigation, or file patent appeals in courts.

Patent Agents work a standard 40-hour week, but sometimes put in additional hours to meet deadlines and complete tasks.

Salaries

Salaries vary, depending on factors such as education, experience, and geographical location. Annual salaries generally range from $50,000 to $100,000 or more.

Employment Prospects

Many Patent Agents are employed by law firms and corporate law departments. They work in various industries, such as the computer, biotechnology, pharmaceuticals, chemical, food manufacturing, agriculture, and telecommunications industries. Some Patent Agents are solo practitioners while others are members of firms that offer patent prosecution services.

The growth in biotechnology and information technology has led to the demand for Patent Agents with strong science and technical backgrounds. Opportunities for Patent Agents are available, particularly in major science and technology research areas, in such locations as New York, Boston, Chicago, Austin, Seattle, San Francisco, and Research Triangle Park in North Carolina.

Advancement Prospects

Opportunities for supervisory and management positions are limited, and Patent Agents usually need to obtain such positions with other employers. Many Patent Agents realize advancement through job satisfaction and by earning higher incomes. Some Patent Agents set up independent practices.

Many Patent Agents enter law school to earn a juris doctor degree and become patent attorneys or intellectual property attorneys.

Education and Training

In order to be eligible for the USPTO bar examination, Patent Agents must possess a bachelor's degree in engineering or a physical or natural science allowed by the USPTO. Employers may require that Patent Agents possess a master's or doctoral degree. Some employers may prefer that candidates hold a law degree in addition to a bachelor's or advanced degree in science or engineering.

Patent Agents typically receive on-the-job training.

Experience, Skills, and Personality Traits

In general, employers hire candidates who have previous work experience in the science or technology fields in which they would be practicing. They also have experience in or are familiar with patent law.

Many scientists and engineers first become technical advisers to patent lawyers in law firms and corporate law departments. As technical advisers, they gain experience by preparing patent applications and becoming familiar with patent law and USPTO procedures. After one or two years in these positions, they are usually ready to pass the USPTO examination to become registered Patent Agents

Patent Agents need excellent writing skills, as they often prepare patent applications that are 30 or more pages long with detailed technical explanations. Analytical, communication, and interpersonal skills are essential for their jobs. Being curious, detail-oriented, organized, and flexible are some personality traits that successful Patent Agents share.

Special Requirements

To practice before the U.S. Patent and Trademark Office, Patent Agents must be registered. This requires passing an entrance bar examination, officially called the "Examination for Registration to Practice in Patent Cases Before the U.S. Patent and Trademark Office," which covers patent law and USPTO procedures. USPTO bar applicants must also pay appropriate fees and fulfill other requirements. For more information, write to the Office of Enrollment and Discipline (OED) at Mail Stop OED, U.S. Patent and Trademark Office, PO Box 2327, Arlington, Virginia 22202-2327. You can also call (703) 306-4097 or visit the USPTO website at http://www.uspto.gov.

Union and Associations

Many Patent Agents join local, state, and national professional associations in the industries in which they serve. Patent Agents are also eligible to join the National Association of Patent Practitioners. By joining professional associations, Patent Agents can take advantage of networking opportunities and other professional services and resources. For contact information to some of these, please see Appendix III.

Tips for Entry

1. As a college student, find out if patent law might interest you by obtaining an internship or getting a part-time job with law firms or corporate law departments that emphasize patent or intellectual property law.
2. Learn about technical adviser or patent agent positions through contacts that you have made with patent practitioners. You can also learn about openings through professional societies that serve the interests of patent practitioners.
3. Some employers provide educational programs to help technical advisers study for the USPTO entrance bar examination.
4. Former USPTO examiners who wish to become registered Patent Agents may be able to waive the examination if they have worked several years with the USPTO.
5. Learn more about Patent Agents on the Internet. Some websites you might visit are United States Patent and Trademark Office, http://www.uspto.gov; and National Association of Patent Practitioners, http://www.napp.org.

TECHNICAL WRITER

CAREER PROFILE

Duties: Develop and produce scientific, technical, or clinical materials, such as manuals, help systems, reports, business plans, promotional materials, and websites; perform duties as required

Alternate Title(s): Technical Communicator, Information Developer, Documentation Specialist

Salary Range: $30,000 to $119,000

Employment Prospects: Good

Advancement Prospects: Good

Prerequisites:

Education or Training—A bachelor's degree in any field

Experience—Have related work experience, or training, or background in one's subject matter; experience with publishing, web development, word processing, and other software tools

Special Skills and Personality Traits—Writing, research, presentation, communication, interpersonal, teamwork, and self-management skills; creative; diplomatic; self-motivated; analytical; organized; flexible; enthusiastic; a quick learner and able to take criticism

Licensure/Certification—None required

CAREER LADDER

```
┌─────────────────────────────────┐
│  Senior Technical Writer or      │
│  Independent Contractor          │
└─────────────────────────────────┘

┌─────────────────────────────────┐
│  Technical Writer                │
└─────────────────────────────────┘

┌─────────────────────────────────┐
│  Junior or Assistant Technical Writer │
└─────────────────────────────────┘
```

Position Description

Technical Writers develop materials about a variety of scientific, technical, or clinical subjects for businesses, companies, government agencies, hospitals, academic institutions, and other organizations. They create written materials, multimedia works, CD-ROMs, and websites for training, reference, informational, and other purposes. For example, Technical Writers might:

- produce operating or repair manuals for technical devices, equipment, machinery, computer hardware, software, or consumer products
- develop help systems that are integrated into software and websites to assist users
- create in-house materials such as employee handbooks, standard operating procedures, training materials, and employee newsletters
- prepare project proposals and business plans
- write scientific, technical, or clinical reports
- write copy for catalogs

- create promotional materials (such as brochures, press releases, and magazine articles) about company products, services, projects, or employees
- develop company websites, which may include writing codes and designing webpages

The audiences, or users of these materials, are generally unfamiliar with the subject matter or are less technically-minded. They may be customers, clients, patients, company employees, a board of directors, bank loan officers, and various others. Thus, Technical Writers are responsible for communicating technical concepts clearly and accurately into language that can be understood by the targeted audiences.

Technical Writers may be permanent employees, temporary workers, or independent contractors. They create materials on a work-for-hire basis. In others words, they do not own the final products. Those belong to their employers or clients who can take full credit for them. Their clients can also make further changes to them or discard them if they don't like the finished products.

Technical Writers are assigned projects which may take several weeks, months, or a few years to complete. Depending on the size of a project, Technical Writers might work alone or with a team of technical communicators, which includes other writers, editors, designers, and artists.

Regardless of the size and complexity of projects, Technical Writers generally begin by defining the scope of a project. They ask such questions as: What are the purpose and objectives of the project? Who is the audience? What is the subject matter? What is the appropriate medium for the task? What form shall it be?

Next, Technical Writers plan and organize the structure of the project. Then they gather information about the subject matter. They interview researchers, technicians and others for relevant information, as well as read literature about the subject matter. If they are writing instructions about a product or procedure, they observe how it works, and sometimes learn how to use it themselves.

Technical Writers draft their manuscripts or web copy according to specific formats and guidelines. They are responsible for writing manuscripts or copy that presents scientific or technical information in a clear and logical matter. They make sure that the complex ideas they are simplifying are accurate and correct. Many Technical Writers produce drawings, graphs, diagrams, and other visual aids to help reinforce the information they are presenting. Some Technical Writers also work on the design and production of the project, which might include text, tables, graphs, drawings, and on-line media. Throughout their projects, Technical Writers meet with scientists, engineers, technicians, and others to discuss ideas and clarify information.

Technical Writers submit drafts to their employers or clients for review. The writers do one or more revisions to incorporate any changes that the employers or clients request. Technical Writers may be also involved in the design and production of the final product.

Technical Writers often work long and irregular hours, which may include working on weekends to meet deadlines.

Salaries

Salaries vary, depending on such factors as education, experience, employer, and geographical location. According to a 2001 salary survey by the Society for Technical Communication (STC), the annual salaries for most of the survey's respondents ranged between $40,000 and $83,000. In STC's 2001 salary survey for independent contractors and temporary employees, most respondents reported annual earnings that ranged from $30,000 to $119,000. The hourly rates for most contractors ranged between $32 and $72 per hour.

Employment Prospects

Many staff openings become available as Technical Writers retire, transfer to other positions, or leave the workforce. The job market for Technical Writers is expected to be good through the coming years due to the continuing development of new technology and scientific discoveries. However, the rate of job growth is dependent on the health of the economy. For example, when the economy is in a downturn, there are fewer job openings and more layoffs for Technical Writers.

Advancement Prospects

Technical Writers can advance to supervisory and managerial positions as team leaders, project managers, and department supervisors. For many writers, their highest ambition is to become successful independent contractors.

Most Technical Writers realize advancement by earning higher incomes, receiving more complicated assignments, and being recognized for the quality of their work.

Education and Training

Employers normally require that Technical Writers possess at least a bachelor's degree, which may be in any field. Many Technical Writers hold a bachelor's and advanced degree in English, communications, engineering, biology, chemistry, physics, computer science, or other science discipline.

Many Technical Writers complete technical writing or technical communication programs sponsored by colleges, universities, continuing education programs, and professional societies.

Employers usually provide on-the-job training to entry-level employees.

Experience, Skills, and Personality Traits

Employers generally hire Technical Writers who have previous work experience related to the position for which they are applying. Many employers hire candidates without experience for entry-level positions as long as they have appropriate technical training or backgrounds in the subject matter about which they would be writing.

Employers seek candidates (both entry-level and experienced) who have experience with publishing, web development, word processing, and other software tools.

Along with possessing excellent writing skills, Technical Writers need strong research, presentation, and communication skills. In addition, they need good interpersonal and teamwork skills, as they must be able to meet and interact with people from diverse backgrounds. Technical writers should have good self-management skills, including the ability to handle stressful situations, work independently, meet deadlines, and prioritize tasks.

Some personality traits that successful Technical Writers have in common are being creative, diplomatic, self-motivated, analytical, organized, flexible, and enthusiastic. Foremost, successful Technical Writers are quick learners and able to handle criticism about their work.

Unions and Associations

Many Technical Writers join local, state, or national professional associations to take advantage of networking opportunities, training programs, job listings, and other professional services and resources. Two general writing organizations that serve the interests of Technical Writers are the Society for Technical Communication and the National Writers Union. Technical Writers also join societies that serve their particular fields, such as the IEEE Professional Communication Society. For contact information on these organizations, please see Appendix III.

Tips for Entry

1. To gain practical experience, consider working with temporary agencies.

2. Many Technical Writers learn about jobs through networking with colleagues at local or regional meetings of professional associations.

3. Create a portfolio that showcases samples of your work. Then bring the portfolio to your interviews to show prospective employers or clients.

4. Use the Internet to learn more about Technical Writers. To get a list of relevant websites to read, enter any of these keywords in a search engine: *technical writers, technical writing,* or *technical communication.*

BUSINESS

ENTREPRENEUR
(SCIENCE AND TECHNOLOGY)

CAREER PROFILE

Duties: Start up and manage new business venture; perform duties as required

Alternate Title(s): Business Owner

Salary Range: $0 to $1,000,000+

Employment Prospects: Good

Advancement Prospects: Fair

Prerequisites:

Education or Training—Business training (formal or informal) is desirable

Experience—Years of experience in the area and industry of the new business venture

Special Skills and Personality Traits—Leadership, management, problem-solving, communication, presentation, writing, interpersonal, and teamwork skills; should a risk taker and visionary; creative; innovative; optimistic; persistent; confident; flexible; self-motivated

Licensure/Certification—Professional licensure may be required; business licenses required

CAREER LADDER

```
┌─────────────────────────────┐
│      Business Owner         │
└─────────────────────────────┘

┌─────────────────────────────┐
│       Entrepreneur          │
└─────────────────────────────┘

┌─────────────────────────────┐
│ Scientist, Engineer, or Other│
│ Science/Technology Professional│
└─────────────────────────────┘
```

Position Description

Many scientists and others working in science and technology reach a point in their careers when they want to be their own boss. They decide to become an Entrepreneur. They have ideas for products or services that they strongly believe would fill a need in certain markets and be profitable. Thus, they are willing to take the risks involved in starting up a new manufacturing company, wholesale establishment, retail firm, or service (business that offers professional expertise and time to perform specific tasks).

To determine whether their proposed ventures are feasible, Entrepreneurs first conduct research. They perform market studies to get an idea of how their target audiences would accept their products or services. They learn about their competition—who they are, how their business would be similar and different from the competition, and so on. In addition, Entrepreneurs gather information to help them determine how to structure their business, what kind of facilities they would need, the types of employees they would need, and how much it would cost to start up their

venture. Entrepreneurs also consult lawyers, accountants, business advisers, and successful business owners for help and advice.

Starting up new businesses also requires much careful planning and decision making by Entrepreneurs. They address various legal issues. If they will be starting a business with other people, they draw up a business contract that formally defines the nature of their partnership. Entrepreneurs also decide on the best legal form—such as solo proprietorship, corporation, or limited liability company—for their business enterprise. Entrepreneurs may choose to form a board of directors to provide advice and guidance over their businesses. (Boards of directors are legally required to be formed for corporations.)

Entrepreneurs obtain all licenses and permits required by local, state, and federal governments for their type of business. Entrepreneurs who plan to sell products that they themselves have invented or created make sure that their exclusive rights to manufacture, use, and sell those products are protected. They obtain patents for inventions from the

U.S. Patent and Trademark Office (USPTO). For creative works, such as books and software, Entrepreneurs formally register their copyrights with the U.S. Copyright Office.

Furthermore, Entrepreneurs are responsible for finding the means to finance their ventures. They might borrow money from themselves, friends, or family members. They might take out business loans from local banks or apply for business grants or loans from government programs. They might also raise money through venture capitalists, who invest money in businesses in exchange for part ownership.

Entrepreneurs prepare business plans, or formal statements, about their proposed ventures. (These are important tools for securing funding for their enterprises.) In these business plans, Entrepreneurs describe the products or services they plan to sell, who their markets and competitors are, and why their products or services are unique or better than the competition. Entrepreneurs also outline how they plan to operate their business. In addition, they provide financial projections for the first few years as well as describe their marketing and sales strategies.

Once their business is up and running, Entrepreneurs now take on another role. As chief executive officers, they handle the overall direction and management of their businesses. Some of their responsibilities entail

- planning and coordinating operational activities, including human resources, finance, accounting, facilities management, information technology, and marketing
- formulating policies and procedures that pertain to the general operations and various divisions
- hiring and training managers, professionals, technical staff, office staff, and other personnel
- making sure all bills and taxes are paid
- troubleshooting problems as they arise in any aspect of their businesses
- promoting their business by joining and networking with trade associations, local chambers of commerce, and other organizations

Most Entrepreneurs are involved in performing professional duties. For example, they might continue developing software products, conducting scientific research, or providing consulting services. As their businesses grow, however, many business owners find themselves focusing solely on management responsibilities.

Some experts say that it generally takes between three to 10 years for businesses to establish themselves in their markets and begin earning profits. Once their business has achieved their goals, Entrepreneurs often seek new challenges. Many Entrepreneurs become involved in acquiring other companies or investing their money in start-up ventures. Some Entrepreneurs sell their businesses and start up new ones to offer totally different products or services to the same markets or to venture into different markets.

Building a successful business takes hard work and dedication. Entrepreneurs typically work long hours each day, and often work six to seven days a week.

Salaries

Annual incomes vary yearly for Entrepreneurs. They can earn as little as nothing or as much as millions of dollars or more. It is also common for Entrepreneurs to lose money during their first years in operation.

Entrepreneurs may receive salaries as executive officers, top-level managers, or consultants from their companies.

Employment Prospects

Many businesses open and close each year. According to the U.S. Small Business Administration (SBA), there were over 600,000 new firms and over 500,000 business closures in the United States in 2000. (Note: Not all closures were due to failure).

Entrepreneurial opportunities in science and technology are readily available for those individuals ready and willing to take advantage of them. Since the 1990s, new technology advancements and scientific discoveries have stimulated the establishment of many start-up companies in information technology (computers, software, semiconductors, communications equipment, and communications services), biotechnology, pharmaceuticals, medical technologies, and health care-related products.

Advancement Prospects

In general, Entrepreneurs measure their success by achieving their business goals for their start-up companies and through gaining recognition for their entrepreneurial talents and skills.

Education and Training

Entrepreneurs need basic business training, whether formal or informal, to succeed well in their ventures. Scientists can learn necessary skills through entrepreneurship courses offered by community colleges, university extension programs, and professional associations. In addition, many books, magazines, and websites about starting businesses are available. Also, many universities offer MBA (master's in business administration) programs specifically designed for scientists and engineers, in which they learn the basics of business tools such as balance sheets and market research.

Experience, Skills, and Personality Traits

Entrepreneurs typically start businesses in industries in which they have many years of experience. They are highly knowledgeable about the products and services that their new ventures offer.

Some skills that Entrepreneurs need to succeed are leadership, management, and problem-solving skills. They also need effective communication, presentation, and writing skills as well as excellent interpersonal and teamwork skills. Successful Entrepreneurs have several personality traits in common. Foremost, they are risk takers and visionaries. In addition, they are creative, innovative, optimistic, persistent, confident, flexible, and self-motivated.

Special Requirements

Entrepreneurs who offer services to the public may be required to hold appropriate professional licensure. For example, engineers, geologists, hydrologists, and soil scientists may be required to be licensed or registered in the states where they practice.

As business operators, Entrepreneurs obtain appropriate local and state business licenses. For specific information about business licenses, contact the local (city or county) government administrative office in the city where you plan to operate your business.

Unions and Associations

Many business owners belong to trade and professional associations to take advantage of networking opportunities, training programs, and other valuable resources and services.

Professional associations for science and technical Entrepreneurs are available in some localities to serve the interests of those living in a particular region.

Tips for Entry

1. Many research universities and other organizations sponsor business incubation programs that help scientists start up and develop their businesses. These programs (sometimes called incubators) offer business and technical support services, assistance with finding finances, office space, shared office services, and so forth. You can learn more about incubators at the National Business Incubation Association website, http://www.nbia.org.

2. The U.S. Small Business Administration (SBA) offers various resources for entrepreneurs. To access its website, go to http://www.sba.gov. To learn about programs aimed at science and technical entrepreneurs, visit the SBA Office of Technology website at http://www.sba.gov/sbir.

3. Learn more about entrepreneurship on the Internet. Some websites you might visit are Startup Journal Center (by the *Wall Street Journal*), http://www.startupjournal.com; and Entreworld.org, http://www.entreworld.org.

MANAGEMENT CONSULTANT

CAREER PROFILE

Duties: Offer consulting services to corporations and other organizations to improve their organizations' performance; provide solutions to complex business problems; conduct research and data analysis; prepare written or oral reports; perform other duties as required

Alternate Title(s): Management Analyst, Research Associate

Salary Range: $58,000 to $100,000

Employment Prospects: Good

Advancement Prospects: Good

Prerequisites:

    Education or Training—MBA or Ph.D. required for entry-level consulting positions

    Experience—Business or industry experience preferred

    Special Skills and Personality Traits—Analytical, problem-solving, communication, writing skills, presentation, interpersonal, leadership, computer, and quantitative skills; self-motivated; creative; tenacious; poised; curious; energetic; enthusiastic; hard worker; passionate about ideas

    Licensure/Certification—None required

CAREER LADDER

```
┌─────────────────────────────────────┐
│     Senior Management Consultant     │
└─────────────────────────────────────┘

┌─────────────────────────────────────┐
│        Management Consultant         │
└─────────────────────────────────────┘

┌─────────────────────────────────────┐
│       Research Associate or          │
│          Junior Consultant           │
└─────────────────────────────────────┘
```

Position Description

The ability to solve problems, create new ideas, and provide advice and suggestions are the services that Management Consultants offer their clients. They provide business advice to private corporations, from small upstart companies to large multinational companies. Many Management Consultants also offer services to government agencies, nonprofit institutions, foreign governments, and other organizations.

Management Consultants may be independent contractors or salaried workers for a management consulting firm, accounting firm, or other business consulting company. Because they are not part of their clients' workforce, Management Consultants are able to remain objective and not be influenced by company politics.

Companies hire Management Consultants to handle a wide range of projects, such as:

- developing strategies for entering new marketplaces or remaining competitive within existing markets
- advising clients about merging, buying, and selling companies
- corporate restructuring
- improving some aspects of their operations such as production, marketing, human resources, and information systems

Some Management Consultants are generalists. They address all types of problems in any industry. Some consultants choose to specialize in specific industries such as health care, nonprofit organizations, biotechnology, and information technology. Others specialize in particular functions, such as organizational strategies, human resources, financial services, sales, and high-tech operations.

Management Consultants are assigned to projects in which they work closely with the clients' managers. With most projects, consultants follow a similar process. They begin by assessing their clients' situation and identifying the specific problems they must tackle. They then conduct research, which includes collecting appropriate client data, such as annual revenues or employment records. They interview executive officers, managers, and employees within the organizations. Consultants also seek information from external sources such as government agencies and trade associations. Consultants also might devise diagnostic surveys and market studies to gather data.

Consultants next analyze and interpret the data to develop solutions to their clients' problems. They use such tools as spreadsheets and mathematical models to gain insight into the problems. Consultants take into account such factors as the nature of an organization, its internal structure, its competition, and market trends as they prepare their recommendations.

Management Consultants submit reports of their findings and recommendations in written or oral form. Clients sometimes retain Management Consultants to help implement the suggestions they have made.

Management Consultants may work on two or more cases at a time. Depending on the projects, they might work independently or with other Management Consultants.

Most Management Consultants are involved in business development. They continually seek out new clients. For example, they might make presentations to potential clients or promote their firms at professional conferences and trade shows. In addition, Management Consultants maintain relationships with existing clients for repeat business.

Management Consultants may be responsible for preparing proposals for prospective work, which describe how consulting firms plan to handle projects. (Companies usually solicit proposals from several firms for projects, and choose the proposal that best suits their needs.) Experienced consultants often perform supervisory, project management, and client relations duties.

Management Consultants typically work long hours, as much as 50 to 60 hours or more per week. Most consultants travel frequently, as they go and work at the clients' work sites, which may be in another city, state, or country. Consultants often spend several weeks or months away from home in order to complete their projects.

Salaries

Salaries vary, depending on such factors as education, experience, type and size of employer, and geographical location. Partners in top consulting firms can expect to earn six-figure annual incomes.

According to a 2000 survey by the Association of Management Consulting Firms, earnings (which include bonuses and profit sharing) in member firms averaged $58,000 for entry-level consultants; $76,300 for management consultants, and $100,300 for senior consultants.

Many firms reward their employees with monetary bonuses for work performance.

Employment Prospects

Management Consultants find employment with large and small management consulting firms. Some firms provide services to corporations in all industries, while others specialize in particular industries (such as biotechnology) or specific functions (such as human resources). Some management consulting firms are affiliated with accounting firms, computer software companies, or technology firms. In addition, computer companies, such as IBM, are developing management consulting divisions. Government agencies also employ Management Consultants, known as management analysts. Furthermore, many Management Consultants are independent contractors.

The job outlook for Management Consultants should be steady over the long term, as organizations rely on outside help to improve their performance. However, the rate of job growth is dependent on the health of the economy. When the economy is on a downturn, there are fewer job openings and more layoffs in consulting firms.

According to the U.S. Department of Labor, job growth is expected to grow in large consulting firms with international expertise and in smaller firms that specialize in biotechnology, mobile commerce, health care, information technology, engineering, telecommunications, human resources, and other specific areas.

Advancement Prospects

Depending on their education and experience, Management Consultants begin their careers at the research associate or junior consultant level. In general, they rise through the ranks as consultants, project managers, and partners. To advance in some firms, research associates may need to obtain further education.

Many Management Consultants use their positions as stepping stones to obtain top management positions in companies, investment banks, or venture capital firms. Those with entrepreneurial ambitions become independent consultants or start their own consulting firms.

Education and Training

Firms hire candidates with a bachelor's or advanced degree. Those with a bachelor's degree are typically hired for research associate positions. For Management Consultant positions, employers typically require that candidates hold a master's in business administration. Many employers also seek candidates with a doctorate in science, engineering, or social science discipline.

Employers typically provide Management Consultants with formal training programs and on-the-job training. Some firms put new hires who are Ph.D. graduates, scientists, engineers, and others with nonbusiness backgrounds through intense business training that last several weeks or months.

Experience, Skills, and Personality Traits

Consulting firms generally seek candidates who have business or industry experience. They hire college graduates, MBAs, and Ph.D.s as well as professionals who have worked several years in their field. Many Management Consultants have switched to consulting from a career in finance, business, actuarial science, life science, chemistry, physics, or engineering.

Employers seek candidates who demonstrate excellent analytical, problem-solving, communication, and writing skills. In addition, they show strong presentation, interpersonal, and leadership skills. Furthermore, prospective consultants need effective computer and quantitative skills.

Being self-motivated, creative, tenacious, poised, curious, energetic, and enthusiastic are some personality traits that successful Management Consultants share. They are also hard workers and passionate about their ideas.

Unions and Associations

Management Consultants might join local, state, or national societies to take advantage of professional services such as education programs and networking opportunities. Some national associations that Management Consultants belong to are the Institute of Management Consultants USA, Inc.,

the Professional and Technical Consultants Association, and the American Association of Healthcare Consultants. For contact information, please see Appendix III.

Tips for Entry

1. Although a consulting job may be years away, you can begin preparing yourself now. You might enroll in or audit business courses. Read business books and publications, such as the *Wall Street Journal* and *Business Week*. Check out websites of consulting firms and talk with management consultants.

2. Contact the consulting firms where you would like to work to learn about their job openings. Also meet with your networking contacts to learn about current and possible upcoming vacancies. In addition, check with college career counseling centers for leads.

3. Consulting firms usually require their prospective job candidates to be interviewed several times by different staff members. One such interview is called the *case interview* in which candidates are given one or more mock business problems to solve. This allows firms to evaluate candidates' problem solving and communication skills as well as their understanding of basic business principles.

4. Use the Internet to learn more about Management Consultants. To get a list of relevant websites, enter the keywords *management consultant* or *management consulting* in a search engine.

MARKET RESEARCH ANALYST

CAREER PROFILE

Duties: Conduct market studies about a company's products or services; design research projects and collect, organize, analyze, and interpret data; make recommendations; write reports; perform other duties as required

Alternate Title(s): Market Analyst, Market Research Specialist

Salary Range: $29,000 to $97,000

Employment Prospects: Good

Advancement Prospects: Good

Prerequisites:
  Education or Training—An advanced degree in marketing, business administration, or a related field
  Experience—Marketing experience preferred
  Special Skills and Personality Traits—Research, problem-solving, writing, presentation, computer, mathematics, statistics, interpersonal, and teamwork skills; curious; patient; persistent; creative; analytical; detail-oriented
  Licensure/Certification—None required

CAREER LADDER

```
┌─────────────────────────────┐
│    Marketing Manager        │
└─────────────────────────────┘

┌─────────────────────────────┐
│  Market Research Analyst    │
└─────────────────────────────┘

┌─────────────────────────────┐
│  MBA Student, Marketing     │
│  Research Associate, or Scientist │
└─────────────────────────────┘
```

Position Description

In business, Market Research Analysts conduct studies about how well products and services perform in the marketplace. They gather and analyze both statistical data as well as opinions from customers. With their findings, companies can make knowledgeable business and marketing decisions. For example, a medical supplies manufacturer might base its decision to change the packaging for its bandages because of the results of a market research study.

Many Market Research Analysts work in marketing departments in companies in various industries. Many others work in firms that offer market research services to companies and other organizations.

Like scientists, Market Research Analysts conduct their investigations in a thorough and methodical manner. First, they define the issues or questions that they must study. For example, Market Research Analysts might be asked to provide information about any of the following:

• the characteristics, dynamics, and trends of particular markets in local, regional, national, or other geographical locations

• their customers or potential customers—what their needs and tastes are, their buying habits, how much purchasing power they have, and so on
• their competitors—what their sales have been like, their marketing methods, their promotional strategies, and so on
• the reactions of customers to new or improved products or services
• methods and strategies to bring products or services into particular markets
• potential sales for products or services

Next, Market Research Analysts design their research plans. They devise research methods and procedures that best suit their purposes. They also create any surveys, questionnaires, and other tools that they may need to solicit opinions from customers.

Market Research Analysts then collect and organize the data. They review statistical information gathered from surveys and questionnaires. They also read relevant written materials from various sources, such as sales data from the companies or demographic data from government agencies. In addition, their studies might require them to read materials about their competitors' products or services. Market Research Analysts might conduct one-on-one interviews or moderate small focus groups with targeted audience members, or direct and supervise trained interviewers.

Market Research Analysts next evaluate and interpret the data. They measure numerical data as well as appraise attitudes of people who have been interviewed. Finally, analysts make recommendations based on their findings, and prepare written reports and statistical charts. They make sure that they have interpreted all technical information accurately and correctly, and present such information in language that is clearly understood by nontechnical individuals.

Depending on their projects, Market Research Analysts may work alone or as part of a research team comprised of statisticians, information technology specialists, interviewers, and other marketing specialists.

Market Research Analysts work 40 hours a week, but often put in additional hours to complete their various tasks and to meet deadlines.

Salaries

Salaries vary, depending on such factors as education, experience, employer, and geographical location. According to the Bureau of Labor Statistics, the estimated annual salary in 2001 for most Market Research Analysts ranged between $28,500 and $96,980.

Employment Prospects

Some employers of Market Research Analysts are marketing research firms, management consulting firms, and advertising companies. Companies in finance, insurance, biotechnology, pharmaceuticals, biomedicine, information technology, computer and data processing, agriculture, health care, and other industries also employ Market Research Analysts. In addition, Market Research Analysts work for government agencies, nongovernmental organizations, political campaign groups, and international organizations (such as the United Nations).

The job outlook for qualified Market Research Analysts is good since they provide organizations with valuable information that they need to stay competitive. Opportunities are expected to be better in marketing research firms, as increasingly more companies outsource marketing research services rather than employ full-time staff. In general, most job openings will become available as workers retire, transfer to another position, or leave the workforce for other reasons.

Advancement Prospects

As they gain appropriate experience, Market Research Analysts can apply for positions in other marketing areas such as sales, brand (or product) management, business development, sales, purchasing, or distribution. Market Research Analysts with management and administrative ambitions can advance to become marketing managers and executives. In some organizations, a doctoral degree is required for top marketing positions. Those with entrepreneurial desires can become independent contractors or start up their own marketing research firms.

Education and Training

Employers generally hire candidates with advanced degrees in marketing, business administration, statistics, economics, or another related discipline. In biotechnology, computer manufacturing, and other technical industries, employers prefer to hire candidates who have a bachelor's or advanced degree in science or engineering combined with a master's degree in business administration.

Many employers provide in-house training programs. Some of them provide opportunities for their employees to enroll in continuing education courses at local colleges and universities.

Market Research Analysts can also take advantage of seminars and conferences provided by professional societies and trade associations.

Experience, Skills, and Personality Traits

In general, Employers prefer to hire candidates who have marketing experience, particularly in the industry in which they would be working. Many employers hire scientists for market research positions with little or no experience, as their scientific training matches the duties they would fulfill as Market Research Analysts.

Market Research Analysts are expected to have excellent research, problem-solving, writing, and presentation skills. They must also have strong computer skills and be proficient in mathematics and statistics. They have strong interpersonal and teamwork skills, as they must work well with others from different backgrounds.

Being curious, patient, persistent, creative, analytical, and detail-oriented are some personality traits that successful Market Research Analysts share.

Unions and Associations

Market Research Analysts might join such professional associations as the Marketing Research Association, the American Marketing Association, and the Qualitative Research Consultants Association. These national societies, as well as those at the local and state levels, offer networking opportunities, training programs, job listings, and other professional services and resources. For contact information, please see Appendix III.

Tips for Entry

1. As a college undergraduate, get an idea if the marketing field is right for you by obtaining a part-time job or internship position with a marketing firm, advertising

agency, public relations firm, or company marketing department. If you are a science major, you might try to obtain an position in the industry in which you would like to work.

2. Talk with marketing researchers who have changed from science and engineering careers. Ask them about their work, how they made the transition, how they got their jobs, what courses they might recommend, and so forth.

3. Contact companies directly about job openings that are currently available or may be available soon. Many firms list current vacancies on their websites.

4. Before going to a job interview, learn as much as you can about the prospective employer and the position. Also practice your interviewing skills by doing a mock interview with a job counselor or friend.

5. Use the Internet to learn more about the field of marketing research. One website you might visit is Marketing Power.com (by American Marketing Association), http//:www.marketingpower.com. To get a list of other websites, enter the keywords *marketing research* or *market research analyst* in a search engine.

SCIENTIFIC OR TECHNICAL SALES REPRESENTATIVE (MANUFACTURER OR WHOLESALE DISTRIBUTOR)

CAREER PROFILE

Duties: Promote and sell products directly to customers in the field; build and maintain a customer base in one's assigned territories; perform duties as required

Alternate Title(s): Technical Sales Representative, Sales Engineer, Manufacturer's Agent, Pharmaceutical Sales Representative, Agricultural Chemical Sales Representative, or other title that reflects a specific field

Salary Range: $28,000 to $106,560

Employment Prospects: Good

Advancement Prospects: Good

Prerequisites:

Education or Training—A bachelor's or advanced degree in science, mathematics, or engineering discipline
   Experience—Several years of sales experience; technical background desirable
   Special Skills and Personality Traits—Interpersonal, communication, leadership, organizational, problem-solving, self-management, math, and computer skills; pleasant; enthusiastic; trustworthy; diplomatic; persuasive; persistent; self-motivated; creative; flexible; able to handle rejection
   Licensure/Certification—None required

CAREER LADDER

```
Sales Manager

Senior Sales Representative

Junior Sales Representative
```

Position Description

Sales Representatives of technical and scientific products are responsible for generating and increasing sales of products for manufacturers and wholesale distributors. They work in the field, promoting products directly to customers—which may be manufacturers, retail establishments, professional businesses, educational institutions, hospitals, construction contractors, government agencies, and other organizations. For example, Sales Representatives in the medical device industry might promote sales of various products to hospitals, medical health centers, HMOs, medical doctors, and other health-care practitioners.

Sales Representatives are experts about the products that they sell. They are comfortable with discussing scientific concepts and using the technical language of their customers. Many Sales Representatives have technical training or backgrounds. Some of them, in fact, have switched from careers as research scientists, technologists, technicians, engineers, and health-care practitioners. Those with engineering backgrounds are sometimes known as sales engineers.

Sales Representatives are assigned to cover geographical regions, or territories, which may consist of several cities, counties, states, and even foreign countries. They are responsible for building up and maintaining a customer (or client) base within their territories. They are also expected to meet with a certain number of customers each day. To find new customers, Sales Representatives follow up leads they obtain from existing customers, their employers, local chambers of commerce, professional and trade associations, and others.

Sales Representatives usually make their initial contact with prospective customers through phone calls or e-mails. They introduce themselves and their products, and schedule appointments to meet with them in person. Sales Representatives generally do research about potential customers before contacting them, so they can discuss how their products may meet the customers' needs.

Meetings with customers are usually brief. Sales Representatives show their products and demonstrate or explain how they can be useful to a customer's business. They accentuate the unique qualities of their products and how they would better suit the customer's needs than would competitors' products.

Making a sale can take several weeks or months. Sales Representatives leave catalogs with their potential customers. These catalogs describe the products, including their prices, availability, and other attractive features. Sales Representatives may also give customers some samples of their products to try out. Sales Representatives follow up their initial meetings with e-mails, phone calls, and additional visits.

For many Sales Representatives, their goal is to establish trusting, long-term relationships with customers for their repeat business. These sales professionals become familiar with their clients' needs and provide them with valuable information that may be useful for developing their businesses. Many Sales Representatives take customers out to lunch or dinner. Some of them occasionally entertain their customers at sports events or other entertainment venues.

Sales Representatives perform a wide range of duties. For example, they:

- schedule appointments with customers and potential customers
- take sales orders as well as negotiate sales contracts
- help customers with problems regarding products and sales deliveries
- prepare sales reports, expense account forms, and other required paperwork
- attend company sales meetings to review sales performance and discuss sales goals
- attend trade shows, professional conferences, and conventions to promote products and make new contacts
- monitor new and existing products being sold by their competitors, checking how well they're selling, and for how much
- keep up with new developments and technologies in their industries

Some Sales Representatives are responsible for installing products, training customers' employees, or providing maintenance service for products. Many Sales Representatives are involved in developing new products, marketing strategies, or promotional programs for their companies.

In some companies, Sales Representatives (without technical backgrounds) and subject-matter experts work together. The Sales Representatives are responsible for performing the regular sales duties, and the experts are responsible for explaining about the products, answering all technical questions, and assisting customers with any problems or concerns.

Some Sales Representatives work on a contractual basis as independent sales agents. They are hired either directly by the manufacturers themselves or by agencies known as manufacturers' agents firms. Independent sales agents often sell different, but complimentary, product lines for two or more manufacturers within the industry.

Sales Representatives work long days and irregular hours. They arrange their own schedules, and often work in the evenings and on weekends to meet with customers. Most Sales Representatives frequently travel by automobile or airplane and sometimes stay away from home for several days or weeks at a time.

Salaries

Earnings vary, depending on a wide array of factors. These include an individual's qualifications, ambition, and sales ability; the type of employer and industry; the products or services being sold and the demand for them in a geographical location; and the general well-being of the economy. Their earnings may also vary from year to year.

Sales Representatives may receive income based on salary, commission, or a combination of both salary and commission. The Bureau of Labor Statistics reports that the estimated annual earnings in 2001 for most Sales Representatives of technical and scientific products ranged between $28,070 and $106,560.

Many companies reward outstanding job performances with monetary bonuses and/or gifts such as free vacation trips. Sales Representatives may be reimbursed for such expenses as meals, lodging, transportation, and home office costs. Many employers provide Sales Representatives with company cars.

Employment Prospects

Scientific and technical Sales Representatives work in such industries as biotechnology, medical devices, pharmaceuticals, chemical processing, computer and data processing services, electrical goods, electronics, industrial machinery and equipment, and others. They may be employed by a company or a manufacturer's agent firm. Many are self-employed manufacturer's agents.

Job openings generally become available to replace professionals who retire or transfer to other positions. Employers will create new positions as they expand their sales force. Job applicants can expect intense competition.

Generally, job opportunities in sales depend upon the health of the economy, consumer preferences, and other factors. The demand for scientific and technical Sales Representatives varies by industry. Currently, the medical, pharmaceutical, and biotechnology industries are strong and job opportunities are expected to be steady for a number of years.

Advancement Prospects

Sales Representatives pursue advancement in various ways. Those interested in administrative and management responsibilities can advance to such positions as sales trainer, sales supervisor, branch manager, district manager, or vice president of sales. Some Sales Representatives have entrepreneurial ambitions and may become an independent manufacturer's agent or establish an independent firm.

Sales Representatives may measure their success by earning higher incomes, meeting or exceeding sales targets, receiving sales accounts or territories of their choice, and becoming top sales representatives for their firms.

Some Sales Representatives use their experience to pursue opportunities in marketing, advertising, purchasing, or consulting.

Education and Training

Many scientific and technical Sales Representatives have a bachelor's or advanced degree in science, mathematics, or engineering discipline.

Employers generally require that scientific and technical Sales Representatives have a bachelor's degree, preferably in a science or engineering field related to the products being sold. Some companies may prefer candidates with a master's degree in business administration. These candidates may not necessarily have an undergraduate degree in science, but they show an aptitude in science or a willingness to master scientific or technical subject matter. Many employers are willing to hire candidates who have no college degrees if they have qualifying sales experience.

Employers usually provide formal training programs for entry-level Sales Representatives, which includes classroom instruction on such topics as sales techniques, marketing, and presentation skills. They also provide technical instruction on the products being sold. New Sales Representatives receive on-the-job training, and work under the supervision of senior representatives for several months before being allowed to work independently.

Experience, Skills, and Personality Traits

The ideal candidate for Sales Representatives of scientific and technical products is someone with several years of sales experience and related background knowledge in science, health, or engineering. Employers are also willing to hire scientists, engineers, and health professionals without sales experience as well as experienced sales people without any technical background if they show enthusiasm and a strong desire to succeed.

In order to generate new business and keep clients, Sales Representatives must have superior interpersonal and communication skills. They should have effective leadership, organizational, and problem-solving skills. They should also have strong self-management skills, such as being able to work independently; manage multiple tasks; handle stressful situations; meet appointments; and manage time efficiently. Adequate math and computer skills are also necessary.

Some personality traits that successful Sales Representatives share are being pleasant, enthusiastic, trustworthy, diplomatic, persuasive, persistent, self-motivated, creative, and flexible. Further, Sales Representatives are thick-skinned—as they must be able to handle rejections that come with the job.

Unions and Associations

Professional associations for Sales Representatives in the different industries are available at the state, regional, and national levels. These societies offer professional services and resources such as education programs, training programs, certification programs, legislative advocacy, and networking opportunities.

Sales Representatives might also join the National Association of Sales Professionals which serves the general interests of Sales Representatives in all industries.

Tips for Entry

1. As a high school student, see if working in the sales field may be something that interests you. For example, you might get a part-time job working as a sales clerk or volunteer in a fund-raising activity for your school or youth group.
2. Many Sales Representatives have found their jobs through word-of-mouth.
3. Job applicants should be prepared to go through several job interviews with a company, which may entail accompanying Sales Representatives on their rounds.
4. Take advantage of the Internet in your job search for a Sales Representative position. You can find job listings as well as information about the companies where you would like to work. To learn if a company has a website, enter its name in a search engine.
5. To learn more about manufacturers' agents, check out these websites: Manufacturers' Agents National Association, http://www.manaonline.org; and Manufacturers' Representatives Educational Research Foundation, http://www.mrerf.org.

EDUCATION AND COMMUNICATIONS

SCHOOLTEACHER, SCIENCE OR MATH

CAREER PROFILE

Duties: Provide instruction for science or math subjects in grades K–12; create lesson plans; prepare lessons, exercises, and activities; perform nonteaching duties as assigned; perform other duties as required

Alternate Title(s): Elementary School Teacher, Middle School Teacher, Junior High School Teacher, High School Teacher; a title that reflects a teaching speciality such as Biology Teacher or Algebra Teacher

Salary Range: $27,000 to $68,000

Employment Prospects: Excellent

Advancement Prospects: Good

Prerequisites:
　Education or Training—Bachelor's degree; for licensed teachers, completion of an accredited teacher education program
　Experience—Student teaching, internship, or other teaching experience
　Special Skills and Personality Traits—Communication, teamwork, interpersonal, management, and organization skills; creative; enthusiastic; dependable; flexible; fair; patient; caring; tolerant
　Licensure/Certification—Teaching credentials required to teach in public schools

CAREER LADDER

```
┌─────────────────────────────┐
│     Mentor Teacher or       │
│   Administrative position   │
└─────────────────────────────┘

┌─────────────────────────────┐
│       Schoolteacher         │
└─────────────────────────────┘

┌─────────────────────────────┐
│ Student Teacher or Substitute Teacher │
└─────────────────────────────┘
```

Position Description

Schoolteachers instruct students in grades kindergarten through 12 (K–12). Two of the core subjects for the K–12 curriculum are science and mathematics. Science Teachers instruct basic concepts and skills in life science, physical science, and earth science. Math Teachers instruct basic concepts and skills in arithmetic, geometry, and algebra.

Schoolteachers work in public, private, and independent schools. Private schools include boarding schools, day schools, military schools, and parochial schools (those that are affiliated with a religious denomination). Independent schools are also private schools, but are not part of other organizations; they have their own board of trustees and develop their own source of funding.

In most school systems, the grades are divided into three levels: elementary school, middle school or junior high school, and high school. Elementary schools may be config-

ured as grades K to three, K to five, K to six, or K to eight. Elementary school teachers are usually responsible for teaching one class of children in all core subjects—math, science, language arts, and social science. Some teachers also provide instruction in computer skills, art, music, and physical education to their students. In many elementary schools, teaching specialists come in once or twice a week to teach those subjects.

Most middle schools are made up of either grades five to eight or six to eight. Typically, teams of two to four middle school teachers are assigned to a class of students (for example, 80 students) at the same grade level. The team is responsible for the instruction of the four core subjects. Each teacher is responsible for teaching one or more subjects. For example, in a two-member team, one might teach math and science while the other teaches language arts and social studies. The exploratory classes—art, music, physical education, foreign language, health, and so on—are taught by specialists.

In some elementary schools and middle schools, science classes are taught by science teaching specialists. They may teach science to different grades in one school or travel to several schools during the week. In addition to teaching classes, science specialists act as resource teachers in the schools they serve. They help other teachers develop and plan science lessons for their classes.

Junior high schools may consist of grades seven and eight or seven to nine, while high schools may be composed of grades nine to ten or ten to twelve. In junior high schools and high schools, the school day is divided into several class periods and students rotate from class to class. Science and Math Teachers are specialists in their subject matter, teaching science or math classes to students in different grade levels. Schoolteachers at these two levels cover advanced topics and skills in science and math.

Science and Math Teachers create daily lesson plans for their classes, following school curriculum guidelines. A lesson plan outlines what the teacher shall teach: the concepts and skills to be taught, the purpose of the lesson, learning objectives, the methods for teaching the lesson, and the exercises and activities that shall reinforce learning.

Teachers must prepare the lessons outlined in their lesson plans. This involves studying topics, gathering teaching materials, creating student materials, setting up demonstrations or experiments, and so on. To help reinforce instruction, teachers may use films, slides, videotapes, and other audiovisual equipment. Many teachers supplement instruction by having students work with computer programs and access the Internet during the class period. Science and Math Teachers also plan field trips to science museums, zoos, environmental centers, and similar venues.

A teacher's day involves various activities. They take attendance, collect homework, review the previous day's lessons, present new lessons through lecture, demonstration, and modeling. Teachers check students' understanding of concepts and skills with written and oral exercises, quizzes, or tests and assign class work, homework, and projects. Schoolteachers also act as mentors to their students.

Schoolteachers are responsible for monitoring students' academic progress. They maintain a record book of students' test scores, grades for class assignments, and so on. At the end of each grading period, teachers evaluate their students' work and assign grades for their performance.

In many public schools, special education students—children with learning, emotional, and physical disabilities—are assigned to general education classrooms. (Recent changes in federal law have mandated that special education students receive their instruction in general education classrooms whenever possible.) With special education students, Math and Science Teachers must follow instructional goals and objectives that are outlined in their students' Individualized Education Programs (IEPs). When needed, they consult with special education teachers for assistance in implementing IEPs.

Schoolteachers have many other tasks, which vary with grade level. They might hold parent-teacher conferences, coach sports, advise after-school clubs, supervise school-grounds during recesses, or supervise school functions. Schoolteachers also participate in department and faculty meetings.

Schoolteachers work beyond the regular school day, and often complete their tasks (making lesson plans, calling parents, grading papers, etc.) during evenings and on weekends. Schoolteachers have a 10-month work schedule. Many schools are in session from September to June. Some schools have year-round sessions.

In most public school systems, teachers receive tenure after completing three to five years of continuous teaching service. With tenure, teachers cannot be fired from their jobs without just cause.

Salaries

Salaries vary and depend on such factors as education, experience, employer, and geographical location. The Bureau of Labor Statistics reports the following estimated salaries for most schoolteachers in 2001:

- secondary school—$27,980 to $67,940
- middle school—$27,790 to $64,270
- elementary school—$27,000 to $64,280

In some schools, teachers can earn extra pay for coaching, being class advisers, sponsoring extracurricular activities, teaching summer school, or performing other jobs.

Employment Prospects

Science (particularly chemistry and physics) and Math Teachers are in demand in many parts of the United States. Jobs are more readily available in inner cities, rural areas, and areas with a high rate of population growth.

Teaching opportunities in public and private schools are expected to continue to increase over the next several years due to the large number of teachers who are reaching retirement age. Opportunities should also grow due to the increasing rate of student enrollment nationwide and the increasing number of states that are passing laws to lower the student-to-teacher ratio.

Advancement Prospects

With further education and licensure, Schoolteachers can become counselors, librarians, curriculum specialists, school psychologists, or other school-related professionals.

Schoolteachers can also advance to positions in school administration. With additional education and licensure, public school teachers can become school principals and district administrators. In private and independent schools, teachers can work their way up to higher positions as school head, division head, or dean of students.

Education and Training
The minimum requirement to become a Schoolteacher in most schools is a bachelor's degree. Many Schoolteachers in public, private, and independent schools hold a master's degree.

Elementary and middle school teachers usually hold a degree in liberal studies. Middle school teachers may have a degree in other fields as long as they have completed the required course work to teach one or more core subjects—math, language arts, science, and social studies. Junior high and high school teachers need at least a bachelor's degree in the primary subject that they are teaching.

All state-licensed teachers must complete an accredited teacher education program that includes a supervised field practicum.

In many schools, beginning teachers are assigned mentor teachers who advise them with curriculum development, classroom management, and so on. Many schools require teachers to attend in-service workshops throughout the year, which cover topics such as new teaching methods and cultural diversity.

Experience, Skills, and Personality Traits
Entry-level Schoolteachers usually have previous teaching experience as student teachers, substitute teachers, or teacher's aides. Many private and independent schools look for candidates who also have a strong background in sports, drama, community service, or other extracurricular activities.

To work with students, staff, and parents, Schoolteachers need excellent communication, teamwork, and interpersonal skills. Additionally, they need strong management and organization skills to complete their many different tasks each day. Successful Schoolteachers share several personality traits, such as being creative, enthusiastic, dependable, flexible, fair, patient, caring, and tolerant.

Special Requirements
To teach in public schools, Schoolteachers must have valid teaching credentials. Elementary school teachers possess elementary education credentials. Middle school teachers hold elementary education, secondary education, or middle-grade credentials, depending on the requirements of their states. Junior high and high school teachers hold secondary education credentials with endorsements in the subjects that they teach.

Licensure requirements vary from state to state. (For specific information, contact the state board of education where

you wish to teach.) Public school teachers may need to complete continuing education units and, eventually, a master's degree for licensure renewal.

An alternative path for teacher licensure is available for those who would prefer to obtain their credentials by teaching full time in classrooms under the supervision of certified educators. To learn more, contact your state board of education or school district office.

Many private schools require certification from the state board of education, school accreditation groups, professional associations, or other recognized organizations. Some schools, such as Montessori school, require internal teaching certifications, which are obtained after completing their training programs.

Schoolteachers can also obtain national certification from the National Board for Professional Teaching Standards (NBPTS). This is on a voluntary basis and does not substitute for state licensure. For more information, call NBPTS at (800) 22TEACH or visit its website at http://www.nbpts.org.

Unions and Associations
Various professional associations at the local, state, and national levels are available to Schoolteachers. They offer such professional services and resources as education programs, teacher resources, and networking opportunities. Most public school teachers belong to either of these teacher unions: the American Federation of Teachers or the National Education Association.

Some societies that serve the interests of Science and Math Teachers are:

- National Council of Teachers of Mathematics
- National Science Teachers Association
- American Association of Physics Teachers
- National Association of Biology Teachers
- National Earth Science Teachers Association
- International Technology Education Association

Science Teachers are also eligible to join scientific societies such as the American Association for the Advancement of Science, the American Chemical Society, the American Geological Institute, and the American Institute of Biological Sciences. See Appendix III for contact information.

Tips for Entry
1. Gain experience working with the age level that you would like to teach. Tutor science students or math students. Obtain paid or volunteer positions working with children in recreational programs, church groups, scouting, 4-H, and so on. Opportunities for working with children or teenagers in zoos, science museums, nature centers, observatories, parks, and other similar institutions may be available in your area.

2. Many schools advertise job openings in local newspapers as well as on their websites.

3. Contact public and private schools where you wish to teach to learn about job vacancies. Submit an application even if jobs are not currently available. Call back from time to time to learn the status of your application.

4. To learn more about teaching in independent schools, contact the National Association of Independent Schools, 1620 L Street, NW, Suite 111, Washington, D.C. 20036. Or phone (202) 973-9700; or visit its website, http//www.nais.org.

5. Use the Internet to learn more about teaching science and mathematics in grades K–12. Some websites you might visit include the Eisenhower National Clearinghouse, http://www.enc.org; the National Science Teachers Association, http://www.nsta.org; and the National Council of Teachers of Mathematics, http://www.nctm.org.

COLLEGE PROFESSOR

CAREER PROFILE

Duties: Provide instruction in science, mathematics, or engineering courses in colleges and universities; perform duties as required of position

Alternate Title(s): Lecturer, Instructor; title that reflects a teaching specialty, such as Botany Professor or Professor of Mathematics

Salary Range: $27,000 to $114,000

Employment Prospects: Good

Advancement Prospects: Fair

Prerequisites:

    Education or Training—Master's or doctoral degree in a math or science specialization

    Experience—Teaching experience needed; research background may be required

    Special Skills and Personality Traits—Communication, presentation, interpersonal, teamwork, social, organization, and management skills; independent; adaptable; curious; flexible; creative

    Licensure/Certification—Teaching credentials may be required to teach in public two-year colleges

CAREER LADDER

```
┌─────────────────────────────┐
│      Professor (Full)       │
└─────────────────────────────┘

┌─────────────────────────────┐
│     Associate Professor     │
└─────────────────────────────┘

┌─────────────────────────────┐
│     Assistant Professor     │
└─────────────────────────────┘

┌─────────────────────────────┐
│          Instructor         │
└─────────────────────────────┘
```

Position Description

Many scientists and mathematicians are employed as College Professors in two-year colleges, four-year colleges, universities, and medical schools. Their primary role is to teach and advise college students as they complete their educational objectives in pursuit of their future careers as scientists, mathematicians, engineers, technologists, technicians, and educators. In addition, many Professors are involved in conducting basic and applied research that lead to important scientific and technological developments and inventions that benefit society. Depending on the college setting, Professors may be responsible for just teaching or for a combination of teaching and conducting research.

Two-year colleges are also known as community colleges, junior colleges, or technical colleges. These colleges serve the educational needs of local communities and provide training for local professions, businesses, industry, and government agencies. Community college professors rarely are required to conduct research. Science and math professors teach courses that fulfill general education require-

ments that lead to associate degrees or occupational certificates. (General education courses in community colleges usually fulfill lower undergraduate requirements in four-year institutions.)

In four-year colleges and universities, Professors teach undergraduate as well as graduate students. Those in small liberal arts colleges focus mostly on teaching while professors at research universities must divide their time among teaching, conducting independent research, and producing scholarly works for publication.

Professors are part of a department or division, corresponding to their subject or field (such as physical geography, animal science, or bioinformatics). For each term, they are assigned to teach courses that are part of a prescribed curriculum. For example, a Math professor at a community college might teach basic arithmetic, finite mathematics, geometry, and applied mathematics for the spring semester.

For each of their courses, Professors develop a course syllabus that outlines the topics and sequence of topics to be taught as well as bibliographies for outside reading assignments. They are also responsible for preparing lectures and laboratory experiments. Depending on the course, Professors lecture to hundreds of students in large halls, supervise students in laboratories, or lead small seminar discussions. Some Professors teach courses on cable or closed-circuit television as well as via the Internet.

Professors perform a wide range of duties, which vary daily. Some general tasks include preparing lectures, reading and critiquing student papers, creating examinations, grading tests, and performing administrative tasks. Professors are required to hold regularly-scheduled office hours to meet with students and advise them on academic and career matters. They also supervise students with their research projects. At large universities, teaching assistants are usually available to help Professors with administering exams, grading exams, and leading discussion sections.

Research Professors conduct studies in areas that interest them. Some research projects are conducted in collaboration with colleagues within their discipline as well as from other disciplines. Professors are responsible for obtaining funds for their research projects. These funds pay for research equipment and supplies, travel to research sites, overhead costs, financial support for themselves and their research assistants, and so on. Therefore, Professors must make time to seek appropriate funding sources (such as the federal government and private corporations) and to prepare grant proposals and budgets. Furthermore, Professors are expected to have the results of their research published in scholarly journals, books, or electronic media.

College professors participate in faculty meetings where they make decisions on curriculum, equipment purchases, hiring, and other departmental matters. Professors also serve on academic and administrative advisory committees which deal with institutional policies. Additionally, they perform community service, such as providing consultation services to community agencies, nonprofit organizations, corporations, government agencies, and other institutions. Many Professors serve on committees, panels, or commissions established by government agencies.

Professors are responsible for keeping up with developments in their fields through independent study, networking with colleagues, and participating in professional conferences and workshops.

Professors have flexible hours that may include teaching courses every day or every other day as well as teaching classes at night or on weekends. They generally teach between 12 to 15 hours per week, but the total number of hours that they actually work can add up to 40 or more hours per week. This includes time spent teaching courses, holding office hours, preparing for classes, grading papers and exams, conducting research, participating in meetings, and so on.

On most campuses, faculty members hold four academic ranks—instructor, assistant professor, associate professor, or (full) Professor. Professors may be hired on a tenure or nontenure track. Tenured Professors are assured jobs at their institutions until they retire or resign. With tenure, they cannot be fired without just cause and due process.

In recent years, colleges and universities have been hiring adjunct (or part-time) instructors to teach general education courses. Adjunct instructors teach one to three courses for an institution. They have limited administrative and student advising duties. Many are not given office space, so they spend little time on campus. Many part-time instructors teach at more than one institution in different parts of a city, county, or region. Some also teach courses for extension programs in community colleges, colleges, or universities.

Salaries

Salaries vary, and depend on factors such as experience, education, academic institution, and geographical location. The Bureau of Labor Statistics reports the following estimated annual salaries in 2001 for most postsecondary Professors in the science, mathematics, and engineering disciplines:

- agricultural science—$34,010 to $99,140
- biological sciences—$31,240 to $114,080
- chemistry—$31,700 to $93,450
- computer science—$26,020 to $90,290
- engineering—$36,090 to $111,960
- environmental science—$32,760 to $95,940
- forestry and conservation science—$38,610 to $98,830
- geography—$33,090 to $89,380
- geoscience (or earth sciences)—$32,740 to $105,890
- mathematics—$27,300 to $88,680
- physics—$34,650 to $105,850

Employment Prospects

In general, job opportunities become available as Professor's retire, resign, or transfer to higher positions. The competition for jobs is high. In recent years, fewer tenure-track positions have become available each year. Due to tight budgets, academic institutions have been hiring more adjunct instructors or have been offering prospective full-time faculty members limited contracts of one to five years which may be renewed.

Advancement Prospects

College Professors must advance through the academic ranks as instructor, assistant professor, associate professor, and finally full professor. Tenure-track positions start at either the instructor or assistant professor level with tenure attained at the associate professor rank. With tenure, Professors have prestige, professional freedom, and job security for the rest of their academic career. Job satisfaction is extremely high, and few tenured Professors leave the profession.

Administrative and management positions are available to those interested in following this career path. Professors can pursue such positions as department chairs, academic deans, administrative directors, provosts, and presidents.

Education and Training

A master's degree is the minimum requirement needed to teach in two-year colleges, but many faculty members hold a doctoral degree. The minimum requirement at four-year colleges and universities is a doctoral degree.

Earning a doctorate takes several years of dedication. In general, students complete four years of undergraduate work, earning a bachelor's degree. This is followed by six to eight years of study for first a master's degree and then a doctoral degree. New Ph.D.s usually spend two or more years completing postdoctoral training before seeking permanent positions.

Experience, Skills, and Personality Traits

Depending on an educational institution's mission, candidates may need to demonstrate that they have a strong teaching or combined teaching and research background. For example, community colleges and smaller liberal arts colleges emphasize teaching over research while research universities are interested in candidates with strong research experience.

Professors must have excellent communication and presentation skills as well as strong interpersonal and teamwork skills to establish rapport with students, colleagues, and administrators. They also need adequate social skills, as Professors attend various college functions. Furthermore, strong organization and management skills are needed to complete their various duties each day.

Successful Professors share several personality traits such as being independent, adaptable, curious, flexible, and creative. They have a strong desire to pursue knowledge in their field as well as to teach and share their knowledge with students.

Special Requirements

Instructors who teach in public two-year colleges may be required to possess valid teaching credentials.

Unions and Associations

Professors belong to different societies to take advantage of networking opportunities and other professional resources and services. They join local, state, and national professional associations. The Mathematical Association of America and the National Science Teachers Association are two organizations that serve the specific interests of science educators.

In addition, many Professors belong to professional associations that serve the general interests of college faculty, such as the American Association for Higher Education, the National Association of Scholars, or the American Association of University Professors. Community college instructors might also join the American Association for Adult and Continuing Education. Professors in public institutions are eligible to join the higher education divisions of the National Education Association or the American Federation of Teachers.

Many Professors also join scientific societies such as the American Association for the Advancement of Science, the American Astronomical Society, the American Geological Institute, the American Institute of Physics, and the American Institute of Biological Sciences. See Appendix III for contact information.

Tips for Entry

1. Preparing Future Faculty (PFF) is a program that offers graduate students an opportunity to experience teaching in colleges and universities at an apprentice level. For more information, check out the program's website at http://www.preparing-faculty.org.

2. To gain work experience, contact institutions about adjunct positions. Many colleges and universities maintain a list of qualified candidates whom they contact when new instructors are needed. It is common for colleges to hire new instructors at the last minute to replace adjunct instructors who have suddenly left for full-time positions.

3. When applying for a position, read the job announcement carefully. Also learn something about the school—whether it is more research-oriented or more teaching-oriented, and so on. Then tailor your résumé and cover letter to fit the position. For example, if you know the school is more interested in teaching, then you would want to emphasize your teaching strengths and experiences.

4. The Internet can provide you with valuable sources for job banks as well as with developments and trends in higher education. Some websites you might want to visit include the American Association for Higher Education, http://www.aahe.org; the American Association of University Professors, http://www.aaup.org; the American Association of Community Colleges, http://www.aacc.nche.edu; and the Chronicle of Higher Education, http://chronicle.com.

SCIENCE EDUCATOR (NONSCHOOL SETTINGS)

CAREER PROFILE

Duties: Develop and implement educational programs in informal settings; plan and teach classes and workshops; develop curriculum; perform other duties as required

Alternate Title(s): Science Education Specialist, Curatorial Assistant of Education; a title that reflects a specialty such as Environmental Educator or Marine Educator

Salary Range: $13,000 to $66,000

Employment Prospects: Fair

Advancement Prospects: Good

Prerequisites:

Education or Training—A bachelor's degree in a science discipline, education, or a related field; an advanced degree may be preferred

Experience—Several years of teaching and program planning experience; background in science

Special Skills and Personality Traits—Interpersonal, teamwork, communication, writing, computer, and self-management skills; creative; organized; flexible; enthusiastic; diplomatic; self-motivated

Licensure/Certification—None required

CAREER LADDER

```
┌─────────────────────────────┐
│   Director (or Curator) of   │
│      Science Education        │
└─────────────────────────────┘

┌─────────────────────────────┐
│  Science Education Specialist or │
│      Program Coordinator      │
└─────────────────────────────┘

┌─────────────────────────────┐
│     Science Educator or       │
│      Outreach Educator        │
└─────────────────────────────┘

┌─────────────────────────────┐
│    Assistant Educator or      │
│      Gallery Explainer        │
└─────────────────────────────┘
```

Position Description

Science Educators are responsible for developing and implementing informal science education programs. Some Science Educators run educational programs in natural history museums, science centers, zoos, aquariums, botanical gardens, planetariums, environmental centers, and other institutions. Other Science Educators manage programs that are sponsored by government agencies (such as NASA), universities and colleges, scientific organizations, and nonprofit groups.

Science Educators develop a wide variety of educational programs and activities around their institution's collections, exhibits, and natural resources. Their objective is to create programs that entertain audiences as well as teach them informally about science and technology. Educational programs include tours, demonstrations, classes, workshops, films, lectures, field trips, and printed materials. Many programs use a hands-on or interactive format in which patrons manipulate objects, complete tasks, handle fossils, run lab experiments, or assist scientists with field studies.

Different programs are developed for different audiences—children, adults, families, and schools. For example, a science museum might offer after-school programs, summer camps, and junior docent programs for young people; family nights at its planetarium; field trips and lecture series aimed specifically for their adult patrons; special tours and workshops for student groups; and on-line learning programs at its website on the Internet.

Some Science Educators are involved in designing and delivering educational outreach programs. They travel to schools, youth centers, community centers, and other organizations and put on workshops and presentations. They use films, slideshows, and other multimedia tools to bring science to life in their lectures. They also utilize fossils, specimens, and other objects that their audiences can experience.

Some Science Educators develop programs that offer science curriculum and instruction support to teachers and other educators in formal settings. For example, environmental educators might conduct workshops for middle school teachers, demonstrating how to do enrichment activities for their lessons about the environment.

Depending on their experience, Science Educators may supervise one or more educational programs. Their duties include scheduling events, finding facilities, obtaining supplies and equipment, managing the program budget, marketing the program, and preparing program evaluations. Science Educators are also responsible for developing and producing teaching materials and activities. They oversee programs on the days they happen, and supervise staff and volunteers that are involved in the program. Most Science Educators teach classes and workshops as well as give presentations and demonstrations.

Science Educators also perform a variety of other tasks, which include:

- helping set up and maintain exhibits
- writing interpretive materials about exhibits, collections, or natural resources
- conducting tours of their facilities
- training and supervising junior staff, volunteers, and interns
- writing grant proposals for future or current programs
- developing marketing and public relations materials such as newsletters, informational brochures, and webpages
- maintaining accurate records, preparing reports, writing correspondence, and completing required paperwork
- attending meetings and conferences

Science Educators work part-time or full-time. They may be required to work evenings, weekends, and holidays. Those working for residential environmental education programs are usually required to live at the camps as well.

Salaries

Salaries vary, and depend on such factors as education, experience, job responsibilities, and type of employer. According to the "Science Center Workforce 2001" (a report by the Association of Science-Technology Centers), the average salary in 2000 for coordinators of public programs was $36,790. Salaries for this position ranged from $13,000 to $65,539. The average salary for coordinators of school programs was $35,669 with salaries ranging from $21,622 to $66,000.

Employment Prospects

Most opportunities become available as Science Educators transfer to other positions. Many jobs are based on the funding of grant proposals, and so may last only for a specific period of time. The turnover rate for Science Educators in informal settings is high, but the competition for available positions is also very high.

Advancement Prospects

Science Educators can advance to supervisory and administrative positions, as program coordinators and directors. Those with higher ambitions can pursue a career path leading to directorships of museums, zoos, aquariums, and so forth.

Education and Training

Employers require that Science Educators have a bachelor's degree in a related science discipline, in another related field, or in education. Some employers require that candidates have a master's degree, but may waive the requirement if candidates have qualifying work experience.

Science Educators are expected to continue their professional growth through self-study, enrollment in training and education programs, networking with colleagues, and so on.

Experience, Skills, and Personality Traits

Employers generally prefer candidates who have several years of teaching experience in informal science programs. They should also have previous experience planning and implementing education or outreach programs in informal settings. In addition, they should have a strong science background.

Science Educators need excellent interpersonal and teamwork skills, as well as strong communication and writing skills. They must be computer literate. In addition, they need good self-management skills, including the ability to handle multiple tasks, prioritize tasks, work independently, and handle stressful situations.

Some personality traits that successful Science Educators share are being creative, organized, flexible, enthusiastic, diplomatic, and self-motivated.

Unions and Associations

Science Educators join different professional societies (at local, state, and national levels) that serve their interests as museum professionals, educators, and scientists. These organizations offer training programs, networking opportunities, and other professional services and resources. Some professional associations at the national level that serve the interests of science educators include the National Science Teachers Association, the North American Association for Environmental Education, and the National Marine Educators Association.

Science Educators are eligible to join associations that serve different types of museums, such as the American Association of Museums, the Association of Science-Technology Centers, the American Association of Botanical Gardens and Arboreta, and the American Zoo and Aquarium Association.

Further, Science Educators can join scientific societies that serve their particular interests, such as the Society for Integrative and Comparative Biology, the American Geophysical Union, the Entomological Society of America, and the Paleontological Society.

See Appendix III for union and association contact information.

Tips for Entry

1. You can start gaining experience in high school and college. Volunteer with education or outreach programs at a science museum, technology center, zoo, or other institution.

2. Many environmental and nature centers hire educators for temporary positions for their residential environmental education programs. These positions usually include room and board along with a weekly salary. Contact environmental organizations in your area for job listings. On the Web, check out job listings at Environmental Career Opportunities, http://www.ecojobs.com.

3. Because Science Educator positions are limited, the job search may be a long one. Many Science Educators were museum volunteers or had worked in such positions as administrative assistants and gallery explainers while doing their job search.

4. Learn more about science education and outreach programs on the Internet. To get a list of relevant websites to visit, enter any of these keywords in a search engine: *science museum* (or *zoo* or *aquarium*) *education program.*

SCIENCE CURATOR

CAREER PROFILE

Duties: Oversee the care and presentation of collections; perform administrative tasks; perform other duties as required of position

Alternate Title(s): Collection Manager

Salary Range: $19,000 to $64,000

Employment Prospects: Poor

Advancement Prospects: Poor

Prerequisites:

Education or Training—A master's or doctoral degree in a science discipline

Experience—Extensive experience working with collections in institutions where they wish to work

Special Skills and Personality Traits—Management, business, research, communication, writing, computer, interpersonal, teamwork, and self-management skills; creative; intuitive; curious; energetic; self-motivated; flexible

Licensure/Certification—None required

CAREER LADDER

```
┌────────────────────────────────────┐
│   Chief Curator (at larger museums) │
└────────────────────────────────────┘

┌────────────────────────────────────┐
│              Curator                │
└────────────────────────────────────┘

┌────────────────────────────────────┐
│   Assistant or Associate Curator    │
└────────────────────────────────────┘
```

Position Description

Science Curators oversee the science and technology collections in museums and other institutions that exhibit these collections for viewing by the general public. Zoos, aquariums, nature centers, botanical gardens, arboretums, natural history museums, planetariums, and science centers are other types of such institutions. Science Curators also work in children's museums which offer interactive exhibits and education programs for young people.

In small institutions, curators are in charge of all collections. In larger institutions, there are usually several curators, with each managing one or more collections. They are assigned to collections in their fields of expertise, such as paleontology, geology, botany, entomology, astronomy, or physics. Very large, specialized institutions may also have curators who only perform research or administrative duties.

Science Curators are responsible for the care and presentation of all the objects, materials, and specimens that are in science and technology collections. For example, a zoo curator oversees collections of live animals. Curators manage collections that belong to their institutions as well as those that are lent to them by donors or by other institutions.

While working with other staff members, Science Curators develop and implement collections programs. Their duties include organizing and preserving collections, describing and classifying items in the collections, conducting research on objects and specimens, and storing collections safely and securely. Science Curators also publish magazine articles, monographs, books, and other materials about the collections for which they are responsible. In addition, they make presentations about their collections at professional conferences as well as at meetings and functions of civic groups.

Science Curators are in charge of developing new exhibits. They work with other staff members to plan and prepare exhibits that bring concepts of science and technology to life and that are easily understood by both children and adults. Science Curators are responsible for choosing appropriate items for exhibits. They do research and write text (or labels) about the items to be displayed. Curators also determine the best way to design exhibits so that they communicate ideas clearly and in an entertaining manner.

Museums and other institutions continually acquire new items by purchasing them, receiving them as gifts, or on loan from other institutions. In the case of live animals and plants, many are acquired through reproduction or are collected in their natural habitats. Science Curators are responsible for deciding which acquisitions to make, after careful research and evaluation of the items being considered. Science Curators also decide which objects should be removed from collections to make way for new ones.

Curators also have administrative tasks to perform, such as administering policies; managing budgets; maintaining collection records; evaluating exhibits and collections programs; training and supervising staff, interns, and volunteers; writing grant proposals; and assisting in fund-raising. Many curators help with public relations and marketing tasks to promote programs, events, and activities at their institutions. For example, they might write press releases or develop informational brochures for patrons. Some Curators participate in the development of science education and public outreach programs for their institutions.

Curators work closely with other staff members, such as directors, archivists, conservators, technicians, and educators.

Some Science Curators are lecturers or adjunct (part-time) instructors at nearby colleges and universities, where they teach in undergraduate, graduate, or continuing education programs. They may teach courses in their field of science or in museum science.

Some science museums, aquariums, and other institutions are connected to research universities. In such cases, Curator positions may be academic appointments. Like other professors, Curators are expected to teach, conduct research projects, produce scholarly work, and fulfill community service obligations.

Salaries

Salaries vary, depending on such factors as education, experience, employer, and geographical location. Curators in large institutions typically earn higher salaries than curators in smaller institutions. The Bureau of Labor Statistics reports that the estimated annual salary in 2001 for most curators ranged between $18,910 and $63,870.

Employment Prospects

The turnover rate for Curators is low; thus competition for any opening is very high, especially for positions with large museums. Most opportunities become available as Curators retire or transfer to other positions.

Because most museums, zoos, aquariums, and similar institutions are nonprofit, positions are dependent on the availability of funding.

Advancement Prospects

Advancement opportunities are limited to obtaining Curator positions with more complicated responsibilities. Thus, for example, Curators in smaller museums might seek positions at larger ones. Curators with administrative and management ambitions can seek to become director of a museum, zoo, or planetarium.

Education and Training

Most employers hire Science Curators who hold a master's or doctoral degree in a relevant science discipline. For example, aquarium curators typically hold an advanced degree in such fields as oceanography, aquatic botany, or marine biology.

Many colleges and universities have graduate programs or certificate-based programs in museum studies with a focus in curatorship.

Experience, Skills, and Personality Traits

Employers choose candidates who have extensive experience working with collections that are similar to those in their type of institution (natural history museums, botanical gardens, and so on).

In order to handle the different aspects of their jobs, Science Curators need management and business skills, as well as research, communication, and writing skills. They also have good computer skills as well as strong interpersonal and teamwork skills. Science Curators need excellent self-management skills, including the ability to handle stressful situations, work independently, prioritize tasks, and meet deadlines.

Being creative, intuitive, curious, energetic, self-motivated, and flexible are some personality traits that successful Science Curators share.

Unions and Associations

Science Curators join professional associations to take advantage of education programs, networking opportunities, and other professional resources and services. Many belong to the American Association of Museums as well as to regional and state museum associations. In addition, Science Curators join associations that serve the interests of different institutions, such as the American Zoo and Aquarium Association, the Society for the Preservation of Natural History Collections, the American Association of Botanical Gardens and Arboreta, and the Association of Science-Technology Centers.

Tips for Entry

1. To gain experience, volunteer at a museum, zoo, or other institution that interests you. Get involved in the different areas of operations, like education, exhibition development, and publications.
2. Many museums have internship programs for college students. If an institution that you're interested in does not have one, contact it anyway and ask about interning there.
3. Get involved with professional organizations and conferences and network with your peers.
4. Learn more about museums on the Internet. Check out websites for the American Association of Museums, http://www.aam-us.org; Association of Science-Technology Centers, http:// www.astc.org; and Global Museum, http://www.globalmuseum.org.

SCIENCE WRITER

CAREER PROFILE

Duties: Write objective and accurate news reports, feature articles, books, documentation, manuals, public relations, or other written materials for general public and professional audiences; perform duties as required of position

Alternate Title(s): A title that reflects an occupation such as Science Reporter, Medical Writer, Technical Writer, or Information Officer

Salary Range: $17,000 to $100,000+

Employment Prospects: Good

Advancement Prospects: Fair

Prerequisites:

Education or Training—A bachelor's degree in a science discipline, journalism, or a related field

Experience—Basic understanding of subject matter; relevant writing experience

Special Skills and Personality Traits—Writing, organization, research, communication, interpersonal, computer, and self-management skills; business skills (for freelancers); creative; observant; flexible; disciplined; self-motivated; persistent

Licensure/Certification—None required

CAREER LADDER

```
┌─────────────────────────────────┐
│ Senior Science Writer, Editor, or │
│        Freelance Writer          │
└─────────────────────────────────┘

┌─────────────────────────────────┐
│         Science Writer           │
└─────────────────────────────────┘

┌─────────────────────────────────┐
│    Entry-level Science Writer    │
└─────────────────────────────────┘
```

Position Description

Science Writers contribute to the general public's understanding of science and technology. They describe and explain scientific concepts and technical terminology in simple, yet accurate, language. They write news articles, magazine features, textbooks, instruction manuals, documentary scripts, grant proposals, marketing materials, content for webpages, and so on.

The field of science writing is made up of several specialties. It is not uncommon for Science Writers to work in several specialized areas throughout their careers.

One specialty is science journalism. Science Writers in this area are commonly known as science reporters or science journalists. They report on current news about scientists, discoveries, inventions, events, issues, and other happenings in the science and technology world. They cover a wide range of topics—including medical studies, health, environmental issues, earthquakes, climate change, space programs, technology, archeological findings, artificial intelligence, science and technology policy, and so on. The stories may take place at the local, state, national, or global level.

Science journalists work for newspapers, magazines, journals, television stations, radio stations, and Internet news services. Their audiences may be the general public or professionals (such as doctors, engineers, chemists, and astrophysicists). Some science journalists are also book authors, producing in-depth reportage about science and technical topics that interest them.

Some Science Writers specialize in the area of public relations and marketing. They are often known as information officers or press writers, and are responsible for communicating the latest scientific research made by their employers to the public media and others. Information officers work for universities, medical centers, pharmaceutical companies, biotechnology firms, high-technology corporations, government agencies, laboratories, research institutes, science museums, and nonprofit health organizations.

Information officers write press releases, and may write articles for in-house publications, speeches for executive officers, scripts for radio and television spots, and copy for their employers' websites. Many information officers are also responsible for creating educational and promotional materials about the products their organizations manufacture and sell.

Still another specialty is medical writing. Medical writers work in various settings, such as biotechnology firms, medical schools, hospitals, pharmaceutical companies, government agencies, and nongovernmental organizations. They create a wide variety of written materials for their employers—for example, clinical study reports, position papers, regulatory documents, investigative drug brochures, and patient handbooks. Many also write articles for newspapers, magazines, and websites.

Furthermore, Science Writers write science textbooks for school and college audiences. Some of them create educational materials for informal educational settings such as science museums, nature centers, and science programs. Other Science Writers specialize in writing grant proposals or developing and writing content for websites. Some Science Writers are involved with writing scripts for documentaries, educational films, and other multimedia. Many are technical writers who develop manuals and other documentation for technical devices, software programs, computer hardware, consumer products, and so forth.

A large part of Science Writers' work involves conducting research. Whether they are writing news articles, grant proposals, or technical manuals, Science Writers need to gather background information. They search through relevant scientific databases and read pertinent literature. They also interview scientists and other experts.

Unless they are writing personal commentary, Science Writers must present the information objectively. They cannot put their own opinions or biases in their writings. In addition, they make sure that the information they are communicating is accurate and correct, and thus they check and often recheck their facts. They revise and edit their writing so that the language is clear and that their products adhere to standard writing formats and guidelines. Further, Science Writers must complete their projects by their deadlines. Most Science Writers are usually juggling several writing projects at the same time, each at different stages.

Many Science Writers are self-employed as freelance writers. They complete writing assignments or writing projects on a contractual basis for different clients. Freelance writers also perform tasks related to running a small business. For example, they do bookkeeping, pay bills and taxes, collect fees from clients, promote business, and maintain office supplies. Furthermore, they set aside time in their schedule just for seeking out future work.

Science Writers are involved in their own professional development. They keep up with science research as well as

continue to improve their writing craft. Many Science Writers also learn new skills such as using graphics software or developing websites.

Salaries

Salaries vary, depending on education, experience, specialty, employer, geographical location, and other factors. According to the Bureau of Labor Statistics, the estimated annual salary in 2001 for most news reporters and correspondents was $17,320 and $68,020; for most public relations specialists: $23,920 to $72,910; for most technical writers: $29,750 to $77,330; and for most writers and authors: $20,570 to $83,180. The Council for Advancement of Science Writers reports that earnings for experienced science writers and correspondents at major newspapers, national magazines, and network television stations may range from $60,000 to $100,000 or more.

Employment Prospects

Most opportunities become available as Science Writers retire or transfer to other positions. Employers create additional science writing positions to meet their growing needs to communicate scientific and technical information.

Advancement Prospects

Science Writers can advance to senior writer and editor positions, which usually involves performing supervisory and management duties.

Many Science Writers measure their success by gaining professional reputations and by earning higher incomes.

Education and Training

Educational requirements vary with the different employers. Minimally, Science Writers should have a bachelor's degree in a scientific discipline, journalism, English, or other relevant field. Many Science Writers have a master's or doctoral degree in a science or engineering discipline.

Experience, Skills, and Personality Traits

Employers prefer to hire Science Writers who have relevant writing experience—such as journalism, public relations, or technical writing—for the position to which they are applying. In addition, Science Writers have a general understanding of the subject matter in which they write.

Science Writers need excellent writing, organization, research, and communication skills. They must have strong interpersonal skills and the willingness to talk with strangers from different backgrounds. Science Writers also need good self-management skills, such as the ability to meet deadlines, work independently, take initiative, and prioritize tasks accordingly. Freelance writers should have adequate business skills.

Some personality traits that successful Science Writers share are being creative, observant, flexible, disciplined, self-motivated, and persistent.

Unions and Associations

Science Writers join professional associations to take advantage of networking opportunities, job banks, and other professional services and resources. Different societies are available to serve the different interests of Science Writers. Some of these societies include:

- National Association of Science Writers
- Society for Technical Communication
- American Medical Writers Association
- Agricultural Communicators in Education
- Association of Health Care Journalists
- Society of Environmental Journalists
- Technology Section of the Public Relations Society of America

Many Science Writers also belong to writing societies such as the National Writers Union and the American Society of Journalists and Authors. Science Writers are also eligible to join scientific societies in their areas of interest, such as the American Geological Institute or the American Institute of Biological Sciences. See Appendix III for contact information.

Tips for Entry

1. As a college student, join a professional writing association to take advantage of networking opportunities and other benefits.
2. Many professional scientific associations offer mass media fellowships for science graduate students and Ph.D.s.
3. Build a portfolio of your published work, as publishers and employers will want to see your writing samples, usually referred to as clips.
4. Contact employers directly about permanent positions or freelance work.
5. Use the Internet to learn more about being a Science Writer. One website you might explore is from the National Association of Science Writers, http://nasw.org. To get a list of other relevant websites, enter the keywords *science writing*.

SCIENCE AND TECHNOLOGY (S&T) POLICY ANALYST

CAREER PROFILE

Duties: Provide policy makers with analyses of science and technology policies, plans, programs, and legislation; conduct research; analyze and interpret data; make oral or written reports; perform other duties as required

Alternate Title(s): Budget Analyst, Policy and Fiscal Analyst, Legislative Analyst, Policy Scientist, Science Policy Analyst, Technology Policy Analyst, Environmental Policy Analyst

Salary Range: $30,000 to $80,000+

Employment Prospects: Good

Advancement Prospects: Good

Prerequisites:

Education or Training—A master's or doctoral degree in a science or engineering discipline

Experience—Experience or substantive knowledge in a particular science or technology; background in policy science; previous experience in public policy preferred

Special Skills and Personality Traits—Research, analytical, quantitative, writing, communication, interpersonal, and teamwork skills; well-organized; creative; objective; self-motivated; quick learner

Licensure/Certification—None required

CAREER LADDER

```
┌─────────────────────────────────────┐
│  Senior or Supervisory Policy Analyst │
└─────────────────────────────────────┘

┌─────────────────────────────────────┐
│           Policy Analyst             │
└─────────────────────────────────────┘

┌─────────────────────────────────────┐
│       Research Assistant or          │
│       Research Associate             │
└─────────────────────────────────────┘
```

Position Description

Policy makers in government, private companies, academia, and nongovernmental organizations make decisions related to science and technology every day. They vote on legislation, make policies, and address problems that concern natural resources, energy supplies, environmental protection, global climate change, nuclear waste disposal, biotechnology, pharmaceuticals, agriculture, fisheries, regulation of the telecommunications industry, infrastructure protection, space programs, science education, and so on.

Science and Technology (S&T) Policy Analysts play an important role in helping policy makers create the most effective science and technology policies. They provide policy makers with analysis of the issues and problems they must address as well as offer alternative solutions. For example, analysts employed by Congress might analyze budget and policy issues related to proposed legislation on biotechnology research.

Policy Analysts are given assignments which they must complete and deliver in a timely matter. They sometimes receive assignments that require a short turnaround time. Analysts begin by finding out what the policy maker wants to accomplish in using the analysis. For example, a legislator may need to vote on a bill on funding genetic research. Policy Analysts must learn the conceptual framework or vision that a policy maker wishes to take. Analysts then define and shape the research to meet the decision maker's objectives. Policy Analysts perform their work objectively at all times. They do not inject their own concepts or beliefs into their assignments.

Analysts next collect data that addresses an assignment. They conduct research alone or with the help of research assistants and associates. They search databases and read appropriate literature. They also conduct interviews with subject matter experts, when necessary. They review, analyze, and interpret data and determine the major issues, costs, benefits, and other interests of their clients.

Policy Analysts prepare reports that are accurate and comprehensive, yet short and clear. They present their reports orally or in written form. The memorandums, reports, or verbal briefs are presented in language that elected officials and managers can understand and use when they present the information to others.

Many S&T Policy Analysts are scientists, mathematicians, and engineers from different disciplines. Some have changed careers, while others continue working as research scientists, professors, and administrators and perform policy analysis on a consulting basis.

Salaries

Salaries vary, depending on education, experience, employer, and other factors. Formal salary information is unavailable for S&T Policy Analysts. In general, entry-level analysts can expect to earn an annual salary between $30,000 and $40,000. An informal survey of a few opportunities listed on the Internet shows that experienced analysts can earn up to $80,000 or more per year.

Employment Prospects

Science and technology policy is a young but growing field. Many S&T Policy Analysts work in the Washington, D.C., area.

In government, S&T Policy Analysts work for executive and legislative branches as well as for government agencies, mostly at the state and federal levels. They are also employed by research and policy institutes, nongovernmental organizations, professional and trade associations, public-interest organizations, academic institutions, and private companies.

Opportunities generally become available as S&T Policy Analysts retire or transfer to other positions. Employers create additional positions to meet growing needs, as long as funding is available.

Advancement Prospects

S&T Policy Analysts can advance to senior positions such as project leader and program administrator. Those with policy-making ambitions can achieve an executive officer position, such as executive director or vice president. S&T Policy Analysts can also become independent consultants and consulting firm owners. Policy analysts often move back and forth between academia, government, industry, and other types of employers as they pursue their careers.

Education and Training

A master's or doctoral degree in science or engineering is generally required of candidates to gain employment as an S&T Policy Analyst. Many employers also hire candidates who hold a master's degree in science and technology policy, public policy, public administration, economics, or another related field. Those interested in a career in higher education should possess a doctoral degree.

Experience, Skills, and Personality Traits

Requirements vary with the different employers. In general, candidates should have experience in or substantive knowledge about a particular area such as space exploration, natural resources, or telecommunications. They should also have a background in policy science and be familiar with issues affecting policies in their fields of interest. Having experience working with legislators and executive officers is preferred by many employers.

S&T Policy Analysts must have excellent research, writing, analytical, and quantitative skills. Additionally, they need superior communication skills and must be able to present complex technical concepts to nontechnical people. Strong interpersonal and teamwork skills are also necessary.

Some personality traits that successful S&T Policy Analysts share are being well organized, creative, objective, and self-motivated. They are also quick learners.

Unions and Associations

Many S&T Policy Analysts belong to scientific societies—such as the American Association for the Advancement of Science—that serve their field of interest. These organizations offer networking opportunities and other professional services and resources.

Tips for Entry

1. To learn more about public policy, talk with professionals in the field. You might also enroll in a public policy course to get an idea if this area interests you.
2. Gain first-hand experience by completing an internship in science and technology policy. Opportunities are available with professional societies, public interest organizations, Congress, state legislatures, and research institutes.
3. Use the Internet to learn more about science and technology policy. Two websites you might visit from the Association for the Advancement of Science (AAAS) are AAAS Center Science, Technology, and Congress, http://www.aaas.org/spp/cstc; and AAAS Science and Policy Programs, http://www.aaas.org/spp. To find other relevant websites, enter the keywords *science and technology policy* or *science policy analysts* in a search engine.

APPENDIXES

APPENDIX I
EDUCATION AND TRAINING: HOW MUCH IS REQUIRED?

In this appendix, you will learn about the educational requirements that are needed for careers in the fields of science, engineering, and mathematics.

HIGH SCHOOL

Many professionals recommend that students should take as many science and math courses as possible to begin preparing for a science or engineering career. These include courses in biology, chemistry, physics, algebra, geometry, precalculus, and computing. In addition, students should also take courses in the humanities, social science, and business to gain a rounded background. High school students should also take courses in English and speech to build up strong reading, writing, and communication skills which are important for survival in college and the work world.

Four-year colleges and universities require college applicants to submit test scores from standardized college entrance exams, which may be the S.A.T. (Scholastic Aptitude Test) or the A.C.T. (American College Test). For further information, talk with your high school counselor. On the Internet, go to http://www.collegeboard.com to learn about the S.A.T. or to http://www.act.org to learn about the A.C.T.

BACHELOR'S PROGRAMS

Research opportunities as technologists, technicians, and research assistants are available to holders of bachelor's degrees. In the applied sciences, as well as in alternative science careers, the bachelor's degree is the minimum requirement for many positions. For example, many actuaries, environmental scientists, forensic scientists, technical writers, and science educators gained entry into their jobs with a bachelor's degree.

Science degree programs are four years long, but many students complete their studies in five or more years, especially if they hold part-time or full-time jobs. The first two years of any bachelor's program are spent fulfilling general requirements in science, social science, the humanities, and English. Students focus on completing coursework for their major during the last two years of their degree programs.

Undergraduate students gain a general background in their areas of interest (physics, geology, biology, mathemat-

ics, and so on). The ability to specialize in a particular subject is found at the graduate level.

To enhance your employability, many professionals suggest that students take a few basic courses in statistics, computers, and data management. In addition, students should continue to build and strengthen their reading, writing, and communication skills.

MASTER'S AND DOCTORAL PROGRAMS

Traditionally, the master's and doctoral degree programs are necessary steps toward becoming a research scientist. The master's program is usually one to two years long in a specialized area of study. Applicants for graduate school must submit their test scores from the Graduate Review Exam (GRE), a standardized graduate entrance exam. For more information, check out the following website: GRE, http://www.gre.org.

Upon completion of their master's program, students enter a doctoral program which generally takes between five to eight years to complete. Doctoral students complete advanced classroom studies and lab research training. They are also required to write a dissertation that involves original research.

To find resources on the Internet related to the world of doctoral students in science, mathematics, and engineering, check out PhDs.org (by Geoff Davis) at http://www.phds.org.

POSTDOCTORAL TRAINING

Many Ph.D. graduates obtain postdoctoral positions for further research, training, and development of scientific skills in their field of interest. They may work in academic, government, industrial, nonprofit, or nongovernmental settings.

Postdoctoral posts are usually one to three years long, and recipients receive either a fellowship or a salary. Many Ph.D.s work in several successive postdoctoral positions before obtaining full-time employment.

To learn more about postdoctoral training positions, check out the following websites:

- The Postdoc Network (Science's Next Wave), http://nextwave.sciencemag.org/pdn
- National Postdoc Association, http://www.nationalpostdoc.org

• Fellowship and Postdoc Opportunities at the National Academies, http://www.nas.edu/opportunities

SCIENCE MASTER'S PROGRAMS

The science master's program is a professional master's of science degree program in science or mathematics, which is offered by many colleges and universities in the United States. It is an alternative option to earning a doctoral degree for individuals who are interested in pursuing careers in industrial settings in such fields as insurance, research management, technology transfer, and consulting.

The science master's program is generally two years long and based in emerging or interdisciplinary fields such as bioinformatics, biotechnology, industrial mathematics, computational science, geographical information systems, industrial microbiology, and environmental sciences.

For further information about the science master's program, talk with your college adviser. You can also find information at the following website: ScienceMasters.com, http://www.sciencemasters.com.

TRAINING FOR CLINICAL RESEARCHERS

To conduct medical (or clinical) research, medical training is usually required. Physician-Scientists, or medical scientists, obtain a medical degree or doctor of osteopathy degree. Many of them obtain a doctoral degree as well.

A bachelor's degree in premedicine or a scientific discipline is the minimum requirement needed to enter medical school. (Many medical schools also accept applicants with other majors if they have met other qualifying requirements.) You will need to take the Medical College Admissions Test before you can apply for medical schools. On the Internet, you can learn more about this test at the Association of American Medical Colleges website. Go to http://www.aamc.org/students/mcat/start.htm.

Medical school is a four-year program. During the first two years, students study anatomy, physiology, pathology, pharmacology and other sciences basic to medicine. They are also introduced to the fundamentals of health care and the examination of patients. Medical students gain practical experience working with patients in office, clinic, and hospital settings in the different medical disciplines during the last two years of medical school. After graduation from medical school, they then complete at least three years in graduate medical education programs (more commonly known as residency programs), where they obtain training in their chosen medical specialty, such as internal medicine or surgery. If they wish to specialize in a subspecialty, such as cardiovascular disease or medical oncology in internal medicine, they complete another one to three more years of training.

Educational training for medical students who also obtain a doctoral degree usually takes between seven to nine years to complete. These students are part of dual degree (M.D./Ph.D.) programs, which are offered at many medical schools. Students initially complete the first two years of medical school. During the next three to five (or more years), they do their graduate work in their chosen fields. After they have completed their dissertations, they then finish the last two years of medical school and complete training in their medical specialties.

For information about medical schools, contact the Association of American Medical Colleges by writing to 2450 N Street, NW, Washington, D.C. 20037; or calling (202) 828-0400; or faxing inquiries to (202) 828-1125; or visiting its website at http://www.aamc.org.

CONTINUING EDUCATION

Throughout their careers, most individuals continue their education to keep up with developments in their fields and to learn new skills. Informally, they read professional books and journals as well as network with colleagues and participate in professional meetings and conferences. They may also enroll in formal training and continuing education programs offered by professional societies, trade associations, colleges, and universities.

Some professionals may need to satisfy continuing education requirements in order to renew professional licensure or certification.

PAYING FOR YOUR EDUCATION

Scholarships, fellowships, grants, and loans are available to help students pay for their college education, from their undergraduate years up through their postdoctoral training. In addition, internship and work-study programs are available, which also give students the opportunity to gain practical work experience in actual work settings. These financial aid programs are sponsored by government agencies, professional societies, trade associations, research institutes, foundations, businesses, and other organizations.

For further information, high school students might consult their high school guidance counselor about state, local, and other scholarships. They might also ask school or public librarians about directories and guides to scholarships, fellowships, grants, and loans. College students should contact their financial aid offices as well as college career centers for information about scholarships, internships, and so on.

APPENDIX II
EDUCATION AND TRAINING RESOURCES

In this appendix, you will learn about Internet sources for education and training programs for some of the occupations that you learned about in this book. To learn about programs for other occupations not listed in this appendix, talk with school or career counselors as well as professionals in the field. You can also consult college directories produced by Peterson's or other publishers, which may be found in your school or public library.

Note: All website addresses were current at the time this book was being written. If a URL no longer works, enter the title of the webpage or the name of the organization or individual to find the new address.

GENERAL RESOURCES
The following websites provide links to various academic programs at the different colleges and universities in the United States:

- The Princeton Review, http://www.princetonreview.com
- Web U.S. Higher Education, a listing of two-year and four-year colleges (maintained by the University of Texas at Austin), http://www.utexas.edu/world/univ
- Peterson's Graduate Schools and Programs, http://iiswinprd01.petersons.com/GradChannel
- GradSchools.com, http://www.gradschools.com

AGRICULTURAL ENGINEERING
The American Society of Agricultural Engineers provides a listing of academic programs in agricultural, food, and biological engineering at http://www.asae.org/membership/students/intlacademic.html.

ASTRONOMY
Dr. Tom Arny (Department of Astronomy, University of Massachusetts) provides a listing of astronomy programs on the following webpages:

- undergraduate programs—http://www.astro.umass.edu/~arny/astro_ugprogs.html
- graduate programs—http://www.astro.umass.edu/~arny/astro_gradprogs.html

BIOCHEMISTRY
The American Society for Biochemistry and Molecular Biology provides a listing of academic departments in molecular biology. To access this list, go to http://www.asbmb.org, and click on the Education link. Then click on the link for List of Schools.

BIOINFORMATICS
The International Society for Computational Biology provides a listing of degree programs in bioinformatics at http://www.iscb.org/univ.shtml.

BIOMEDICAL ENGINEERING
The following organizations provide listings of biomedical engineering programs:

- Whitaker Foundation, http://summit.whitaker.org/cgi-bin/lookup.cgi
- American Society of Biomechanics, http://www.asb-biomech.org/gradinfo/index.html

BIOPHYSICS
The American Physical Society's Division of Biological Physics provides a listing of biophysics programs at http://www.aps.org/DBP/graduate.html.

CHEMICAL ENGINEERING
The American Institute of Chemical Engineers posts a listing of chemical engineering programs at http://www.aiche.org/education/abet.htm.

CHEMISTRY
The American Chemical Society provides a database of chemistry-based master's degree programs at http://center.acs.org/applications/masters_survey/browse.cfm.

CLIMATOLOGY
The Association of American Geographer's Climate Specialty Group provides a listing of graduate climatology programs at http://www.geog.ku.edu/AAG/Csg/csghome.htm.

COMPUTER SCIENCE (OR COMPUTING SCIENCE)

Here are two websites where you can learn about some academic programs in computing science:

- The Accreditation Board for Engineering & Technology (ABET) provides a listing for computing science programs accredited by ABET at http://www.abet.org/cac1.html
- The Department of Computer Science and Electrical Engineering at the University of Maryland, Baltimore County provides a listing of graduate programs in computing programs at http://www.cs.umbc.edu/csgradinfo.html

EARTH SCIENCES (OR GEOSCIENCES)

Listings of various academic programs in the earth sciences can be found at the following websites:

- American Geophysical Union, http://agu.org/sci_soc/phd_urls.html
- Geoscience Departments WWW Directory–U.S. and Canada (maintained by Timothy Heaton, University of South Dakota), http://www.usd.edu/esci/geodepts.html

ENGINEERING

For a listing of engineering programs accredited by the Accreditation Board for Engineering & Technology, go to its webpage at http://www.abet.org/eac1.html.

ENTOMOLOGY

A listing of academic programs in entomology can be found at these websites:

- Entomology Departments around the World (maintained by Jason Bishop, Colorado State University), http://www.colostate.edu/Depts/Entomology/colleges.html
- University Entomology Departments in the United States (maintained by Jun Fan, Virginia Tech), http://atum.isis.vt.edu/~fanjun/text/Link_dept.html

ENVIRONMENTAL SCIENCE

The following organizations provide listings of environmental science, environmental engineering, and related environmental programs at their websites:

- EnviroEducation.com: The Environmental Education Directory, http://www.enviroeducation.com
- Air and Waste Management Association, http://www.awma.org/resources/education

EPIDEMIOLOGY

A listing of epidemiology programs can be found at the following website: The World-Wide Virtual Library: Epidemiology (maintained by Department of Epidemiology and Biostatistics, University of California, San Francisco), http://www.epibiostat.ucsf.edu/epidem/epidem.html.

FOOD SCIENCE

The Institute of Food Technologists provides a listing of undergraduate and graduate programs in food science at http://www.ift.org/education.

FORENSIC ANTHROPOLOGY

For listings of some programs in forensic anthropology, go to the following websites:

- American Board of Forensic Anthropology, http://www.csuchico.edu/anth/ABFA
- Graduate Education in Forensic Anthropology (Health Science Library, University of Utah), http://medlib.med.utah.edu/kw/osteo/resources/resources.html

For a listing of graduate programs in physical anthropology, visit the American Association of Physical Anthropology at http://physanth.org/gradprogs.

FORENSIC PSYCHIATRY

The American Academy of Psychiatry and the Law provides a listing of forensic psychiatry training programs at http://www.emory.edu/AAPL/training.htm.

FORENSIC SCIENCE

The American Academy of Forensic Sciences provides a listing of undergraduate and graduate programs in forensic science at http://www.aafs.org/Education/schools1.htm.

FOREST SCIENCE

The Society of American Foresters provides a listing of bachelor's and advanced programs in forest science at http://www.safnet.org/educate/edguide.htm.

GENETICS

The American Society of Human Genetics provides a listing of graduate and postgraduate training programs in human genetics at http://www.faseb.org/genetics/ashg/pubs/tpguide/intro.shtml.

HORTICULTURE
The American Society for Horticultural Science provides a listing of academic horticulture programs at http://www.ashs.org/hortprograms.html.

MEDICAL PHYSICS
The American Association of Physicists in Medicine provides a listing of medical physics programs at http://www.aapm.org/educ.

MEDICAL SCIENCE
To learn about the Medical Scientist Training Program sponsored by the National Institutes of Health, a federal agency, go to the following webpage: http://www.nigms.nih.gov/funding/mstp.html.

MEDICINE
For listings of medical programs, visit these websites:

- Association of American Medical Colleges, http://www.aamc.org/meded/medschls/start.htm
- The Princeton Review, http://www.princetonreview.com/medical/default.asp

For listings of graduate medical education programs (or residency programs) and sponsoring institutions, go to the following webpage at the Accreditation Council for Graduate Medical Education website at http://www.acgme.org/adspublic.

METEOROLOGY (OR ATMOSPHERIC SCIENCES)
The National Weather Association provides a listing of academic programs in meteorology or atmospheric science at http://www.nwas.org/links/universities.html.

MOLECULAR BIOLOGY
The American Society for Biochemistry and Molecular Biology provides a listing of academic departments in molecular biology. To access this list, go to http://www.asbmb.org, and click on the Education link. Then click on the link for List of Schools.

OCEANOGRAPHY (OR AQUATIC SCIENCES)
The American Society of Limnology and Oceanography provides a listing of graduate programs in limnology or oceanography at http://www.aslo.org/links/academic.html.

OPERATIONS RESEARCH AND MANAGEMENT SCIENCES
The Institute for Operations Research and the Management Sciences provides a listing of educational programs in operations research and the management sciences at http://www.informs.org/Edu/Programs.

PATHOLOGY
For listings of pathology programs visit the following websites:

- Intersociety Committee on Pathology, http://www.pathologytraining.org
- College of American Pathologists: go to http://www.cap.org/superlinks, and then click on the Pathology Departments link.

PHARMACOLOGY
American Society for Pharmacology and Experimental Therapeutics provides a listing of undergraduate and graduate programs in pharmacology at http://www.aspet.org/public/training_programs/training_programs.html.

RANGE MANAGEMENT
The Society for Range Management provides a list of professional programs in range management education at its website. To access the list, first go to http://www.rangelands.org, then click on the Programs & Services link.

REGULATORY AFFAIRS
The Regulatory Affairs Professionals Society provides a list of some graduate programs in regulatory affairs at http://www.raps.org/careers/grad.cfm.

SCIENCE AND TECHNOLOGY POLICY
For a list of U.S. graduate programs, check out Guide to Graduate Education in Science, Engineering and Public Policy by the American Association for the Advancement of Science. To access this guide on the Internet, go to http://www.aaas.org/spp/sepp.

SCIENCE COMMUNICATION
A listing of science communication programs and courses can be found at:

- School of Journalism and Mass Communication, University of Wisconsin, Madison, http://murrow.journalism.wisc.edu/dsc

- The Society of Environmental Journalists, http://www.sej. org/careers/index.htm

SPACE PHYSICS
The American Geophysical Union's Space Physics and Aeronomy Section provides a listing of colleges and universities offering advanced degrees in space physics fields at http://spaweb.space.swri.edu/universities.html.

STATISTICS
The American Statistical Association provides a list of colleges and universities in the United States and Canada that offer degree programs in statistics at http://www.amstat.org/education/SODS.

TECHNICAL WRITING (OR TECHNICAL COMMUNICATION)
The Society for Technical Communication has a database of academic programs in technical communication at http://www.stc.org/academic.asp.

TOXICOLOGY
The Society of Toxicology provides a listing of academic programs in toxicology at http://www.toxicology.org/publicoutreach/careerresources/careerprograms.html.

APPENDIX III
PROFESSIONAL ASSOCIATIONS

In this appendix, you will find contact information and website addresses for the professional organizations that are mentioned in this book. Most of these organizations offer information about careers, job opportunities, training programs, educational resources, professional certification programs, and so on.

Many of these organizations have a main office (or headquarters) with branch offices throughout the United States. Contact an organization's headquarters or contact person to find out if there is a branch in your area. Other local, state, regional, and international professional associations also represent many of the professions discussed in this book. To learn about other relevant professional societies and unions, contact local professionals.

Note: All contact information and website addresses were current when the book was being written. If you come across a URL that is no longer valid, you may be able to find an organization's new website by entering its name in a search engine.

BIOLOGICAL SCIENCES

American Arachnological Society
http://www.americanarachnology.org

American Association for Higher Education
1 Dupont Circle
Suite 360
Washington, DC 20036
Phone: (202) 293-6440
Fax: (202) 293-0073
http://www.aahe.org

American Association for the Advancement of Science
1200 New York Avenue, NW
Washington, DC 20005
Phone: (202) 326-6400
http://www.aaas.org

American Fisheries Society
5410 Grosvenor Lane
Bethesda, MD 20814
Phone: (301) 897-8616
Fax: (301) 897-8096
http://www.fisheries.org

American Institute of Biological Sciences
1444 I Street, NW
Suite 200
Washington, DC 20005
Phone: (202) 628-1500
Fax: (202) 628-1509
http://www.aibs.org

American Mosquito Control Association
143-A Wayside Road
Tinton Falls, NJ 07724
Mailing Address:
P.O. Box 234
Eatontown, NJ 07724
Phone: (732) 932-0667
Fax: (732) 542-3267
http://www.mosquito.org

American Physiological Society
9650 Rockville Pike
Bethesda, MD 20814
Phone: (301) 634-7164
http://www.the-aps.org

American Society for Biochemistry and Molecular Biology
9650 Rockville Pike
Bethesda, MD 20814
Phone: (301) 634-7145
Fax: (301) 634-7126
http://www.asbmb.org

American Society for Horticultural Science
113 South West Street
Suite 200
Alexandria, VA 22314
Phone: (703) 836-4606
Fax: (703) 836-2024
http://www.ashs.org

American Society for Microbiology
1752 N Street, NW
Washington, DC 20036
Phone: (202) 737-3600
http://www.asmusa.org

American Society for Virology
E-mail: ASV@mcw.edu
http://www.mcw.edu/asv

American Society of Agronomy
677 South Segoe Road
Madison, WI 53711
Phone: (608) 273-8080
Fax: (608) 273-2021
http://www.agronomy.org

American Society of Animal Science
1111 North Dunlap Avenue
Savoy, IL 61874
Phone: (217) 356-9050
Fax: (217) 398-4119
http://www.asas.org

American Society of Human Genetics
9650 Rockville Pike
Bethesda, MD 20814
Phone: (800) HUM-GENE or (301) 571-1825
http://www.faseb.org/genetics/ashg/ashgmenu.htm

American Society of Limnology and Oceanography
5400 Bosque Boulevard
Suite 680
Waco, TX 76710
Phone: (800) 929-2756 or (254) 399-9635
Fax: (254) 776-3767
http://www.aslo.org

American Society of Plant Biologists
15501 Monona Drive
Rockville, MD 20855
Phone: (301) 251-0560
Fax: (301) 279-2996
http://www.aspb.org

Animal Behavior Society
Animal Behavior Society Central Office
Indiana University
2611 East 10th Street, #170
Bloomington, IN 47408
Phone: (812) 856-5541
Fax: (812) 856-5542
http://www.animalbehavior.org

**Association for Computing
  Machinery**
1515 Broadway, 17th Floor
New York, NY 10036
Phone: (800) 342-6626 or (212)
  626-0500
http://www.acm.org

**Association of Applied Insect
  Ecologists**
P.O. Box 10880
Napa, CA 94581
Phone/Fax: (707) 265-9349
http://aaie.net

**Association of Professors of Human
  or Medical Genetics**
E-mail: glfeldman@genetics.wayne.edu.
http://www.faseb.org/genetics/aphmg/
  aphmg1.htm

Botanical Society of America
1735 Neil Avenue
Columbus, OH 43210
Phone: (614) 292-3519
Fax: (614) 247-6444
http://www.botany.org

Coleopterists Society
Contact: Terry Seeno, Treasurer
3294 Meadowview Road
Sacramento, CA 95832
E-mail: treasurer@coleopsoc.org
http://www.coleopsoc.org

Ecological Society of America
1707 H Street, NW
Suite 400
Washington, DC 20006
Phone: (202) 833-8773
Fax: (202) 833-8775
http://www.esa.org

Entomological Society of America
9301 Annapolis Road
Lanham, MD 20706
Phone: (301) 731-4535
Fax: (301) 731-4538
http://www.entsoc.org

Genetics Society of America
Contact: Elaine Strass, Executive Director
E-mail: estrass@genetics-gsa.org
http://www.genetics-gsa.org

**International Society for Computational
  Biology**
c/o the San Diego Supercomputer Center
UC San Diego
9500 Gilman Drive
La Jolla, CA 92093
Phone: (858) 822-0852
Fax: (858) 822-5407
http://www.iscb.org

North American Benthological Society
Contact: Tracy Candelaria
E-mail: tcandelaria@allenpress.com
http://www.benthos.org

Society for Conservation Biology
4245 N. Fairfax Drive
Arlington, VA 22203
Phone: (703) 276-2384
Fax: (703) 995-4633
http://conbio.net

Society for Industrial Microbiology
3929 Old Lee Highway
Suite 92A
Fairfax, VA 22030
Phone: (703) 691-3357
Fax: (703) 691-7991
http://www.simhq.org

**Society for Integrative and
  Comparative Biology**
1313 Dolley Madison Boulevard
Suite 402
McLean, VA 22101
Phone: (800) 955-1236 or (703) 790-1745
Fax: (703) 790-2672
http://www.sicb.org

Society for Marine Mammalogy
http://www.marinemammalogy.org

Society of General Physiologists
P.O. Box 257
Woods Hole, MA 02543
Phone: (508) 540-6719
Fax: (508) 540-0155
http://www.emory.edu/CELLBIO/SGP/
  sgp.htm

Society of Wetland Scientists
1313 Dolley Madison Boulevard
Suite 402
McLean, VA 22101
Phone: (703) 790-1745
Fax: (703) 790-2672
http://www.sws.org

CHEMISTRY

**American Association for Clinical
  Chemistry**
2101 L Street, NW
Suite 202
Washington, DC 20037
Phone: (800) 892-1400 or (202)
  857-0717
Fax: (202) 887-5093
http://www.aacc.org

**American Association for Higher
  Education**
1 Dupont Circle
Suite 360
Washington, DC 20036
Phone: (202) 293-6440
Fax: (202) 293-0073
http://www.aahe.org

**American Association for the
  Advancement of Science**
1200 New York Avenue, NW
Washington, DC 20005
Phone: (202) 326-6400
http://www.aaas.org

**American Association of Cereal
  Chemists**
3340 Pilot Knob Road
St. Paul, MN 55121
Phone: (651) 454-7250
Fax: (651) 454-0766
http://www.aaccnet.org

**American Association of University
  Professors**
1012 Fourteenth Street, NW
Suite 500
Washington, DC 20005
Phone: (202) 737-5900
Fax: (202) 737-5526
http://www.aaup.org

American Chemical Society
1155 Sixteenth Street, NW
Washington, DC 20036
Phone: (800) 227-5558
Fax: (202) 872-4615
http://www.chemistry.org/portal/Chemistry

American College of Toxicology
9650 Rockville Pike
Bethesda, MD 20814
Phone: (301) 571-1840
Fax: (301) 571-1852
http://www.actox.org

American Institute of Biological Sciences
1444 I Street, NW
Suite 200
Washington, DC 20005
Phone: (202) 628-1500
Fax: (202) 628-1509
http://www.aibs.org

American Institute of Chemical Engineers
3 Park Avenue
New York, NY 10016
Phone: (212) 591-7338
Fax: (212) 591-8897
http://www.aiche.org

American Institute of Chemists
1620 I Street, NW
Suite 615
Washington, DC 20006
Phone: (202) 833-1838
Fax: (202) 463-8498
http://www.theaic.org

American Society for Biochemistry and Molecular Biology
9650 Rockville Pike
Bethesda, MD 20814
Phone: (301) 634-7145
Fax: (301) 634-7126
http://www.asbmb.org

Association for Government Toxicologists
http://www.agovtox.org

Association of Formulation Chemists
PO Box 15235
Hattiesburg, MS 39404
Phone: (601) 268-1629
Fax: (601) 296-1352
http://www.afc-us.org

Geochemical Society
Department of Earth and Planetary Sciences
Washington University
1 Brookings Drive
St. Louis, MO 63130
Phone: (314) 935-4131
Fax: (314) 935-4121
http://gs.wustl.edu

National Association of Scholars
221 Witherspoon Street, Second Floor
Princeton, NJ 08542
Phone: (609) 683-7878
Fax: (609) 683-0316
http://www.nas.org

Society of Cosmetic Chemists
120 Wall Street
Suite 2400
New York, NY 10005
Phone: (212) 668-1500
Fax: (212) 668-1504
http://www.scconline.org

Society of Environmental Toxicology and Chemistry
1010 North 12th Avenue
Pensacola, FL 32501
Phone: (850) 469-1500
Fax: (850) 469-9778
http://www.setac.org

Society of Forensic Toxicologists
P.O. Box 5543
Mesa, AZ 85211
Phone/Fax: (480) 839-9106
http://www.soft-tox.org

Society of Toxicology
1767 Business Center Drive
Suite 302
Reston, VA 20190
Phone: (703) 438-3115
Fax: (703) 438-3113
http://www.toxicology.org

Society of Women Engineers
230 E Ohio Street
Suite 400
Chicago, IL 60611
Phone: (312) 596-5223
Fax: (312) 644-8557
http://www.swe.org

PHYSICS AND ASTRONOMY

Acoustical Society of America
Suite 1NO1
2 Huntington Quadrangle
Melville, NY 11747
Phone: (516) 576-2360
Fax: (516) 576-2377
http://asa.aip.org

American Association for Higher Education
1 Dupont Circle
Suite 360
Washington, DC 20036
Phone: (202) 293-6440
Fax: (202) 293-0073
http://www.aahe.org

American Association for the Advancement of Science
1200 New York Avenue, NW
Washington, DC 20005
Phone: (202) 326-6400
http://www.aaas.org

American Association of Physicists in Medicine
1 Physics Ellipse
College Park, MD 20740
Phone: (301) 209-3350
Fax: (301) 209-0862
http://www.aapm.org

American Association of University Professors
1012 Fourteenth Street, NW
Suite 500
Washington, DC 20005
Phone: (202) 737-5900
Fax: (202) 737-5526
http://www.aaup.org

American Astronomical Society
2000 Florida Avenue, NW
Suite 400
Washington, DC 20009
Phone: (202) 328-2010
Fax: (202) 234-2560
http://www.aas.org

American Geophysical Union
2000 Florida Avenue, NW
Washington, DC 20009
Phone: (800) 966-2481 or (202) 462-6900
Fax: (202) 328-0566
http://www.agu.org

American Geophysical Union Space Physics and Aeronomy Section
2000 Florida Avenue, NW
Washington, DC 20009
http://spaweb.space.swri.edu/index.html

American Institute of Physics
1 Physics Ellipse
College Park, MD 20740
Phone: (301) 209-3100
Fax: (301) 209-0843
http://www.aip.org

American Nuclear Society
555 North Kensington Avenue
La Grange Park, IL 60526
Phone: (708) 352-6611
Fax: (708) 352-0499
http://www.ans.org

American Physical Society
1 Physics Ellipse
College Park, MD 20740
Phone: (301) 209-3200
Fax: (301) 209-0865
http://www.aps.org

American Physical Society Division of Biological Physics
1 Physics Ellipse
College Park, MD 20740
http://www.aps.org/DBP

American Physical Society Division of Nuclear Physics
1 Physics Ellipse
College Park, MD 20740
http://dnp.nscl.msu.edu

Biophysical Society
9650 Rockville Pike
Bethesda, MD 20814
Phone: (301) 530-7114
Fax: (301) 530-7133
http://www.biophysics.org

Institute for Nuclear Theory
University of Washington
Physics/Astronomy Building
Box 351550
Seattle, WA 98195
Phone: (206) 685-3360
Fax: (206) 685-3730
http://int.phys.washington.edu

International Association of Geomagnetism and Aeronomy
http://www.ngdc.noaa.gov/IAGA

International Union for Pure and Applied BioPhysics
http://www.iupab.org

National Association of Scholars
221 Witherspoon Street, Second Floor
Princeton, NJ 08542
Phone: (609) 683-7878
Fax: (609) 683-0316
http://www.nas.org

EARTH SCIENCES

Air Weather Association
http://www.airweaassn.org

American Association for Higher Education
1 Dupont Circle
Suite 360
Washington, DC 20036
Phone: (202) 293-6440
Fax: (202) 293-0073
http://www.aahe.org

American Association of Petroleum Geologists
1444 South Boulder Avenue
Tulsa, OK 74114
Mailing Address:
P. O. Box 979
Tulsa, OK 74101
Phone: (800) 364-2274 or (918) 584-2555
Fax: (918) 560-2665
http://www.aapg.org

American Association of Stratigraphic Palynologists
http://www.palynology.org

American Association of University Professors
1012 Fourteenth Street, NW
Suite 500
Washington, DC 20005
Phone: (202) 737-5900
Fax: (202) 737-5526
http://www.aaup.org

American Congress on Surveying and Mapping
6 Montgomery Village Avenue
Suite 403
Gaithersburg, MD 20879
Phone: (240) 632-9716
Fax: (240) 632-1321
http://www.acsm.net

American Geographical Society
120 Wall Street
Suite 100
New York, NY 10005
Phone: (212) 422-5456
Fax: (212) 422-5480
http://www.amergeog.org

American Geological Institute
4220 King Street
Alexandria, VA 22302
Phone: (703) 379-2480
Fax: (703) 379-7563
http://www.agiweb.org

American Geophysical Union
2000 Florida Avenue, NW
Washington, DC 20009
Phone: (800) 966-2481 or (202) 462-6900
Fax: (202) 328-0566
http://www.agu.org

American Institute of Hydrology
2499 Rice Street
Suite 135
St. Paul, MN 55113
Phone: (651) 484-8169
Fax: (651) 484-8357
http://www.aihydro.org

American Institute of Professional Geologists
8703 Yates Drive
Suite 200
Westminster, CO 80031
Phone: (303) 412-6205
Fax: (303) 412-6219
http://www.aipg.org

American Meteorological Society
45 Beacon Street
Boston, MA 02108
Phone: (617) 227-2425
Fax: (617) 742-8718
http://www.ametsoc.org/AMS

American Society of Civil Engineers
1801 Alexander Bell Drive
Reston, VA 20191
Phone: (800) 548-2723 or (703) 295-6300
Fax: (703) 295-6222
http://www.asce.org

American Society of Limnology and Oceanography
5400 Bosque Boulevard
Suite 680
Waco, TX 76710
Phone: (800) 929-2756 or (254) 399-9635
Fax: (254) 776-3767
http://aslo.org

American Society of Mechanical Engineers
3 Park Avenue
New York, NY 10016
Phone: (800) 843-2763 or (973) 882-1167
http://www.asme.org

American Water Resources Association
4 West Federal Street
P.O. Box 1626
Middleburg, VA 20118
Phone: (540) 687-8390
Fax: (540) 687-8395
http://www.awra.org

Association for Women Geoscientists
P.O. Box 30645
Lincoln, NE 68503-0645
http://www.awg.org

Association of American Geographers
1710 16th Street, NW
Washington, DC 20009
Phone: (202) 234-1450
Fax: (202) 234-2744
http://www.aag.org

Association of American Geographers Cartography Specialty Group
Contact: Rex Cammack
Department of Geography, Geology, and Planning
Southwest Missouri State University
Springfield, MO 65804
E-mail: rexcammack@smsu.edu
http://www.csun.edu/~hfgeg003/csg

Association of American Geographers Climate Specialty Group
Contact: Brent Yarnal
Department of Geography
302 Walker Building
Pennsylvania State University
University Park, PA 16802
E-mail: alibar@essc.psu.edu
http://www.geog.ku.edu/AAG/Csg/csghome.htm

Association of Engineering Geologists
720 S. Colorado Boulevard
Suite 960-S
Denver, CO 80246
Phone: (303) 757-2926
Fax: (303) 757-2969
http://www.aegweb.org

Environmental and Engineering Geophysical Society
720 S. Colorado Boulevard
Suite 960-South Tower
Denver, CO 80246
Phone: (303) 756-3143
Fax: (303) 691-9490
http://www.eegs.org

Cartography and Geographic Information Society
6 Montgomery Village Avenue
Suite 403
Gaithersburg, MD 20879
Phone: (240) 632-9716
Fax: (301) 632-1321
http://www.acsm.net/cagis/index.html

Geological Society of America
3300 Penrose Place
Boulder, CO 80301
Mailing Address:
P.O. Box 9140
Boulder, CO 80301
Phone: (303) 447-2020
Fax: (303) 357-1070
http://www.geosociety.org

Institute of Electrical and Electronic Engineers
445 Hoes Lane
Piscataway, NJ 08854
Phone: (732) 981-0060
Fax: (732) 981-1721
http://www.ieee.org

International Association of Broadcast Meteorologists
http://www.iabm.org

International Association of Seismology and Physics of the Earth's Interior
Contact: Dr. E. R. Engdahl, IASPEI Secretary-General
Department of Physics
University of Colorado
Campus Box 390
Boulder, CO 80309
E-mail: engdahl@lemond.colorado.edu
http://www.iaspei.org

International Association of Volcanology and Chemistry of the Earth's Interior
http://www.iavcei.org

Marine Technology Society
5565 Sterrett Place
Suite 108
Columbia, MD 21044
Phone: (410) 884-5330
Fax: (410) 884-9060
http://www.mtsociety.org

National Association of Black Geologists and Geophysicists
4212 San Felipe
Suite 420
Houston, TX 77027
http://nabgg.com

National Association of Scholars
221 Witherspoon Street, Second Floor
Princeton, NJ 08542
Phone: (609) 683-7878
Fax: (609) 683-0316
http://www.nas.org

National Council of Industrial Meteorologists
Contact: Dr. George E. McVehil
44 Inverness Drive East, Building C
Englewood, CO 80112
E-mail: gmcvhel@mcvehil-monnett.com
http://www.wxresearch.com/ncim

National Groundwater Association
601 Dempsey Road
Westerville, OH 43081
Phone: (800) 551-7379 or (614) 898-7791
Fax: (614) 898-7786
http://www.ngwa.org

National Weather Association
1697 Capri Way
Charlottesville, VA 22911
Phone/Fax: (434) 296-9966
http://www.nwas.org

Oceanic Engineering Society
Contact: Jim Collins, OES Membership Development Chair
University of Victoria
Dept. of Electrical and Computer Engineering
P.O. Box 3055
Victoria, B.C. V8W 3P6
Canada
E-mail: j.s.collins@ieee.org
http://www.oceanicengineering.org

Oceanography Society
P.O. Box 1931
Rockville, MD 20849
Phone: (301) 251-7708
Fax: (301) 251-7709
http://www.tos.org

Paleontological Society
Contact: Mr. Dean Frazier, Business Manager
E-mail: afrazier@allenpress.com
http://www.paleosoc.org

Seismological Society of America
201 Plaza Professional Building
El Cerrito, CA 94530
Phone: (510) 525-5474
Fax: (510) 525-7204
http://www.seismosoc.org

Society of Exploration Geophysicists
8801 South Yale
Tulsa, OK 74137
Mailing Address:
P.O. Box 702740
Tulsa, OK 74170

Phone: (918) 497-5500
Fax: (918) 497-5557
http://www.seg.org

Society of Naval Architects and Marine Engineers
601 Pavonia Avenue
Jersey City, NJ 07306
Phone: (800) 798-2188 or (201) 798-4800
Fax: (201) 798-4975
http://www.sname.org

Society of Vertebrate Paleontology
60 Revere Drive
Suite 500
Northbrook, IL 60062
Phone: (847) 480-9095
Fax: (847) 480-9282
http://www.vertpaleo.org

MATHEMATICS

American Academy of Actuaries
1100 Seventeenth Street, NW, Seventh Floor
Washington, DC 20036
Phone: (202) 223-8196
Fax: (202) 872-1948
http://www.actuary.org

American Association of University Professors
1012 Fourteenth Street, NW
Suite 500
Washington, DC 20005
Phone: (202) 737-5900
Fax (202) 737-5526
http://www.aaup.org

American Mathematical Society
201 Charles Street
Providence, RI 02904
Phone: (800) 321-4AMS or (401) 455-4000
Fax: (401) 331-3842
http://www.ams.org

American Society of Pension Actuaries
4245 North Fairfax Drive
Suite 750
Arlington, VA 22203
Phone: (703) 516-9300
Fax: (703) 516-9308
http://www.aspa.org

American Statistical Association
1429 Duke Street
Alexandria, VA 22314
Phone: (888) 231-3473 or (703) 684-1221

Fax: (703) 684-2037
http://www.amstat.org

Association for Women in Mathematics
4114 Computer and Space Sciences Building
University of Maryland
College Park, MD 20742
Phone: (301) 405-7892
Fax: (301) 314-9363
http://www.awm-math.org

Casualty Actuarial Society
1100 North Glebe Road
Suite 600
Arlington, VA 22201
Phone: (703) 276-3100
Fax: (703) 276-3108
http://www.casact.org

Caucus for Women in Statistics
http://depts.washington.edu/wcaucus

Conference of Consulting Actuaries
1110 W. Lake Cook Road
Suite 235
Buffalo Grove, IL 60089
Phone: (847) 419-9090
Fax: (847) 419-9091
http://www.ccactuaries.org

Institute for Operations Research and the Management Sciences
901 Elkridge Landing Road
Suite 400
Linthicum, MD 21090
Phone: (800) 4IN-FORMS
Fax: (410) 684-2963
http://www.informs.org

Institute of Mathematical Statistics
Business Office
P.O. Box 22718
Beachwood, OH 44122
Phone: (216) 295-2340
Fax: (216) 921-6703
http://www.imstat.org

Mathematical Association of America
1529 Eighteenth Street, NW
Washington, DC 20036
Phone: (800) 741-9415 or (202) 387-5200
Fax: (202) 265-2384
http://www.maa.org

National Association of Scholars
221 Witherspoon Street, Second Floor
Princeton, NJ 08542
Phone: (609) 683-7878

Fax: (609) 683-0316
http://www.nas.org

Society for Industrial and Applied Mathematics
3600 University City Science Center
Philadelphia, PA 19104
Phone: (800) 447-SIAM or (215) 382-9800
Fax: (215) 386-7999
http://www.siam.org

Society of Actuaries
475 North Martingale Road
Suite 800
Schaumberg, IL 60173
Phone: (847) 706-3500
Fax: (847) 706-3599
http://www.soa.org

COMPUTER SCIENCE

American Association for Artificial Intelligence
445 Burgess Drive
Menlo Park, CA 94025
Phone: (650) 328-3123
Fax: (650) 321-4457
http://www.aaai.org

American Association for Higher Education
1 Dupont Circle
Suite 360
Washington, DC 20036
Phone: (202) 293-6440
Fax: (202) 293-0073
http://www.aahe.org

American Society of Mechanical Engineers
3 Park Avenue
New York, NY 10016
Phone: (800) 843-2763 or (973) 882-1167
http://www.asme.org

Association for Computing Machinery
1515 Broadway, 17th Floor
New York, NY 10036
Phone: (800) 342-6626 or (212) 626-0500
http://www.acm.org

Association for Computing Machinery Special-Interest Group in Software Engineering
Contact: Ginger Ignatoff, ACM-SIGSOFT Program Director
Association for Computing Machinery
1515 Broadway, 17th Floor
New York, NY 10036

Phone: (212) 626-0613
Fax: (212) 302-5826
E-mail: ignatoff@acm.org
http://www.acm.org/sigsoft

Association for Computing Machinery Special-Interest Group for Artificial Intelligence
Contact: Alisa Rivkin, ACM-SIGART
    Program Director
Association for Computing Machinery
1515 Broadway, 17th Floor
New York, NY 10036
Phone: (212) 626-0607
Fax: (212) 302-5826
E-mail: rivkin@acm.org
http://www.acm.org/sigart

Association for Women in Computing
41 Sutter Street
Suite 1006
San Francisco, CA 94104
Phone: (415) 905-4663
http://www.awc-hq.org

Institute of Electrical and Electronic Engineers (IEEE) Computer Society
1730 Massachusetts Avenue, NW
Washington, DC 20036
Phone: (202) 371-0101
Fax: (202) 728-9614
http://www.computer.org

Institute of Electrical and Electronic Engineers Robotics and Automation Society
1730 Massachusetts Avenue, NW
Washington, DC 20036
Phone: (732) 562-3900
Fax: (732) 981-1769
http://www.ncsu.edu/IEEE-RAS

National Association of Scholars
221 Witherspoon Street, Second Floor
Princeton, NJ 08542
Phone: (609) 683-7878
Fax: (609) 683-0316
http://www.nas.org

National Society of Professional Engineers
420 King Street
Alexandria, VA 22314
Phone: (703) 684-2800
http://www.nspe.org

Technical Council on Software Engineering
(part of IEEE Computer Society)
1730 Massachusetts Avenue, NW
Washington DC 20036
Phone: (202) 371-0101
http://www.tcse.org

AGRICULTURAL SCIENCE AND FOOD SCIENCE

American Chemical Society
1155 Sixteenth Street, NW
Washington, DC 20036
Phone: (800) 227-5558
Fax: (202) 872-4615
ACS: http://www.chemistry.org/portal/
Chemistry

American Dairy Science Association
1111 North Dunlap Avenue
Savoy, IL 61874
Phone: (217) 356-5146
Fax: (217) 398-4119
http://www.adsa.org

American Meat Science Association
1111 North Dunlap Avenue
Savoy, IL 61874
Phone: (217) 356-5368
http://www.meatscience.org

American Society for Horticultural Science
113 South West Street
Suite 200
Alexandria, VA 22314
Phone: (703) 836-4606
Fax: (703) 836-2024
http://www.ashs.org

American Society of Agricultural Engineers
2950 Niles Road
St. Joseph, MI 49085
Phone: (269) 429-0300
Fax: (269) 429-3852
http://www.asae.org

American Society of Agricultural Engineers Professional Engineering Institute
2950 Niles Road
St. Joseph, MI 49085
Phone: (269) 429-0300
Fax: (269) 429-3852
http://www.asae.org/pei

American Society of Agronomy
677 South Segoe Road
Madison, WI 53711
Phone: (608) 273-8080
Fax: (608) 273-2021
http://www.agronomy.org

American Society of Animal Science
1111 North Dunlap Avenue
Savoy, IL 61874
Phone: (217) 356-9050
Fax: (217) 398-4119
http://www.asas.org

Association of Women Soil Scientists
http://AWSS.homestead.com

Botanical Society of America
1735 Neil Avenue
Columbus, OH 43210
Phone: (614) 292-3519
Fax: (614) 247-6444
http://www.botany.org

Crop Science Society of America
677 South Segoe Road
Madison, WI 53711
Phone: (608) 273-8086
Fax: (608) 273-2021
http://www.crops.org

Institute of Food Technologists
525 West Van Buren
Suite 1000
Chicago, IL 60607
Phone: (312)782-8424
Fax: (312) 782-8348
http://www.ift.org

National Society of Consulting Soil Scientists, Inc.
PMB 700
325 Pennsylvania Avenue, SE
Washington, DC 20003
Phone: (800) 535-7148
http://www.nscss.org

National Society of Professional Engineers
420 King Street
Alexandria, VA 22314
Phone: (703) 684-2800
http://www.nspe.org

Poultry Science Association
1111 North Dunlap Avenue
Savoy, IL 61874
Fax: (217) 398-4119
http://www.poultryscience.org

Society of Flavor Chemists
86 Watertower Plaza, #343
Leominster, MA 01453
Phone: (978) 840-8596
Fax: (978) 383-0580
http://www.flavorchemist.org

Soil Science Society of America
677 South Segoe Road
Madison, WI 53711
Phone: (608) 273-8095
Fax: (608) 273-2021
http://www.Soils.org

MEDICAL SCIENCE

**American Academy of Pediatrics—
    Epidemiology Section**
141 Northwest Point Boulevard
Elk Grove Village, IL 60007
Phone: (847) 434-4000
Fax: (847) 434-8000
http://www.aap.org/sections/epidemiology

**American Association for the
    Advancement of Science**
1200 New York Avenue, NW
Washington, DC 20005
Phone: (202) 326-6400
http://www.aaas.org

**American Association of
    Pharmaceutical Scientists**
2107 Wilson Boulevard
Suite 700
Arlington, VA 22201
Phone: (703) 243-2800
Fax: (703) 243-9650
http://www.aaps.org

**American Association of Physicists in
    Medicine**
1 Physics Ellipse
College Park, MD 20740
Phone: (301) 209-3350
Fax: (301) 209-0862
http://www.aapm.org

**American College of Clinical
    Engineering**
5200 Butler Pike
Plymouth Meeting, PA 19462
Phone: (610) 825-6067
http://www.accenet.org

**American College of Clinical
    Pharmacology**
Contact: Susan Ulrich, R.Ph.
E-mail: accp1ssu@aol.com
http://www.accp1.org

American College of Epidemiology
1500 Sunday Drive
Suite 102
Raleigh, NC 27607
Phone: (919) 861-5573
Fax: (919) 787-4916
http://www.acepidemiology.org

**American College of Medical
    Physics**
11250 Roger Bacon Drive
Suite 8
Reston, VA 20190
Phone: (703) 481-5001
Fax: (703) 435-4390
http://www.acmp.org

**American College of Preventative
    Medicine**
1307 New York Avenue, NW
Suite 200
Washington, DC 20005
Phone: (202) 466-2044
Fax: (202) 466-2662
http://www.acpm.org

American College of Radiology
1891 Preston White Drive
Reston, Virginia 20191
Phone: (800) 227-5463
Fax: (703) 620-6329
http://www.acr.org

**American Institute for Medical and
    Biological Engineering**
1901 Pennsylvania Avenue, NW
Suite 401
Washington, DC 20006
Phone: (202) 496-9660
Fax: (202) 466-8489
http://www.aimbe.org

**American Institute of Chemical
    Engineers**
3 Park Avenue
New York, NY 10016
Phone: (212) 591-7338
Fax: (212) 591-8897
http://www.aiche.org

American Medical Association
515 N. State Street
Chicago, IL 60610
Phone: (312) 464-5000
http://www.ama-assn.org

American Physical Society
1 Physics Ellipse
College Park, MD 20740

Phone: (301) 209-3200
Fax: (301) 209-0865
http://www.aps.org

**American Psychological Association—
    Division of Psychopharmacology
    and Substance Abuse**
750 First Street, NE
Washington, DC 20002
Phone: (800) 374-2721 or (202)
    336-5500
http://www.apa.org/divisions/div28

**American Public Health Association—
    Epidemiology Section**
800 I Street, NW
Washington, DC 20001
Phone: (202) 777-APHA
Fax: (202) 777-2534
http://www.human.cornell.edu/pam/apha/
    index.htm

**American Society for Clinical
    Pathology**
2100 West Harrison Street
Chicago, IL 60612
Phone: (312) 738-1336
http://www.ascp.org

**American Society for Clinical
    Pharmacology and Therapeutics**
528 N. Washington Street
Alexandria, VA 22314
Phone: (703) 836-6981
Fax: (703) 836-5223
http://www.ascpt.org

**American Society for Investigative
    Pathology**
9650 Rockville Pike
Bethesda, MD 20814
Phone: (301) 634-7130
Fax: (301) 634-7990
http://www.asip.org

**American Society for Pharmacology
    and Experimental Therapeutics**
9650 Rockville Pike
Bethesda, MD 20814
Phone: (301) 634-7060
Fax: (301) 634-7061
http://www.aspet.org

American Society of Biomechanics
Contact: Gary Heise, Communications
    Committee Chairperson
E-mail: gary.heise@unco.edu
http://asb-biomech.org

Association for Molecular Pathology
9650 Rockville Pike
Bethesda, MD 20814
Phone: (301) 634-7939
Fax: (301) 634-7990
http://www.ampweb.org

Association for Pathology Informatics
9650 Rockville Pike
Bethesda MD 20814
Phone: (301) 571-1880
http://www.pathologyinformatics.org

Association for Professionals in Infection Control and Epidemiology, Inc.
1275 K Street, NW
Suite 1000
Washington, DC 20005
Phone: (202) 789-1890
Fax: (202) 789-1899
http://www.apic.org

Biomedical Engineering Society
8401 Corporate Drive
Suite 225
Landover, MD 20785
Phone: (301) 459-1999
Fax: (301) 459-2444
http://www.bmes.org

Biophysical Society
9650 Rockville Pike
Bethesda, MD 20814
Phone: (301) 530-7114
Fax: (301) 530-7133
http://www.biophysics.org

College of American Pathologists
325 Waukegan Road
Northfield, IL 60093
Phone: (800) 323-4040 or (847) 832-7000
http://www.cap.org

Council of State and Territorial Epidemiologists
2872 Woodcock Boulevard
Suite 303
Atlanta, GA 30341
Phone: (770) 458-3811
Fax: (770) 458-8516
http://www.cste.org

Health Physics Society
1313 Dolley Madison Boulevard
Suite 402
McLean, VA 22101
Phone: (703) 790-1745
Fax: (703) 790-2672
http://hps.org

Institute of Electrical and Electronic Engineers—Engineering in Medicine and Biology Society
EMBS Executive Office
445 Hoes Lane
Piscataway, NJ 08855
Phone: (732) 981-3454
http://www.eng.unsw.edu.au/embs

National Society of Professional Engineers
420 King Street
Alexandria, VA 22314
Phone: (703) 684-2800
http://www.nspe.org

Rehabilitation Engineering and Assistive Technology Society of North America
1700 North Moore Street
Suite 1540
Arlington, VA 22209
Phone: (703) 524-6686 or (703) 524-6639 (TTY)
Fax: (703) 524-6630
http://www.resna.org

Society for Cardiovascular Pathology
E-mail: webmaster@scvp.net
http://scvp.net

Society for Epidemiological Research
P.O. Box 990
Clearfield, UT 84098
Phone: (801) 525-0231
Fax: (801) 774-9211
http://www.epiresearch.org

Society for Pediatric Pathology
c/o United States and Canadian Academy of Pathology (USCAP)
3643 Walton Way Extension
Augusta, GA 30909
Phone: (706) 364-3375
Fax: (706) 733-8033
http://www.spponline.org

Society of Nuclear Medicine
1850 Samuel Morse Drive
Reston, VA 20190
Phone: (703) 708-9000
Fax: (703) 708-9015
http://www.snm.org

Tissue Engineering Society International
http://www.tesinternational.org

United States and Canadian Academy of Pathology
3643 Walton Way Extension
Augusta, GA 30909
Phone: (706) 733-7550
Fax: (706) 733-8033
http://www.uscap.org

ENVIRONMENTAL PROTECTION AND CONSERVATION

Air and Waste Management Association
420 Fort Duquesne Boulevard
One Gateway Center, 3rd Floor
Pittsburgh, PA 15222
Phone: (412) 232-3444
Fax: (412) 232-3450
http://www.awma.org

American Academy of Environmental Engineers
130 Holiday Court
Suite 100
Annapolis, MD 21401
Phone: (410) 266-3311
Fax: (410) 266-7653
http://www.enviro-engrs.org

American Association for the Advancement of Science
1200 New York Avenue, NW
Washington, DC 20005
Phone: (202) 326-6400
http://www.aaas.org

American Chemical Society
1155 Sixteenth Street, NW
Washington, DC 20036
Phone: (800) 227-5558
Fax: (202) 872-4615
http://www.chemistry.org/portal/Chemistry

American Chemical Society—Division of Environmental Chemistry
http://www.acs-envchem.duq.edu

American Forage and Grassland Council
P.O. Box 94
Georgetown, TX 78627
Phone: (800) 944-2342
Fax: (512) 931-1166
http://www.afgc.org

American Institute of Biological Sciences
1444 I Street, NW
Suite 200
Washington, DC 20005

Phone: (202) 628-1500
Fax: (202) 628-1509
http://www.aibs.org

**American Institute of Chemical
  Engineers**
3 Park Avenue
New York, NY 10016
Phone: (212) 591-7338
Fax: (212) 591-8897
http://www.aiche.org

American Institute of Chemists
1620 I Street, NW
Suite 615
Washington, DC 20006
Phone: (202) 833-1838
Fax: (202) 463-8498
http://www.theaic.org

American Planning Association
122 South Michigan Avenue
Suite 1600
Chicago, IL 60603
Phone: (312) 431-9100
Fax: (312) 431-9985
http://www.planning.org

American Society of Agronomy
677 South Segoe Road
Madison, WI 53711
Phone: (608) 273-8080
Fax: (608) 273-2021
http://www.agronomy.org

American Society of Civil Engineers
1801 Alexander Bell Drive
Reston, Virginia 20191
Phone: (800) 548-2723 or (703) 295-6300
Fax: (703) 295-6222
http://www.asce.org

**American Society of Mechanical
  Engineers**
3 Park Avenue
New York, NY 10016
Phone: (800) 843-2763 or (973) 882-1167
http://www.asme.org

American Water Works Association
6666 West Quincy Avenue
Denver, CO 80235
Phone: (303) 794-7711
Fax: (303) 794-3951
http://www.awwa.org

**Association of Consulting Foresters of
  America**
732 North Washington Street
Suite 4-A
Alexandria, VA 22314

Phone: (703) 548-0990
Fax: (703) 548-6395
http://www.acf-foresters.com

Ecological Society of America
1707 H Street, NW
Suite 400
Washington, DC 20006
Phone: (202) 833-8773
Fax: (202) 833-8775
http://www.esa.org

Forest Stewards Guild
P.O. Box 8309
Santa Fe, NM 87504
Phone: (505) 983-3887
Fax: (505) 986-0798
http://www.foreststewardsguild.org

Geological Society of America
3300 Penrose Place
Boulder, CO 80301
Mailing Address:
P.O. Box 9140
Boulder, CO 80301
Phone: (303) 447-2020
Fax: (303) 357-1070
http://www.geosociety.org

**National Association of Environmental
  Professionals**
P.O. Box 2086
Bowie, MD 20718
Phone: (888) 251-9902 or (301) 860-1140
Fax: (301) 860-1141
http://www.NAEP.org

**National Association of Local
  Government Environmental
  Professionals**
1350 New York Avenue, NW
Suite 1100
Washington, DC 20005
Phone: (202) 638-6254
Fax: (202) 393-2866
http://www.nalgep.org

National Ground Water Association
601 Dempsey Road
Westerville, OH 43081
Phone: (800) 551-7379 or (614) 898-7791
Fax: (614) 898-7786
http://www.ngwa.org

**National Society of Professional
  Engineers**
420 King Street
Alexandria, VA 22314
Phone: (703) 684-2800
http://www.nspe.org

Society for Range Management
445 Union Boulevard
Suite 230
Lakewood, CO 80228
Phone: (303) 986-3309
Fax: (303) 986-3892
http://www.rangelands.org

Society of American Foresters
5400 Grosvenor Lane
Bethesda, MD 20814
Phone: (301) 897-8720
Fax: (301) 897-3690
http://www.safnet.org

Society of Wetland Scientists
1313 Dolley Madison Boulevard
Suite 402
McLean, VA 22101
Phone: (703) 790-1745
Fax: (703) 790-2672
http://www.sws.org

Soil and Water Conservation Society
7515 NE Ankeny Road
Ankeny, IA 50021
Phone: (515) 289-2331
Fax: (515) 289-1227
http://www.swcs.org

Water Environment Federation
601 Wythe Street
Alexandria, VA 22314
Phone: (800) 666-0206 or (703) 684-2452
Fax: (703) 684-2492
http://www.wef.org

FORENSIC SCIENCE

**American Academy of Forensic
  Sciences**
410 North 21st Street
Suite 203
Colorado Springs, CO 80904
Mailing Address:
P.O. Box 669
Colorado Springs, CO 80901
Phone: (719) 636-1100
Fax: (719) 636-1993
http://www.aafs.org

**American Academy of Psychiatry and
  the Law**
1 Regency Drive
P.O. Box 30
Bloomfield, CT 06002
Phone: (800) 331-1389 or (860) 242-5450
Fax: (860) 286-0787
http://www.emory.edu/AAPL

American Anthropological Association
4350 North Fairfax Drive
Suite 640
Arlington, VA 22203
Phone: (703) 528-1902
Fax: (703) 528-3546
http://www.aaanet.org

American Association of Physical Anthropology
AAPA Membership
P.O. Box 1897
Lawrence, KS 66044
http://physanth.org

American College of Forensic Examiners
2750 East Sunshine
Springfield, MO 65804
Phone: (417) 881-3818
Fax: (417) 881-4702
http://www.acfe.com

American Medical Association
515 North State Street
Chicago, IL 60610
Phone: (312) 464-5000
http://www.ama-assn.org

American Psychiatric Association
1000 Wilson Boulevard
Suite 1825
Arlington, VA 22209
Phone: (888) 35-PSYCH or (703) 907-7300
http://www.psych.org

American Society of Questioned Document Examiners
P.O. Box 382684
Germantown, TN 38183
Phone: (901) 759-0729
Fax: (901) 737-2643
http://www.asqde.org

American Society of Safety Engineers
1800 East Oakton Street
Des Plaines, IL 60018
Phone: (847) 699-2929
Fax: 847-768-3434
http://www.asse.org

Association of Firearm and Toolmark Examiners
http://www.afte.org

International Association of Bloodstain Pattern Analysts
12139 East Makohoh Trail
Tucson, AZ 85749
Phone: (520) 760-6620

Fax: (520) 760-6621
http://www.iabpa.org

National Academy of Forensic Engineers
174 Brady Avenue
Hawthorne, NY 10532
Phone: (866) 623-3675 or (866) 741-0633
Fax: (877) 741-0633)

National Society of Professional Engineers
420 King Street
Alexandria, VA 22314
Phone: (703) 684-2800
http://www.nspe.org

Society for Applied Anthropology
P.O. Box 2436
Oklahoma City, OK 73101
Phone: (405) 843-5113
Fax: (405) 843-8553
http://www.sfaa.net

Society of Forensic Toxicologists
P.O. Box 5543
Mesa, AZ 85211
Phone/Fax: (480) 839-9106
http://www.soft-tox.org

INDUSTRY

American Chemical Society—Division of Chemical Technicians
1155 Sixteenth Street, NW
Washington, DC 20036
Phone: (800) 227-5558
Fax: (202) 872-4615
http://www.chemistry.org/portal/Chemistry

American Society for Quality
600 North Plankinton Avenue
Milwaukee, WI 53203
Mailing Address:
P.O. Box 3005
Milwaukee, WI 53201
Phone: (800) 248-1946
Fax: (414) 272-1734
http://www.asq.org

Institute of Electrical and Electronic Engineers—Professional Communication Society
E-mail: b.w.moeller@ieee.org
http://www.ieeepcs.org

Institute of Food Technologists
525 West Van Buren
Suite 1000
Chicago, IL 60607

Phone: (312) 782-8424
Fax: (312) 782-8348
http://www.ift.org

National Association of Patent Practitioners
4680-18i Monticello Avenue
PMB 101
Williamsburg, VA 23188
Phone: (800) 216-9588
Fax: (757) 220-3928
http://www.napp.org

National Writers Union
National Office East
113 University Place, 6th Floor
New York, NY 10003
Phone: (212) 254-0279
Fax: (212) 254-0673
National Office West
337 17th Street, #101
Oakland, CA 94612
Phone: (510) 839-0110
Fax: (510) 839-6097
http://www.nwu.org

Project Management Institute
4 Campus Boulevard
Newtown Square, PA 19073
Phone: (610) 356-4600
Fax: (610) 356-4647
http://www.pmi.org

Regulatory Affairs Professionals Society
11300 Rockville Pike
Suite 1000
Rockville, MD 20852
Phone: (301) 770-2920
Fax: (301) 770-2924
http://www.raps.org

Society for Technical Communication
901 North Stuart Street
Suite 904
Arlington, VA 22203
Phone: (703) 522-4114
Fax: (703) 522-2075
http://www.stc.org

BUSINESS

American Association of Healthcare Consultants
5 Revere Drive
Suite 200
Northbrook, IL 60062
Phone: (888) 350-2242
http://www.aahc.net

American Marketing Association
311 South Wacker Drive
Suite 5800
Chicago, IL 60606
Phone: (800) AMA-1150
http://www.marketingpower.com

Institute of Management Consultants USA, Inc.
2025 M Street, NW
Suite 800
Washington, DC 20036
Phone: (800) 221-2557 or (202) 367-1134
Fax: (202) 367-2134
http://www.imcusa.org

Marketing Research Association
1344 Silas Deane Highway
Suite 306
P.O. Box 230
Rocky Hill, CT 06067
Phone: (860) 257-4008
Fax: (860) 257-3990
http://www.mra-net.org

National Association of Sales Professionals
8300 North Hayden Road
Suite 207
Scottsdale, AZ 85258
Phone: (480) 951-4311
http://www.nasp.com

Professional and Technical Consultants Association
1060 North Fourth Street
San Jose, CA 95112
Phone: (800) 74-PATCA or (408) 971-5902
Fax: (408) 999-0344
http://www.patca.org or
    http://www.patca.com

Qualitative Research Consultants Association
11240 Waples Mill Road, #200
Fairfax, VA 22030
Phone: (888) 674-7722 or (703) 934-2155
Fax: (703) 359-7562
http://www.qrca.org

EDUCATION AND COMMUNICATIONS

Agricultural Communicators in Education
University of Florida
Building 116, Mowry Road
P.O. Box 110811
Gainesville, FL 32611

Phone: (352) 392-9588
Fax: (352) 392-7902
http://www.aceweb.org

American Association for Adult and Continuing Education
4380 Forbes Boulevard
Lanham, MD 20706
Phone: (301) 918-1913
Fax: (301) 918-1846
http://www.aaace.org

American Association for Higher Education
1 Dupont Circle
Suite 360
Washington, DC 20036
Phone: (202) 293-6440
Fax: (202) 293-0073
http://www.aahe.org

American Association for the Advancement of Science
1200 New York Avenue, NW
Washington, DC 20005
Phone: (202) 326-6400
http://www.aaas.org

American Association of Botanical Gardens and Arboreta
100 West 10th Street
Suite 614
Wilmington, DE 19801
Fax: (302) 655-8100
http://www.aabga.org

American Association of Museums
1575 I Street, NW
Suite 400
Washington, DC 20005
Phone: (202) 289-1818
Fax: (202) 289-6578
http://www.aam-us.org

American Association of Physics Teachers
1 Physics Ellipse
College Park, MD 20740
Phone: (301) 209-3311
Fax: (301) 209-0845
http://www.aapt.org

American Association of University Professors
1012 Fourteenth Street, NW
Suite 500
Washington, DC 20005
Phone: (202) 737-5900
Fax: (202) 737-5526
http://www.aaup.org

American Astronomical Society
2000 Florida Avenue, NW
Suite 400
Washington, DC 20009
Phone: (202) 328-2010
Fax: (202) 234-2560
http://www.aas.org

American Chemical Society
1155 Sixteenth Street, NW
Washington, DC 20036
Phone: (800) 227-5558
Fax: (202) 872-4615
http://www.chemistry.org/portal/
    Chemistry

American Federation of Teachers
555 New Jersey Avenue, NW
Washington, DC 20001
Phone: (202) 879-4440
http://www.aft.org

American Geological Institute
4220 King Street
Alexandria, VA 22302
Phone: (703) 379-2480
Fax: (703) 379-7563
http://www.agiweb.org

American Geophysical Union
2000 Florida Avenue, NW
Washington, DC 20009
Phone: (800) 966-2481 or (202) 462-6900
Fax: (202) 328-0566
http://www.agu.org

American Institute of Biological Sciences
1444 I Street, NW
Suite 200
Washington, DC 20005
Phone: (202) 628-1500
Fax: (202) 628-1509
http://www.aibs.org

American Institute of Physics
1 Physics Ellipse
College Park, MD 20740
Phone: (301) 209-3100
Fax: (301) 209-0843
http://www.aip.org

American Medical Writers Association
40 West Gude Drive
Suite 101
Rockville, MD 20850
Phone: (301) 294-5303
Fax: (301) 294-9006
http://www.amwa.org

American Society of Journalists and Authors
1501 Broadway
Suite 302
New York, NY 10036
Phone: (212) 997-0947
Fax: (212) 768-7414
http://www.asja.org

American Zoo and Aquarium Association
8403 Colesville Road
Suite 710
Silver Spring, MD 20910
Phone: (301) 562-0777
Fax: (301) 562-0888
http://www.aza.org

Association of Health Care Journalists
204 Murphy Hall
University of Minnesota
206 Church Street, SE
Minneapolis, MN 55455
Phone: (612) 624-8877
Fax: (612) 626-8251
http://www.ahcj.umn.edu

Association of Science-Technology Centers
1025 Vermont Avenue, NW
Suite 500
Washington, DC 20005
Phone: (202) 783-7200
Fax: (202) 783-7207
http://www.astc.org

Entomological Society of America
9301 Annapolis Road
Lanham, MD 20706
Phone: (301) 731-4535
Fax: (301) 731-4538
http://www.entsoc.org

International Technology Education Association
1914 Association Drive
Suite 201
Reston, VA 20191
Phone: (703) 860-2100
Fax: (703) 860-0353
http://www.iteawww.org

Mathematical Association of America
1529 Eighteenth Street, NW
Washington, DC 20036
Phone: (800) 741-9415 or (202) 387-5200
Fax: (202) 265-2384
http://www.maa.org

National Association of Biology Teachers
12030 Sunrise Valley Drive
Suite 110
Reston VA 20191
Phone: (800) 406-0775 or (703) 264-9696
Fax: (703) 264-7778
http://www.nabt.org

National Association of Scholars
221 Witherspoon Street, Second Floor
Princeton, NJ 08542
Phone: (609) 683-7878
Fax: (609) 683-0316
http://www.nas.org

National Association of Science Writers
P.O. Box 890
Hedgesville, WV 25427
Phone: (304) 754-5077
Fax: (304) 754-5076
http://nasw.org

National Council of Teachers of Mathematics
1906 Association Drive
Reston, VA 20191
Phone: (703) 620-9840
Fax: (703) 476-2970
http://www.nctm.org

National Earth Science Teachers Association
P.O. Box 2194
Liverpool, NY 13089
http://www.nestanet.org

National Education Association
1201 16th Street, NW
Washington, DC 20036
Phone: (202) 833-4000
Fax: (202) 822-7974
http://www.nea.org

National Marine Educators Association
P.O. Box 1470
Ocean Springs, MS 39566
http://www.marine-ed.org

National Science Teachers Association
1840 Wilson Boulevard
Arlington, VA 22201
Phone: (703) 243-7100
http://www.nsta.org

National Writers Union
National Office East
113 University Place, 6th Floor
New York, NY 10003
Phone: (212) 254-0279
Fax: (212) 254-0673

National Office West
337 17th Street, #101
Oakland, CA 94612
Phone: (510) 839-0110
Fax: (510) 839-6097
http://www.nwu.org

North American Association for Environmental Education
410 Tarvin Road
Rock Spring, GA 39739
Phone: (706) 764-2926
Fax: (706) 764-2094
http://naaee.org

Paleontological Society
Contact: Mr. Dean Frazier, Business Manager
E-mail: afrazier@allenpress.com
http://www.paleosoc.org

Society for Integrative and Comparative Biology
1313 Dolley Madison Boulevard
Suite 402
McLean VA 22101
Phone: (800) 955-1236 or (703) 790-1745
Fax: (703) 790-2672
http://www.sicb.org

Society for Technical Communication
901 North Stuart Street
Suite 904
Arlington, VA 22203
Phone: (703) 522-4114
Fax: (703) 522-2075
http://www.stc.org

Society for the Preservation of Natural History Collections
Contact: Lisa Palmer
P.O. Box 797
Washington, DC 20044
http://www.spnhc.org

The Society of Environmental Journalists
P.O. Box 2492
Jenkintown, PA 19046
Phone: (215) 884-8174
Fax: (215) 884-8175
http://www.sej.org

Technology Section of the Public Relations Society of America
33 Irving Place
New York, NY 10003
Phone: (212) 460-1482
http://www.tech.prsa.org

APPENDIX IV
RESOURCES ON THE WORLD WIDE WEB

Listed in this appendix are websites and webpages that can help you learn more about many of the professions that are discussed in this book. You will also find some resources that offer career and job search information.

Note: All website addresses were current when this book was being written. For a website address that no longer works, you may be able to find its new one—try entering the name of the organization or webpage in a search engine.

GENERAL INFORMATION

Wikipedia (the Free Encyclopedia)
http://www.wikipedia.org

World Book Encyclopedia Online
http://www.aolsvc.worldbook.aol.com

CAREER AND JOB INFORMATION

GOVERNMENT RESOURCES

Occupational Employment Statistics (Bureau of Labor Statistics)
http://www.bls.gov/oes/2000/oes_nat.htm

Bureau of Labor Statistics
http://www.bls.gov

California Occupational Guides
http://www.calmis.ca.gov/htmlfile/subject/guide.htm

National Academy Press
http://www.nap.edu/info/browse.htm

Occupational Outlook Handbook (Bureau of Labor Statistics)
http://www.bls.gov/oco/home.htm

CAREER INFORMATION

Career Fields (UC Berkeley Career Center)
http://career.berkeley.edu/CareerExp/CareerFields.stm

CareerJournal (from the *Wall Street Journal*)
http://www.careerjournal.com

Next Step Magazine
http://www.nextstepmagazine.com

The Princeton Review
http://www.princetonreview.com

Science News, Careers in Science, and Cancer Information (by Megan Brown)
http://www.geocities.com/CapeCanaveral/Hangar/4707/index.html

Science's Next Wave
American Association for the Advancement of Science
http://nextwave.sciencemag.org

WetFeet.com
http://www.wetfeet.com

JOB SEARCH/JOB BANK RESOURCES

America's Job Bank
http://www.jobsearch.org

BioMedNet Science Jobs
http://jobs.bmn.com

College Grad Job Hunter
http://www.collegerad.com

JobStar: Job Search Guide
http://jobstar.org

Medzilla.com
http://www.medzilla.com

Monster
http://www.monster.com

Scijobs.org: The Scientist's Employment Network
http://www.scijobs.org

USA Jobs
U.S. Office of Personnel Management
http://www.usajobs.opm.gov

GENERAL SCIENCE

U.S. GOVERNMENT RESOURCES

National Academies
http://www.nas.edu

National Academy of Engineering
http://www.nae.edu

National Academy of Sciences
http://www4.nationalacademies.org/nas/
nashome.nsf

National Science Foundation
http://www.nsf.gov

MISCELLANEOUS

Alfred P. Sloan Foundation
http://www.sloan.org/main.shtml

Discover Engineering Online
http://www.discoverengineering.org

Engineer Girl
National Academy of Sciences
http://www.engineergirl.org

Eric Weisstein's World of Science
A Wolfram Web Resource
http://scienceworld.wolfram.com

Mad Scientist Network
http://www.madsci.org

PBS Scientific American Frontiers
http://www.pbs.org/saf

Public Library of Science
http://www.publiclibraryofscience.org

Real Science!
KTEH San Jose Public TV
http://www.realscience.org

BIOLOGICAL SCIENCES

GENERAL RESOURCES

BioExchange.com
http://bioexchange.com

Biology Links
Department of Molecular and Cellular
Biology
Harvard University
http://mcb.harvard.edu/BioLinks.html

**BioRap: Biological Research for
Animals and People**
Connecticut United for Research
Excellence, Inc.
http://www.biorap.org

**Federation of American Societies for
Experimental Biology**
http://www.faseb.org

**The Organization of Biological Field
Stations**
http://www.obfs.org

MICROBIOLOGIST

American Board of Medical Laboratory
http://www.asmusa.org/acasrc/aca25.htm

**American Board of Medical
Microbiology**
http://www.asmusa.org/acasrc/aca24.htm

American College of Microbiology
http://www.asmusa.org/acasrc/college.htm

American Society for Cell Biology
http://www.ascb.org

**American Society of Clinical
Pathologists**
http://www.ascp.org

Microbe Library
http://www.microbelibrary.org

Microbe World
http://www.microbeworld.org/mlc

National Registry of Microbiologists
http://www.asmusa.org/acasrc/aca23.htm

BOTANIST

American Society of Plant Biologists
http://www.aspb.org

American Society of Plant Taxonomists
http://www.sysbot.org

Internet Directory for Botany
http://www.botany.net/IDB

ZOOLOGIST

The Animal Diversity Web
http://animaldiversity.ummz.umich.edu

Ark Animals: Animal Tracks Magazine
http://www.arkanimals.com

Biosis
http://www.Biosis.org

Careers in Zoology
Oregon State University
http://osu.orst.edu/dept/zoology/careers.
htm

Online Zoologists
by Wesley R. Elsberry and Diane J.
Blackwood
http://www.rtis.com/nat/user/elsberry

AQUATIC BIOLOGIST

Animal Information Database
Sea World/Busch Gardens
http://www.seaworld.org

Aquatic Network
http://www.aquanet.com

LakeNet
http://www.worldlakes.org

**National Marine Educators
Association**
http://www.marine-ed.org

ENTOMOLOGIST

**American Board of Forensic
Entomology**
http://www.missouri.edu/~agwww/
entomology

Bug Bios: Insects on the Web
http://www.insects.org

Bugwood Network
Department of Entomology, University
of Georgia
http://www.bugwood.org

**Iowa State Entomology Index of
Internet Resources**
http://ent.iastate.edu/list

PHYSIOLOGIST

**International Union of Physiological
Sciences**
http://iups.mcw.edu

GENETICIST

**American Board of Genetic
Counseling**
http://www.faseb.org/genetics/abgc/
abgcmenu.htm

American Board of Medical Genetics
http://www.abmg.org

Association of Genetic Technologists
http://www.agt-info.org

Genetics Societies
http://www.faseb.org/genetics

Genetic Education Center
Kansas Medical Center
http://www.kumc.edu/gec/geneinfo.html

Human Genome Project Information
http://www.ornl.gov/hgmis

MOLECULAR BIOLOGIST

Cell and Molecular Biology Online
by Pamela Gannon
http://www.cellbio.com

BIOINFORMATICS SCIENTIST

**BioPlanet—The Bioinformatics
Homepage**
http://www.bioplanet.com

Bioinformatics.org
http://bioinformatics.org

**National Center for Biotechnology
Information**
http://www.ncbi.nlm.nih.gov

ECOLOGIST

Ecology.com
http://www.ecology.com

The Ecology WWW Page
http://www.people.fas.harvard.edu/
~brach/Ecology-WWW.html

Society for Ecological Restoration
http://www.ser.org

CHEMISTRY

GENERAL RESOURCES

American Board of Clinical Chemistry
http://www.aacc.org/abcc

National Registry of Certified Chemists
http://www.nrcc6.org

**World Wide Web Resources in
Chemistry**
Hiram College Library
http://library.hiram.edu/sub_chem.htm

CHEMICAL ENGINEER

Chemical Engineers' Resource Page
http://www.cheresources.com

TOXICOLOGIST

American Board of Forensic Toxicology
http://www.abft.org

American Board of Toxicology
http://www.abtox.org

**American Board of Veterinary
Toxicology**
http://www.abvt.org

**EXTOXNET—The Extension
Toxicology Network**
http://ace.orst.edu/info/extoxnet

Toxicology Online
http://www.toxicologyonline.com

PHYSICS AND ASTRONOMY

GENERAL RESOURCES

Argonne National Laboratory
U.S. Department of Energy laboratory
http://www.anl.gov

The Net Advance of Physics
http://web.mit.edu/redingtn/www/netadv

PhysLink.com
http://www.physlink.com

Department of Energy
http://www.energy.gov

BIOPHYSICIST

Biophysics Textbook
http://www.biophysics.org/btol/become.
html

NUCLEAR PHYSICIST

The ABCs of Nuclear Science
http://www.lbl.gov/abc

Division of Nuclear Physics
U.S. Department of Energy
http://www.sc.doe.gov/production/henp/
np/index.html

Institute for Nuclear Theory
http://int.phys.washington.edu

ASTRONOMER/SPACE PHYSICIST

American Association of Amateur Astronomers
http://www.corvus.com

American Association of Variable Star Observers
http://www.aavso.org

Astronomical Observatory Links
http://www.ngcic.com/obs.htm

Astronomical Society of the Pacific
http://www.astrosociety.org

The Astronomy Cafe
http://www.theastronomycafe.net

Center for Science Education
Space Sciences Laboratory (UC Berkeley)
http://cse.ssl.berkeley.edu/scientists.html

NASA—Hubble Space Telescope Project
http://hubble.nasa.gov

NASA Polar, Wind, and Geotail Projects
http://www-istp.gsfc.nasa.gov

National Space Science Data Center
http://nssdc.gsfc.nasa.gov

Oulu Space Physics Textbook (Space Physics Group of Oulu)
http://www.oulu.fi/~spaceweb/textbook

Universities Space Research Association
http://www.usra.edu

National Aeronautics and Space Administration (NASA)
http://www.nasa.gov

EARTH SCIENCES

GENERAL RESOURCES

Employment Resources in the Earth, Atmospheric and Oceanic Sciences
by Elizabeth Wallace, Syracuse University Library
http://libwww.syr.edu/research/internet/earth/jobs.html

Earth Science Resources: Geology Oceanography, Astronomy and Ecology
by R. Hays Cummins, Miami University
http://jrscience.wcp.muohio.edu/html/earthsci.html

National Association of State Boards of Geology
http://www.asbog.org

National Geographic Society
http://www.nationalgeographic.com

U.S. Bureau of Land Management
http://www.blm.gov

U.S. Department of Interior
http://www.doi.gov

U.S. Geological Survey
http://www.usgs.gov

U.S. Fish and Wildlife Service
http://www.fws.gov

U.S. National Park Service
http://www.nps.gov

U.S. National Oceanic and Atmospheric Administration
http://www.noaa.gov

PALEONTOLOGIST

The PaleoNet Pages
http://www.ucmp.berkeley.edu/Paleonet

Paleontology and Fossils Resources
by Jack D. Mount, University of Arizona
http://www.u.arizona.edu/~jmount/paleont.html

SEISMOLOGIST

National Earthquake Information Center
U.S. Geological Survey
http://neic.usgs.gov

Center for Earthquake Research and Information
The University of Memphis
http://www.ceri.memphis.edu/index.shtml

VOLCANOLOGIST

Alaska Science Forum: Volcanoes Index
http://www.gi.alaska.edu/ScienceForum/volcanoes.html

Volcano Hazards Program
U.S. Geological Survey
http://volcanoes.usgs.gov

Volcano World
http://volcano.und.nodak.edu

OCEANOGRAPHER/OCEAN ENGINEER

Center for Coastal Environmental Health and Bimolecular Research
U.S. National Oceanic and Atmospheric Administration
http://www.chbr.noaa.gov/Index.htm

National Marine Fisheries
http://www.nmfs.noaa.gov

Marine Careers.net
http://www.marinecareers.net

Scripps Institute of Oceanography
http://www.scilib.ucsd.edu/sio/guide/career.html

HYDROLOGIST

Global Hydrology Resource Center
http://ghrc.msfc.nasa.gov

The Hydrology Web
http://terrassa.pnl.gov:2080/hydroweb.html

Water Resources of the United States
U.S. Geological Survey
http://water.usgs.gov

METEOROLOGIST

Meteorology Guide: The Online Guides
Department of Atmospheric Sciences, University of Illinois at Urbana-Champaign
http://ww2010.atmos.uiuc.edu/(Gh)/guides/mtr/home.rxml

National Weather Service
http://www.nws.noaa.gov

University Corporation for Atmospheric Research
http://www.ucar.edu

CLIMATOLOGIST

Climate Organizations
Virginia State Climatology Office
http://climate.virginia.edu/orgs.htm

National Climatic Data Center
http://lwf.ncdc.noaa.gov/oa/ncdc.html

CARTOGRAPHER

American Congress on Surveying and Mapping
http://www.acsm.net

National Center for Geographic Information and Analysis
UC Santa Barbara
http://www.ncgia.ucsb.edu

MATHEMATICS

GENERAL RESOURCES

The Math Forum
Drexel University
http://www.mathforum.com

Mathematics Science Career Information
http://www.ams.org/careers

OPERATIONS RESEARCH ANALYST

INFORMS Online
http://www.informs.org

IFORS On-Line Encyclopedia
International Federation of Operational Research Societies
http://www.ifors.org/ioe/index.html

Operations Research
http://or.pubs.informs.org

ACTUARY

Actuary.com
http://www.actuary.com

Be an Actuary
http://www.BeAnActuary.com

COMPUTER SCIENCE

GENERAL RESOURCES

ACM Career Resource Center
Association for Computing Machinery
http://campus.acm.org/crc

The Ada Project
http://tap.mills.edu

Computing Research Association
http://www.cra.org

Graduating Engineer and Computer Careers Online
http://www.GraduatingEngineer.com

Institute for Certification of Computing Professionals
http://www.iccp.org

MIT Laboratory for Computer Science
http://www.lcs.mit.edu

SOFTWARE ENGINEER

SEWeb: Software Engineering Resources
IEEE Computer Society
http://www.computer.org/SEweb

Software Engineering Institute
Carnegie-Mellon University
http://www.sei.cmu.edu

Software Engineering Resources
by R.S. Pressman and Associates, Inc.
http://www.rspa.com/spi

ARTIFICIAL INTELLIGENCE SCIENTIST

AI Topics
American Association for Artificial Intelligence
http://www.aaai.org/AITopics/aitopics.html

Artificial Intelligence Depot
http://ai-depot.com/Main.html

Artificial Intelligence Resources
Institute for Information Technology, National Research Council of Canada
http://www.iit.nrc.ca/ai_point.html

ROBOTICS RESEARCHER

Internet Robot Resources
NASA Space Telerobotics Program
http://ranier.hq.nasa.gov/telerobotics_page/internetrobots.html

Robot Information Central
by Arrick Robotics
http://www.robots.com/robots.html

Robotics Industries Association
http://www.robotics.org

Web Resources on Robotics
ORNL Research Libraries
http://www.ornl.gov/Library/robotics.htm

AGRICULTURAL SCIENCE AND FOOD SCIENCE

GENERAL RESOURCES

AgJobsUSA
http://www.agjobsusa.com

Agriculture 21
http://www.fao.org/ag/default.htm

Agriculture Network Information Center
http://www.agnic.org

Agricenter International: Agriculture, Technology, and Community
http://www.agricenter.org

American Farm Bureau
http://www.fb.com

American Farmland Trust
http://www.farmland.org

Council for Agricultural Science and Technology
http://www.cast-science.org

enPlant: Home of Awesome Careers
Department of Horticulture and Crop Science, Ohio State University
http://enplant.osu.edu

Sustainable Agriculture Network
http://www.sare.org

U.S. Agricultural Research Service
http://www.ars.usda.gov

U.S. Animal and Plant Health Inspection Service
http://www.aphis.usda.gov

U.S. Department of Agriculture
http://www.usda.gov

U.S. National Agricultural Library
http://www.nal.usda.gov

U.S. Cooperative State Research, Education, and Extension Service
http://www.reeusda.gov

The World of Food Science
http://www.worldfoodscience.org

HORTICULTURAL SCIENTIST

American Horticultural Society
http://www.ahs.org

Botany.Com: Encyclopedia of Flowers and Plants
http://www.botany.com

Center for New Crops and Plant Products
Purdue University
http://www.hort.purdue.edu/newcrop

Horticulture: The Horticultural Web
http://www.horticulture.com

International Society for Horticultural Science
http://www.ishs.org

Jobs in Horticulture
http://www.hortjobs.com

CROP SCIENTIST

American Seed Trade Association
http://www.amseed.com

Food and Agriculture Organization
United Nations
http://www.fao.org

Weed Science Society of America
http://www.wssa.net

SOIL SCIENTIST

Soil Science Education
by Dr. Elissa Levine, Goddard Space Flight Center
http://ltpwww.gsfc.nasa.gov/globe/index.htm

National Soil Survey Center
http://soils.usda.gov

ANIMAL SCIENTIST

The Aquaculture Network Information Center
http://aquanic.org

American Fisheries Society
http://www.fisheries.org

American Registry of Professional Animal Scientists
http://www.arpas.org

Animal Agriculture Links
AgricultureLaw.com
http://www.agriculturelaw.com/links/animalag.htm

Federation of Animal Science Societies
http://www.fass.org

Livestock Virtual Library
Oklahoma State University
http://www.ansi.okstate.edu/library

FOOD SCIENTIST

U.S. Center for Food Safety and Applied Nutrition
http://www.cfsan.fda.gov

U.S. Food and Nutrition Information Center
http://www.nal.usda.gov/fnic

U.S. Food Safety and Inspection Service
http://www.fsis.usda.gov

MEDICAL SCIENCE

GENERAL RESOURCES

Accreditation Council for Graduate Medical Education
http://www.acgme.org

American Board of Medical Specialties
http://www.abms.org

Association of American Medical Colleges
http://www.aamc.org

American Academy of Osteopathy
http://www.academyofosteopathy.org

American Osteopathic Association
http://www.aoa-net.org

BioMedNet News and Comment
http://news.bmn.com

Institute of Medicine
http://www.iom.edu

MedBio World
http://www.medbioworld.com

U.S. National Institutes of Health
http://www.nih.gov

U.S. Centers for Disease Control and Prevention
http://www.cdc.gov

U.S. Commissioned Corps
Department of Health and Human Services
http://www.usphs.gov

U.S. Food and Drug Administration
http://www.fda.gov

PATHOLOGIST

American Board of Pathology
http://www.abpath.org

American College of Veterinary Pathologists
http://www.acvp.org

Intersociety Committee on Pathology Information
http://www.pathologytraining.org

PHARMACOLOGIST

American Board of Clinical Pharmacology
http://abcp.net

Medicines by Design: The Biological Revolution in Pharmacology
http://www.nigms.nih.gov/news/science_ed/medbydes.html

Pharmaceutical Education and Research Institute
http://www.peri.org

EPIDEMIOLOGIST

The World-Wide Web Virtual Library: Epidemiology
http://www.epibiostat.ucsf.edu/epidem/epidem.html

BIOMEDICAL ENGINEER

Biomedical Engineering Network
http://www.bmenet.org

Institute of Biological Engineering
http://www.ibeweb.org

National Institute of Biomedical Imaging and Bioengineering
http://www.nibib1.nih.gov

Whitaker Foundation
http://www.whitaker.org

MEDICAL PHYSICIST

American Board of Medical Physics
http://www.acmp.org/abmp/abmp.html

American Board of Radiology
http://www.theabr.org

International Organization for Medical Physics
http://www.iomp.org

ENVIRONMENTAL PROTECTION AND CONSERVATION

GENERAL RESOURCES

ECO World: Global Environmental Community
http://www.ecoworld.com

Envirolink: The Online Environmental Community
http://www.envirolink.org

Environmental Careers Organization
http://www.eco.org

The Environmental Education Directory
http://www.enviroeducation.com

Institute of Professional Environmental Practice
http://www.ipep.org

The Nature Conservancy
http://nature.org

National Registry of Environmental Professionals
http://www.nrep.org

Ubiquity Environmental Page
by Nicholas D'Amato
http://www.geocities.com/RainForest/8974/homepage.htm

U.S. Environmental Protection Agency
http://www.epa.gov

ENVIRONMENTAL CHEMIST

National Registry of Certified Chemists
http://www.nrcc6.org

EnvironmentalChemistry.com
http://environmentalchemistry.com

ENVIRONMENTAL PLANNER

Center for Urban Policy and the Environment
http://www.urbancenter.iupui.edu/container.htm

Cyburbia: The Urban Planning Portal
http://www.cyburbia.org

Planetizen: The Planning and Development Network
http://www.planetizen.com

Planners Network
http://www.plannersnetwork.org

FORESTER

American Forests
http://www.americanforests.org

Davies and Company
Karl Davies
http://www.daviesand.com

National Association of State Foresters
http://www.stateforesters.org

USDA Forest Service
http://www.fs.fed.us

RANGE SCIENTIST

**Natural Resources Conservation
    Service**
http://www.nrcs.usda.gov

**Rangelands of the Western
    United States**
http://ag.arizona.edu/agnic

USDA Forest Service Rangelands
http://www.fs.fed.us/rangelands/index.html

FORENSIC SCIENCE

GENERAL RESOURCES

**Carpenter's Forensic Science
    Resources**
http://www.tncrimlaw.com/forensic

Forensic Education.com
http://www.forensiceducation.com/index.
    htm

National Center for Forensic Science
University of Central Florida
http://ncfs.ucf.edu

Reddy's Forensic Page
http://www.forensicpage.com

Zeno's Forensic Site
http://forensic.to/forensic.html

Young Forensic Scientists Forum
http://www.aafs.org/yfsf

CRIMINALIST

American Board of Criminalistics
http://www.criminalistics.com/abc

**American Society of Crime Laboratory
    Directors**
http://www.ascld.org

Crime Scene Investigation
http://www.crime-scene-investigator.net/
    index.html

**International Association for
    Identification**
http://www.theiai.org

FORENSIC ENGINEER

**Society of Forensic Engineers and
    Scientists**
http://www.forensic-society.org

FORENSIC ANTHROPOLOGIST

**American Board of Forensic
    Anthropology**
http://www.csuchico.edu/anth/ABFA

ForensicAnthro.com
http://www.forensicanthro.com

FORENSIC PSYCHIATRIST

**American Board of Psychiatry and
    Neurology**
http://www.abpn.com

Forensic Psychiatry Resource
by Dr. James Hooper, University of
    Alabama
http://ua1vm.ua.edu/~jhooper

Forensic Psychiatry Resources
compiled by Myron Pulier
http://www.umdnj.edu/psyevnts/forensic.
    html

WILDLIFE FORENSIC SCIENTIST

Federal Wildlife Officers Association
http://www.fwoa.org

Marine Forensics Branch
Center for Coastal Environmental Health
    and Biomolecular Research
http://www.chbr.noaa.gov/
    MarineForensics.html

**National Fish and Wildlife Forensics
    Laboratory**
http://www.laboratory.fws.gov

Fish and Wildlife Service
http://www.fws.gov

INDUSTRY

Bio.com Career Center
http://career.bio.com/careercenter/index.
    jhtml

Biotechnology Web site
developed by Dr. Paul DeAngelis,
    University of Oklahoma
Health Sciences Center
http://w3.uokhsc.edu/biotechhighschool/
    intro.html

Industry Week.com
http://www.iwgc.com

**Pharmaceutical Research and
    Manufacturers of America**
http://www.phrma.org

**U.S. Consumer Product Safety
    Commission**
http://www.cpsc.gov

PROJECT MANAGER

**ALLPM: The Project Managers
    Homepage**
http://www.allpm.com

**gantthead.com: The Online
    Community for IT project
    managers**
http://www.gantthead.com

Project Magazine
http://www.projectmagazine.com

Project Management.com
http://www.projectmanagement.com

Project-Manager
WMB Publishing
http://www.project-manager.com

QUALITY PROFESSIONALS

CyberQuality Resource
by Bill Casti
http://www.quality.org

International Organization for Standardization
http://www.iso.ch/iso/en/ISOOnline.openerpage

REGULATORY AFFAIRS SPECIALIST

Center for Bio/Pharmaceutical and Biodevice Development
San Diego State University
http://www.cbbd.sdsu.edu/index.html

Drug Information Association
http://diahome.org

European Society of Regulatory Affairs
http://www.esra.org

Food and Drug Law Institute
http://www.fdli.org

U.S. Food and Drug Administration (FDA)
http://www.fda.gov

Office of Regulatory Affairs
U.S. FDA
http://www.fda.gov/ora

PATENT AGENT

From Patent to Profit
http://www.frompatenttoprofit.com

Patent Cafe
http://www.patentcafe.com

U.S. Patent and Trademark Office
http://www.uspto.gov

TECHNICAL WRITER

Newbie Techwriter
by Paul Dunham
http://www.cloudnet.com/~pdunham/newbietechwriterhome.html

TECHWR-L
RayComm, Inc. Resource
http://www.raycomm.com/techwhirl

Technical Writers Anonymous
by Andrew Angelopoulos
http://www.technicalwritersanonymous.com

BUSINESS

ENTREPRENEUR

Entrepreneur.com
http://www.entrepreneur.com

Entreworld.org
http://www.entreworld.org

The Invention Dimension
Massachusetts Institute of Technology
http://web.mit.edu/invent/www/links_pg2.html

National Business Incubation Association
http://www.nbia.org

SBA Office of Technology
http://www.sba.gov/sbir

Startup Journal Center
by the *Wall Street Journal*
http://www.startupjournal.com

Technology Capital Network
http://www.tcnmit.org

U.S. Small Business Administration
http://www.sba.gov

MANAGEMENT CONSULTANT

MCNI: Information Central for Management Consulting Worldwide
http://www.mcninet.com

MARKET RESEARCH ANALYST

Council of American Survey Research Organizations
http://www.casro.org

Marketing Power.com
American Marketing Association
http://www.marketingpower.com

SALES REPRESENTATIVE

Manufacturers' Agents National Association
http://www.manaonline.org

Manufacturers' Representatives Educational Research Foundation
http://www.mrerf.org

Sales Vault: The Sales and Marketing Portal
http://www.salesvault.com

EDUCATION AND COMMUNICATIONS

SCHOOL TEACHER/SCIENCE EDUCATOR

ASTC Resource Center: Education Index
http://www.astc.org/resource/educator/educmain.htm

Education Week on the Web
http://www.edweek.org

Eisenhower National Clearinghouse for Mathematics and Science Education
http://www.enc.org

ERIC Clearinghouse for Science, Mathematics, and Environmental Education
Educational Resources Information Center
http://www.ericse.org

Electronic Journal of Science Education
http://unr.edu/homepage/jcannon/ejse/ejse.html

National Association of Independent Schools
http//www.nais.org

National Board for Professional Teaching Standards
http://www.nbpts.org

Office of Science Education
U.S. Department of Energy
http://www.scied.science.doe.gov/scied/sci_ed.htm

The Science Page
Murray Hart
http://sciencepage.org

Teacherplanet.com
http://teachersplanet.com

What's Cool?
Office of Legislative and Public Affairs, National Science Foundation
http://www.nsf.gov/od/lpa/events/start.htm

U.S. Department of Education
http://www.ed.gov

COLLEGE INSTRUCTOR

Association of American Colleges and Universities
http://www.aacu-edu.org

American Association of Community Colleges
http://www.aacc.nche.edu

Chronicle of Higher Education
http://chronicle.com

Preparing Future Faculty
http://www.preparing-faculty.org

SCIENCE CURATOR

Global Museum Webzine
http://www.globalmuseum.org

SCIENCE WRITER

ACE (Agricultural Communicators in Education) International Headquarters
http://www.aceweb.org/homepage

Science Writing and Net Resources Links
by Larry Krumenaker
http://nasw.org/users/larryk/swlinks.htm

Writing Resources on the World Wide Web
Massachusetts Institute of Technology
http://web.mit.edu/uaa/www/writing/links

SCIENCE AND TECHNOLOGY POLICY ANALYST

AAAS Center Science, Technology, and Congress
http://www.aaas.org/spp/cstc

AAAS Science and Policy Programs
http://www.aaas.org/spp

Christine Mirzayan Science and Technology Policy Internship Program
The National Academies
http://www7.nationalacademies.org/internship

National Council for Science and the Environment
http://www.NCSEonline.org

Science and Technology Policy Institute
http://www.rand.org/scitech/stpi

Office of Science and Technology Policy
http://www.ostp.gov

APPENDIX V
GLOSSARY

A.A.   Associate of Arts, a degree granted by a two-year college.

actuarial science   The application of mathematics to identify financial risks, uncertainties, and probabilities that could occur in the future.

adjunct instructor   An individual who teaches part-time at a college or university.

agronomy   The study of plants and soils in their surrounding environments.

anatomy   The study of the internal structure of living organisms.

animal science   The study of animals that are used for food, fiber, work, recreation, and companionship.

applied research   Scientific studies that are conducted for practical purposes, such as developing new products, methodologies, or technologies.

applied sciences   Science fields in which scientific principles are used for practical purposes; for example, medical science, biotechnology, horticulture, and forensic science.

artificial intelligence (AI)   The study of computational models that describe human thinking processes.

astronomy   The study of the solar system and the universe; this discipline is also known as astrophysics.

astrophysics   Another name for astronomy.

atmospheric science   Another name for meteorology, the study of the Earth's atmosphere.

B.A.   Bachelor of Arts.

B.S.   Bachelor of Science.

basic research   Scientific studies that are conducted to gain new knowledge and understanding about a particular subject.

biochemistry   The study of how chemicals combine and react within the cells.

bioinformatics   The scientific management of all biological information that is stored in computer databases.

biological sciences   Life sciences; the various disciplines and subdiscipines of biology.

biology   The study of humans, animals, plants, and one-celled organisms.

biomedical research   Scientific studies which involve finding ways to prevent, treat, and cure human diseases and conditions.

biophysics   The application of physics to the study of life systems.

bioscientist   A scientist who studies biology or one of its disciplines or subdisciplines.

biotechnology   The study and practice of using living cells and materials to create pharmaceutical, diagnostic, agricultural, and other products.

botany   The study of plants.

BLS   Bureau of Labor Statistics; an agency in the U.S. Department of Labor.

cartography   The study and practice of making of maps.

chemistry   The study of chemicals, or substances, which make up all living and nonliving matter.

climatology   The study of the climate, the pattern of weather that occurs over a long period of time in a geographical area.

clinical research   Studies which involve testing experimental drugs and treatments on human subjects; the final stages of development of new drugs.

communication skills   The speaking and listening abilities a worker needs to successfully perform his or her job.

compliance   The meeting of requirements set forth by a specific law or regulation.

computational model   A mathematical model, or equation, that represents the components in a problem and their relationship to each other.

computer hardware   All physical parts of a computer; also all computer-related equipment such as a printer or modem.

computer model   A computer program used to create a mathematical, or computational, model.

computer science   The study of computational foundations upon which the operation and design of computers and computer systems are based.

conservation   The protection of air, water, soil, and other natural resources.

criminalistics   The application of science to the analysis, identification, and evaluation of physical evidence that is collected at a crime scene.

crop science   The study and application of growing and managing field crops such as wheat, rice, potatoes, legumes, and cotton.

DNA   Deoxyribonucleic acid; the genetic code of a living organism.

D.O.   Doctor of Osteopathy.

data   Information, including facts and figures.

discipline   A field of study, such as biology, geology, or soil science.

earth sciences   The scientific disciplines that study the Earth, its oceans, and its atmosphere; may also include the disciplines that study space and the solar system.

ecology   The study of how ecosystems are organized and how plants and animals interact with each other in their surroundings.

ecosystem   A geographical area and all living and nonliving things that reside within that area.

entomology   The study of insects and related arthropods such as spiders, ticks, and centipedes.

entrepreneurial   Being willing to risk starting a new business.

environmental science   The study of how human activities affect the environment as well as the practice of preventing, treating, and controlling environmental problems such as air pollution or the depletion of natural resources.

EPA   Environmental Protection Agency; the U.S. agency that enforces federal environmental laws.

epidemiology   The study of human health and disease.

expert witness   An individual whom a court recognizes as having the required knowledge, expertise, and credentials to address specific issues in a court trial.

FDA   Food and Drug Administration; a branch of the U.S. Department of Health and Human Services.

food science   The application of science to the development and production of safe, healthy, and tasty food products that meet customers' satisfaction.

forensic   Having to do with the law.

forensic science   The application of sciences to the study of legal and regulatory matters.

forest science   The study and practice of forest conservation and management.

GIS   Geographic Information Systems; the collection of geographic information that is stored in computer databases.

GPS   Global Positioning Systems; the use of satellites to automatically pinpoint locations anywhere on Earth.

General Schedule (GS)   The pay schedule used for most federal employees.

genetics   The study of heredity, or how traits, are passed between generations.

geography   The study of the physical processes and human activities that occur on the Earth's surface.

geology   The study of the structure, composition, processes, and history of the Earth.

geophysics   The application of physics to study the Earth's interior.

geosciences   Another name for the earth sciences.

graduate medical education   Medical residency; the years of medical training that medical graduates perform to gain practical experience.

horticulture   The study of growing fruits, vegetables, and ornamental plants.

hydrology   The study of the water cycle, or hydrologic cycle, which is the circulation of water from the atmosphere to the surface of the Earth and back.

independent contractor   A self-employed, or freelance, professional.

independent research   Scientific studies in which scientists can choose the topics they wish to research.

interpersonal skills   The abilities a worker needs to communicate and work well with others on the job.

life process   Circulatory, respiratory, or other life system that performs a specific function to keep an organism alive.

life science   The study of living things—humans, animals, plants, and microscopic organisms.

life system   The cells, tissues, and organs that work together to perform a specific function in a living organism; for example, the circulatory, respiratory, or skeletal system.

M.A.   Master of arts.

M.D.   Doctor of Medicine.

M.S.   Master of science.

market   A specific group of people or organizations that have been targeted as likely buyers for a particular product or service.

mathematical model   A mathematical equation that describes the components of a problem and their relationship to each other; also called a computational model.

mathematics   The study of measurement, properties, and relationships of quantities and sets.

medical physics   The application of radiation, heat, lasers, and other physical tools to the study of diagnosing and treating human diseases and health problems.

medical sciences   The scientific disciplines that are involved in the study of medicine.

meteorology   The study of the Earth's atmosphere.

methodology   A particular set of procedures.

microbe   A microorganism such as a virus, mold, alga, or bacterium.

microbiology   The study of bacteria, viruses, fungi, and other microbes (or microorganisms).

molecular biology   The study of the structure and function of DNA, RNA, and the proteins that reside in the cell nucleus.

natural resources   Air, water, food, shelter, and all other things that are produced in nature and that living organisms need in order to survive.

natural sciences   The science disciplines that study natural phenomena.

nongovernmental organization   A nonprofit organization that is not part of a government agency or business.

nuclear physics   The study of the nucleus of the atom.

oceanography   The study of the Earth's oceans and coastal environments.

operations research   The application of mathematics and other sciences to solve complex problems related to running organizations; this discipline is also known as management science or decision technology.

organism   A living thing—human, animal, plant, or microbe.

P.E.   Professional Engineer; an engineer who is licensed in the state where he or she practices; he or she can perform engineering services which may involve the health, safety, and welfare of the general public.

Ph.D.   Doctor of Philosophy.

paleontology   The study of fossils of microbes, plants, and animals that lived on Earth over thousands or millions of years ago.

pathology   The study of how cells and tissues are altered by disease; also a medical practice.

pharmacology   The study of drugs and how they can best treat or prevent disease and illness.

physical anthropology   The study of how the human body has adapted, changed, and evolved over time; this discipline is both a biological science and a social science.

physical sciences   The sciences, such as physics and astronomy, that study the nonliving world.

physics   The study of matter and energy.

physiology   The study of the life processes (such as the respiratory system) that keep organisms alive.

principle   A basic truth, rule, or law.

problem-solving skills   The abilities a worker needs to analyze, interpret, and solve problems on the job.

production   The process of manufacturing products.

project management   The oversight and coordination of the activities for a work project.

protocol   A standard operating procedure.

psychiatry   The medical practice that diagnoses and treats patients with mental problems.

quality   Having all the required characteristics; being free of any defects or deficiencies.

quality assurance program   All the activities involved in ensuring the quality standards of raw materials, production processes, and final products.

quality control program   All the activities involved in checking quality of raw materials, packaging, and products during the production processes.

R.G.   Registered Geologist; a geologist who is licensed in the state where he or she practices; he or she can perform geological services which may involve the health, safety, and welfare of the general public.

RNA   Ribonucleic acid; the molecules that transmit the DNA code to other parts of the cell.

range science   The study and practice of the conservation and management of rangelands such as grasslands, wetlands, and savannas.

regulatory   Having to do with government regulations.

research   A scientific investigation.

research and development   The process of developing new products or improving existing products for commercial purposes.

research assistant   An individual who provides research and administrative support to research scientists; he or she has at least a bachelor's degree.

research associate   An individual who performs complicated research tasks under the supervision of scientists.

research grant   Money given by a government agency, corporation, or other organization to researchers so that they may complete their research projects.

research scientist   A scientist who is primarily involved in conducting research in a particular science discipline.

robotics   The scientific study and practical application of robots.

seismology   The study of earthquakes.

social sciences   The scientific disciplines (such as psychology, sociology, economics, and geography) that study people and their interactions and activities.

software   Programs that instruct computers how to operate automatically; also programs that allow computer users to perform specific tasks such as word processing.

soil science   The study of soils within their environments.

space physics   The study of the physical processes that occur in space between the Sun and the planets in the solar system.

specialist   An individual who has expertise in a particular occupation; for example, a regulatory affairs specialist.

start-up venture   A new business or company.

statistics   The study of the collection, organization, analysis, and interpretation of large masses of numerical data.

subdiscipline   A field of study that is part of a major area of study; for example, physical oceanography, marine chemistry, and marine biology are subdisciplines of oceanography.

teamwork skills   The abilities a worker needs to work as part of a group on a job or on a work project.

technician   An individual who has the practical technical knowledge and skills of a particular occupation; for example, a chemical technician.

technique   A technical method used in conducting scientific research.

technologist   A scientist who is involved in the practical application of a science; for example, a food technologist.

technology   The application of science for practical purposes.

toxicology   The study of poisonous, or toxic, substances.

translational research   Applied research.

USDA   United States Department of Agriculture.

USPTO   United States Patent and Trademark Office.

volcanology   The study of volcanoes.

wildlife forensics   The application of science to the solving of crime in which the victims are animals.

zoology   The study of the animal kingdom.

APPENDIX VI
BIBLIOGRAPHY

A. PERIODICALS

MAGAZINES

Listed below are a few of the scientific and technical magazines that are available in libraries and on magazine stands.

American Scientist
Subscription Department
P.O. Box 13975
Research Triangle Park, NC 27709
Phone: (800) 282-0444 or (919) 549-0097
Fax: (919) 547-5284
http://www.sigmaxi.org/amsci/amsci.html

Discover
P.O. Box 37281
Boone, IA 50037
http://www.discover.com

National Geographic
Phone: (800) NGS-LINE or (813) 979-6845.
http://www.nationalgeographic.com

Nature
P.O. Box 5055
Brentwood, TN 37024
Phone: (866) 839-0194
http://www.nature.com/nature

New Scientist
Customer Services
Two Rector Street, 26th Floor
New York, NY 10006
Phone: (888) 822-3242
Fax: (800) 327-9021
http://www.newscientist.com

Nuts and Volts
430 Princeland Court
Corona, CA 92879
http://www.nutsvolts.com

Popular Science
Phone: (800) 289-9399
http://www.popsci.com/popsci

Science Magazine
American Association for the Advancement of Science (AAAS)
Subscriber Services
Phone: (202) 326-6417

Fax: (202) 842-1065
http://www.sciencemag.org

Science News Online
http://www.sciencenews.org

Science Week
http://www.scienceweek.com

Science's Next Wave (an on-line career resource)
AAAS Subscriber Services
Phone: (202) 326-6417
Fax: (202) 842-1065
http://nextwave.sciencemag.org

Scientific American
P.O. Box 3186
Harlan, IA 51593
Phone: (800) 333-1199
Fax: (712) 755-7118
http://www.sciam.com

Sky & Telescope
49 Bay State Road
Cambridge, MA 02138
Phone: (800) 253-0245 or (617) 864-7360
Fax: (617) 864-6117
http://www.skypub.com

Technology Review
P.O. Box 420007
Palm Coast, FL 32142
Phone: (800) 877-5230
http://www.techreview.com

ZDNET (news about current technology and computers)
http://www.zdnet.com

JOURNALS

Many scientific and technical journals are available to every profession. Here are some things you might do to find journals specific to a profession in which you are interested.

1. Talk with librarians, professors, and professionals for recommendations.
2. Check out professional and trade associations. Many of them publish professional journals, newsletters, magazines, and other publications.

3. The following are a few publishers who produce many scientific and technical journals. Visit their websites to view a listing of what they offer:

Academic Press (imprint of Elsevier Science)
http://www.apnet.com/journals

Oxford University Press
http://www3.oup.co.uk/jnls

Wiley InterScience (imprint of John Wiley & Sons)
http://www.interscience.wiley.com

Nature Publishing Group
http://www.nature.com

4. The following websites and webpages provide listings of various scientific and technical periodicals:

American Medical Association
http://www.ama-assn.org/med_link/peer.htm

High Wire (Library of the Sciences and Medicine, Stanford University)
http://highwire.stanford.edu

MedBio World
http://www.medbioworld.com

PubMed Central
http://www.pubmedcentral.nih.gov

Enviornmental Expert.com
http://www.environmental-expert.com/magazines.htm

Scientific Journals and Magazines listings from Google
http://directory.google.com/Top/Science/Publications/Journals_and_Magazines/?tc=1

B. BOOKS

Listed below are some book titles that can help you learn more about science and science careers. To find other books, ask a librarian for help. You might also ask professionals to recommend titles for you to read.

GENERAL INFORMATION

Derry, Gregory Neil. *What Science Is and How It Works.* Princeton, N.J.: Princeton University Press, 1999.

DK editors. *Ultimate Visual Dictionary 2000.* New York: DK Publishing, Inc., 1999.

Isaacs, Alan; John Daintith; and Elizabeth Martin; editors. *A Dictionary of Science, 4th edition.* Oxford, England: Oxford University Press, 1999.

Reader's Digest Association. *Reader's Digest: How in the World?* Pleasantville, N.Y.: Reader's Digest Assocization, 1990.

Yount, Lisa. *Contemporary Women Scientists.* New York: Facts On File, Inc., 1994.

CAREER INFORMATION

Committee on Science, Engineering, and Public Policy, National Academy of Sciences, National Academy of Engineering, Institute of Medicine. *Careers in Science and Engineering.* Washington, D.C.: National Academy Press, 1996.

Easton, Thomas A. *Careers in Science.* Lincolnwood, Ill.: VGM Career Horizons, NTC Publishing Group, 1996.

Feibelman, Peter J. *A Ph.D. Is Not Enough! A Guide to Survival in Science.* Reading, Mass: Addison-Wesley Publishing Co., 1993.

Fiske, Peter S., Ph.D. *Put Your Science to Work: The Take-Charge Career Guide for Scientists.* Washington, D.C.: American Geophysical Union, 2001.

Goldreich, Gloria, and Esther Goldreich. *What Can She Be? A Scientist.* New York: Holt, Rinehart and Winston, 1981.

Kelsey, Jane. *Science.* Lincolnwood, Ill.: VGM Career Horizons, NTC Publishing Group, 1997.

Kreeger, Karen Young. *Guide to Nontraditional Careers in Science.* Philadelphia, Penn.: Taylor & Francis, 1999.

Louise, Chandra B. *Jump Start Your Career in BioScience.* Durham, N.C.: Peer Productions, 1998.

National Academy of Science. *Careers in Science and Engineering: A Student Planning Guide to Grad School and Beyond.* Washington, D.C.: National Academy Press, 1996. (An on-line version can be found at http://www.nap.edu/readingroom/books/careers.)

Reeves, Diane Lindsey. *Career Ideas for Kids Who Like Science.* New York: Checkmark Books, Facts On File, Inc., 1998.

Robbins-Roth, Cynthia, editor. *Alternative Careers in Science: Leaving the Ivory Tower.* San Diego, Calif.: Academic Press, 1998.

Shenk, Ellen. *Outdoor Careers: Exploring Occupations in Outdoor Fields.* Harrisburg, Penn.: Stackpole Books, 1992.

U.S. Bureau of Labor Statistics, *Occupational Outlook Handbook 2002–2003.* Washington, D.C.: Bureau of Labor Statistics, 2000. (http://stats.bls.gov/oco/home.htm)

BIOLOGICAL SCIENCES

Camenson, Blythe. *Careers for Plant Lovers and Other Green Thumbs.* Lincolnwood, Ill.: VGM Career Horizons, NTC Publishing Group, 1995.

Higginson, Mel. *Scientists Who Study Wild Animals.* Vero Beach, Fla.: The Rourke Corporation, Inc., 1994.

Imes, Rick. *The Practical Entomologist.* New York: Simon and Schuster/Fireside, 1992.

Janovy, John, Jr. *On Becoming a Biologist.* New York: Harper & Row, Publishers, 1985.

Maynard, Thane. *Working with Wildlife: A Guide to Careers in the Animal World.* New York: Franklin Watts, Grolier Publishing, 1999.

Miller, Louise. *Careers for Animal Lovers and Other Zoological Types.* Chicago, Ill.: VGM Career Books, 2001.

Raven, Peter H., and George B. Johnson. *Biology, 3rd edition.* St. Louis, Mo.: Mosby-Year Book, Inc., 1992.

Reeves, Diane Lindsey, and Nancy Heubeck. *Career Ideas for Kids Who Like Animals and Nature.* New York: Checkmark Books, Facts On File Inc., 2000.

Tagliaferro, Linda. *Genetic Engineering Progress in Peril.* New York: Lerner Publications Company, 1997.

Winter, Charles A. *Opportunities in Biological Science Careers.* Lincolnwood, Ill.: VGM Career Horizons, NTC/Contemporary Publishing Co., 1998.

CHEMISTRY

Breslow, Ronald. *Chemistry Today and Tomorrow: The Central, Useful, and Creative Science.* Washington, D.C.: American Chemical Society, 1977.

Friary, Richard J. *Jobs in the Drug Industry: A Career Guide for Chemists.* San Diego, Calif.: Academic Press, 2000.

Woodburn, John H. *Opportunities in Chemistry Careers.* Lincolnwood, Ill.: VGM Career Horizons, 1997.

PHYSICS AND ASTRONOMY

Hawking, Stephen W. *A Brief History of Time: From the Big Bang to Black Holes.* New York: Bantam Books, 1998.

Orange, Daniel, Ph.D., and Gregg Stebben; Denis Boyles, Series Editor. *Everything You Need to Know about Physics.* New York: Pocket Books, 1999.

Stott, Carole, and Amie Gallagher. *The New Astronomer.* New York: DK Publishing, 1999.

Tribble, Alan C. *Tribble's Guide to Space.* Princeton, N.J.: Princeton University Press, 2000.

EARTH SCIENCES

Bolt, Bruce A. *Earthquakes, 4th edition.* New York: W. H. Freeman and Co., 1999.

Camenson, Blythe. *Great Jobs for Geology Majors.* Lincolnwood, Ill.: VGM Career Horizons, 1999.

Decker, Robert, and Barbara Decker. *Volcanoes, 3rd edition.* New York: W. H. Freeman and Co., 1997.

Krueger, Gretchen Dewailly. *Opportunities in Petroleum Careers.* Lincolnwood, Ill.: VGM Career Horizons, NTC Publishing Group, 1990.

Lambert, David. *The Field Guide to Geology.* New York: Checkmark Books, Facts On File, 1998.

Novacek, Michael. *Time Traveler: In Search of Dinosaurs and Ancient Mammals from Montana to Mongolia.* New York: Farrar, Straus, and Giroux, 2002.

Thurman, Harold V., and Alan P. Trujillo. *Essentials of Oceanography, 7th edition.* New York: Prentice Hall, 2001.

Whybrow, Peter J., editor. *Travels with the Fossil Hunters.* New York: Cambridge University Press, 2000.

Wyckoff, Jerome. *Reading the Earth: Landforms in the Making.* Mahwah, N.J.: Adastra West, Inc., 1999.

MATHEMATICS

Reeves, Diane Lindsey. *Career Ideas for Kids Who Like Math.* New York: Checkmark Books, Facts On File Inc., 2000.

Sterrett, Andrew, editor. *101 Careers in Mathematics.* Washington, D.C.: The Mathematical Association of America, 1996.

COMPUTER SCIENCE

Bone, Jan. *Opportunities in Robotics Careers.* Lincolnwood, Ill.: VGM Career Horizon, NTC Publishing Group, 1993.

Darling, David. *Beyond 2000: Computers of the Future.* Parsippany, N.J.: Dillon Press, 1996.

Hawkins, Lori, and Betsy Dowling. *100 Jobs in Technology.* New York: Macmillan, Inc., 1996.

Henderson, Harry. *Career Opportunities in Computers and Cyberspace.* New York: Checkmark Books, Facts On File, Inc., 1999.

Jefferis, David. *Artificial Intelligence: Robotics and Machine Evolution.* New York: Crabtree Publishing Co., 1999.

Maupin, Melissa. *Computer Engineer.* Mankato, Minn.: Capstone Books, 2001.

Reeves, Diane Lindsey, and Peter Kent. *Career Ideas for Kids Who Like Computers.* New York: Checkmark Books, Facts On File, Inc., 1998.

Stair, Lila B. *Careers in Computers.* Lincolnwood, Ill.: VGM Career Horizons, 1996.

Wickelgreen, Ingrid. *Ramblin' Robots: Building a New Breed of Mechanical Beasts.* New York: Franklin Watts, 1996.

AGRICULTURAL SCIENCE AND FOOD SCIENCE

Garner, Jerry. *Careers in Horticulture and Biology.* Lincolnwood, Ill.: VGM Career Horizons, NTC/Contemporary Publishing Group, Inc., 1997.

Golderg, Jan. *Opportunities in Horticultural Careers.* Lincolnwood, Ill.: VGM Career Horizons, NTC Publishing Group, 1995.

MEDICAL SCIENCE

Gable, Fred. *Opportunities in Pharmacy Careers.* Lincolnwood, Ill.: VGM Career Horizons, NTC/Contemporary Publishing, 1998.

Snook, I. Donald, Jr., and Leo D'Orazio. *Opportunities in Health and Medical Careers.* Lincolnwood, Ill.: VGM Career Horizons, NTC/Contemporary Publishing Group, Inc., 1998.

Stonier, Peter D., editor. *Discovering New Medicines: Careers in Pharmaceutical Research and Development.* New York: John Wiley and Sons, 1995.

Zannos, Susan. *Careers in Science and Medicine.* Bear, Del.: Mitchell Lane Publishers, 2001.

ENVIRONMENTAL PROTECTION AND CONSERVATION

Basta, Nicholas. *The Environmental Career Guide: Job Opportunities with the Earth in Mind.* New York: John Wiley and Sons, Inc., 1991.

Environmental Careers Organization. *The Complete Guide to Environmental Careers in the 21st Century.* Washington, D.C.: Island Press, 1997.

Fanning, Odom. *Opportunities in Environmental Careers.* Lincolnwood, Ill.: VGM Career Horizons, NTC Publishing Group, 1996.

Nelson, Corinna. *Working in the Environment.* Minneapolis, Minn.: Lerner Publications, 1999.

Quintana, Debra. *100 Jobs in the Environment.* New York: Macmillan Publishing Company, Inc., 1996.

FORENSIC SCIENCE

Camenson, Blythe. *Opportunities in Forensic Science Careers.* Chicago, Ill.: VGM Career Books, 2001.

Echaore-McDavid, Susan. *Career Opportunities in Law Enforcement, Security, and Protective Services.* New York: Checkmark Books, Facts On File, Inc.; 2000.

Echaore-McDavid, Susan. *Career Opportunities in the Law and the Legal Industry.* New York: Checkmark Books, Facts On File, Inc., 2002.

Jackson, Donna M. *The Bone Detectives: How Forensic Anthropologists Solve Crimes and Uncover Mysteries of the Dead.* Boston, Mass.: Little, Brown, and Co., 1996.

Saferstein, Richard. *Criminalistics: An Introduction to Forensic Science.* Upper Saddle River, N.J.: Prentice Hall, 1998.

Thomas, Peggy. *Talking Bones: The Science of Forensic Anthropology.* New York: Facts On File, Inc.; 1995.

Ubelaker, Douglas H. and Henry Scammell. *Bones: A Forensic Detective's Casebook.* New York: Harper Paperbacks, 2000.

INDUSTRY

Baker, Sunny, and Kim Baker. *The Complete Idiot's Guide to Project Management.* 2d ed. New York: Alpha Books, Macmillan USA, Inc., 2000.

Brown, Sheldon S.; revised by Mark Rowh. *Opportunities in Biotechnology Careers.* Chicago, Ill.: VGM Career Books, 2001.

Chirico, JoAnn. *Opportunities in Science Technician Careers.* Lincolnwood, Ill.: VGM Career Horizons, NTC Publishing Group, 1996.

Goldberg, Jan. *Opportunities in Research and Development Careers.* Lincolnwood, Ill.: VGM Career Horizons, NTC Publishing Group, 1997.

Lindsell-Roberts, Sheryl. *Technical Writing for Dummies.* New York: John Wiley and Sons, 2001.

Pringle, Alan S.; Sarah S. O'Keefe; and Bill Burns. *Technical Writing 101: A Real-World Guide to Planning and Writing Technical Documentation.* Research Triangle Park, N.C.: Scriptorium Press, 2000.

Wells, Donna. *Biotechnology.* Tarrytown, N.Y.: Benchmark Books, 1996.

BUSINESS

Karlson, David. *Consulting for Success: A Guide for Prospective Consultants.* Los Altos, Calif.: Crisp Publications, 1991.

Mariotti, Steve, with Debra DeSalvo and Tony Towle. *The Young Entrepreneur's Guide to Starting and Running a Business.* New York: Times Books, 2000.

Sindermann, Carl J., and Thomas K. Sawyer. *The Scientist as Consultant: Building New Career Opportunities.* New York: Plenum Press, 1997.

Steinberg, Margery. *Opportunities in Marketing Careers.* Lincolnwood, Ill.: VGM Career Horizons, 1994.

EDUCATION AND COMMUNICATIONS

Barker, Kathy. *At the Helm: A Laboratory Navigator.* Cold Spring Harbor, N.Y.: Cold Spring Harbor Laboratory, 2002.

Blum, Deborah, and Mary Knudson, editors. *A Field Guide for Science Writers.* New York: Oxford University Press, 1998.

Echaore-McDavid, Susan. *Career Opportunities in Education.* New York: Checkmark Books, Facts On File, Inc., 2001.

Reis, Richard M. *Tomorrow's Professor: Preparing for Academic Careers in Science and Engineering.* New York: IEEE Press, 1997.

C. BOOKLETS, PAMPHLETS, AND BROCHURES

Listed below are some titles of booklets, pamphlets, and brochures about science careers. Those produced by professional societies can usually be obtained for free. Some societies may have a web version of their materials at their websites.

BIOLOGICAL SCIENCES

"Your Career in Microbiology: Unlocking the Secrets of Life." Booklet may be obtained from American Society for Microbiology, 1752 N Street, NW, Washington, DC 20036; phone: (202) 737-3600; http://www.asmusa.org.

"Careers in Botany: A Guide to Working with Plants." Booklet may be obtained from Botanical Society of America, 1735 Neil Avenue, Columbus, OH 43210; phone: (614) 292-3519; http://www.botany.org.

"Careers in Animal Biology." Booklet may be obtained from Society for Integrative and Comparative Biology, 1313 Dolley Madison Boulevard, Suite 402, McLean, VA 22101; phone: (800) 955-1236 or (703) 790-1745; fax: (703) 790-2672; http://www.sicb.org.

PHYSICS AND ASTRONOMY

"A New Universe to Explore: Careers in Astronomy." Booklet may be obtained from American Astronomical Society, 2000 Florida Avenue, NW, Suite 400, Washington, DC 20009-1231; phone: (202) 328-2010; fax: (202) 234-2560; http://www.aas.org.

"Careers in Biophysics." Booklet may be obtained from Biophysical Society, 9650 Rockville Pike, Bethesda, MD 20814; phone: (301) 530-7114; fax: (301) 530-7133; http://www.biophysics.org.

EARTH SCIENCES

"Cartographers." Brief 199. Monrovia, NY: Chronicle Guidance Publications, Inc., 2001. (Address is 66 Aurora Street, Moravia, NY 13118-3576; phone: (800) 622-7284; fax: (315) 497-3359; http://www.ChronicleGuidance.com)

"Geographers." Brief 155. Monrovia, NY: Chronicle Guidance Publications, Inc., 1997. (Address is 66 Aurora Street, Moravia, NY 13118-3576; phone: (800) 622-7284; fax: (315) 497-3359; http://www.ChronicleGuidance.com)

AGRICULTURAL SCIENCE

"Exploring Careers in Agronomy, Crops, Soils, and Environmental Sciences." Booklet may be obtained from American Society of Agronomy, 677 South Segoe Road, Madison, WI 53711; phone: (608) 273-8080; fax: (608) 273-2021; http://www.agronomy.org.

"Food Scientists." Brief 114. Monrovia, NY: Chronicle Guidance Publications, Inc., 2001. (Address is 66 Aurora Street, Moravia, NY 13118-3576; phone: (800) 622-7284; fax: (315) 497-3359; http://www.ChronicleGuidance.com)

"Careers in Food Science and Technology." For brochure, contact: Institute of Food Technologists, 525 West Van Buren, Suite 1000, Chicago, IL 60607; phone: (312) 782-8424; fax: (312) 782-8348; http://www.ift.org.

"Soils Sustain Life." For career brochure, contact Soil Science Society of America, 677 South Segoe Road, Madison, WI 53711; phone: (608) 273-8095; fax: (608) 273-2021. http://www.Soils.org

MEDICAL SCIENCE

"Explore Pharmacology: Graduate Studies in Pharmacology." For career booklet, contact American Society for Pharmacology and Experimental Therapeutics, 9650 Rockville Pike, Bethesda, MD 20814-3995; phone: (301) 634-7060; fax: (301) 634-7061; http://www.aspet.org.

ENVIRONMENTAL PROTECTION AND CONSERVATION

"Careers in Range Science and Range Management." For career brochure, contact Society for Range Management, 445 Union Boulevard, Suite 230, Lakewood, CO 80228; phone: (303) 986-3309; fax: (303) 986-3892; http://www.rangelands.org.

INDEX